MW00810026

New Life in the Risen Christ

Wesleyan and Methodist Explorations

EDITORS

Daniel Castelo
Robert W. Wall

DESCRIPTION

The *Wesleyan and Methodist Explorations* series will offer some of the best Methodist Wesleyan scholarship for the church and academy by drawing from active participants in the international guilds of Methodist scholarship (Oxford Institute of Methodist Studies, Wesleyan Theological Society, American Academy of Religion—Methodist Studies Section, and others).

There is an urgent need within Wesleyan Methodist scholarship for constructive theological work that will advance the field into interdisciplinary and creative directions. The potential for the series is vast as it will seek to establish possible future directions for the field.

Another key concern of this series will be to tap the emerging field of theological interpretation of Scripture located in and for particular ecclesial traditions. Theological interpretation offers insight to historical study, especially the reception of Scripture and its effects within the Methodist church, as well as exploring the epistemic gains to particular biblical texts and themes. Theological interpretation offers insight into the holy ends of these gains for the life of the church in worship, instruction, mission, and personal devotions for a people called Methodist.

The series will seek out great monographs, while also considering superior and adapted doctoral dissertations and well-conceived and tightly focused edited volumes.

EDITORIAL ADVISORY BOARD

Carla Works   Hal Knight III
Karen Winslow   Priscilla Pope-Levison
Sangwoo Kim   Sharon Grant
Matt Sigler   Frederick L. Ware
Ashley Dreff   Dennis Dickerson

New Life in the Risen Christ

A Wesleyan Theology of Baptism

GENERAL EDITOR

Jonathan A. Powers

CASCADE *Books* · Eugene, Oregon

NEW LIFE IN THE RISEN CHRIST
A Wesleyan Theology of Baptism

Wesleyan and Methodist Explorations

Copyright © 2023 Wipf and Stock Publishers. All rights reserved. Except for brief quotations in critical publications or reviews, no part of this book may be reproduced in any manner without prior written permission from the publisher. Write: Permissions, Wipf and Stock Publishers, 199 W. 8th Ave., Suite 3, Eugene, OR 97401.

Cascade Books
An Imprint of Wipf and Stock Publishers
199 W. 8th Ave., Suite 3
Eugene, OR 97401

www.wipfandstock.com

PAPERBACK ISBN: 978-1-6667-3597-0
HARDCOVER ISBN: 978-1-6667-9370-3
EBOOK ISBN: 978-1-6667-9371-0

Cataloguing-in-Publication data:

Names: Powers, Jonathan A., editor.

Title: New life in the risen Christ : a Wesleyan theology of baptism / edited by Jonathan A. Powers.

Description: Eugene, OR : Cascade Books, 2023 | Series: Wesleyan and Methodist Explorations | Includes bibliographical references.

Identifiers: ISBN 978-1-6667-3597-0 (paperback) | ISBN 978-1-6667-9370-3 (hardcover) | ISBN 978-1-6667-9371-0 (ebook)

Subjects: LCSH: Methodist Church—Doctrines. | Theology, Doctrinal. | Baptism. | Baptism—History.

Classification: BX8331.3 .N47 2023 (print) | BX8331.3 .N47 (ebook)

Common English Bible. Copyright © 2012 by Common English Bible and/or its suppliers. All rights reserved.

New King James Version®. Copyright © 1982 by Thomas Nelson. Used by permission. All rights reserved.

New Living Translation. Copyright © 1996, 2004, 2015 by Tyndale House Foundation. All rights reserved.

New Revised Standard Version Bible. Copyright © 1989 by National Council of the Churches of Christ in the United States of America. Used by permission. All rights reserved worldwide.

For Audrey and Elizabeth.
Remember your baptism,
and be thankful.

...the virtue of this free gift,
the merits of Christ's life and death,
are applied to us in baptism.

— JOHN WESLEY

Table of Contents

List of Contributors

Peter J. Bellini is Professor of Church Renewal and Evangelization in the Heisel Chair, United Theological Seminary, Dayton, Ohio.

Steven D. Bruns is a pastor in Waynesboro, Mississippi, and an Adjunct Professor for Asbury Theological Seminary, Wesley Biblical Seminary, and Asbury University.

Frederick David Carr is the Assistant Professor of Biblical Studies at Northeastern Seminary in Rochester, New York.

Dion A. Forster is the Professor of Public Theology and Ethics, and the Chair of the Department of Systematic Theology and Ecclesiology in the Faculty of Theology at Stellenbosch University in Stellenbosch, South Africa.

Laura Garverick is a PhD student in systematic theology at Calvin Theological Seminary, the assistant editor of the *Wesleyan Theological Journal*, and aided in the editing work of the present volume.

Felicia Howell LaBoy is the Lead Pastor/Life Coach of the historic First United Methodist Church in Elgin, Illinois.

Henry H. Knight III is the Donald and Pearl Wright Professor of Wesleyan Studies and E. Stanley Jones Professor of Evangelism at Saint Paul School of Theology in Roeland Park, Kansas.

Sarah Heaner Lancaster is the Werner Professor of Theology at the Methodist Theological School in Delaware, Ohio.

Michael Pasquarello III is the Methodist Chair of Divinity, Director of the Robert Smith Jr. Preaching Institute, and Director of the Doctor of Ministry program at Beeson Divinity School, Samford University, in Birmingham, Alabama.

Brent D. Peterson is the Dean of the College of Theology and Christian Ministries and Professor of Theology at Northwest Nazarene University in Nampa, Idaho.

Jonathan A. Powers is the Assistant Professor of Worship Studies and the Associate Dean of the E. Stanley Jones School of Mission and Ministry at Asbury Theological Seminary in Wilmore, Kentucky.

Daniel D. Shin is the Associate Professor of Theology and World Christianity and the E. Stanley Jones Chair of Evangelism at Drew Theological School in Madison, New Jersey.

R. Matthew Sigler is the Associate Professor of Wesleyan Theology and United Methodist Liaison at Seattle Pacific University and Seminary in Seattle, Washington.

David F. Watson is the Academic Dean and Vice President for Academic Affairs and Professor of New Testament at United Theological Seminary in Dayton, Ohio.

Karen B. Westerfield Tucker is the Professor of Worship at Boston University School of Theology in Boston, Massachusetts.

Acknowledgments

IT TAKES A VILLAGE to raise a child, a church to baptize a person, and a team to publish a book. Many people, therefore, need to be acknowledged as part of this publishing endeavor. Firstly, I am grateful to each contributor for lending their time, energy, and expertise to this book. Your writings are a great blessing to both the academy and the church. I would be remiss to not express my appreciation to Laura Garverick for her assistance in editing this volume. Her keen mind for theological matters along with her acute eye to detail have helped strengthen the book in ways beyond what I could have done alone.

Acknowledgment must be given to Kathy Armistead for supporting my vision for this book, to the late Billy Abraham for first planting the idea in my head of publishing a volume on Wesley's theology of baptism, and to Daniel Castelo and Rob Wall for the encouragement, support, and patience they have given to my work as the general editor of the book. Matthew Wimer, George Callihan, Chelsea Lobey, Heather Carraher and the team at Cascade also have been critical in getting this volume published.

I am grateful to Kenneth Collins, Ryan Danker, Jessica LaGrone, Stacy Minger, Teddy Ray, Lester Ruth, Bob Stamps, Timothy and Julie Tennent, Jason Vickers, and Taylor Zimmerman for our numerous conversations on the sacrament of baptism. My hope is that this book will serve to spur similar discussions among others. Thank you to my wife, Faith, and to my daughters, Audrey and Elizabeth, for your love and care for me as I have worked on editing this book, and for the ways you live into and live out your baptism every day. Finally, thanks be to our loving God, who adopts us into his family through baptism and by his Spirit raises us to new life in Jesus Christ.

Introduction

THERE IS A TERM used in literary studies for a story in which the overall plot follows the protagonist through an experience of cultural or spiritual relocation. In German, this type of story is called a *Bildungsroman*.[1] In English it is known as an *initiation story*. The primary emphasis in this genre of literature is the change and transformation a person undergoes as they shift from one way of life to another. A *Bildungsroman* story details the protagonist's formative years and/or spiritual education as the narrative moves in three primary stages: 1) an initial occurrence that forces change and spurs the protagonist toward growth; 2) an education process where the protagonist must leave behind their place of physical, cultural, and/or spiritual origin in order to mature and gain a distinct identity; 3) a place of maturity where the protagonist is now able to help others with their newfound experience and wisdom.

Crucial to the narrative of a *Bildungsroman* story is some kind of initiatory act or situation. This singular moment serves as the turning point and driving force of the entire tale. Whether the story is about a respectable yet reserved hobbit whose life is interrupted by a wizard who encourages him to go on an adventure—or whether it is about a young white girl whose eyes are opened to racism in the Jim Crow South after her father is chosen to defend a black man accused of assault—some outside force creates a shift in the protagonist's life. The protagonist is forced either to reject their new reality or embrace it and learn to live into it. Every choice and action from that point forward is indicative of

---

1. The word *Bildungsroman* is a combination of the German word *bildung*, meaning formation, and *roman*, meaning novel. For more on the literary genre of *Bildungsroman*, see Buckley, *Season of Youth*; Engel, "Variants of the Romantic 'Bildungsroman,'" 263–95; and Madden, "Bildungsroman," 18–19.

this juncture. Regardless of what the character chooses, their life has been forever altered by that initiatory moment.

Whereas the term *Bildungsroman* is used primarily as a way of classifying literature, the concept can also be used to characterize Christian life. Spiritual stories—especially conversion accounts—often fit within the purview of *Bildungsroman*. For example, consider Jesus's encounter with the disciples on the road to Emmaus, the conversion of the Apostle Paul, or the *Confessions* of Saint Augustine. All of these stories emphasize a spiritual awakening and relocation. In each, an outside force (God) instigates a change in a person's life. This person then gains new insights and wisdom along with a new perspective on life as the narrative progresses. By the conclusion of the story, the person has changed and is found sharing their newfound insight with others.

Truly, every Christian's story is a *Bildungsroman*. The sacramental rite of baptism represents the defining act of initiation. John Wesley claims as much in his "Treatise on Baptism" when he calls baptism the "initiatory sacrament" that enters a person into covenantal relationship with God.[2] In particular, baptism serves as a sign of divine grace that initiates Christian faith and life. It fashions the Christian in the death and resurrection of Jesus Christ, unites the Christian to the church, and inaugurates a new, permanent reality that illumines the whole of the Christian's existence, namely life in the risen Christ. It is thus crucial for Christians to understand the gravity and worth of their baptism.

This book has been put together as a resource for exploring both the meaning of the sacramental act of baptism as well as baptism's significance in daily Christian life. Distinguished Wesleyan scholars from around the world are brought together in this volume to offer a clear and comprehensive theological vision of baptism. The book has been divided into three parts: Baptism and the Triune God; Baptism and the Christian Life; and Baptism and the Church. While each of the three categories overlap and cannot be separated from the others, this organizational method was chosen as a way of emphasizing particular aspects of baptism. In part one, baptism is examined in connection with the Persons

---

2. Wesley, "Treatise on Baptism," 188. The current volume utilizes "A Treatise on Baptism" found in the Thomas Jackson edition of *The Works of John Wesley*. The treatise also appears in the more recently published *Bicentennial Edition of The Works of John Wesley*. See J. Wesley, "A Treatise on Baptism," in *Bicentennial Edition of the Works of John Wesley*, vol. 14, *Doctrinal and Controversial Treatises III*, edited by Sarah Heaner Lancaster, Randy L. Maddox, and Kelly Diehl Yates. Nashville: Abingdon, 2022.

and work of the Triune God. Michael Pasquarello provides a beautiful liturgical and theological introduction to the volume, situating baptism as initiation and immersion into the love of the Trinity. Steven Bruns and Sarah Heaner Lancaster then carefully discern John Wesley's thought on God's work in baptism, especially as it relates to regeneration and justification respectively. Peter Bellini concludes the first part of the book with a study on the sacramental relationship in baptism between the outward sign of water and the inward work of the Holy Spirit.

Part two of the book reflects on the implications of baptism for the Christian life. Frederick David Carr opens the section with an examination of baptism in the New Testament. In his chapter, Carr provides insights to the meaning of baptism in emerging Christianity and prompts us to consider implications for theology and practice today. Carr's work is followed by a chapter I have written on the inseparable link between baptism and Christian discipleship, especially as it relates to the maintenance of holy life and love in the church. Daniel Shin then observes the connection between baptism and evangelism, casting a vision for the reign of God in the church's service and witness in the world. In her chapter, Laura Garverick sets forth a theological vision for social justice as a necessary outworking of transforming, baptismal grace. Felicia LaBoy accompanies Garverick with a chapter on the sacramental emphasis in Wesley's practical divinity in light of his views on social holiness. Henry Knight then examines baptism and the means of grace, considering how baptism itself is a means of grace and serves as the normative link to all other means of grace within the Christian community. David Watson finishes part two with a profound essay on the implications of baptism for people with developmental disabilities, particularly considering Wesley's views on infant baptism.

Part three of the book looks at baptism in the life of the church. The section begins with Dion Forster's treatment of baptism and ecclesiology. In his chapter, Forster addresses the theological problem that has come about due to the way contemporary understandings of the human person have reshaped relationships to social structures, which includes the church. R. Matthew Sigler then details the connection between baptism and the Eucharist, examining why the Eucharist historically has been the rite of the baptized and showing how John Wesley preserved the sacramental sequence throughout his ministry. Next, Brent Peterson offers a study on the eschatological scope of baptism, considering how baptism joins the Christian to Christ's life, death, and resurrection as initiation into the martyr-church whereby cosmic healing occurs. In the final chapter of the book, Karen Westerfield Tucker engages the topic of baptism and ecumenism as she details sacramental dialogues that have taken place in recent decades among various Christian groups, offering insights from these conversations for those within the Wesleyan tradition.

In addition to the three parts that comprise the body of the book, an appendix has been included that contains two works by John Wesley: "A Treatise on Baptism" and his sermon "The New Birth." These two works are essential to Wesley's theological treatment of baptism and are cited often throughout the volume. I encourage you to read them first, especially if you are unfamiliar with either.

In closing, as you make your way through the material in this book, I pray it leads you to behold the beauty and richness of the Triune God who meets you in the sacraments and who bestowed in your baptism the grace that initiates you into new life with the risen Christ.

Jonathan A. Powers
Epiphany 2023

Bibliography

Buckley, J. H. *Season of Youth: The Bildungsroman from Dickens to Golding.* Cambridge: Harvard University Press, 1974.

Engel, Manfred. "Variants of the Romantic 'Bildungsroman' (with a Short Note on the 'Artist Novel')." In *Romantic Prose Fiction*, vol. 23. *A Comparative History of Literatures in European Languages*, edited by Gerald Gillespie et al., 263–95. Philadelphia: John Benjamins, 2008.

Madden, David. "Bildungsroman." In *A Primer of the Novel: For Readers and Writers*, 18–19. Metuchen: Scarecrow, 1980.

Wesley, John. "A Treatise on Baptism." In *Works of John Wesley*, vol. 10, *Letters, Essays, Dialogs, Addresses,* edited by Thomas Jackson, 188–201. Grand Rapids: Zondervan, 1958–59.

PART I

Baptism and the Triune God

CHAPTER 1

Baptism and the Trinity

Immersion in the Life of Divine Love

MICHAEL PASQUARELLO III, SAMFORD UNIVERSITY

Sacraments ordained of Christ are not only badges or tokens of Christian men's profession, but rather they are certain signs of grace, and God's good will toward us, by which he doth work invisibly in us, and doth not only quicken, but also strengthen and confirm, our faith in him.[1]

Baptism is not only a sign of profession and mark of difference whereby Christians are distinguished from others that are not baptized; but it is also a sign of regeneration or the new birth.[2]

Remembering the Future

ROWAN WILLIAMS, FORMER ARCHBISHOP of Canterbury, has written of the "charismatic memory" of the church.[3] By this he means the historical memory activated by the Holy Spirit in the body of Christ as a form of

1. The United Methodist Church, "Of the Sacraments," Article XVI.
2. The United Methodist Church, "Of the Sacraments," Article XVII.
3. Williams, *Why Study the Past?*, 93.

grace. Williams sees this memory at work in worshipping communities where the Bible, as the primary record of God's self-communication, is read not just as a relic of the past, but as bearing the present communication of God. In a very real sense, worship is a time when the church remembers its future before God.

The language of worship is thus not merely contemporary—where praise is offered not only in words that are straightforwardly our own, that is, in today's words—it is also offered in words used in and inherited from psalms, canticles, hymnody, sermons, liturgies, and prayers. Williams notes the habit of charismatic memory and inherited speech tells us how and why the two false certainties that characterize much modern thinking, either the certainty of the present or the certainty of the past, are false for a people called to participate in God's mission through history and time as sanctified by God's incarnate presence.[4] As Williams comments on the gift of Christian speech:

> We speak because we are called, invited, and authorized to speak, we speak what we have been given, out of our new "belonging," and this is a "dependent" kind of utterance, a responsive speech. But it is not a dictated or determined utterance: revelation is addressed not so much to a will called upon to submit as to an imagination called upon to "open itself." . . . The integrity of theological utterance . . . does not fall into line with an authoritative communication, but in the reality of its rootedness, its belonging in the new world constituted in the revelatory event or process. . . . God "speaks" in the response as the primary utterance: there is a dimension of "givenness," generative power, and the discovered new world in the work of the imagination opening itself.[5]

For example, the following baptismal hymn of Charles Wesley calls upon God, the Father, Son, and Holy Spirit to be present, to act graciously for and in the baptized, the remarkable advent of a new creation:

> Father, Son, and Holy Ghost,
> In solemn power come down!
> Present with thy heavenly host,
> Thy ordinance to crown.

4. Williams, *Why Study the Past?*, 93.
5. Williams, *On Christian Theology*, 146–47.

See a sinful worm of earth!
Bless to him the cleansing flood!
Plunge him, by a second birth,
Into the depths of God.

Let the promised inward grace
Accompany the sign;
On his new born soul impress
The character divine!

Father all thy love reveal!
Jesus, all thy name impart!
Holy Ghost, renew and dwell
Forever in his heart![6]

Wesley gives voice to an important piece of "charismatic memory" that may yet assist us to see and hear the astonishing reality of the "baptismal covenant" effected in the church's public prayer and praise to the Triune God. As the *United Methodist Hymnal* states, "The baptismal covenant is God's word to us, promising our adoption by grace, and our word to God promising our response of faith and love."[7]

Moreover, at the beginning of the "baptismal covenant," the pastor says the following words, pointing clearly to the gratuitous initiative of God who incorporates and renews the baptized as participants in the body of Christ. "Through the sacrament of baptism we are initiated into Christ's holy church. We are incorporated into God's mighty acts of salvation and given new birth through water and the Spirit. All this is God's gift, offered to us without price."[8] And in the "congregational reaffirmation of the baptismal covenant," the pastor adds these words, "Through the reaffirmation of our faith we renew the covenant declared at our baptism, acknowledging what God is doing for us, and affirm our commitment to Christ's holy church."[9] Finally, a closing blessing in "Baptismal Covenant III" states, "God the Father, God the Son, and God the Holy Spirit bless, preserve, and keep you, now and evermore."[10]

We can conclude from the language of our United Methodist Church liturgies that the shared life of the baptized is rooted in the Triune

---

6. Wesley, "Father, Son, and Holy Ghost, In Solemn Power Come Down!"

7. *United Methodist Hymnal*, 32.

8. *United Methodist Hymnal*, 33.

9. *United Methodist Hymnal*, 50.

10. *United Methodist Hymnal*, 49.

God's mighty acts of salvation encompassing past, present, and future. Moreover, we can hear God's work in the life of the baptized affirmed beautifully by the "Thanksgiving over the Water," which follows the congregational profession of the church's Trinitarian faith. This astonishing narrative is remembered as an act of praise for the action of the Father, Son, and Holy Spirit in the creation, redemption, and consummation of all things.

> Eternal Father:
> When nothing existed but chaos,
> You swept across the dark waters
> and brought forth light.
> In the days of Noah
> you saved those on the ark through water.
> After the flood you set in the clouds a rainbow.
> When you saw your people as slaves in Egypt,
> you led them to freedom through the sea.
> Their children you brought through the Jordan
> to the land which you promised.
>
> In the fullness of time you sent Jesus,
> nurtured in the water of a womb.
> He was baptized by John and anointed by your Spirit.
> He called the disciples
> to share in the baptism of his death and resurrection
> and to make disciples of all nations.
>
> Pour out your Holy Spirit,
> To bless this gift of water and those who receive it,
> to wash away their sin
> And clothe them in righteousness
> throughout their lives,
> that, dying and being raised with Christ,
> they may share in his final victory.[11]

This liturgical formula is clearly Trinitarian. But it is also important to note that the biblical event of baptism, and the life bestowed upon the baptized, is also Trinitarian in shape. Here, a theological observation by Albert Outler regarding what can be seen as an example of the "charismatic memory" of John Wesley is helpful. Outler notes, "it seems clear that Wesley's conception of the *ordo salutis* (order of salvation) is deeply influenced by Irenean doctrine," and "His [Wesley's] basic idea of the 'order of salvation'—as the process of the restoration to the image of God is

---

11. "Baptismal Covenant I," *The United Methodist Hymnal*, 36.

obviously an adaptation of St. Ireaneaus's doctrine of . . . the recapitula-
tory work of Christ as the ground of all salvation."[12]

Outler is referring to Irenaeus, second-century Bishop of Lyon, who
was a salutary exemplar of classical Bible reading according to the rule
of faith, the interpretation of Scripture as a single, unified, coherent narrative which witnesses to the God of Jesus Christ within the baptismal,
eucharistic, and kerygmatic patterns of the church's liturgical life.

Arguably the first great post-biblical theologian of the church, Irenaeus summarized the Apostolic witness to Triune God by means of a
rule of faith or truth which: 1) identifies the one Creator who rules heav-
en and earth and is worshiped by the church in the acts of baptism and
Eucharist; 2) guides its interpretation of Scripture; 3) informs the content
of its preaching, and shapes its faith, imagination, and life.[13] Rowan Greer
observes that Irenaeus was the first witness to a Christian Bible and a
framework for its interpretation.

> The church came to insist that the God of Israel was the God of
> Jesus Christ and also that the significance of the Hebrew Scrip-
> tures lay in the testimony they bore to Christ. . . . For Christians,
> the dialogue between God and his people found its fullest ex-
> pression in Christ, and so Christ became the key to the whole of
> Scripture. The theological and even christological convictions
> that determined how a Christian Bible was to be constituted
> then became central in shaping the interpretation of that Bible.[14]

For Irenaeus, the church's theology begins with the gracious movement
of the Triune God toward creation and humanity. This personal knowledge is received and transmitted in the church's worship and sacraments,
its prayers and catechesis, and by the words, images, and stories of the
biblical narrative. Thus, the fundamental source of the vision or knowledge of God's glory revealed in Christ crucified and raised from the dead
was what was accomplished and experienced in the prayer and praise of
the church.

Ireneaus viewed the church's worship, doctrine, and life as intimately related by the new reality entrusted to and experienced by the apostles;

---

12. Oden and Longden, *Wesleyan Theological Heritage*, 104–5; see also Outler,
Sermons I, 75.

13. For good discussions of Irenaeus see Osborn, *Irenaeus of Lyons*; Studer, *Trinity
and Incarnation*; Greer, *Broken Lights*; Behr, *Formation of Christian Theology*; O'Keefe
and Reno, *Sanctified Vision*.

14. Greer, "Christian Bible," 111.

the continued presence of the crucified and risen Lord received in assemblies that followed the Lord's command to baptize and to celebrate a supper of bread and wine in remembrance of him. Jeremy Driscoll summarizes this dynamic of worship and believing: "baptism and eucharist—it is the Lord's command that makes this a *lex orandi* (law of prayer). On the foundation of what God the Trinity accomplishes in these celebrations, and from the communities' experience of them there developed a history of thought, a history of theology. Some ways of understanding things eventually became normative themselves: a *lex credendi* (law of believing)."[15]

The liturgy thus gave rise to both the interpretive framework and interpretation of the Christian Bible, the apostolic witness to the Gospel of Jesus Christ received through the medium of Scripture according to the pattern of the *regula fidei* or "rule of faith."[16] For Irenaeus, then, Christian worship, the sacraments, Scripture, preaching, Christian virtue, and devotion were all congruent with a Trinitarian rule of faith.[17] The rule or canon for understanding and measuring the scriptural pattern of God's truth is most positively set forth by Irenaeus in a catechetical handbook, *The Proof or Demonstration of the Apostolic Preaching*, which provides a "summary memorandum" of Christian teaching, "the preaching of truth so as to strengthen your faith . . . to understand all the members of the body of truth . . . and receive the exposition of the things of God, so that . . . it will bear your own salvation like fruit."[18]

The *Demonstration* clearly and comprehensively unfolds the content of the Scriptures, the Old Testament, which points to the revelation of Jesus Christ as proclaimed by the apostles. Irenaeus thus sought to assist Christians in recognizing and following the scriptural authority of that preaching by demonstrating that the apostles' proclamation of what has been fulfilled in the death and resurrection of Christ, shaped as it is by Scripture, was indeed prophesied by the same God who created the world, elected Israel, and inspired the Law and the Prophets.[19] Because the true meaning of Scripture is theological, Irenaeus begins by confessing the Triune God as the source of Christian faith, hope, and love:

15. Driscoll, "Uncovering the Dynamic," 214–15.

16. Driscoll, "Uncovering the Dynamic," 219.

17. See the excellent introduction in Greer, *Broken Lights*, 1–20.

18. Irenaeus, *Apostolic Preaching*, 39.

19. Behr, *Formation of Christian Theology*, 112–13.

> We must keep the rule (canon of faith) unswervingly, and per-
> form the commandments of God, believing in God and fearing
> him; for he is the Lord, and loving Him. . . . Faith exhorts us to
> remember that we have received baptism for the remission of
> sins, in the name of God the Father and in the name of Jesus
> Christ, the Son of God, who was incarnate, and died, and was
> raised, and in the Holy Spirit of God, and that this baptism is the
> seal of eternal life and rebirth to God.[20]

Irenaeus's confession of the Triune name leads to a reading of Eph 4:6
that illumines his liturgical and theological vision of Scripture: "One God
and Father, who is above all and with all and in us all." This enabled Irenaeus to affirm that everything is created by the Father through his Word,
while the Holy Spirit who is received in baptism enables us to cry, "Abba,
Father," and forms us to the likeness of God.[21]

Irenaeus's great theological accomplishment was the assertion of
concrete, material conclusions—regarding the truth of God and humanity—drawn from the whole economy of divine grace. In its Trinitarian
dimensions, the economy extends from the creation of all things to the
creative work of the Spirit in baptism and moves to anticipating Christ's
return in glory to consummate the peace and righteousness of God on
earth.[22]

According to Irenaeus, these three articles—God the Father, the
Son Christ Jesus, and the Holy Spirit—order Christian faith and life and
are connected intimately to what happens in the liturgical experience of
the church.[23] This is summed up in the scriptural story expressing the
continuity of Adam and Christ, of creation and redemption, as one all-
encompassing divine economy or history embodied in the rule of faith,
which finds its fullness in the new humanity of the incarnate Word.[24]

> And this is the order of our faith, the foundation of the edifice
> and the support of our conduct: God, the Father, uncreated,
> uncontainable, invisible, one God, the Creator of all: this the
> first article of our faith. And the second article: The Word of
> God, the Son of God, Christ Jesus our Lord, who was revealed
> by the prophets according to the character of their prophecy

---

20. Irenaeus, *Apostolic Preaching*, 3.
21. Irenaeus, *Apostolic Preaching*, 5.
22. Driscoll, "Uncovering the Dynamic," 218.
23. Driscoll, "Uncovering the Dynamic," 217. Also Irenaeus, *Apostolic Preaching*, 7.
24. Greer, *Broken Lights*, 26–27.

and according to the nature of the economies of the Father, by whom all things were made, and who, in the last time, to recapitulate all things, became a man amongst men, visible and palpable, in order to abolish death, to demonstrate life, and to effect communion between God and man. And the third article: the Holy Spirit, through whom the prophets prophesied and the patriarchs learnt the things of God and the righteous were led in the path of righteousness, and who, in the last times, was poured out in a new fashion upon the human race renewing man, throughout the world, to God.[25]

Of critical importance for Irenaeus is that the one God who is Creator and Redeemer of all things is known in the church's liturgical actions of baptism and eucharist. Thus, in the saving activity of the Trinity, those who bear the Spirit are led to the Son and the Son presents them to the Father: both the substance and goal of salvation is communion with the Triune God.[26]

It is the liturgical knowledge of the Trinity received in baptism that provides the key or rule for understanding the whole Bible. As Robert Wilken concludes, "The rule of faith had a Trinitarian structure whose narrative identified God by the things recorded in the Scriptures, the creation of the world, the inspiration of the prophets, the coming of Christ in the flesh, and the outpouring of the Holy Spirit. . . . The Bible is thus oriented toward a future still unfolding."[27]

The Trinitarian Faith of Methodists

As a priest of the Church of England who was the reluctant leader of a movement that sought its evangelical reform, Wesley was "traditioned" into the life of the church within a context constituted by Scripture, the confession of doctrine, the liturgy and sacraments, and works of piety and mercy; means of grace through which the Spirit creates and sustains a holy people across time.[28] In many ways, Methodism was a consequence of reform that began in England at the turn of the sixteenth century, serving as a renewing force in parishes, working with common pastoral aims, and participating in an educational *and* missional endeavor that

25. Irenaeus, *Apostolic Preaching*, 6.
26. Irenaeus, *Apostolic Preaching*, 7.
27. Wilken, *Spirit of Early Christian Thought*, 66–67.
28. Holmer, *Te Grammar of Faith*, 203–4.

underwrote the dissemination and transmission of evangelical faith and life.[29]

It is significant, moreover, that the English reformers maintained a robust commitment to a doctrine of the Trinity that affirmed the Apostles', Nicene, and Athanasian Creeds. In addition, the *Book of Common Prayer* is itself pervaded by Trinitarian discourse for use in liturgical settings for the purpose of conveying a vision of God's saving activity, thus leading to joyful contemplation and loving obedience in communion with God.[30] In other words, by coming to know, love, and enjoy God within the economy of grace, worshippers are made participants in the Triune mystery and mission. Equally significant is that the Anglican Thirty-Nine Articles of Religion speak of Scripture only after confessing faith in the Trinity, the incarnate Word, the descent of Christ into hell, Christ's resurrection from the dead, and the economy of the Spirit.

The existence of the church's being and life within the Triune relations is primary for arriving at a view of Scripture as a sufficient rule and instrument of salvation which affects living faith that bears fruit in love and good works. Rather than beginning with the apologetic arguments of Protestant scholasticism surrounding the Bible, Wesley affirmed that Holy Scripture speaks through the Spirit's testimony to generate and nurture communion with the Trinitarian God. In other words, Scripture functions "sacramentally," or as a means of grace, thus mediating Christ and the fullness of his saving work through the "oracles of God."[31] The primary aim of both theology *and* pastoral ministry is to assist the Spirit's work of teaching, forming, and building up Christian communities through attentive receptivity to the Word of God, which informs and guides the use of the means of grace.

Jason Vickers argues persuasively that post-reformation theology in England was marked by increasing distance between the Trinity, scriptural interpretation, and the Christian life due to an academic separation of theological reflection on the being of God from consideration of the work of God.[32] His discussion points toward recovery of a traditional understanding of the Trinity as the personal name of God—the "Father,

---

29. Gregory, "Making of a Protestant Nation."

30. Vickers, *Invocation and Assent*, 37–38.

31. Dorrien, *Remaking of Evangelical Theology*, 165–67.

32. This is one of the primary concerns addressed in Vickers' book *Invocation and Assent*.

Son, and Holy Spirit"—and its accompanying identifying descriptions of God's economy of creation and salvation.

Of particular importance is Vickers' documentation of the shift in English Protestantism by which the church's rule of faith increasingly referred to Scripture rather than personal trust in and appropriate response to God and God's saving activity in Christ and the Spirit. In other words, for much of Christian tradition salvation was not limited to intellectual assent to doctrinal propositions contained in Scripture, thus viewed as an epistemological concern with how we know and how we prove what can be known. On the other hand, salvation was, for the Wesleys, constituted by coming to know, trust, and love the Triune God in the sacramental practices of the church, or the means of grace, in an ontological and doxological way of knowing that is participatory and transformative.[33]

Vickers' work calls our attention to the role Wesley played in recovering the Trinitarian name in hymns, prayers, and sermons, a vital reminder of the rightful home of Trinitarian discourse in the liturgical life of the church to the end of knowing, loving, and enjoying God. In other words, the Trinity, Scripture, the rule of faith, and salvation were integrally related in the church's worship, sacraments, preaching, evangelism, catechesis, and service.[34] As Wesley affirms in his reading of the Sermon on the Mount, "to worship God in spirit and in truth means to love him, to delight in him, to desire him, with all our heart and mind and soul and strength, to imitate him we love by purifying ourselves, even as he is pure; and to obey him whom we love, and in whom we believe, both in thought and word and work."[35]

A hymn by Charles Wesley for use during a service of Christian baptism demonstrates the imaginative response of invoking the gracious action of the Triune God for and in the life of the baptized.

> Come, Father, Son, and Holy Ghost,
> Honour the means ordained by thee!
> Make good our apostolic boast,
> And own thy glorious ministry.
>
> We now thy promised presence claim,
> Sent to disciple all mankind,

---

33. Vickers, *Invocation and Assent*, 37–38.

34. Vickers, *Invocation and Assent*, 169–90. Vickers devotes most of his work to Charles rather than John. My point is that John's work also displays a Trinitarian rule.

35. Wesley, "Upon Our Lord's Sermon on the Mount, IV," 544.

Sent to baptize in thy name,
We now thy promised presence find.

Father, in these reveal thy Son;
In these, for whom we seek thy face,
The hidden mystery make known,
The inward, pure, baptizing grace.

Jesus, with us thou always art;
Effectuate now the sacred sign,
The gift unspeakable impart,
And bless the ordinance divine.

Eternal Spirit, descend from high,
Baptizer of our spirits thou!
The sacramental seal apply,
And witness with the water now!

O that the souls baptized therein
May now thy truth and mercy feel,
May rise, and wash away their sin—
Come, Holy Ghost, their pardon seal![36]

Wesley's hymn raises theological questions requiring pastoral attentiveness and care in the teaching and the practice of baptism. For example, in a collection of essays on the pastoral use of Scripture, the practice of the early Methodists is described in the following manner:

> While preaching remained central to their project, Sacraments and a high view of the church office fell by the wayside; and for all of the education of the leadership; the incipient experiential pragmatism of the movement raised obvious questions about the need for education over against the ability to produce the desired effect. It was, one might say, at root an anti-intellectual and therefore anti-doctrinal movement. The exegetical and theological skills . . . crucial for any kind of pastoral ministry was ultimately to prove unnecessary within a Christianity conceived of in terms of revivalism.[37]

36. Wesley, "Come Father, Son, and Holy Ghost, Honour the Means Ordained by Thee!", 646–47.

37. Trueman, "Impact of the Reformation," 93. For an insightful narrative that traces the development of Protestant theology and theological education, including that of Pietism, see Howard, *Protestant Theology*.

While this assessment does not deal justly with either the Wesleys' theology or their practice, it does offer a valid description of how the practices of Methodists have often been perceived. What has evolved into a kind of conventional wisdom poses significant challenges for how we envision the relation of doctrine and the life of the church, what Charles Wesley aptly described as the union of "sound knowledge and vital piety":

> Unite the pair so long disjoined,
> Knowledge and vital piety:
> Learning and holiness combined,
> And truth and love, let all men see
> In those whom up to thee we give,
> Thine, wholly thine, to die and live.[38]

We need to reclaim the Wesley's vision of "practical divinity" as different than the modern theological paradigm that has divided theology, the knowledge and love of God in Christ, into discrete, academic disciplines more often oriented to professional guilds than to the praise of God in Christian worship, doctrine, and life. As Thomas Langford notes, "Theology, for John Wesley, was intended to transform life. . . . Theology is important as it serves the interest of Christian formation. Theology is never an end, but is always a means for understanding and building transformed life. Theology, in [Wesley's] understanding was to be preached, sung, and lived."[39]

Attending to the relation of the theology and practice—particularly the Trinity and baptism—in the Wesleyan tradition will involve us in a conversation beginning with the early church and extending through the sixteenth century for which theology—*theologia*—was a practical habit, or *habitus*, an aptitude of the intellect, heart, and will having the primary characteristic of knowledge seeking wisdom in love. In earlier times some saw this as a gift infused directly by God, which was intimately tied to worship, the sacraments, prayer, virtue, and desire for God. Later, with

---

38. Wesley, "Come Father, Son, and Holy Ghost, To Whom We for Our Children Cry," 644.

39. Langford, *Practical Divinity*, 22–23. See also the recent study by Colon-Emeric, *Wesley, Aquinas & Christian Perfection*. Colon-Emeric describes Wesley's practical divinity as a "practically practical science" (or existential) in comparison with Aquinas, whose work he describes as a "speculatively practical science" (contemplative). In the end, these are both necessary and complementary. D. Stephen Long provides an extensive discussion of Wesley's union and integration of knowledge and love, or theology and ethics, in Long, *John Wesley's Moral Theology*.

the advent of formal theological investigation, others saw it as a form of wisdom, which could be promoted, deepened, and extended by human study and argument.

However, the meaning of theology did not displace the more primary sense of the term; theology as a practical *habitus*, a habitual or methodical attentiveness to and awareness of the Father's saving wisdom through Christ by the work of the Holy Spirit in the worship, sacraments, teaching, and life of the church.[40] As Mark McIntosh comments, "For many Christians across the centuries, this [the knowledge of God] has meant that theology is really a form of prayer or communion with God, in which, ultimately the thinking of the theologian about God comes to life as God's presence within the life of the theologian."[41]

Rather than a specialized academic discipline limited to a few courses in the curriculum, theology is for all Christians understood as both a knowledge and disposition that orients the mind and heart to loving communion with God and neighbors as the goal of all human knowledge, desire, and action. Here the Wesleys' practical divinity resonates well with contemporary reflection on theology, which focuses on practical theology as a larger framework within which all the disciplines converse and work together: biblical studies, history, systematics, and church practices—including baptism and holy communion as well as preaching, praying, and singing.[42]

This integration of theological and practical wisdom unites Wesley the Oxford Don and Wesley the pastor. However, the division of these two images betrays a pervasive theory/practice split that continues to generate concern regarding the irrelevance of theology for the church, as well as concern regarding non-theologically oriented practices of ministry. We may see in this the problem of reducing the preparation for ministry to training professionals, in that it "may easily be described and maintained apart from any convictions about God, any commitment to a distinctive community patterned in the life, death, and resurrection of Jesus, any awareness of responsibility to serve the laity in their vocations, or any directedness toward the coming kingdom of God."[43]

---

40. Farley, *Theologia*, 33–39; See also the discussion of theology in Nichols, *Shape of Catholic Theology.*

41. McIntosh, *Divine Teaching*, 13.

42. Gelder, "Theological Education," 44.

43. Jones and Armstrong, *Resurrecting Excellence*, 85.

Baptized into the Life of Triune Love

Understanding the relation of the Trinity and baptism will benefit from the vision of Wesley's "practical divinity" in which faith, learning, and ministry are pervaded by theology that serves the transformation of women and men into the obedience of holy love. As Robert Cushman observes, Wesley's practical divinity maps a way of salvation in which "doctrine comes to life, the creed is made incarnate, and humanity participates in the divine nature."[44] While a certain amount of professional training for ministry is necessary, it is not sufficient in itself to generate faithful ministry that serves the Holy Spirit's work of calling, forming, and building up the church to be a sign and witness to the reign and mission of the Triune God as affirmed in the "covenant of baptism."

Fundamental for Wesley was a conviction that faith and holy living are the fruit of the Father's self-giving in the Son by the Spirit who indwells the church through the means of grace. Recognizing that a world without saints will not know how to praise, know, and glorify God as its source and end, Wesley expected Methodist preachers to spend significant time in prayer and study for "transcribing" the knowledge of God in Christ into their lives and ministry according to the beliefs, affections, and practices of true religion; love of God and neighbor.[45] This new way of being is centered in the affections as motivating dispositions that integrate the rational and emotional dimensions of life; the heart purified by divine grace from which flow holy thoughts, words, and actions pleasing to God.[46]

Wesley directs our attention to a "family style" of faith, learning, and pastoral practice that reorients the classical disciplines—biblical, theological, and historical—toward seeing the church's worship and sacramental life as a participation in the life of the Triune God through the means of grace.[47] And while this may not be acceptable by the standards of modern theology and its division into discrete academic disciplines, it may be precisely what is needed to reunite theology and the church, particularly the Trinity and baptism, within a shared vision of God's saving wisdom shining forth in the world through the living witness of the

44. Cushman, *John Wesley's Experimental Divinity*, 10.

45. Maddox, *Responsible Grace*, 113.

46. Maddox, *Responsible Grace*, 113.

47. Here I am indebted to the work of Thompson, *Struggle for Theology's Soul*, 15–21.

baptized. Wesley offers this description of a life that is holy and happy in God, irreducible to either knowing or doing but rather rooted in Trinitarian love:

> this happy knowledge of the true God is only another name for religion; I mean Christian religion, which indeed is the only one that deserves the name. Religion, as to the nature or essence of it, does not lie in this or that set of notions, vulgarly called "faith"; nor in a round of duties, however carefully "reformed" from error and superstition. It does not consist in any number of outward actions. No; it properly and directly consists in the knowledge and love of God, as manifested in the Son of his love, through the eternal Spirit. And this naturally leads to every heavenly temper, and to every good word and work.[48]

Shaped by an evangelical message and way of life that is ordered by the Trinitarian confession of the whole church, a Wesleyan public witness of baptism is at home within the vocation of nurturing mature love for God and neighbor, or holiness of heart and life. It is not surprising, then, that Wesley's theological vision encompassed the whole of Methodists' life: worshiping, preaching, praying, singing, reading, teaching, conversing, communing, conferencing, visiting the sick, serving the poor, ministering to prisoners, working, buying and selling, marrying, raising children, and caring for loved ones. In all of these activities, Wesley longed to see the fruit of God's holy love reigning over, in, and through the life of the baptized. As seen from this perspective, the intelligibility of the relation of Trinitarian doctrine and the sacrament of baptism is correlative to the existence of a holy people raised up by the Spirit to know, love, and enjoy God in Christ: the gospel becoming a people.

Emphasizing living faith expressed in works of love, Wesley's practical divinity exceeds the "information + skill = practical application," which operates within a "cause and effect" paradigm of ministry and contributes to a misunderstanding of the church's sacraments as mere external ritual. Lost in this is the nature of the sacraments as divine gifts, received inwardly by the gift of faith, and manifested outwardly in lives shaped by the truth and goodness of God's love abundantly poured out by the Spirit upon the baptized. As William Abraham comments on Wesley's vision, "The link between [ministry] and doctrine is clear. It is in encounter with this gracious and deeply mysterious reality mediated in

---

48. Wesley, "Sermon 77, 'Spiritual Worship,'" 99.

Word, sacrament, liturgy, and holiness that the church rediscovers the truths which lie buried in its doctrinal heritage."[49]

Thus, God's generous self-communication, mediated by the crucified and risen Christ through the Spirit's witness in Scripture is enacted in the church's sacramental life, engendering living faith informed by God's knowledge and infused by God's love.[50] Amazingly, by the power of the Holy Spirit, the self-giving love of God in Christ received in baptism becomes the very order and movement of a new kind of thinking, speaking, living, and being with one another.[51]

Given a lifelong loyalty to the doctrine of the Church of England, it is not surprising that John Wesley did not seek to be original in his "Treatise on Baptism."[52] However, I want to conclude this chapter by pointing to Wesley's important sermon, "The New Birth," which supplements the baptismal treatise.[53] The text used as the basis for "The New Birth" (John 3:7) was very familiar to Wesley in his preaching: "Ye must be born again." The sermon conveys a strong commitment to the intimate relation of the Triune God and the life of the baptized; of the need for ongoing conversion by the Spirit who effects both inward and outward holiness that results from and points to the new creation in Christ. Wesley thus takes up the matter of vital religion or living faith. He acknowledges this is a divine mystery, and that the manner of its happening cannot be defined. "Thou mayest be as absolutely assured of the fact of the blowing of the wind; but the precise manner of how it is done, how the Holy Spirit works this in the soul, neither thou nor the wisest of the children of men is able to explain."[54]

---

49. Abraham, "Revitalization of United Methodist Doctrine," 49.

50. Lash, *Voices of Authority*, 11–12.

51. McIntosh, "Faith, Reason, and the Mind of Christ," 139.

52. See the discussion of Wesley's "Treatise on Baptism" in Heitzenrater, *Wesley and the People*, 200–201, 206. "Not surprisingly, then, Wesley's expressed views on baptism are essentially in agreement with those of the Church [of England]" (200). See also Oh, *John Wesley's Ecclesiology*, 173–79; I have been helped in my understanding of Wesley's views (and their tensions) on the Trinity and baptism by Wainwright, *Worship with One Accord*, 105–26. Readers will see that I have chosen to limit the scope of this essay to the Trinitarian nature and scope of baptism and the living faith it effects. I have not addressed the historical controversies related to baptism during either Wesley's ministry or in the Wesleyan tradition.

53. Wesley, "Sermon 45, 'The New Birth,'" 186–201.

54. John Wesley, "Sermon 45, 'The New Birth,'" 190–91.

Wesley affirms what he had previously stated in a *Sermon on the Trinity*—that the knowledge of the Triune God is interwoven with all true Christian faith, or vital religion, which at its heart entails the witness of the Holy Spirit who witnesses with the spirit of believers that they are children of God.[55] According to Wesley, this is all of God:

> It is the great change which God works in the soul when he brings it into life: when he raises it from the death of sin to the life of righteousness. It is the change wrought in the whole soul by the almighty Spirit of God when it is "created anew in Christ Jesus"; when it is renewed after the image of God; in righteousness and true holiness, when the love of the world is changed into the love of God, pride into humility, passion into meekness; hatred, envy, malice, into sincere, tender disinterested love for all mankind. In a word it is that change whereby the earthly, sensual, devilish mind is turned into the "mind which was in Christ." This is the nature of the new birth. "So is everyone that is born of the Spirit."[56]

This grand affirmation of new birth leads Wesley to address the matter of baptism. He asserts baptism is not the same as the new birth. Baptism is a sacrament, an outward sensible or material sign. And while the act of baptism signifies the new birth, it is distinct from regeneration, which is the thing signified. Following the *Catechism of the Church of England*, Wesley distinguishes but does not divide the external act, "In the name of the Father, Son, and Holy Spirit," from the inward act of the Triune God whose name is invoked in baptism, "A death unto sin, and a new birth unto righteousness."[57] In other words, Wesley's interpretation sought to preserve both the freedom of divine grace and the human necessity of receiving and responding to God's gracious initiative. Neither right opinion regarding the Trinity nor right conduct of the sacrament is able to produce the effects of living faith that are generated by the Father's self-giving in Christ and the Spirit. This, of course, raises all sorts of pastoral questions that Wesley addresses only briefly. The new birth, which is of God, may indeed occur in baptism, although it may not always accompany it. In addition, a person may be "born of water," undergoing the external act, but without being "born of the Spirit," undergoing the inward change. What appears to concern Wesley, and which is deserving of our consideration,

55. John Wesley, "Sermon 55, 'On the Trinity,'" 386.
56. Wesley, "Sermon 45, 'The New Birth,'" 193–94.
57. Wesley, "Sermon 45, 'The New Birth,'" 196–97.

is the intimate relation of the Trinity and the life of the baptized. As he states, "The tree is known by its fruits." He does not attempt to explain this tension, but rather rests upon the living demonstration of Christian lives that manifest the reality of the Spirit's grace, the knowledge of Christ that is received and lived among the children of God.[58]

Wesley goes so far as to address church members who have been baptized—those who pray, listen to sermons, sing hymns, read Scripture, receive the Eucharist, and seek to do no harm while seeking to do good. He does not deny the importance of what we know and do. However, these are not sufficient in themselves. The means of grace, including baptism, are just that, the means rather than the source and end of living faith.[59] As the Spirit's gift, living faith receives the Father's gratuitous and generous self-giving in the Son and responds in love for God and neighbor, comprising a way of life shaped and oriented by the truth and goodness of the Son's joyful obedience to the Father.[60]

Wesley's reflections are an invitation to remember and be thankful for our baptism; for the life of self-communicative love into which we have been graciously immersed—in the name of the Father, the Son, and the Holy Spirit. In Wesley's own words:

> God is continually breathing, as it were, upon his [sic] soul, and his soul is breathing unto God. Grace is descending into his heart, and prayer and praise ascending into heaven. And by this intercourse between God and man, this fellowship with the Father and the Son, as by a kind of spiritual respiration, the life of God in the soul is sustained, and the child grows up till he comes to the full "measure of the stature of Christ."[61]

Bibliography

Abraham, William J. "The Revitalization of United Methodist Doctrine and the Renewal of Evangelism." In *Theology and Evangelism in the Wesleyan Heritage*, edited by James C. Logan, 35–50. Nashville: Abingdon, 1994.

Behr, John. *The Formation of Christian Theology: The Way to Nicea*, volume 1. Crestwood: St. Vladimir's Seminary Press, 2001.

58. Wesley, Sermon 45, 'The New Birth,'" 197–99.
59. Wesley, "The New Birth," 194–196.
60. Wesley, "The New Birth," 198–201.
61. Wesley, "The New Birth," 193.

Colon-Emeric, Edgardo A. *Wesley, Aquinas & Christian Perfection: An Ecumenical Dialogue*. Waco: Baylor University Press, 2009.

Cushman, Robert E. *John Wesley's Experimental Divinity: Studies in Methodist Doctrinal Standards*. Nashville: Abingdon, 1989.

Dorrien, Gary. *The Remaking of Evangelical Theology*. Louisville: Westminster John Knox, 1998.

Driscoll, Jeremy, OSB. "Uncovering the Dynamic *Lex Orandi—Lex Credendi* in the Baptismal Theology of Irenaeus." *Pro Ecclesia* 12.2 (Spring 2003) 214–15.

Farley, Edward. *Theologia: The Fragmentation and Unity of Theological Education*. Philadelphia: Fortress, 1983.

Greer, Rowan A. *Broken Lights and Mended Lives: Theology and Common Life in the Early Church*. University Park: Pennsylvania State University Press, 1986.

———. "The Christian Bible and Its Interpretation." In *Early Biblical Interpretation*, edited by Wayne Meeks, 107–208. Philadelphia: Westminster, 1986.

Gregory, Jeremy. "The Making of a Protestant Nation: 'Success' and 'Failure' in England's Long Reformation." In *England's Long Reformation: 1500–1800*," edited by Nicholas Tyacke, 307–33. London: UCL, 1998.

Heitzenrater, Richard P. *Wesley and the People Called Methodists*. Nashville: Abingdon, 1995.

Holmer, Paul L. *The Grammar of Faith*. San Francisco: Harper and Row, 1978.

Howard, Thomas Albert. *Protestant Theology and the Making of the Modern German University*. Oxford: Oxford University Press, 2006.

Ireneaus of Lyons. *On the Apostolic Preaching*. Translated by John Behr. Crestwood: St. Vladimir's Press, 1997.

Jones, L. Gregory, and Kevin R. Armstrong. *Resurrecting Excellence: Shaping Faithful Christian Ministry*. Grand Rapids: Eerdmans, 2006.

Langford, Thomas A. *Practical Divinity: Theology in the Wesleyan Tradition*. Nashville: Abingdon, 1983.

Lash, Nicholas. *Voices of Authority*. Eugene, OR: Wipf and Stock, 2005.

Long, D. Stephen. *John Wesley's Moral Theology: The Quest for God and Goodness*. Nashville: Abingdon, 2005.

Maddox, Randy L. *Responsible Grace: John Wesley's Practical Theology*. Nashville: Abingdon, 1994.

McIntosh, Mark A. *Divine Teaching: An Introduction to Christian Theology*. Oxford: Blackwell, 2008.

———. "Faith, Reason, and the Mind of Christ." In *Reason and the Reasons of Faith*, edited by Paul J. Griffiths and Reinhard Hutter, 119–42. New York and London: T&T Clark, 2005.

Nichols, Aidan, OP. *The Shape of Catholic Theology: An Introduction to Its Sources, Principles, and History*. Collegeville, MN: Liturgical, 1991.

Oden, Thomas C., and Leicester R. Longden, eds. *The Wesleyan Theological Heritage: Essays of Albert C. Outler*. Grand Rapids: Zondervan, 1991.

Oh, Gwang Seok. *John Wesley's Ecclesiology: A Study in Its Sources and Development*. Vol. 27, *Pietist and Wesleyan Studies*. Lanham, MD: Scarecrow, 2008.

O'Keefe, John, and R. R. Reno. *Sanctified Vision: An Introduction to Early Christian Interpretation of the Bible*. Baltimore: Johns Hopkins University Press, 2005.

Outler, Albert C. "Introduction." In *Bicentennial Edition of the Works of John Wesley*. Vol. 1, *Sermons I*, edited by Albert C. Outler, 1–100. Nashville: Abingdon, 1984.

Osborn, Eric. *Irenaeus of Lyons*. Cambridge: Cambridge University Press, 2001.

Studer, Basil. *Trinity and Incarnation: The Faith of the Early Church*. Edited by Andrew Louth. Collegeville, MN: Liturgical, 1994.

Thompson, William M. *The Struggle for Theology's Soul: Contesting Scripture in Christology*. New York: Crossroad, 1996.

Trueman, Carl. "The Impact of the Reformation and Emerging Modernism." In *The Bible in Pastoral Practice: Readings in the Place and Function of Scripture in the Church*, edited by Paul Ballard and Stephen R. Holmes, 78–96. Grand Rapids, MI: Eerdmans, 2005.

The United Methodist Church. "Of the Sacraments: Our Doctrinal Heritage." In *The Book of Discipline of the United Methodist Church, 2008*, 63–64. Nashville: United Methodist Publishing, 2008.

Van Gelder, Craig. "Theological Education and Missional Leadership Formation: Can Seminaries Prepare Missional Leaders for Congregations?" In *The Missional Church and Leadership Formation*, edited by Craig Van Gelder, 11–44. Grand Rapids: Eerdmans, 2009.

Vickers, Jason E. *Invocation and Assent: The Making and Remaking of Trinitarian Theology*. Grand Rapids: Eerdmans, 2008.

Wainwright, Geoffrey. *Worship with One Accord: Where Liturgy and Ecumenism Embrace*. Oxford: Oxford University Press, 1997.

Wesley, Charles. "Come Father, Son, and Holy Ghost, Honour the Means Ordained by Thee!" In *Bicentennial Edition of the Works of John Wesley*. Vol. 7, *A Collection of Hymns for the Use of the People Called Methodists*, edited by Franz Hildebrandt and Oliver A. Beckerlegge, 646–47. Nashville: Abingdon, 1983.

———. "Come Father, Son, and Holy Ghost, To Whom We for Our Children Cry." In *Bicentennial Edition of the Works of John Wesley*. Vol. 7, *A Collection of Hymns for the Use of the People Called Methodists*, edited by Franz Hildebrandt and Oliver A. Beckerlegge, 644. Nashville: Abingdon, 1983.

———. "Father, Son, and Holy Ghost, In Solemn Power Come Down!" In *Bicentennial Edition of the Works of John Wesley*. Vol. 7, *A Collection of Hymns for the Use of the People Called Methodists*, edited by Franz Hildebrandt and Oliver A. Beckerlegge, 647–48. Nashville: Abingdon, 1983.

Wesley, John. "Sermon 24, 'Upon Our Lord's Sermon on the Mount, IV.'" In *Bicentennial Edition of the Works of John Wesley*. Vol. 1, *Sermons I*, edited by Albert C. Outler, 531–49. Nashville: Abingdon, 1984.

———. "Sermon 45, 'The New Birth.'" In *Bicentennial Edition of the Works of John Wesley*. Vol. 2, *Sermons II*, edited by Albert C. Outler, 186–201. Nashville: Abingdon, 1985.

———. "Sermon 55, 'On the Trinity.'" In *Bicentennial Edition of the Works of John Wesley*. Vol. 2, *Sermons II*, edited by Albert C. Outler, 373–86. Nashville: Abingdon, 1985.

———. "Sermon 77, 'Spiritual Worship.'" In *Bicentennial Works of John Wesley*. Vol. 2, *Sermons II*, edited by Albert C. Outler, 88–102. Nashville: Abingdon, 1985.

Williams, Rowan. *On Christian Theology*. Oxford: Blackwell, 2000.

———. *Why Study the Past? The Quest for the Historical Church*. Grand Rapids: Eerdmans, 2005.

Wilken, Robert Louis. *The Spirit of Early Christian Thought: Seeking the Face of God*. New Haven: Yale University Press, 2003.

CHAPTER 2

Baptism and Regeneration

The Waters of New Birth

STEVEN D. BRUNS,

ASBURY THEOLOGICAL SEMINARY

"VERY TRULY, I TELL you, no one can enter the kingdom of God without being born of water and Spirit." This statement of Jesus, recorded in John 3:5, is simple, straightforward, and tremendously hard to theologically parse. Regarding the sacrament of baptism, it has led to understandings that range from the act of baptism in water automatically conveying eternal and undeniable salvation upon a person to the opposite extreme; that is, the act of baptism itself meaning nothing and the spiritual state of one's beliefs conveying salvation upon a person. The underlying question seeking to be addressed here is: What is the relationship between baptism and regeneration?

A Wesleyan theology on baptism, as with every other issue, is multifaceted in its approach to the issue of regeneration. Often times those different facets complement one another, and sometimes they are in opposition to one another. This is seen in the various strands and branches of the Wesleyan-Methodist movement today in the varied ways in which they approach the issue of baptism and regeneration. However, each contemporary branch of the tradition inherited these diverse theological opinions from the foundation of the movement itself, diverse opinions of how baptism and regeneration are linked together as implied in John 3:5. Since the Wesleyan theological heritage had its beginnings in Anglicanism—itself a blend of Roman Catholicism, Continental Reformation theology, and evangelical pietism—it is no wonder discussions on baptism within the Wesleyan tradition are rough waters to navigate. Add post-colonial revivalism and the liturgical renewal movement into the mix and baptismal discourse becomes an almost perfect theological storm.

Before looking at Wesley's own views on baptism, it is helpful to briefly examine the sacramental stance of each of the previously mentioned traditions in order to provide some theological context. To begin, in Roman Catholic practice it is believed that a sacrament as a means of grace works *ex opera operato*, meaning it communicates God's grace "from the work worked." In other words, by the very act of performing the sacrament it *necessarily* works for its stated intention. In the case of baptism, the act itself is equated with regeneration. From the Continental Reformation perspective, baptism is a means of grace, yet does not work simply because of the rite itself. Personal faith is necessary for God's grace to be communicated to the one being baptized and for regeneration to occur. Evangelical pietism emphasizes that, unlike national citizenship, citizenship in the kingdom of heaven must be a choice; therefore, one must be a believer to be a recipient of baptism; that is, one must have consciously made a decision to accept the tenets of Christianity and affirm the desire to conform to them. Post-colonial revivalism upheld that a believer had to have a definitive, cognitive experience of conversion to which the rite of baptism was merely representative and illustrative. Essentially, in this framework, baptism itself was not necessary. The only item necessary for regeneration is the personal conversion experience. Baptism *could* be administered, but it was only to show publicly that the converted person was now a part of the Christian faith. Finally, in the liturgical renewal movement there was a concerted effort to recapture the sacramental essence of baptism, realizing that scripturally and traditionally something happened to a person when baptized, even if it was not clear what that *something* was. No doubt about it, with all of these crosscurrents, baptismal discourse is a theological storm indeed.

A necessary anchor to help stabilize the discussion on baptism for those in the Wesleyan tradition is John Wesley himself. Speaking to the relationship between regeneration and baptism, throughout his sermons and writings Wesley continually focuses on the necessity of the new birth—i.e., regeneration—always distinguishing regeneration as something that comes exclusively from God. Conversion is a human act of will, but the new birth is the free gift of God's grace in a person's life.[1] Wesley also makes a significant distinction between the new birth and justification. Justification, in Wesley's understanding, is what God does *for* humans in declaring their sins forgiven and in restoring relationship with the Triune God. Regeneration is what God does *in* humans, making them new creations and enabling them to overcome sin and temptation throughout the rest of their lives as they progress on toward sanctification.[2] Beyond this distinction, though, there is much debate surrounding the exact nature of regeneration, including when and how it occurs.

When dealing with baptism from a Wesleyan perspective, it is vitally important to remember baptism is a sacrament. The classic definition of a sacrament is that it is made up of two parts: a sign and a thing signified by that sign. In the case of baptism, the sign is the imposition of water and the thing signified is the grace of God. Thus, it is also vitally important to remember that as a sacrament, baptism is a means of grace. It is one of the established ways God chooses to communicate divine grace to human beings. Because baptism is a sacrament, Wesley was adamant it should not be confused with the new birth. Rather, baptism is a sign that points to the new birth. It is an outward sign of inward grace.

In the Wesleyan tradition there is also the practice of differentiating "different" graces based on God's activity in a person's life: prevenient grace, convicting grace, justifying grace, and sanctifying grace.[3] The logical place to put baptism is with justifying grace. While Wesley did point out the fact that justification and regeneration were separable only insofar as discussion made it necessary to separate them, in actuality he believed they always went together in the life of a believer.[4] Herein lies the issue: Do justification and regeneration happen congruently with baptism? In other words, does the sign *necessarily* coincide with the grace signified?

To further complicate the relationship between baptism and regeneration, there are different times when baptism may occur: as an infant or as an adult.[5] Though particular denominational practices and doctrines

1. Wesley, "Sermon 45, 'The New Birth,'" 196–97.

2. Wesley, "Sermon 45, 'The New Birth,'" 198.

3. There truly are no different types of grace, but these theological delineations are made for ease of discussion on how grace works in an individual's life at any given time.

4. Wesley, "Sermon 45, 'The New Birth,'" 187.

5. By *adult*, the meaning is anyone who can cognitively answer for herself or himself. This would also include older children and teens.

vary, by and large these two different ages for baptism have their own sets of presuppositions attached to them. One has at its core a conscious dependence upon a covenant community for life in the kingdom of God. The other has at its core a conscious decision to respond to God on the part of the one being baptized. Even with these two different starting points for the baptisms, however, the church still confesses along with Paul in Eph 4:5 that there is "one Lord, one faith, one baptism." While there may only be one baptism, it will be much more beneficial for the discussion if these two types of baptism are treated separately.

Infant Baptism and Regeneration

The concept of baptism and regeneration in infants is the less complex of the two types of baptism in Wesleyan practice. An important assumption made in this discussion is that infant baptism is a valid expression of the Christian faith and life. The biblical, theological, and historical evidence for infant baptism as an integral part of the church's life from its earliest days is staggering.[6] The Wesleyan tradition stands firmly within the aforesaid historic stream of theological thought and ecclesiological practice. This is not to say that every branch of the Wesleyan tradition views infant baptism in the same light. On the contrary, as will be seen in the contemporary issues surrounding baptism and regeneration later in the chapter, differences in theology and practice emerge in the various offshoots claiming a Wesleyan heritage. Nevertheless, most of the Wesleyan family of churches, in continuity with the historic church, do have as a part of their official theology the practice of infant baptism. However, there are a number of questions that must be answered regarding the practice, for instance: What about people who were baptized as infants and later left the faith? Of what value was their baptism? Are infants who are baptized automatically saved? If it is a sacrament, what kind of grace is being represented in the baptism? Does this child need to do anything later in life for a relationship with Christ? Essentially, does an infant experience the new birth, being regenerated when baptized?

For Wesley, the answer to the last question was an unequivocal "yes." He had no problem stating that infants experienced regeneration

6. Church fathers such as Irenaeus, Tertullian, Hippolytus, and Origen all wrote about infant baptism from a diverse geographic spread throughout the second century. After these, the practice is universally recorded and attested in the life of the church. For an excellent treatment, see McKnight, *It Takes a Church to Baptize.*

because his Anglican heritage affirmed it, and he found confirmation of it in his readings from the early church.[7] Additionally, Wesley firmly believed infants suffered from the effects of original sin. This fact alone was enough for him to see and proclaim the validity of the sacrament for infants. If all were under the curse brought about by original sin, then all needed the laver of regeneration in the waters of baptism. In Wesley's understanding of original sin, which was based in Augustinian thought, every single person, from conception to death, suffered from the effects of original sin. He differed from Augustine, however, since he did not believe humans bore the *guilt* of Adam's original actions throughout the duration of their lives, rather just the effects of that original sin (a distinction Wesley made, but which he still labeled *guilt*, thereby using the same word with two slightly different meanings).[8] Despite the difference, the net result is the same in that Wesley believed all humans are under sin's curse and must be born anew. Since the Bible and Christian tradition as a whole knew of no age of accountability before which the effects (or guilt) of original sin were not felt, Wesley saw infants as appropriate recipients of the grace of regeneration for the expiation of original sin's effects. Wesley wrote, "And as the *corruption* of our nature evidences the absolute necessity of *regeneration*, so the necessity of regeneration proves the corruption of our nature. For why should a man need a *second* birth if his nature were not ruined in the *first* birth? Even infants must be born again, for this rule admits of no exception. . . . And now by the appointment of Christ they are to be baptized; which shows they are unclean, and that there is no salvation for them but 'by the washing of regeneration, and renewing of the Holy Ghost.'"[9]

There are differences between the service of infant baptism Wesley sent to America in his *Sunday Service* and the service of infant baptism found in the 1662 Anglican *Book of Common Prayer*. However, the differences are not contradictory. As an abridgment of the 1662 *Book of Common Prayer*, Wesley removed in his *Sunday Service* several statements in the baptismal rite, specifically those that made it sound as if the infant

---

7. See Wesley, "Treatise on Baptism," 193; Wesley, "Sermon 45, 'The New Birth,'" 197. Also see Wesley, "The Doctrine of Original Sin, Part VI (1757)," 441: "A denial of original sin not only renders baptism needless with regard to infants, but represents a great part of mankind as having no need of Christ or the grace of the new covenant."

8. John Wesley, "The Doctrine of Original Sin, Part III (1757)," 307.

9. John Wesley, "The Doctrine of Original Sin, Part VII (1757)," 454–55.

baptized could never fall away from being a part of the body of Christ.[10] Additionally, Wesley removed language that presumed regeneration necessarily happened because water was being poured over the child. This fits exactly with Wesley's differentiation between the sign (the water) and the thing signified (the grace of God). While Wesley's language in differentiating these two aspects of the sacrament, most emphatically in his sermon "The New Birth," was mostly directed to adults and baptism, this instance shows that he applied that understanding to the rite given to the American Methodists for their infants. It also fits with Wesley's experiences throughout his ministry in which he encountered people who had been baptized as infants but were not living as members of Christ's body. Regardless, Wesley retained language in the service such as:

> I beseech you to call upon God the Father, through our Lord Jesus Christ, that of his bounteous mercy he will grant to *this Child* that thing which by nature *he* cannot have; that *he* may be baptized with water and the Holy Ghost. . . .
>
> We beseech thee, for thine infinite mercies, that thou wilt look upon *this Child*; wash *him* and sanctify *him* with the Holy Ghost. . . .
>
> We call upon thee for *this Infant*, that *he*, coming to thy holy baptism, may receive remission of *his* sins by spiritual regeneration.
>
> Give thy Holy Spirit to *this Infant*, that *he* may be born again, and be made *an heir* of everlasting salvation. . . .[11]

Again, the language in the *Sunday Service* was ameliorated to the point it would not be assumed the infant was being regenerated at the moment of baptism (i.e., the ever-present specter of the Roman Catholic *ex opera operato*); however, the expectation of regeneration of the infant remained present because Wesley understood regeneration to be necessary to the

---

10. Wesley omitted statements such as "Dearly beloved, ye have brought this child here to be baptized; ye have prayed that our Lord Jesus Christ would vouchsafe to receive him, to release him of his sins, to sanctify him with the Holy Ghost, to give him the kingdom of heaven, and everlasting life. Ye have heard also, that our Lord Jesus Christ hath promised in his Gospel to grant all these things that ye have prayed for: which promise, he for his part will most surely keep and perform." He also removed the word "regenerate" in reference to the newly baptized infant in the two places it occurred. Wesley made a similar move in omitting from the Articles of Religion any article that tended to be more Calvinist in its theology. See *Book of Common Prayer*, 1662.

11. Wesley, *Sunday Service of the Methodists*, 139–41.

human condition. All humans were born with the stain of sin, thus all humans needed to be washed from it. Infant baptism, as a means of grace, was therefore the outward sign of the inward grace of regeneration that gave the child a clean slate for living in the world without suffering the personal consequences of original sin. To put it another way, Wesley believed in baptismal regeneration in infants, even if it was not done *ex opera operato*.

This unequivocal and unapologetic stance on baptismal regeneration in infants did not bind Wesley into thinking that all who were baptized were necessarily saved, though. As Wesley saw the disastrous lifestyles of supposedly "Christian" people in England, Ireland, and Scotland he knew that a person, once baptized, could fall away from that grace, and indeed often did. He even said of himself that he "sinned away" the grace he received in baptism by the time he was ten years old.[12] In fact, Wesley used both of these arguments in defending the Methodist movement in an open letter to William Warburton, the Bishop of Gloucester.[13] In that letter, Wesley wrote it was the expected theological position of the Church of England that all its members would receive the Holy Spirit through baptism, as evidenced by the Thirty-Nine Articles, the Homilies, and the rites of the church pertaining to baptism and confirmation. He also took great care to point out to the bishop that hardly any of the members of the church were regenerate, to the point it was questionable whether or not England could honestly be described as a "Christian" country. This reality gives the rationale for why Wesley engaged in ministry as he did and founded the Methodist movement. It also gives the primary reason why Wesley's baptismal understanding was convoluted between regeneration in infants and a necessity of Christian experience in adults. If infant baptism did not produce adult Christians, something must be missing in the traditional understanding of baptism and regeneration.

Adult Baptism and Regeneration

While Wesley was straightforward in his understanding of baptismal regeneration in infant baptism, with adult baptism the theology becomes more opaque. In several instances, when preaching to large crowds of people, Wesley's recourse was to dissuade his hearers from relying upon

12. Wesley, "May 24, 1738," 242–43.
13. Wesley, "Letter to the Right Reverend," 335–51.

the fact that they had been baptized as infants.[14] In his mind it was necessary to have a transformative experience with the Living God that could be described as the new birth. For those who professed that they had been born again in baptism as infants, the message was clear: you must be born again, again.

Wesley also seemed to use the same terminology, being born again, for two different experiences within the life of one who was growing in grace with God. First, there was being born again in the "lower sense." This was receiving the forgiveness of sins, also called justification, often in conjunction with a conversion experience or baptism. Second, there was being born again in the "higher sense." This was experiencing the sanctifying work of the Holy Spirit in regeneration. These two experiences can be seen most clearly in Wesley's journal entry for January 25, 1739. He wrote:

> Of the adults I have known baptized lately, one only was at that time born again, in the full sense of the word; that is, found a thorough, inward change, by the love of God filling her heart. Most of them were only born again in a lower sense; that is, received the remission of their sins. And some (as it has since too plainly appeared) neither in one sense nor the other.[15]

It seems that the ideal method of how God works in lives—justification and regeneration happening concurrently—was not always observed in the people to whom Wesley ministered.

Pragmatist that Wesley was, if the people did not fit the ideal of the theological plan, then the theological plan was tweaked to describe what was happening with the people. Wesley's theological descendants followed him in this practice. As a result, this is where the theological heirs of Wesley and the early Methodist movement encounter problems when looking at the issue of baptismal regeneration. If an actual evangelical experience was necessary in the life of a person to be regenerate, then the issue of baptism becomes optional in the life of the believer. Yet, that is not how Wesley saw the sacrament, since he insisted upon it and gave the Methodist Episcopal Church a rite for baptizing infants. Nevertheless, an actual evangelical experience was exactly what Wesley preached.

---

14. Wesley, "Sermon 45, 'The New Birth,'" 199–201.

15. Wesley, "January 25, 1739," 32. See also Wesley, "Sermon 40, 'Christian Perfection,'" 106. In it, Wesley also speaks of being born again in a lower and more perfect sense.

As a result, the "lower" and "higher" views of being regenerate morphed into second blessings or second definitive works of grace. Regeneration, as a theological concept of being born again, was divorced from the act of baptism in adults. Either it was something, in Wesley's mind at least, that was experienced in infant baptism, or it was an experience that was distinct from baptism and the water merely was the outward confirmation of that experience that had already taken place in the life of the adult believer.

Baptism and Regeneration Today

If John Wesley's nuanced theology concerning baptism and regeneration is the anchor for a Wesleyan understanding of the topics, it is wise to see how some of the major contemporary expressions of that theology are congruent or incongruent with it. Did the anchor hold? In this case, the fullest treatment of the topic of baptism from a Wesleyan perspective is the 1996 document *By Water and the Spirit: A United Methodist Understanding of Baptism.*[16] Besides this document, there are also other denominational understandings of baptism, although not as explicitly articulated, in the Free Methodist Church, the Wesleyan Church, and the Nazarene Church.

If baptism is a sacrament, and a sacrament by definition is a means of grace, then which kind of grace is mediated through the sacrament of baptism? In the United Methodist document *By Water and the Spirit*, it is understood that for infants the grace to be mediated is prevenient grace. It states:

> Infant baptism rests firmly on the understanding that God prepares the way of faith before we request or even know that we need help (prevenient grace). The sacrament is a powerful expression of the reality that all persons come before God as not more than helpless infants, unable to do anything to save ourselves, dependent upon the grace of our loving God. The faithful community of the church serves as a means of grace for those whose lives are impacted by its ministry. Through the church, God claims infants as well as adults to be participants in the gracious covenant of which baptism is the sign.[17]

16. United Methodist Church, *By Water and the Spirit.*
17. United Methodist Church, *By Water and the Spirit*, 10.

The document proceeds to explain that the baptism of infants is retained within the life of the church because of historical continuity with the church through the ages and the theological justification is that God is always at work in people's lives as the primary mover. Even before any human being recognizes God's love for her or him, that divine presence is actively reaching out to the person. Infant baptism becomes a sign of that reality and that activity of grace within the life of the individual and the life of the congregation.

There is a major problem with this theological understanding of infant baptism, though. In Wesleyan theology, *all of humanity* receives God's prevenient grace. This is by definition. Prevenient grace is the grace that goes before an awareness of conviction or a need of a savior. This was Wesley's corrective to the Calvinist doctrine of total depravity. It avoided the logical conclusion total depravity and a sovereign God created, namely that anyone who was saved was foreordained to be saved by God. Prevenient grace was freely given to enable all humans to freely choose for or against God. A child, by experiencing baptism with this understanding, is absolutely no different than a child who has not experienced baptism. This is quite simply because they both receive God's prevenient grace. The only difference is that the baptized child, apart from getting wet, is now a member of a local congregation (although not in the following three denominations, as will be seen below). This is a far different understanding of God's grace and baptism as a means of that grace than Wesley's theological framework. There, infant baptism was the means of receiving regeneration because of the reality of the effects of original sin in the lives of all humans, infants included. With the neglect, or repudiation, of an understanding of the effects of original sin on humanity, the efficaciousness of baptism for infants is moot. In an effort to distance the church from medieval ideas of unbaptized infants in limbo, the church has emptied the sacrament of theological meaning that is consistent with the rest of Wesleyan theology.

To be fair to the document, *By Water and the Spirit* also contains the confusion about infant baptism that is prevalent within contemporary Methodism. Immediately after declaring that the understanding of infant baptism is based upon prevenient grace, the document proceeds stating, "The church affirms that children being born into the brokenness of the world should receive the cleansing and renewing forgiveness of God no less than adults. The saving grace made available through Christ's atonement is the only hope of salvation for persons of any age."[18] This would seem to imply that there is more at work in an infant's baptism than merely an outward reminder of prevenient grace at work in that child. While not as explicit as Wesley in his attempt to balance infant regeneration and the necessity for all people to truly experience a new birth and live as those who have been regenerated by the power and presence of God, this shows that the authors of the document still have the same issue in mind. The document further states:

> The United Methodist Church does not accept either the idea that only believer's baptism is valid or the notion that the baptism of infants magically imparts salvation apart from active personal faith. Pastors are instructed by the Book of Discipline to explain our teaching clearly on these matters, so that parent(s) or sponsors might be free of misunderstandings.[19]

Unfortunately, the document itself does not help pastors be able to explain clearly an understanding of infant baptism theologically, as noted above.

On the other end of the spectrum, with adult baptism, *By Water and the Spirit* also claims that regeneration does not always coincide with baptism. It may precede baptism, coincide with it, or come subsequent to it. This, again, exports any sacramental meaning out of the act of baptism. It ceases to be a means of grace and merely becomes a rite within the church that signifies membership. This is not the fault of the modern church, though. In this aspect, contemporary ecclesial understanding is firmly within Wesley's delineation of baptism as being an outward act signifying justification, conversion, and regeneration. This is the logical position of any Christians who would stand against the concept of *ex opera operato*.

The Free Methodist Church has not created a document the likes of *By Water and the Spirit*, yet it has given some theological reflection to the issue of baptism and regeneration. This is most clearly seen in its Articles of Religion. Because the Free Methodist Church (as well as the Wesleyan Church and the Nazarene Church) does not have a restrictive rule freezing the Articles of Religion in their 1808 version, the Free Methodist Church has modified and expanded the original Methodist

18. United Methodist Church, *By Water and the Spirit*, 9.
19. United Methodist Church, *By Water and the Spirit*, 11.

Articles. The Article entitled "baptism" in the Free Methodist Church's *Book of Discipline* states:

> Water baptism is a sacrament of the church, commanded by our Lord, signifying acceptance of the benefits of the atonement of Jesus Christ to be administered to believers as a declaration of their faith in Jesus Christ as Savior.
>
> Baptism is a symbol of the new covenant of grace as circumcision was the symbol of the old covenant; and, since infants are recognized as being included in the atonement, they may be baptized upon the request of parents or guardians who shall give assurance for them of necessary Christian training. They shall be required to affirm the vow for themselves before being accepted into church membership.[20]

This Article then needs to be taken in conjunction with the article specifically on regeneration, which itself is an article that further explicates the Free Methodist understanding of "New Life in Christ" as defined by the articles for each of the terms of justification, regeneration, adoption, and sanctification.

> Regeneration is a biological term which illustrates that by a new relationship in Christ, one does in fact have a new life and a new spiritual nature capable of faith, love and obedience to Christ Jesus as Lord. The believer is born again and is a new creation. The old life is past; a new life is begun.[21]

Together these two Articles are fairly straightforward in the understanding that, for a Free Methodist understanding of regeneration and baptism, the normal process is that someone becomes a believer in Christ, is therefore born again, and subsequently undergoes baptism as a sign and confirmation of that regenerate state. This takes seriously Wesley's distinction between the outward sign of baptism and the inward act of God's grace being communicated to the one baptized.[22] It is codified, though, in an understanding that the outward sign will occur *after* the inward grace has been received.

The case of infant baptism and regeneration for the Free Methodists is more in line with *By Water and the Spirit*. Here, for the Free Methodist Church, the focus is on membership. The difference between the two

---

20. Free Methodist Church USA, *2019 Book of Discipline*, para. 124.

21. Free Methodist Church, *Book of Discipline*, para. 117.

22. Wesley, "Sermon 45, 'The New Birth,'" 196–97.

expressions of infant baptism, though, is that for the Free Methodists, an infant baptism signifies membership only within the covenant community of God, not the church as an institution. Membership in the church requires a profession of faith by the child herself or himself. In addition to this curious facet of Free Methodist polity, it is debatable whether infant baptism is a means of grace at all since the article states that "infants are recognized as being included in the atonement." This could mean that the atonement is open to infants, and thus it is appropriate for them to receive baptism. On the other hand, it could mean that somehow a child is already saved through the death and resurrection of Christ. That would mean the issue for infant baptism is not even one of prevenient grace as the child is apparently already a participant in the atoning work of Christ. As a result, there is no need for regeneration. The article is vague in this area.

The Wesleyan Church goes one step further than the Free Methodist Church in its *Book of Discipline*. The Article of Religion specifically titled "The Atonement" states when discussing the crucifixion and its effects upon the whole world, "This atonement . . . is unconditionally effective in the salvation of those mentally incompetent from birth, of those converted persons who have become mentally incompetent, and of children under the age of accountability. But it is effective for the salvation of those who reach the age of accountability only when they repent and exercise faith in Christ."[23] For the Wesleyan Church, infant baptism is not even a case of prevenient grace. Rather, by their official theology children are in no need of any grace prior to "the age of accountability." While there is no mention of what that age is, regeneration is necessary only after reaching that age. As a result, and consistent with the article on the atonement, the Wesleyan Article of Religion on Baptism states, "We believe that water baptism is a sacrament of the church, commanded by our Lord and administered to believers. It is a symbol of the new covenant of grace and signifies acceptance of the benefits of the atonement of Jesus Christ. By means of this sacrament, believers declare their faith in Jesus Christ as Savior."[24] By this definition of baptism, the Wesleyan Church explicitly affirms what the Free Methodist Church also affirms that the normal and expected way of God's working in someone's life is for that person to respond to the call upon her or his life, to experience regeneration, and

23. Wesleyan Church, *Discipline*, para. 226.
24. Wesleyan Church, *Discipline*, para. 42.

then to undergo baptism as the outward sign of that inward grace already received.

Interestingly, however, is the curious way in which the Wesleyan Church words its article on baptism. A plain reading of the article would lead to the conclusion that baptism for infants is not permitted within the denomination. However, under the heading "Observance of Sacraments" the Wesleyan Church makes this statement:

> All persons to be baptized shall have the choice of baptism by immersion, pouring, or sprinkling. Since children are born into this world with natures inclined to sin, and yet the prevenient grace of God provides for their redemption during the period before reaching the age of accountability, those parents who so choose may testify to their faith in God's provision by presenting their small children for baptism, while those who prefer to emphasize baptism as a testimony by individual believers to their own act of faith may present their children for dedication.[25]

Here, as in *By Water and the Spirit* as well as the Free Methodist Church's understanding, infants can be baptized as evidence of God's prevenient grace working in the lives of those small children. Consistent with the Free Methodist Church specifically, to be a member in the Wesleyan Church one must have "Confession of faith in Jesus Christ as evidenced by an inner witness of new birth through the Holy Spirit and a commitment to pursue holiness in all things."[26] In other words, since the possibility of regeneration is limited to a conscious decision on the part of person at or beyond the age of accountability, infant baptism (without any connotation of regeneration) does not allow one to be a member of the local congregation.

The Church of the Nazarene makes extremely explicit to all of its members how it understands regeneration and baptism with respect to infants. Not having to parse out what its theology means in the everyday life of its members, the Nazarene Church includes this statement within the ritual for baptism of infants: "While we do not hold that baptism imparts the regenerating grace of God, we do believe that Christian baptism signifies for this young child God's acceptance within the community of Christian faith on the basis of prevenient grace."[27] This coincides with

25. Wesleyan Church, *Discipline*, para. 290.

26. Wesleyan Church, *Discipline*, para. 297.

27. Nazarene Church, *Church of the Nazarene Manual, Sacraments and Rituals*, para. 700.2.

its Article of Faith on the atonement which states, "The Atonement is graciously efficacious for the salvation of those incapable of moral responsibility and for the children in innocency but is efficacious for the salvation of those who reach the age of responsibility only when they repent and believe."[28] This is identical in sentiment, if not language, with the Wesleyan Church's understanding of atonement as evidenced in their article above. It is also in agreement with *By Water and the Spirit* and the Free Methodist Church in its placement of prevenient grace as the type of grace for which baptism is the means of an infant's participation. This is interesting since, like the Wesleyan Church, there is no real need to specify that prevenient grace is given through baptism since the Nazarene Church states that infants are covered by Christ's atonement on the cross until they come of age and need to make a conscious decision whether or not to follow Christ. This was highlighted by Karen Westerfield Tucker, in her comprehensive work *American Methodist Worship*, who noted:

> Indeed, given the argument sometimes advanced that infants, prior to baptism, were already beneficiaries of Christ's universal atonement (increasingly identified—incorrectly—as Wesley's doctrine of prevenient grace), any notion of infant regeneration was, in fact, redundant.[29]

Also congruent with the Wesleyan Church is the statement the Nazarene Church makes in its article on regeneration. It states, "We believe that regeneration, or the new birth, is that gracious work of God whereby the moral nature of the repentant believer is spiritually quickened and given a distinctively spiritual life, capable of faith, love, and obedience."[30] This shows that the Nazarene Church's understanding of regeneration is that it is something that happens in the life of a believer once that person has repented of sin and converted to a life following Jesus Christ. In line with the Free Methodist Church and the Wesleyan Church, the Nazarene Church understands that baptism for those who have made a decision is a sign that comes *after* the person has been regenerated. Their article on baptism states as much when it says, "We believe that Christian baptism,

28. Nazarene Church, *Church of the Nazarene Manual, Sacraments and Rituals*, para. 6.

29. Westerfield Tucker, *American Methodist Worship*, 106. In fact, Westerfield Tucker provides and in-depth journey from Wesley to the contemporary scene in her chapter "The Rites of Christian Initiation." That background of theological and ritual development is indispensable for this topic.

30. Nazarene Church, *Church of the Nazarene Manual, Articles of Faith*, para. 9.1.

commanded by our Lord, is a sacrament signifying acceptance of the benefits of the atonement and incorporation into the Body of Christ. . . . It is to be administered to believers indicating their full purpose of obedience in holiness and righteousness."[31]

Through these four examples of an understanding of baptism and regeneration in the United Methodist document *By Water and the Spirit*, the Free Methodist Church's Articles of Religion, the Wesleyan Church's Articles of Religion, and the Nazarene Church's Articles of Faith, it is possible to articulate a contemporary Wesleyan theology of baptism and regeneration. This contemporary understanding is congruent in some ways and incongruent in other ways with Wesley and the original Methodist movement. The similarity is that in adults there has always been a call to be born again. There is a necessity for regeneration and new birth in the lives of all who would call themselves Christian. There is also a realization that this regeneration does not necessarily correspond to the act of baptism. In some of the traditions, the expectation is that regeneration will have already occurred in a person's life prior to the sacramental act of baptism. The main dissimilarity is that Wesley, and the early Methodists, understood infant baptism to be regenerative in nature whereas the contemporary expressions of Methodism understand infant baptism to convey prevenient grace and not be regenerative in any way.

This is the fine line Christians of all traditions need to walk, not the least Wesleyans. As Westerfield Tucker notes, "A tension occurs whenever the church both baptizes infants and expects personal faith of its members."[32] Baptism as a sacrament is something instituted by Jesus Christ. It has traditionally been understood to be not only the entry point into the life of the Christian community of faith but also the means by which people were regenerated into a new creation and born from above, for both infants and adults. Nevertheless, after two thousand years of experience, the church understands that not everyone who is baptized becomes new creation. The act of baptism is not a magical ritual that always works (just as a "sinner's prayer" is not a magical incantation that always works). Wesley and the Methodist movement have tried to walk that tightrope of acknowledging the necessity of baptism on the one hand and declaring the necessity of a conscious yielding of will to God on the

---

31. Nazarene Church, *Church of the Nazarene Manual, Articles of Faith*, para. 12.

32. Westerfield Tucker, *American Methodist Worship*, 116.

other hand. The balance is between the sign and the thing signified. It is the heart of what a sacrament actually is.

Theological Issues

The main issue with which the contemporary Wesleyan-Methodist family needs to deal is the issue of infant baptism. The reason for this is simple. If baptism is a means of grace and the grace that is understood to be received by the infant in her or his baptism is prevenient grace, there is no real point for the infant in having the baptism at all. In order to be consistent with theology and the understanding of grace in the lives of people, Christians in the Wesleyan theological tradition have to admit that all humanity receive prevenient grace. There is no sacrament that is the means of that grace at all. The modern linking of prevenient grace to the sacrament of baptism is a major reordering of the understanding of grace for the Wesleyan tradition and brings an inconsistency to the understanding of prevenient grace into the tradition. Either people now need to undergo baptism as infants to receive prevenient grace or infant baptism does not act as a means of grace distinct from any other person's experience who does not receive baptism as an infant. The majority theological stance in the four modern traditions above is the latter. This means that the weight of the sacrament becomes one of fulfilling the desires of the parents. It has become an ordinance that the church does because of commandment and tradition. In essence, infant baptism has simply become infant dedication with water. This is very different from Wesley and his theology.

Part of the reason for this discrepancy in the theology surrounding infant baptism and regeneration is the basic issue: from what do humans need to be regenerated? Wesley was clear that all of humanity was affected by original sin. Only Adam and Eve were guilty of that original sin, but all humanity suffer the consequences of that sin in that as a race, human nature is now stained with sin. Even infants need to be washed to remove that stain, Wesley thought. This is why he published his father's "Treatise on Baptism." Indeed, it is also why Wesley included a service for the baptism of infants in the worship book he sent to America for the creation of the Methodist Episcopal Church in America. Even with the changes he made to the service, it is still expected that infants who are baptized will be regenerated by the agency of the Holy Spirit.

The modern Wesleyan theological tradition must make a serious inquiry into what it actually believes concerning infant baptism as a means of grace and as a sacrament. One of the emphases Wesleyans have had in their theology is that they stand in the general flow of the history of the church. They affirmed the major theological truths of the historic church. Wesley and the early Methodists also claimed to be following in that tradition, hearkening back to "primitive Christianity" when necessary, and keeping the contemporary reality when appropriate. By removing regeneration from infant baptism, the modern traditions have embraced more of an almost Anabaptist theology regarding baptism. To be sure, a call for a conscious decision about accepting God's grace and regenerative transformation was always a part of Wesley's preaching to adults, but likewise the reality of regeneration in infants was also always a part of the Wesleyan tradition. Either the contemporary situation needs to return to the original understanding, or infant baptism needs to be explained in such a way that it is understood with language that reflects the current theological position: ordinance, not sacrament; dedication with water, not regeneration.

Bibliography

The Free Methodist Church USA. *2019 Book of Discipline*. Indianapolis: Free Methodist Church, 2019.

McKnight, Scot. *It Takes a Church to Baptize: What the Bible Says about Infant Baptism*. Grand Rapids: Brazos, 2018.

The Nazarene Church. *Church of the Nazarene Manual 2017–2021*. Kansas City: The Foundry, 2017.

The United Methodist Church. *By Water and the Spirit: A United Methodist Understanding of Baptism*. Nashville: General Board of Discipleship, 1996.

Wesley, John. "The Doctrine of Original Sin, Part III (1757)." In *Bicentennial Edition of the Works of John Wesley*. Vol. 12, *Doctrinal and Controversial Treatises I*, edited by Randy L. Maddox, 306–51. Nashville: Abingdon, 2012.

———. "The Doctrine of Original Sin, Part VI (1757)." In *Bicentennial Edition of the Works of John Wesley*. Vol. 12, *Doctrinal and Controversial Treatises I*, edited by Randy L. Maddox, 424–47. Nashville: Abingdon, 2012.

———. "The Doctrine of Original Sin, Part VII (1757)." In *Bicentennial Edition of the Works of John Wesley*. Vol. 12, *Doctrinal and Controversial Treatises I*, edited by Randy L. Maddox, 448–82. Nashville: Abingdon, 2012.

———. "January 25, 1739." In *Bicentennial Edition of the Works of John Wesley*. Vol. 19, *Journals and Diaries II (1738–1743)*, edited by W. Reginald Ward and Richard P. Heitzenrater, 32. Nashville: Abingdon, 1976).

———. "A Letter to the Right Reverend the Lord Bishop of Gloucester [William Warburton] (1747)." In *Bicentennial Edition of the Works of John Wesley*. Vol.

11, *The Appeals to Men of Reason and Religion and Certain Related Open Letters*, edited by Gerald R. Cragg, 459–63. Nashville: Abingdon, 1987.

———. "May 24, 1738." In *Bicentennial Edition of the Works of John Wesley*. Vol. 18, *Journals and Diaries I (1735–1738)*, edited by W. Reginald Ward and Richard P. Heitzenrater, 242–50. Nashville: Abingdon, 1990.

———. "Sermon 40, 'Christian Perfection.'" In *Bicentennial Edition of the Works of John Wesley*. Vol. 2, *Sermons II*, edited by Albert C. Outler, 97–124. Nashville: Abingdon, 1985.

———. "Sermon 45, 'The New Birth.'" In *Bicentennial Edition of the Works of John Wesley*. Vol. 2, *Sermons II*, edited by Albert C. Outler, 186–201. Nashville: Abingdon, 1985.

———. *The Sunday Service of the Methodists in North America*. Reprint ed. Nashville: United Methodist Publishing, 1984.

———. "A Treatise on Baptism." In *Works of John Wesley*. Vol. 10, *Letters, Essays, Dialogs, Addresses*, edited by Thomas Jackson, 188–201. Grand Rapids: Zondervan, 1958–59.

The Wesleyan Church. *The Discipline of the Wesleyan Church 2016*. Indianapolis: Wesleyan Church, 2016.

Westerfield Tucker, Karen B. *American Methodist Worship*. New York: Oxford University Press, 2001.

CHAPTER 3

Baptism and Justification

Evangelical Conversion and Infant Baptism

SARAH HEANER LANCASTER,

METHODIST THEOLOGICAL SCHOOL IN OHIO

AT THE HEART OF John Wesley's theological reflection on the way of salvation lies the experience of justification.[1] Knowing God has pardoned us so that we may know ourselves as children of God provides us with assurance of God's love and assurance of our salvation. John Wesley learned the importance of this experience from the Moravians, and it became the focal point for how he understood what it meant to be an "altogether" or "real" Christian.[2] Connecting this experience with baptism is not a straightforward task, however, especially when infant baptism is widely practiced within the Wesleyan-Methodist tradition. Because Wesley accepted the importance of baptizing infants without explicitly reflecting on the way the practice worked with the evangelical experience that the Methodist movement called people to, churches in the Wesleyan-Methodist tradition are left with some tension in our

1. Wesley defines justification as pardon in "Sermon 43, 'The Scripture Way of Salvation,'" 153–69. In the same place Wesley describes justification and sanctification as the "two general parts" of salvation.

2. Podmore, *Moravian Church*, 42. For Wesley's description of an altogether Christian see "Sermon 2, 'The Almost Christian,'" 131–41.

thinking and practice. This chapter will explore this tension in an attempt to make sense of the practice of infant baptism, which has been widely retained in the Wesleyan-Methodist tradition.[3]

As Wesley developed his understanding of the way of salvation, he found it important to distinguish justification from regeneration or new birth. He explains in his sermon "The New Birth" that while justification and new birth often occur together, they are distinct works of God. Justification is God's work "*for us*, in forgiving our sins," and new birth is instead God's work "*in us*, in renewing our fallen nature."[4] In a logical sense, justification precedes new birth, even if they occur together temporally, because God does something *for* us to initiate the work *in* us. Even with their distinct purposes, justification and regeneration are closely related precisely because they work together to bring us into the way of salvation.[5] For this reason, both realities have long been understood to accompany the sign of baptism.[6] This chapter, however, will focus primarily on justification—that is, it will focus on God's work "*for* us" more than God's work "*in* us"—but some account of the latter will be necessary to see the connection with the former.

The Need for Justification

For Wesley, justification is rooted in the human problem. He follows the long tradition of the church in interpreting the account of Adam and Eve in Gen 3 as a description of how human beings not only broke relationship with God but also distorted human nature to be something other than what God intended it to be. In his sermon "The Image of God," Wesley describes how human beings were created for holiness and happiness. Wesley notes that we are holy when we are filled with the holy love of God so thoroughly our deepest responses to the world around us are motivated and directed by holy love. In the original state of righteousness, Adam's will was perfectly in line with God's will. Thus, Adam both knew what was good, and he wanted what was good. With this alignment

---

3. World Methodist Council ecumenical dialogue presupposes infant baptism among Methodists. See *Encountering Christ the Savior*, para. 30.c.

4. Wesley, "Sermon 45, 'The New Birth,'" 186–201.

5. I have also treated the connection between justification and regeneration in baptism in "Baptism and Justification," 1–19.

6. United Methodist Church, *By Water and the Spirit*, para. 30–31.

of wills, Adam did not suffer from what Wesley describes as disturbed mental or emotional states, meaning that as a result of his being holy, he was also happy.[7] He was what he was created to be.

In the fall, Adam's disobedience destroyed this holy and happy state, and human nature was changed into something other than what God had intended. In Wesley's view, the effects of the fall were both physical and spiritual. The human body became prone to sickness and would finally fail in death. The human soul, because its alignment with God was skewed, began to misunderstand the world and was drawn to love other things more than God. Because of this misdirected love toward things that cannot satisfy and are not secure, mental and emotional states were disrupted, as one cannot help but be disappointed and unfulfilled by the things being desired in the place of God. The result of this change in human nature is that human beings live in misery rather than the true happiness God intends.[8] Wesley's theology is intensely concerned with this spiritual condition. Wesley refers to its correction as restoring the threefold moral image of God.[9]

As eighteenth-century Enlightenment philosophers were drawn to more optimistic assessments of the human condition, Wesley maintained the central importance for Christian theology of original sin resulting from the fall.[10] He retained the article "Of Original Sin or Birth Sin," renumbered as VII in the Articles of Religion, which he sent to the newly forming church in North America after the colonies had won their independence. Notably, Wesley's longest treatise was on original sin.[11] He recognized that for salvation to be a meaningful goal there must be something to be saved from, and the doctrine of original sin provided the account of the problem for which Jesus Christ is Savior. Sin requires forgiveness, so justification is essential to God's saving work.

Justification, though, is not the whole of salvation for Wesley. Instead, salvation for Wesley consists in being restored to what humanity was made to be: namely, creatures that were made for loving God above all else and for loving other creatures in accordance with our love for

---

7. Wesley, "Sermon 141, 'The Image of God,'" 290–303.

8. Wesley, "Sermon 141, 'The Image of God,'" 1–5.

9. Wesley, "Sermon 62, 'The End of Christ's Coming,'" 471–84.

10. See Wesley, "Sermon 114, 'The Unity of the Divine Being,'" 60–71, for Wesley's assessment of the "rational religion" of his time.

11. Wesley could also use the language of "inbeing" sin. For a discussion of what Wesley meant by that terminology, see Maddox, *Responsible Grace*, 74–82.

God. He says that having the image of God restored to what it should be is "the one thing needful."[12] The "way of salvation" then, is the theological description of how in Christ humanity can regain what has been lost, not only after death but also in this life. For this reason, Wesley could refer to salvation as "a present thing," and he could speak of its scope as "the entire work of God, from the first dawning of grace in the soul until it is consummated in glory."[13] By showing us that we are forgiven, accepted children of God, justification opens the way for God to work in us for this restoration. The reason justification opens the further work of sanctification is that God's expression of love to us calls forth our love in return.[14]

The Need for Pardon

As serious as the human problem is, it is easy to go through life without noticing it. We deal with our misery by settling for temporary satisfaction in the things around us rather than in God. Wesley describes the condition of most people as being asleep, unaware, and unconcerned with the way we fail to be what God wants us to be.[15] The first thing God has to do in order to save us is to wake us up to our predicament so that we will begin to seek help in Christ. Wesley believed God's grace provides every person with a conscience so that we can tell right from wrong, and then grace works further to "convince" us of how thoroughly we are controlled by sin so we are motivated to seek the forgiveness of God.[16] The need for pardon must be recognized before we will seek pardon. This is why Wesley insisted on a place for repentance in the way of salvation. We are justified (pardoned) by faith, but repentance precedes pardon.[17]

12. See Wesley, "Sermon 146, 'The One Thing Needful,'" 351–59.

13. Wesley, "Sermon 43, 'The Scripture Way of Salvation,'" 153–69. Acknowledging the scope of salvation in the entire work of God, including prevenient grace, is an important point for understanding the position he takes with regard to unbaptized infants who die, covered in another section of this chapter.

14. See Wesley, "Sermon 43, 'The Scripture Way of Salvation,'" 153–69, I.4.

15. See Wesley, "Sermon 9, 'The Spirit of Bondage and Adoption,'" 248–66, where Wesley describes the "natural man" as being asleep.

16. Wesley, "Sermon 9, 'The Spirit of Bondage and Adoption,'" 248–66, especially II.2. In "On Working Out Our Own Salvation," Wesley connects "natural conscience" to "preventing grace," saying "No man living is entirely destitute" of it. See Wesley, "Sermon 85, 'On Working Out Our Own Salvation,'" 199–209.

17. Wesley, "Sermon 43, 'The Scripture Way of Salvation,'" 153–69. Wesley defines justification as pardon in I.3.

Because Wesley was leading a movement in which he was preaching mostly to people who had already been baptized in the Church of England, he saw and addressed the need for people to recognize that they were failing to be what God created them to be. Wesley never denied that God had brought the baptized into covenant with himself through baptism; rather, Wesley pointed out that the baptized had not responded to this call and act of God in the way that they should. In this way, Wesley's revival movement aimed to wake up and bring back to life all those who had failed to respond to the claim God made upon their lives in baptism. Many of the baptized had failed to respond to God's baptismal claim on their lives by either turning openly to sin or by misunderstanding the opportunity baptism opened up to them by thinking that generally decent lives and church-going were the fulfillment of the life God intended for them.[18] In both cases, people failed to recognize that baptism opened the possibility of cultivating relationship with God by using the means of grace available in the church. As means of grace, actions such as prayer, searching Scripture, and receiving the Lord's Supper, are ways through which we come to know and trust in God's love so that we may grow in our love for God. Open sinners may neglect the use of these means altogether, and others may use them, thinking them to be ends in themselves rather than means for relationship.

In either case, because persons are not filled with love of God, they are not being restored to the life of love God created us for. So, they fail to receive the one thing needed for salvation. Not loving and trusting God with one's whole heart is the essence of sin.[19] Wesley often speaks of sin as rooted in desire, and he categorizes three desires as especially important for leading people away from God. First, desire of the flesh or seeking physical pleasure replaces God with bodily experiences. Second, desire of the eye, seeking pleasure in less physical ways (for instance the enjoyment we feel in having the latest fashion or gadget) replaces God with less tangible gratifications. Finally, the pride of life, which Wesley describes as desire of praise, replaces God with the esteem of other people. Each of these desires draws one away from God by directing their love and trust

18. These are the two options Wesley names in "Sermon 45, 'The New Birth,'" 186–201.

19. See Wesley, "Sermon 44, 'Original Sin,'" 170–85, especially section II. Wesley describes atheism not as intellectual rejection of God but rather as failure to know and love God, so we fall into idolatry. The three desires are expressions of our love of the world instead of God.

to something else. So whether openly violating the commands of God or settling for going through the motions of religious life, all need to be forgiven for looking to something other than God for fulfillment.

For the adults Wesley addressed in his preaching, the need for justification was evident. Because most of his hearers had already been baptized, his theological understanding of justification developed primarily in connection with evangelical preaching that called people to repentance and faith. In that situation, his main concern was to get people to an honest self-examination of their lives before God so they would open themselves to the grace God offered. He did not rebaptize them, so his theology of justification did not explicitly link justification and baptism. However, as his movement became a church that baptized infants, he had to give some thought to baptism. Although he never explicitly developed the connection between justification and infant baptism, some points of contact can be shown.

Original Sin and Baptism

Ever since Christian theology linked the transmission of original sin to infants, the need for baptism for the remission of sin for infants has been a pressing concern. If infants are born with original sin, and therefore share in the guilt of sin, then they need to be pardoned. In times of high infant mortality, this way of thinking about original sin presses parents toward baptizing infants as early as possible so if they die, they will not be damned for original guilt. John Wesley was well aware of this problem, and his theology developed in the direction of a generous understanding for infants, even as he continued to insist on the serious problem of original sin.

Although he never settled on a specific theory about the mechanism for transmission, Wesley did accept the universal scope of the problem.[20] It seemed obvious that because infants were vulnerable to illness and death, they shared in the way sin distorted the original state humans had in God's original creation. He was reluctant, though, to accept that the pardon infants receive was because of damning guilt. As much as Wesley affirmed the need to talk about original sin, when he edited the Church of England's article "Of Original Sin or Birth Sin" for the Articles of Religion

---

20. For a discussion of the options Wesley explored, see Maddox, *Responsible Grace*, 75–81.

that he sent to North America, he removed reference to how original sin deserves "God's wrath and damnation."[21] Similarly, when Wesley edited and published his father's "Treatise on Baptism," he retained the idea of guilt but removed the adjective "damning."[22] Wesley accepted that infants share in the human problem, but he stopped short of attributing condemnation to them. Because human nature even for infants is affected by the fall, they need God's grace in order to grow into the life of holiness and happiness God intends for all of humanity. Even without the threat of damnation, baptism as a sign of God's work for salvation was not to be denied to infants.

In Wesley's own time, the emphasis of the Protestant Reformation on being saved by faith had made infant baptism a disputed practice. Given the choice between baptizing infants and waiting until an age when a profession of faith could be made, the emphasis of Wesley's movement on being justified by faith might have made believer's baptism appear to be more suitable. Wesley, though, in publishing an extract of William Wall's *Thoughts Upon Infant Baptism*, accepted the arguments of his time in favor of infant baptism; for instance, that infant baptism for children of Christian parents was an ancient practice in the church and also that baptism of infants indicates inclusion in the new covenant for Christians, just as the circumcision of infant Jewish boys meant infants are included in God's covenant with Israel.[23] When it became evident that Methodists in North America would have to constitute themselves as a church, Wesley included infant baptism in the liturgy he sent for that purpose.

The Sunday Service Wesley sent to North America included both a ritual of baptism for infants as well as a ritual for persons of "riper years." For infants, the corruption of original sin has not yet manifested itself in actual sins, whereas for those of riper years it surely has. This difference is reflected in the wording of the two rituals. In the ritual for those of riper years, the minister directly addresses the persons being baptized regarding how baptism releases them from their sins.[24] Not only is di-

21. The original wording of the article may be found in The Book of Common Prayer or online at https://www.churchofengland.org/prayer-and-worship/worship-texts-and-resources/book-common-prayer/articles-religion.

22. Maddox, *Responsible Grace*, 224. Maddox also points out Wesley stopped publishing this treatise after 1770, even though he continued to publish *Thoughts Upon Infant Baptism*.

23. Wesley, *Thoughts Upon Infant Baptism*.

24. Wesley, *Sunday Service*, 144.

rect questioning not possible for infants, such a matter is not necessary either. References to justification (pardon) are not absent, though, in the ritual for infants. This ritual speaks of washing and being delivered from God's wrath, and it sets baptism in the context of Christ's dying for the forgiveness of sins.[25] In light of how Wesley removed reference to wrath and damnation in the article "Of Original Sin or Birth Sin," the presence of the word "wrath" in the ritual for infants may seem odd. This apparent discrepancy may be reconciled with the recognition that God disapproves of the presence of sin in human life (even in infants), so there is wrath, but this wrath is not punishing anger.[26] God forgives the presence of sin, and so opens up the possibility of relationship. Because of what Christ has done, the presence of sin at the very beginning of life was not damning. This point is addressed more fully in the paragraphs below about unbaptized infants. The ritual also refers to being an adopted child of God, the basis for one's assurance of God's love that was such a hallmark of the experience of justification for the revival movement.[27] Thus, even for infants, baptism acts as a sign of justification.

For infants who could be baptized, God works through this sacrament to offer both justification and regeneration to baptized infants, as they grow and develop in the company of the Christian community, can begin to journey along the way of salvation God provides in Jesus Christ. Though no human can escape the bodily vulnerability that is one effect of original sin, baptized infants are forgiven children of God who can know and depend on God's gracious presence in their lives. Similar to the experience of justification for people of riper years, in infant baptism God is doing something for us followed by work that is in us. Infants who are unable to be baptized will be discussed below.

Because the effect of the fall not only leaves human beings vulnerable physically but also spiritually, the justification and regeneration of baptism can be lost. Indeed, this was the problem Wesley called people to consider through his evangelical preaching: not what were you made in

25. Wesley, *Sunday Service*, 139–41.

26. This is not to say Wesley disregarded or minimized God's wrath. The condition for being admitted to a Methodist society was "a desire to flee from the wrath to come." See "The General Rules of the Methodist Church," in the *Book of Discipline of The United Methodist Church*. Rather, it is to point out Wesley must have thought about wrath somewhat differently for infants than for persons of riper years, and this is a suggestion for an understanding of the wrath of God that fits with infant baptism.

27. Wesley, *Sunday Service*, 143.

your baptism, but what are you now?[28] Our distorted natures are prone
to sin ("inclined to evil" in the words of Article VII), so we incur guilt
for actual sins as we go through life, and we will remain prone to sin
unless and until God fully heals our natures. Baptism is neither a vac-
cination against actual sin nor forgiveness for future sin. The question
Wesley asked to people of riper years, "What are you now?" does not
call into question God's work in baptism; rather it calls us to examine
our response to God's work in us. Have we in fact stayed on the way of
salvation that God initiated in us at baptism? If we have not, then we
must start the journey again by being justified and regenerated again.
God's design for Methodism, as it is recorded in the "Large Minutes,"
"to reform the nation, and in particular the Church, to spread scriptural
holiness over the land," was essentially understood as a mission to call
baptized Christians in a nation with an established church back to the
way of salvation.[29] The scope of God's salvation covers not only the guilt
of sin (justification), but also sin's power (sanctification). As Wesley says,
sin remains after justification, but it does not rule.[30] Sanctification is the
process of being empowered by God to resist the rule that sin keeps trying to exert. When we neglect to make use of the power God provides to
us to resist sin, we can fall back under its sway. Infant baptism does not by
itself "fix" the human problem. Rather, it puts the baptized in a position
to work with God's work in them, using the means of grace available in
the church along with the support and accountability of others who are
also on the way.

As a sacrament, baptism is a sign-act of God's justification and regeneration. It is a visible means that brings us into the invisible presence
and power of God, but as a sign, it is also distinct from that which it
signifies. The reality we need in order to be saved is God's grace to forgive
us and renew our natures. Although the visible sign of water expresses
and conveys this grace, it is not the grace itself. Wesley made use of the
distinction he had learned in the Church of England between the sign
and the thing signified in his sermon "The New Birth."[31] In this sermon,
his concern is for those who are of riper years, having in mind persons
who receive the sign of water at a mature time in life but who continue

28. See Wesley, "Sermon 18, 'Marks of the New Birth,'" 415–30.

29. Wesley, "Large Minutes," 836–935, section 4.

30. Wesley, "Sermon 43, 'Scripture Way of Salvation,'" 153–69. See also Wesley,
"Sermon 13, 'On Sin in Believers,'" 314–34.

31. Wesley, "Sermon 45, 'The New Birth,'" 186–201, IV.1.

in sin just as they did before they were baptized. He uses the distinction in this context to make the point that when a person who is of an age to resist God's grace is baptized the sign and the thing signified "do not constantly go together"; in other words, a person of riper years may receive the visible sign of water without accepting the offered invisible reality of grace.[32] He makes sure to say, though, that in the case of infant baptism, the church does affirm that the two realities go together, presumably because infants are not able to resist grace the way people who have come to an age of accountability can. In this sermon, the particular work of grace under discussion is regeneration, although the logic of the distinction holds for justification as well.

Wesley does not explicitly draw upon the distinction between sign and thing signified with regard to infants who have not been baptized, but he does implicitly rely on the logic of that distinction in order to make sense of the problem of those who do not have access to the sacrament. Persons in that situation are not brought into the church by baptism, so they cannot be led to faith by the church. Late in his life, Wesley began publishing *The Arminian Magazine*, in which he promoted God's offer of "universal redemption" with the intent to counter certain Calvinist ideas, namely those that by maintaining the security of the elect also inevitably doomed many to damnation without any chance of redemption.[33] Across several issues of the magazine, Wesley published extracts from John Plaifere's "An Appeal to the Gospel for the true Doctrine of Divine Predestination, concorded with the Orthodox Doctrine of God's Free Grace, and Man's Free Will." In February 1779 (the second year of the magazine's publication), Wesley published a section of Plaifere's work entitled, "Concerning the Salvability of the Heathen." In this portion of his work, Plaifere argued "that God, for the merit of Christ will accept the sincere endeavors of all men who live according to their best abilities, though he was not pleased to bless all with the light of Revelation." Plaifere's central conviction is in the goodness of God who cannot be doubted to look with compassion on those who are outside the church but nevertheless who act according to the best light they have. Plaifere connects the situation of those outside the church to infants who have died without being baptized

---

32. Wesley, "Sermon 45, 'The New Birth,'" 186–201, IV.2.

33. Gunter, "Annotated Content Index." I do not think by "universal redemption" Wesley meant simply everyone was saved. He objected to "universal salvation" among the Moravians. His concern against the Calvinists was to show everyone has the possibility of being saved.

as well as to those who do not have the mental capacities to ever come to faith, offering the comfort: "a good and wise God can require nothing of any, which he knows to be impossible."[34]

In the same issue, Wesley included a poem written by a father as an elegy to his dead infant with the implied endorsement, "I have left out some stanzas, but have not altered a line." Because it is conveyed in poetic verse, the situation of the dying infant is not stated with precision, but the poem describes the baby just opening its eyes and then its soul departing. Under such circumstances, there would be neither time for baptism nor an act of faith, but the father is confident that God will regard the child as innocent. In this poem, the father also extends innocence to infants not born to Christian parents, saying:

> Will God, their common Maker, think ye, deal
> So differently with these, as yours to save,
> And send the heathen infant's soul to hell,
> Whene'er he sends its body to the grave?

The father recognizes the problem of original sin and God's justice in punishing the whole human race, but he goes on to stress the mercy and goodness in Christ's redemption, saying:

> For as thro' the offence of Adam, all
> (He and his unborn seed) were doom'd to die
> Ev'n so, the righteousness of Jesus shall
> Retrieve them all, and freely justify.

For this father, the ransom provided by Christ is the basis for God to act in mercy to forgive us of that for which we are justly accountable.[35] This mercy is available to every infant whether born to Christian parents or not.

Although neither Plaifere's extract nor the poem are Wesley's own words, their presence in the magazine over which he exercised editorial control shows Wesley at least did not reject the generous view of salvation from damnation which they represent.[36] The reality of justification was

34. Anonymous, *Arminian Magazine*, 57. Compare Plaifere's point to Wesley's recognition that there must be "time and opportunity" for fruits meet for repentance to be necessary for justification in Wesley, "Sermon 43, 'Scripture Way of Salvation,'" 153–69.

35. Anonymous, "Elegiac Stanzas," 96–103. See also note 10 above.

36. Maddox provides several examples of what we can tell of Wesley's own thoughts about baptism with regard to damnation for original sin from examining how he edited others in *Responsible Grace*, 223–34.

God's to give, whether or not the sign of baptism had been administered. Without Wesley's own explicit argument, it is only possible to infer what he would think, but his confidence in God's goodness to work for human salvation, even apart from the very means that God established in the church for this purpose, seems clear from his choices of what to address in his magazine.[37] This confidence did not undermine the need to make use of those means when they are available, but it does remind us that the means are not under our control. It is God who makes the reality of grace available, when and where God will. Baptism is a sign of this reality, but the reality exceeds the sign.

Sin is a real problem from which we need to be saved, and this problem is so serious it impacts us from the very beginning of our lives. Wesley understood we all need to be saved, but his theological point is precisely that Jesus Christ came to save all, not just some. Because of the work of Christ, those who are unable to follow the way of salvation Wesley preached are nonetheless salvagable in the sense of not facing eternal damnation. Although they may not receive the fullness of salvation available to us in this life (the present assurance of God's loving acceptance and full restoration of the image of God in this life), they are not doomed eternally just because of Adam's sin.[38] Baptism is a genuine sign of the reality of God's forgiving grace, and it is to be offered by the church as a means for God to use, but God's forgiveness is not restricted to the offering of the sign.

The Need for Ongoing Justification

Because the Methodist movement was a movement to spread scriptural holiness among people who for the most part had already been baptized, Wesley's theological reflection was focused on what he needed to say within the context of that movement. In this section, the need for

37. Like Plaifere, Wesley presumes in "Sermon 85, 'On Working Out Our Own Salvation,'" that every person has some glimmer of God's light because prevenient grace gives every human a conscience. This does not mean Wesley would draw the same conclusion Plaifere did, but it shows they share an openness about God working in everyone.

38. It is well to keep in mind Wesley conceives salvation as having a very large scope that includes not only what happens after we die but also what God does to renew our natures while we live on this earth. See Wesley, "Sermon 43, 'The Scripture Way of Salvation,'" 153–69.

ongoing justification for Methodists in a movement is explored to see how it might guide thinking about ongoing justification after infant baptism. I extend Wesley's theology beyond his original context here as I try to think with him about how to address a new situation.

In Wesley's original context, the need for ongoing justification arose as a question about the sin that remains after persons who have reached an age of accountability receive the powerful evangelical experience of justification but have not yet been perfected. The sermons "On Sin in Believers" and "The Repentance of Believers" especially address this question. In these two sermons, Wesley focuses on the sin that remains in believers' lives tainting but not controlling them. He does not here speak of committing outward sins (deliberate violations of God's commands), but rather only of inward sins (dispositions) that show sin has not been finally destroyed.[39] Wesley had long insisted that even a babe in Christ would not commit outward sin.[40] That is, newly justified Christians would not deliberately engage in behavior they knew God would prohibit. But because he does not hold that justification eliminates sin itself, but rather justification suspends or stuns sin so that sin does not have control over us, Wesley needed to consider the presence of sin in those who are justified.[41]

To do so, Wesley must make a case for why he says sin remains even in those who are justified. He notes that Scripture itself acknowledges the continued struggle with sin, and this struggle continues to be attested in the experience of believers.[42] The work of God in us that begins at the same time we are justified gives us the capacity to resist sin so we do not commit acts God prohibits, but because sin is not gone, it continues to try to exert control over us. Its very being is a danger we must recognize and guard against.[43] In his doctrine of perfection, Wesley holds out hope that

39. Wesley was pressed to think carefully about types of sin in the face of his interaction with Count Zinzendorf, who had stated believers were wholly justified and wholly sanctified at the same time. Wesley's insistence sin remained after justification had to be explained, so he defined sin in ways to account for different expressions of it. The typology he developed may not be fully descriptive of the human struggle, but he sets an example of nuanced reflection. Important definitions of outward and inward sin may be found in Wesley, "Sermon 19, 'The Great Privilege,'" 431–43, II.2 and Wesley, "Sermon 13, 'On Sin in Believers,'" 314–33, II.2.

40. Wesley, "Sermon 40, 'Christian Perfection,'" 97–124.

41. Wesley, "Sermon 43, 'Scripture Way of Salvation,'" 153–69.

42. Wesley, "Sermon 13, 'On Sin in Believers,'" 314–33.

43. Wesley, "Sermon 13, 'On Sin in Believers,'" 314–33, IV.4, IV.10.

God can finally eradicate the very being of sin from our lives, but unless and until that happens, our responsibility is not to give way to it.[44]

In this period between justification and perfection, believers are in need of repentance. They do not repent in the same way as before justification—namely repenting of sins committed that would lead to their eternal destruction—but rather Wesley speaks of repentance after justification as "self-knowledge," an awareness that sin remains and tries to exert itself in our desires in order to turn us from God.[45] Sin "cleaves" to all our actions, no matter how outwardly good, so we are not fully who we ought to be.[46] Under the presumption that where there is sin there is also guilt, the very presence of sin (even if we do not act on it) in our lives requires forgiveness. Because believers have been adopted as children of God, there is no condemnation for this guilt. God continues to forgive. But because believers know that sin remains in their lives, they also know that they bear its guilt and deserve to be punished for it.[47]

Knowledge of the sin that remains reminds them of their predicament and how helpless they are to do anything about it. The process of sanctification continues, and Wesley maintains that God can clean even the remains of sin from human lives, but unless and until it pleases God to do so, even believers remain guilty and in need of forgiveness.[48] This self-knowledge causes them to turn to Christ as their only hope for deliverance from this sin.[49] Because the experience of justification enables believers to know that they are children of God, they can trust in God's ongoing forgiveness as they repent. Believers are not haunted by fear for their souls, but they see themselves honestly and continue to seek the help of God daily. Therefore, justification does not simply lie in the past, but is an ongoing call upon our lives to keep turning to God.

This need for ongoing justification until God has finished the entire work of salvation can inform how the Wesleyan-Methodist tradition thinks about God's work after infant baptism. Because God works to justify and regenerate infants in baptism, baptized infants are in a similar position to justified adults. The presence of sin is forgiven, but it has not

44. Wesley, "Sermon 14, 'Repentance of Believers,'" 335–52, I.20.

45. Wesley, "Sermon 14, 'Repentance of Believers,'" 335–52, I.1.

46. Wesley, "Sermon 14, 'Repentance of Believers,'" 335–52, I.11.

47. Wesley, "Sermon 14, 'Repentance of Believers,'" 335–52, II.6.

48. Wesley, "Sermon 14, 'Repentance of Believers,'" 335–52, I.20.

49. Wesley, "Sermon 14, 'Repentance of Believers,'" 335–52, I.16–18.

been eliminated. It remains and continues to try to exert control. Baptized infants are forgiven children of God who may depend on God's ongoing forgiveness as they continue to struggle with sin as they go through their lives. Children who are still maturing as they grow are in a different life situation than mature, fully accountable adults, so their struggle may be somewhat different, but they also may keep turning to God daily for strength, guidance, and repentance as self-knowledge, and they may trust as children of God that God will empower and forgive.

This insight underscores why baptism is not an automatic "fix" to the human problem. Within the church, infant baptism puts young baptized members in the very position that justified members of the Methodist movement were in—forgiven and growing in sanctification, but still vulnerable to the existence of sin that remains. In light of this situation, attention to children's spiritual lives becomes very important.

Conclusion

John Wesley's theological writings were shaped by issues he needed to think about in his time and place. In his context, he primarily reflected on how best to call people away from being satisfied with anything less than the full salvation God offers in this life: namely an assurance of God's holy love that enables our own holy love in return and leads to the holiness and happiness for which we were made. In order to enjoy this full salvation, one needs to be justified and regenerated so that one can be sanctified. In the context of the established Church of England, Wesley encountered people who may have been baptized in the church but had not continued along the way of salvation. In that situation, Methodists did not need to baptize but to call the baptized back to the way. That call was to an evangelical experience. Given the pressing concern of the movement, Wesley did not need to reflect much on baptism with regard to the way of salvation. The reflection he did was mostly to help people see that they could not simply rely on their baptism in the church for their justification and regeneration because sin continued to exert control in their lives.

Given the controversy over infant baptism in his time, Wesley did take a position in support of infant baptism in the Church of England. As Methodism needed to take ecclesial form in North America, Wesley modeled the resources he sent to North America after the Church of England. At that time, he did not explicitly address the connection between infant baptism and the way of salvation he had reflected on for years. This chapter has attempted to show this connection can be made so we can see Wesley's bequest of infant baptism to the newly forming church in North America was not a mistake or lapse of consistency. Despite his commitment to infant baptism in the church, Wesley was also attentive to God's ability to work apart from the sign. He did not restrict justification to baptism, even as he trusted that it was a means God used to justify. In this way, Wesley recognized that justification was God's to give.

The way of salvation as Wesley conceived it includes the entire work of God in human life. For most people to whom Wesley preached, the way of salvation began with an experience of justification and regeneration. This experience was the opening of the possibility of regaining the one thing needful, namely the moral image of God. Infant baptism also opens this possibility by offering justification and regeneration. At any stage of life, we are always vulnerable to letting sin regain power over us, so infant baptism is not a guarantee of remaining on the way God has set us on. The community, then, becomes extremely important for holding us accountable and supporting us along the way. Early Methodists supported each other in society, and the church is now responsible for supporting children after baptism. As a sign of the assurance and acceptance of God's love, baptism opens us to respond to God's ongoing work of sanctification in us and puts us in a community where that can happen. If we fail to respond, we need to be called back to start again. As long as we continue to respond, we may be confident in God's power and presence in our lives to give us the one thing needful to become who God created us to be.

Bibliography

Anonymous. *The Arminian Magazine* 2 (February 1779, reprint 2015) 57.

Anonymous. "Elegiac Stanzas on the Death of an Infant." *The Arminian Magazine* 2 (1789, reprint 2015), 96–103.

Gunter, Stephen W. "An Annotated Content Index." *The Arminian Magazine* vols. 1–20 (1778–1797). https://divinity.duke.edu/sites/divinity.duke.edu/files/documents/cswt/Arminian_Magazine_vols_1-20.pdf.

Lancaster, Sarah Heath. "Baptism and Justification: A Methodist Understanding." *Ecclesiology* 4 (2008) 1–19.

Maddox, Randy L. *Responsible Grace: John Wesley's Practical Theology*. Nashville: Abingdon, 1994.

Podmore, Colin. *The Moravian Church in England 1728–1760.* Oxford: Clarendon, 1998.

The United Methodist Church. *By Water and the Spirit: A United Methodist Understanding of Baptism.* Nashville: General Board of Discipleship, 1996.

Wesley, John. "The Large Minutes." In *Bicentennial Edition of the Works of John Wesley.* Vol. 10, *The Methodist Societies, The Minutes of Conference,* edited by Henry D. Rack, 836–935. Nashville: Abingdon, 2011.

————. "Sermon 2, 'The Almost Christian.'" In *Bicentennial Edition of the Works of John Wesley.* Vol. 1, *Sermons I,* edited by Albert C. Outler, 131–41. Nashville: Abingdon, 1984.

————. "Sermon 9, 'The Spirit of Bondage and Adoption.'" In *Bicentennial Edition of the Works of John Wesley.* Vol. 1, *Sermons I,* edited by Albert C. Outler, 248–66. Nashville: Abingdon, 1984.

————. "Sermon 13, 'On Sin in Believers.'" In *Bicentennial Edition of the Works of John Wesley.* Vol. 1, *Sermons I,* edited by Albert C. Outler, 314–34. Nashville: Abingdon, 1984.

————. "Sermon 14, 'The Repentance of Believers.'" In *Bicentennial Edition of the Works of John Wesley.* Vol. 1, *Sermons I,* edited by Albert C. Outler, 335–52. Nashville: Abingdon, 1984.

————. "Sermon 18, 'Marks of the New Birth.'" In *Bicentennial Edition of the Works of John Wesley.* Vol. 1, *Sermons I,* edited by Albert Outler, 415–30. Nashville: Abingdon, 1984.

————. "Sermon 19, 'The Great Privilege of Those That Are Born of God.'" In *Bicentennial Edition of the Works of John Wesley.* Vol. 1, *Sermons I,* edited by Albert C. Outler, 431–43. Nashville: Abingdon, 1984.

————. "Sermon 40, 'Christian Perfection.'" In *Bicentennial Edition of the Works of John Wesley.* Vol. 2, *Sermons II,* edited by Albert C. Outler, 97–124. Nashville: Abingdon, 1985.

————. "Sermon 43, 'The Scripture Way of Salvation.'" In *Bicentennial Edition of the Works of John Wesley.* Vol. 2, *Sermons II,* edited by Albert C. Outler, 153–69. Nashville: Abingdon, 1985.

————. "Sermon 44, 'Original Sin.'" In *Bicentennial Edition of the Works of John Wesley.* Vol. 2, *Sermons II,* edited by Albert C. Outler, 170–85. Nashville: Abingdon, 1985.

————. "Sermon 45, 'The New Birth.'" In *Bicentennial Edition of the Works of John Wesley.* Vol. 2, *Sermons II,* edited by Albert C. Outler, 186–201. Nashville: Abingdon, 1985.

————. "Sermon 62, 'The End of Christ's Coming.'" In *Bicentennial Edition of the Works of John Wesley.* Vol. 2, *Sermons II,* edited by Albert C. Outler, 471–84. Nashville: Abingdon, 1985.

————. "Sermon 85, 'On Working Out Our Own Salvation.'" In *Bicentennial Edition of the Works of John Wesley.* Vol. 3, *Sermons III,* edited by Albert C. Outler, 199–209. Nashville: Abingdon, 1986.

————. "Sermon 114, 'The Unity of the Divine Being.'" In *Bicentennial Edition of the Works of John Wesley.* Vol. 4, *Sermons IV,* edited by Albert C. Outler, 60–71. Nashville: Abingdon, 1987.

————. "Sermon 141, 'The Image of God.'" In *Bicentennial Edition of the Works of John Wesley.* Vol. 4, *Sermons IV,* edited by Albert C. Outler, 290–303. Nashville: Abingdon, 1987.

————. "Sermon 146, 'The One Thing Needful.'" In *Bicentennial Edition of the Works of John Wesley*. Vol. 4, *Sermons IV*, edited by Albert C. Outler, 351–59. Nashville: Abingdon, 1987.

————. *The Sunday Service of the Methodists in North America*. Reprint ed. Nashville: United Methodist Publishing, 1984.

————. *Thoughts Upon Infant Baptism: Extracted from a Late Writer* (William Wall). Bristol: Farley, 1751.

World Methodist Council. *Encountering Christ the Savior: Church and Sacraments*. Lake Junaluska, NC: World Methodist Council, 2011. http://worldmethodistcouncil. org/wp-content/uploads/2014/10/Encountering-Christ-the-Saviour-Church-and-Sacraments.pdf.

CHAPTER 4

Baptism and Pneumatology

Holy Water

PETER J. BELLINI, UNITED THEOLOGICAL SEMINARY

Except a man be born of water and of the Spirit—*Except he experience that great inward change by the Spirit, and be baptized (wherever baptism can be had) as the outward sign and means of it.* —Wesley's *Notes* on John 3:5[1]

Introduction: Wesley, a Practical Theologian of Holiness

JOHN WESLEY AND THE people called Methodists had one primary, providential purpose and mission. Upon it hung all of their doctrine, spirit, and discipline. Full sanctification, "this doctrine is the grand depositum which God has lodged with the people called Methodists; and for the sake of propagating this chiefly He appeared to have raised us up."[2] The Methodist Connexion was asked at Conference, "What may we reasonably believe to be God's design in raising up the Preachers called Methodist?" The answer offered was: "To reform the nation, particularly

---

1. John Wesley, "John 3:5," 218.
2. Wesley, "John Wesley to Robert Carr Brackenbury," 9.

the church, and to spread scriptural holiness over the land."[3] Wesley also realized that the mission of scriptural holiness "could never be wrought in us, but by the power of the Holy Ghost."[4] This essay is primarily about the sacramental relationship between the outward sign of water and the inward regenerating work of the Spirit, and how both are related to holiness. A Wesleyan theology of baptism and regeneration is located in the larger Spirit-led *ordo* of holiness that informs the nature of the sacrament, its nuances and tensions, and its ultimate goal for Wesley. The grace of baptism launches one on a soteriological journey of personal and social holiness of heart and life that manifests the kingdom of heaven on earth.

As we begin an analysis of Wesleyan pneumatology and baptism, two premises need to be established from the onset regarding John Wesley as a theologian. First, John Wesley was not a systematic or doctrinal theologian in a way that Calvin was systematic with his *Institutes* or in a way that Aquinas was doctrinal with his *Summa*.[5] Prior to Albert Outler, Wesley had long been marginalized as not being a serious theologian for such reasons. However, Outler credited Wesley as a significant theologian in his own right but yet labeled him modestly a "folk theologian."[6] More recently, major Wesleyan historical theologians such as Frank Baker,[7] Randy Maddox,[8] and Kenneth Collins,[9] among others, have esteemed him as a practical theologian, recognizing how Wesley understood himself and giving him his just due. In Wesley's own words, he considered his task to be "practical divinity."[10]

Second, Wesley as a practical theologian was primarily concerned about doing theology within a soteriological framework, specifically honing in on the core themes of grace (the means) and holiness or holy love (the end).[11] Wesley's theological emphasis on grace and holiness

3. Wesley, "Large Minutes," 299.

4. Wesley, "Thoughts Upon Methodism," 238.

5. Rack, *Reasonable Enthusiast*, 381.

6. Outler, "Towards a Re-Appraisal," 40–43.

7. Baker, "Practical Divinity," 7–16.

8. Maddox, "Practical Theologian?" 122–47.

9. Collins, *Theology of John Wesley*, 1–3.

10. Wesley cited by Maddox, "John Wesley: Practical Theologian?" 128.

11. Adding to Outler's axial theme of grace, Ken Collins rightfully identifies the "axial" themes of grace and holiness around which Wesley's theology turns. Collins, *Theology of John Wesley*, 5–12. Wesley often used the Johannine phrase "perfect love" and even the term "holy love" to express best the mutually defining conjunction holiness and love in Wesley's theology.

shaped early Methodist teaching and practices in terms of its *ordo salutis/ via salutis*[12] with the two main loci, justification and sanctification. These theological sites are located on an upward continuum of grace, fueled and supported by the means of grace. Wesley put it this way, "Our main doctrines, which include all the rest, are three—that of repentance, of faith, and of holiness. The first of these we account, as it were, the porch of religion; the next the door, the third, religion itself."[13]

For Wesley, salvation was ministered by God's grace through the Spirit from its prevenient stages to its *telos* in Christian perfection and glorification.[14] The goal of salvation is to restore humanity to the original image of righteousness and holiness. Along this trajectory of grace, Wesley's soteriology nuances various tensions that emerge along the *ordo salutis*. Among others, such tensions, or conjunctions, include grace and works, justification and sanctification, instantaneous and process, and sacrament (outward) and the work of the Spirit (inward).[15] For Wesley, it is clear that "it is the office of the Holy Ghost to sanctify."[16] Again, in making us holy, it is the "Holy Ghost, called the 'Spirit of Truth' . . . in establishing his faith, and in perfecting his obedience; or in other words should sanctify him to redemption."[17] It is within this larger soteriological

12. There is an ongoing debate regarding terminology. Namely, which phrase is more accurate of Wesley's theology: *ordo salutis* (recognizing crisis and process, promoted by Outler and Collins) or *via salutis* (more of a gradual process perspective, promoted by Maddox)? See Collins, *Theology of John* Wesley, 307–312. Wesley's development of grace is best represented as a process of salvation with two key foci and crises, justification and sanctification. Thus, for Wesley, salvation involves both process and crises. Yet, *via salutis* is a term that reflects the title and content of Wesley's most published and definitive theological sermon, "The Scripture Way of Salvation." This sermon in no way differs from the process-crisis dynamic noted above in the *ordo salutis*, highlighting the two foci and crises of justification and sanctification. In this light, I am thinking of the two idioms interchangeably to describe the process-crisis continuum of grace and salvation in Wesley. The way of salvation, for Wesley, involves growth in grace with the two experiences of justification and sanctification. However, as to not confuse the reader, I will be consistent and use *ordo*, but I could just as easily use *via*, and according to my definition, they mean the same thing. See Wesley, "Sermon 43, 'Scripture Way of Salvation,'" 153–69.

13. Wesley, "Principles of a Methodist," 227.

14. Wesley understood the entire work of salvation beginning with prevenient grace and ending with glorification, though grace continues in that state eternally. Wesley, "Sermon 43, 'Scripture Way of Salvation,'" 153–69.

15. Collins, *Theology of John Wesley*, 4–16.

16. Wesley, "Farther Appeal," 108.

17. Wesley, "Letter to the Right Reverend," 459.

scheme, with holiness as its *telos* and grace, or the work of the Spirit, as the means to attain the goal, that a Wesleyan construal of baptism is located.

Lycurgus Starkey, commenting on Wesley's pneumatology, declares, "All virtue and growth in Christian holiness is by the power of the Holy Spirit which is the imparted presence of God-in-Christ in human life."[18] Within a Wesleyan scheme of theology, the Holy Spirit is not only the divine presence of holy love,[19] but also the "agent or administrator of redemption."[20] Starkey elaborates, "As the bearer of the redemptive effects of the historical atonement initiated by the Father and effected by the Son, the personal agency of the Holy Spirit is crucial."[21] Wesley recognized the Spirit as the chief executor of the grace-empowered work of salvation wrought by Christ in the heart and life. In Johannine pneumatology, which Wesley often draws upon, the Spirt of Truth—as presence—presents the person of Christ and reveals, witnesses, and applies the saving work of Christ in the world and in the church, beginning at baptism leading to holiness.[22]

In the *oikonomia* of God, it is the third person of the Trinity, the Holy Spirit, who is the divine agent of grace and our experience of salvation, initiating in baptism.[23] Baptism is the initiating grace either accompanying baptismal regeneration in an infant or potentially accompanying conversion in an adult that begins the salvation journey to Christian perfection. The inward change wrought through the outward sign of baptism is the dynamic work of the Holy Spirit, the divine agent of redemption. Wesley iterates, "This beginning of that vast, inward change, is usually termed, the new birth. Baptism is the outward sign of this inward grace."[24] Thus, baptism is a conversation about water and the Spirit; a reality in which the outward sign of baptism is joined with the inward work of the Holy Spirit. Furthermore, in Wesleyan theology, this reality results in regeneration on the way to Christian perfection. Simply put, for Wesleyans, "Baptism is the doorway to the sanctified life."[25]

18. Starkey, *Work of the Holy Spirit*, 34.

19. Collins, *Theology of John Wesley*, 121.

20. Starkey, *Work of the Holy Spirit*, 26.

21. Starkey, *Work of the Holy Spirit*, 26.

22. John 14–16. Wesley, "Farther Appeal," 163–76; Wesley, "Gloucester," 148–73.

23. Wesley, "Farther Appeal," 107–8. The entire work of salvation is the operation of the Holy Spirit.

24. Wesley, "Farther Appeal," 107.

25. United Methodist Church, *By Water and the* Spirit, 8.

Wesley and the Holy Spirit

Prior to examining in more detail Wesley's connection between water and the Spirit, one first needs to examine more closely Wesley's understanding of the Holy Spirit. Wesley, unlike many Pentecostals and charismatics today, did not speak of the third person of the Trinity in isolation, a quasi-pneumatological unitarianism. The Spirit of Truth did not come to reveal or speak of himself but of the Son, who receives all things from the Father (John 16:13–15). Wesley's pneumatology was always properly moored to a larger trinitarian economy.

When the orthodox status of the doctrine of the Trinity was hotly contested in Wesley's day, the founder of Methodism, in the words of Geoffrey Wainwright, defended the doctrine and "refused his hand to Arians, Socinians, and Deists, for their heart was not right with his heart."[26] Wesley was a resolved trinitarian and held to the divinity and personhood of the Holy Spirit.[27] As mentioned above, Wesley was not a speculative theologian and that applies to his trinitarianism as well. Wesley did not often wax on the dogmatic dynamics of the Trinity proper nor rigidly use its related technical terms, though he did on occasion use the terms "Trinity" and "Triune." However, he did not insist upon the use of traditional language, such as "Trinity" or "Person"[28] but preferred the plain term, "Three-One God." Rob Staples may be slightly overstating the case regarding the Trinity when he claims, "He turns quickly from such doctrinal matters as the nature, personality, and procession of the Holy Spirit, and the place of the Holy Spirit within the Trinity, to those subjects more directly related to the *ordo salutis* and the work of the Spirit in Christian experience."[29]

---

26. Wainwright, "Why Wesley," 27.

27. In Wesley's sermon, "Sermon 138, 'On Grieving the Holy Spirit,'" he regularly refers to the Spirit using personal pronouns. See also his *Notes* on John 15:26 in which he acknowledges the *filioque* and attributes divinity, double procession, and personhood to the Holy Spirit. For example, see *Poetical Works of John and Charles Wesley*, 7:248–49, cited by Starkey, *Work of Holy Spirit*, 24. This Trinitarian hymn on John 14:20, written by Charles and approved by John, clearly affirms the divinity of the Spirit as well as the Spirit's procession from both the Father and the Son.

28. Wesley, "Sermon 55, 'On the Trinity,'" 375. He claimed to use these terms not by insistence but because "I know of none better."

29. Staples, "John Wesley's Doctrine of the Holy Spirit," 91–115. Wesley at times, though infrequently, did address some of the more dogmatic aspects of the doctrine. See Maddox, *Responsible Grace*, 136–43.

Although his main interest was soteriological, Wesley highly valued the overarching significance of the doctrine of the Trinity asserting, "The knowledge of the Three-One God is interwoven with all true Christian faith," and "[i]t enters into the very heart of Christianity: It lies at the root of all vital religion."[30] The grammar of Trinitarian theology is implicit and assumed by Wesley, undergirding his soteriology throughout his literary corpus.[31] Wainwright asserts:

> Our salvation is for Wesley the differentiated but united work of the Three Persons of the Godhead; it sets us into an appropriate relation to each Person, and it gives us, as will shortly be insisted, a share in their divine communion. The Holy Trinity appears, therefore, as both the origin and goal of soteriology.[32]

Hypothetically, Wesley could affirm *"opera trinitatis ad extra sunt indivisa"* (external works of the *Trinity* are undivided), and he also seems to uphold the doctrine of appropriation, recognizing the will of the Father in the work done *for* us by Christ on the cross in justification and the work of the Spirit done *in* us through sanctification.[33]

Wesley's functional, but clearly not modal,[34] trinitarian-soteriological grammar communicates that salvation is wrought by the will of the Father in the work of the Son through the power of the Spirit, reflecting the liturgy's triune baptismal formula. Wesley's penchant for practical theology is echoed in his interest in the soteriological work of the Trinity that makes persons holy. Thus, for Wesley, the work of the Holy Spirit is situated within the *oikonomia* of the Trinity, particularly the triune work of salvation beginning with prevenient grace and culminating in entire sanctification and ongoing growth in grace throughout one's life. Trinity

---

30. Wesley, "Sermon 55, 'On the Trinity,'" 384.

31. Although Wesley only wrote one sermon specifically employing the word "Trinity" in the title, he often preached on the subject in other sermons, such as "The Unity of the Divine Being" or "Justification by Faith." He also expounds on the doctrine throughout his *Notes,* (e.g., John 15:26; Phil 2:1; Heb 9:14; 1 Joh 1:3; 5:7–8; Rev 4:8) and in many of his *Letters,* (e.g., "A Letter to a Roman Catholic"), as well as in Methodist hymns and prayers. He also leaves the Anglican Article "Of Faith in the Holy Trinity" unchanged for the American Methodists in the reworking of the Articles. For a thorough examination of Wesley's theology of the Trinity, and even dogmatic concerns regarding the Trinity in Wesley's works, see also Tan, "Doctrine of the Trinity," 3–14. See also Bryant, "Doctrine of the Trinity," 64–73.

32. Wainwright, "Why Wesley," 35.

33. Wesley "Justification by Faith," 187; Williams, *John Wesley's Theology,* 100.

34. See Tan, "Doctrine of the Trinity," 6–14.

shapes the way of salvation; it is authored and willed by the Father, accomplished in the atoning work of the Son, and revealed, appropriated,
and witnessed by the Spirit. Further, it is the work of the Spirit that yields
the experience of our salvation. For Wesley, scriptural Christianity is a
religion of the Spirit and the heart. He operated out of an epistemology
of theology that allowed for the Spirit's illumination to support both the
inner perception and assurance of the Spirit's immediate work and the
sanctified reason to think theologically about the experience of grace.[35]
Salvation is fulfilled and authenticated in the heart and life of the believer
by the converting and sanctifying work of the Spirit and realized through
the indirect and direct witness of the Spirit.

Simply put, Wesleyan pneumatology is disclosed in the *oikonomia*
and culminates with the life of holiness. The Holy Spirit is God present.
The person of the Spirit is the divine presence sent in our world. As the
"Holy" Spirit, he is 'presenting' divine, holy love to the world.[36] Also, in
his presenting, he is presenting and implementing the work of the Son
and the will of the Father on earth as it is in heaven, ultimately to make
humanity holy.[37] Wesley penned in his sermon, "On Grieving the Holy
Spirit," that "[t]he title 'holy,' applied to the Spirit of God, does not only
denote that he is holy in his own nature, but that he makes us so; that he
is the great fountain of holiness to his church."[38] Linking holiness to the
work of the Spirit, Wesley also writes in a "Letter to a Roman Catholic":

> I believe the infinite and eternal Spirit of God, equal with the
> Father and the Son, to be not only perfectly holy in himself, but
> the immediate cause of all holiness in us; enlightening our un-
> derstandings, rectifying our wills and affections, renewing our
> natures, uniting our persons to Christ, assuring us of the adop-
> tion of sons, leading us in our actions; purifying and sanctifying
> our souls and bodies, to a full and eternal enjoyment of God.[39]

35. "The testimony of the Spirit is an inward impression on the soul, whereby the
Spirit of God directly witnesses to my spirit, that I am a child of God; that Jesus Christ
hath loved me, and given himself for me; and that all my sins are blotted out, and I,
even I, am reconciled to God." Wesley, "Sermon 10, 'The Witness of the Spirit, I,'" 280.

36. See Maddox, *Responsible Grace*, 121–23. See also Collins, *Theology of John
Wesley*, 124–27.

37. Wesley, "Letter to a Roman Catholic," 82.

38. Wesley, "Sermon 138, 'On Grieving the Holy Spirit,'" 486.

39. Wesley, "Letter to a Roman Catholic," 82.

The Holy Spirit serves as the divine agent and chief executor of the *ordo salutis* with holiness as its *telos*.

> There can be no point of greater importance to him who knows that it is the Holy Spirit which leads us into all truth and into all holiness than to consider with what temper of soul we are to entertain his divine presence . . . the conversion and entire sanctification of our hearts and lives.[40]

By grace, the Spirit goes before us, convincing us of sin and the righteousness found in Christ (John 16:8). Further, he leads us to repentance and faith; applies the merits of Christ for our justification; regenerates our nature in the new birth, symbolized in baptism; bears witness to our adoption; grants us assurance; convinces us of the need for further deliverance from sin; and sanctifies our soul of sin in perfect, holy love, bringing us into full assurance.

The *missio Spiritus* begins in water (baptism), propelled by the wind (in regeneration), and culminates in fire (entire sanctification). Even further, eschatologically, Wesley anticipated a general deliverance for humanity through the universal spread of the gospel that would result in a new creation, by which he meant a new cosmos, a new heaven and earth.[41] A Wesleyan pneumatology recognizes that from creation to the new cosmos the Holy Spirit is the agent of transformation, sanctifying and transfiguring, making all things new and fashioning humanity in the image (*eikon*) of God in Christ. It is within this upward, transcending trajectory of radical grace propelled by the Spirit that the sacrament of baptism is distinguished as the sacrament of initiation into this grace.

The Holy Spirit and Grace

The Holy Spirit is the primary actor in baptism, initiating grace. Grace as gift, or givenness, specifically the giving of God's self, is inextricably linked to, and in places seemingly synonymous with, the agency of the Holy Spirit. Wesley often uses the term "grace" for the "power of the Spirit" that restores humanity to his image and makes humanity holy that

40. Wesley, "Sermon 138, 'On Grieving the Holy Spirit,'" 485.

41. See Wesley "Sermon 50, 'The General Deliverance,'" 436–50; Wesley, "Sermon 63, 'The General Spread of the Gospel,'" 485–99; and Wesley, "Sermon 63, 'The New Creation,'" 500–510.

we may love God and others.[42] Starkey notes for Wesley, "The Holy Spirit and the grace of God are never separated from one another."[43] Similarly, Randy Maddox calls the Holy Spirit, "the presence of responsible grace" and an "empowering presence."[44] Wesley elaborates:

> "By the grace of God" is sometimes to be understood that free love, that unmerited mercy, by which I a sinner, through the merits of Christ, am now reconciled to God. But in this place it rather means that power of God the Holy Ghost, which "worketh in us both to will and to do of his good pleasure." As soon as ever the grace of God in the former sense, His pardoning love, is manifested to our souls, the grace of God in the latter sense, the power of His Spirit, takes place therein. And now we can perform God what to man was impossible. Now we can order our conversation aright. We can do all things in the light and power of that love through Christ which strengtheneth us.[45]

In Wesley's words, one notes the relative change stemming from justifying grace and further the real change wrought inwardly by the regenerating grace and power of the Spirit in which he equates "grace" with the "power of God." These two notions of grace are further developed in Wesley's work and often characterized by Wesley scholars as juridical, Protestant, relative change, or monergistic, and the latter notion as therapeutic, Catholic/Orthodox, real change, or synergistic (cooperant).[46] Wesley's

42. Wesley, "Sermon 10, 'The Witness of the Spirit, I,'" 281–82.

43. Starkey, *Work of the Holy Spirit*, 37.

44. Maddox, *Responsible Grace*, 119.

45. Wesley, "Sermon 12, The Witness of Our Own Spirit,'" 309.

46. These distinctions are often made by various Wesley scholars. Maddox uses the term "responsible grace" for the co-operant (Outler's term) nature of grace and salvation. Maddox also identifies in Wesley a therapeutic focus of salvation in which the goal of salvation is healing of the entire person from the sickness of sin resulting in sanctification or *theosis*. See Maddox, *Responsible Grace*, 141–48. On the other hand, Kenneth Collins identifies a tension of both notions of grace operative in Wesley, as Wesley works from two different paradigms. There is the Catholic emphasis of cooperant grace and the Protestant emphasis of free grace. In cooperant grace, God initiates action and that is followed synergistically by a human response to the divine initiative. Collins sees this dynamic of synergism, for example, in the convincing grace of the Spirit that requires a human response of repentance and faith (and works if possible). The Protestant or free grace emphasis is one in which God acts alone, a monergism, and the work is usually immediate. Collins identifies this understanding of grace in Wesley's teaching on justification by faith and entire sanctification by faith; both experiences are solely the work of God and are completed in an instant. See Collins, *Theology of John Wesley*, 288–93.

operative notion of grace seems to be working from both frameworks though held in tension. Likewise, this tension also carries over to Wesley's theology of baptism in which he holds sacramental (infant and adult baptismal grace) and evangelical (new birth) views together. Outler summarizes how Wesley joined saving grace with sacrament: "The Christian Life, in Wesley's view, is empowered by the energy of grace: prevenient, saving, sanctifying, sacramental."[47]

Wesley on Baptism

In order to truly understand Wesley's conjunctive view of baptism, it is necessary to grasp both his sacramental and evangelical views on baptism, the nature of their distinctions, and how Wesley attempted to hold them together in a larger soteriological framework that was fashioned to foster holiness. On one hand, Wesley held a high church, sacramental view of baptism and baptismal regeneration that he inherited from Anglicanism, which received it from Rome. On the other hand, Wesley, following his Aldersgate experience in 1738, adopted an evangelical perspective that still valued infant and adult baptism as an outward sign but further insisted on the inward grace of regeneration that is solely ministered by the Spirit. In his own case as a youth and in the instances of many around him, he realized that one often sinned away the grace received in infant baptism and needed subsequently to be born again.

Wesley's journal entry for May 24, 1738 gives account of Aldersgate and a brief overview of the years leading up to the experience. Wesley begins that entry referencing his infant baptism, later gradual fall into outward sin, and his quest for holiness. Here, he is obviously interpreting and rethinking his infant baptism in light of his recent conversion experience: "I believe, till I was about ten years old I had not sinned away that "washing of the Holy Ghost" which was given me in baptism . . ."[48] Wesley's theology and practice of baptism were developed over time as he attempted to hold these two views conjunctively in tension but not

---

47. Outler, *John Wesley*, 33.
48. Wesley, "May 24, 1738," 98.

without ambiguity at times.[49] Increasingly, over time, in emphasizing the distinction between the new birth and water baptism, he put more weight on the transformation of the new birth over the outward sign and even over the incipient regeneration received in infant baptism. The new birth sufficiently effected the change needed to go on to perfection, which was always the goal.[50]

As an Anglican priest, Wesley ministered the sacrament to infant and adult alike as needed in the Georgia mission and throughout the Methodist revival. Wesley considered the practice of infant baptism to be upheld by both Scripture and the tradition of the early church. He understood baptism, specifically infant baptism, as the New Testament circumcision,[51] and cited its practice in the book of Acts and in Christian tradition for the first eighteen hundred years.[52] During his lifetime, Wesley published two pieces that specifically reflected his views on baptism. The first is his "Thoughts Upon Infant-Baptism" (1751, 1780, and 1791), a short work he edited and republished from William Wall's *History of Infant Baptism*. The second work is entitled "A Treatise on Baptism" (1756, 1758),[53] an abridgement of his father Samuel Wesley's *The Pious Communicant Rightly Prepared . . .* (1698). He also included instructions for infant and adult baptism in the *Sunday Service of the Methodists in the United States of America* (1784, 1786). Further, he expounded on the topic in his *Notes*, in many of his sermons, and throughout his works.[54] Although as a good Anglican, Wesley identified baptism as one of the two sacraments and upheld its significance, he did not include baptism in the

49. Scholars debate as to whether Wesley's views were consistent, altered, contradictory, or ambiguous. See chapter 1 of Gayle Carlton Fenton's *This Gift of Water* for more on this conversation as well as a detailed treatment of other facets of Wesley's practice of baptism. Felton, *This Gift of Water*. See also Maddox, *Responsible Grace*, 221–24 for the sacramental versus evangelical debate regarding baptism, the weight placed on various editions of his published works on baptism, and Wesley's consistency regarding these two views. See also Williams, *John Wesley's Theology*, 116–22.

50. See Maddox, *Responsible Grace*, 222, 224, especially Wesley's editing of the *Sunday Service* in these regards.

51. Wesley, "Treatise on Baptism," 191.

52. Wesley, "Treatise on Baptism," 193–98. Wesley cites, St. Austin, Origen, Cyprian, Athanasius, Chrysostom, and others.

53. To his "Treatise on Baptism," Wesley added a smaller work entitled, "Serious Thoughts Concerning Godfathers and Godmothers (1752)." See Wesley, "Serious Thoughts," 235–36.

54. As exemplified and cited throughout this chapter.

means of grace[55] listed in the *General Rules*, probably because it was not a repeatable practice like the other means of grace. Reasonably, many early Methodists were already baptized as infants in the institutional church. Nonetheless, Wesley claimed that the sacrament was indeed a means of grace employed by the Spirit for regeneration.

In "A Treatise on Baptism" Wesley defines baptism as "the initiatory sacrament, which enters us into covenant with God. It was instituted by Christ, who alone has power to institute a proper sacrament, a sign, a seal, pledge, and means of grace, perpetually obligatory of all Christians."[56] baptism, as a sign and means of grace, initiates a person into a covenant with God in which they partake of five basic benefits. The first benefit is "the washing away the guilt of original sin, by the application of the merits of Christ's death."[57] Wesley applied this to all in Adam, including infants. The inconsistency in this claim is that, elsewhere, Wesley attributed the removal of guilt from original sin to prevenient grace as an unconditional benefit.[58] Maddox reasons that by Wesley omitting the guilt as "damning" from Samuel's Wesley's original work he contended that the guilt "was universally cancelled at birth by Prevenient Grace."[59] Likewise, Collins points out that for Wesley the "soteriological significance" of infant baptism "was diminished somewhat by his understanding of prevenient grace" that removes the penalty of eternal death for original sin.[60] More so, this unconditional benefit of the atonement indicates two things. First, that baptism is not juridically essential, nor did Wesley insist on it necessarily for salvation (i.e., the unbaptized regenerated Quaker).[61] Two,

---

55. John Wesley defines the means of grace as "outward signs, words, or actions, ordained of God, and appointed for this end, to be the ordinary channels whereby He might convey to men, preventing, justifying and sanctifying grace." See Wesley, "Sermon 16, 'The Means of Grace,'" 381.

56. Wesley, "Treatise on Baptism," 188.

57. Wesley, "Treatise on Baptism," 190.

58. "Therefore no infant ever was or will be sent to hell for the guilt of Adam's sin seeing it is cancelled by the righteousness of God as soon as they are sent into the world." Wesley, "John Wesley to John Mason," 453.

59. Maddox, *Responsible Grace*, 224.

60. Collins, *Theology of John Wesley*, 264.

61. John Wesley, "Oct. 16, 1756," 387. Early Methodists attracted many Quakers. Wesley did not believe these converts were damned because they were not baptized. However, since baptism is commanded as well as the testimony of a good conscience from a new convert (1 Pet 3:21), Wesley baptized Quakers that came into the Methodist fold.

that our representation in Christ extends greater grace through universal atonement over against the universal condemnation in Adam. Although the punishment of death is passed onto all through the disobedience of one man, the obedience of one righteous man brought righteousness and life to all (Rom 5:18).[62]

The second benefit is New Testament circumcision: baptism brings one into covenant with God. For Wesley, this New Testament covenant is one in which God promises to "give them a new heart and a new spirit, to sprinkle clean water upon them," a reality "of which the baptismal is only a figure."[63] Here Wesley is making a distinction between the renewal of the heart, which is an inward work of the Spirit, and baptism, which is a "figure" that represents or points to inner renewal. The third and fourth benefits confer admission into the church, or membership in the body of Christ, and adoption into the family of God for those born of water and of the Spirit.[64] Again, Wesley makes a distinction between the outward sign (water) and the inward grace (Spirit). In this way, Wesley often uses the term "baptism" in two senses. One is pejorative, the mere outward sign of the water, which alone is ineffective. Two is the proper sense, baptism as the sacrament that joins the outward sign of water with the inward grace of the Spirit. Wesley illustrates, "By water then, as a means, the water of baptism, we are regenerated or born again; whence it is called by the apostle, 'the washing of regeneration.' Our Church therefore ascribes no greater virtue to baptism than Christ himself has done. Nor does she ascribe it to the outward washing, but to the inward grace, which, added thereto, makes it a sacrament. Herein a principle of grace is infused, which will not be wholly taken away, unless we quench the Holy Spirit of God by long-continued wickedness."[65] Wesley insisted that the outward washing of the water alone does not result in the "washing of regeneration." It is the infusion of grace by the power of the Spirit through the elements of the water that makes it a regenerating holy act,

62. Note that an atonement, which is for all, or a universal atonement, is different than universalism or universal salvation, which instead declares that all are saved. Christ's death for all provides unconditional benefits, such as prevenient grace that restores a degree of freedom to respond to God's grace and also removes Adamic guilt. Thus, death is merited due to our own sin and not that of Adam. Also, universal atonement means that Christ died for all, so that whoever believes on him will have eternal life.

63. John Wesley, "A Treatise on Baptism," 191.

64. John Wesley, "A Treatise on Baptism," 191–92.

65. John Wesley, "A Treatise on Baptism," 192.

a sacrament. Neither the water nor the practice[66] can do the work by itself or together (an *ex opere operato*),[67] the inward work of grace by the Spirit's power is essential to work the efficacy of regeneration. The two aspects, water and the Spirit, though not synonymous, nor always joined, need to work together in the sacrament.

Finally, with the fifth benefit, "we are heirs of the kingdom of heaven" and to all of the promises of God. All of these benefits are provided "in baptism, the ordinary instrument of our justification."[68] Although debated, Wesley maintained throughout his ministry the importance and normativity of baptism and its need to be linked with regeneration. The sacrament proper contains both the outward sign and the inward grace, and thus, only in this sense is regeneration connected with baptism, not as an outward sign alone. However, he did not equate the two; neither did the Church of England. In his sermon "The New Birth," the language is unequivocal:

> First, it follows, that baptism is not the new birth: They are not one and the same thing. Many indeed seem to imagine that they are just the same; at least, they speak as if they thought so. . . . Certainly it is not by any within these kingdoms, whether of the established Church, or dissenting from it. The judgment of the latter is clearly declared in their large Catechism: –Q. "What are the parts of a sacrament? A. the parts of a sacrament are tow: The one an outward and sensible sign; the other, an inward and spiritual grace, thereby signified. –Q What is baptism? A. Baptism is a sacrament, wherein Christ hath ordained the washing with water, to be a sign and seal of regeneration by his Spirit." Here it is manifest, baptism, the sign, is spoken of as distinct from regeneration the thing signified.[69]

Not only are baptism and the new birth not the same, but also the new birth "does not always accompany baptism."[70] They do not constantly go together. A man may possibly be "born of water," and yet not be "born of

66. In his sermon "The New Birth," Wesley uses the phrase, "an act of man, purifying the body," for the external visible washing of the water. Wesley, "Sermon 45, 'The New Birth,'" 197.

67. According to Gayle Carlton Felton, and I concur, "Wesley thoroughly repudiated any interpretation of baptism which implied an *ex opere operato* view." See Felton, *Gift of Water,* 33.

68. Wesley, "Treatise on Baptism," 191.

69. Wesley, "Sermon 45, 'The New Birth,'" 196.

70. Wesley, "Sermon 45, 'The New Birth,'" 197.

the Spirit." There may sometimes be the outward sign, where there is not the inward grace. I do not speak with regard to infants: "It is certain our Church supposes that all who are baptized in their infancy are at the same time born again; and it is allowed that the whole office for the baptism of Infants proceeds upon this supposition."[71] Wesley consistently affirmed this distinction between the new birth and adult baptism. However, he acknowledged that infant baptism, as an initiatory sacrament, was the "ordinary way" one was initiated in Christ and regenerating grace. Yet, as an initiatory work, infant baptism was not a seal that completed regeneration or salvation. Wesley observed that many baptized as infants sinned away their baptismal grace, like he did at ten years of age, and needed the new birth. Wesley responds to the one who relies on their infant baptism, "Lean no more on the staff of that broken reed, that ye were born again in baptism. Who denies that ye were then made children of God, and heirs of the kingdom of heaven? But not withstanding this, ye are now children of the devil."[72] Wesley encountered many who claimed baptism in word but denied it by their deeds,[73] and did not have the marks of new birth, which are "power over outward sin," faith, hope, and love.[74] The fruit of the Spirit, rather than water, signifies the true mark of regeneration.

Baptism: Sacramental and Evangelical

The need for the new birth in one's latter years does not dismiss or negate the initial grace at infant baptism, and neither does infant baptism negate that later in life one must be born again. What is initiated in infant baptism needs to be completed as the child develops morally and matures into adulthood. The untested face temptation and usually fall into inward and even outward sin at some point.[75] Repentance, faith, and regenerating grace are then needed. This seeming incongruence of infant baptism and the new birth in Wesley has been theorized differently by many.[76] In places, Wesley juxtaposes the initiatory or incipient grace in

---

71. Wesley, "Sermon 45, 'The New Birth,'" 197.

72. Wesley, "Sermon 18, 'Marks of the New Birth,'" 430.

73. Wesley, "Sermon 18, 'Marks of the New Birth,'" 221–22; cf. Wesley, "Sermon 45, 'The New Birth,'" 200.

74. Wesley, "Sermon 18, 'Marks of the New Birth,'" 428.

75. United Methodist Church, *By Water and the Spirit*, 1:3–5; 4:17–18.

76. See Maddox, *Responsible Grace*, 224–25.

infant baptism alongside the regenerating grace in new birth in a way that leads some scholars like Bernard Holland to propose two different types of regeneration, an "elemental" one in infant baptism and a "full" one in the new birth. However, it does not seem Wesley is intimating this distinction. God is not doling out a second-class, lower-grade quality of grace at infant baptism and releasing a higher-octane type in the new birth. Maddox contests Holland on two counts. One, Holland assumes all children will sin away their baptism. Maddox seems to disagree, while Wesley would agree. Pastorally, Wesley placed greater weight on conversion because many of early Methodists, including himself, were Anglicans who were baptized as infants but were not living up to the grace given to them. For Maddox to hope for more is wishful thinking, considering the gravity of universal and thorough depravity.

Second, Maddox, in regard to falling away, would say that Wesley "did not attribute the cause to insufficiency of baptismal grace but to their neglect of that grace."[77] I concur. God's grace at every stage, from prevenient to repenting to regenerating and sanctifying, prepares us for more grace, grace upon grace, as it coincides with our spiritual development. An infant is not ready for convincing grace, as one newly regenerated usually is not ready for entire sanctification. Grace normatively is intended, given, and works alongside our cognitive, moral, and spiritual development to invite our participatory response. Wesley exhorts, "Stir up the spark of grace which is now in you, and he will give you more grace."[78] Baptismal grace, as initiatory, is not insufficient or an inferior grace but with development requires our participatory response, or it can be lost. Wesley continues, "So that no man sins because he has not the grace, but because he does not use the grace which he hath. . . . But for him that hath not,—that does not improve the grace already given,—shall be taken away wat he assuredly hath."[79]

Wesley still contends that infant baptism is the ordinary means of regeneration ordained by God.[80] Baptismal grace in an infant is an initiatory sacrament that "initiates" into a trajectory of grace that intends toward entire sanctification and full assurance[81] but does not guarantee

77. Maddox, *Responsible Grace*, 225.

78. Wesley, "Sermon 85,' Working Out Our Own Salvation,'" 208.

79. Wesley, "Sermon 85,' Working Out Our Own Salvation,'" 207.

80. Felton, *Gift of Water*, 44.

81. Wesley, "Sermon 76, 'On Perfection,'" 75–76.

it. No state of grace is irresistible, static, or supersedes our freedom to say "no." Maddox puts it this way, "While the grace of baptism is *sufficient* for initiating Christian life, it becomes *efficient* only as we responsively participate."[82] Felton similarly claims Wesley was convinced "that the grace of infant baptismal regeneration was insufficient to effect salvation for mature persons."[83] Even adult baptism, if accompanied by repentance, faith, and the new birth, yields forgiveness of sin and brings one into regenerating grace yet still needs to be completed in sanctifying grace.[84] Regenerating grace does not guarantee one will go on to perfection. Continual growth in grace is essential. For this reason, Wesley established the means of grace: instituted (i.e., prayer), prudential (i.e., class and band meetings), and general (i.e., self-denial) to disciple, nurture, encourage, and exhort the faithful to go on to perfection. On the upward continuum of grace, the purpose of the outward work of baptism is to be joined with the new birth, and the purpose of the new birth is entire sanctification, holiness.[85]

The Dove must descend into the water as modeled in Christ's baptism, fulfilling all righteousness (John 1:31–32). The Spirit sanctifies the water and turns it from ordinary elements into new wine. The real presence of the Spirit and his empowering and sanctifying work through the water is the dynamism of the sacrament.[86] Baptismal water is not mere H2O; it is living water. What makes the baptismal water living water? The

---

82. Maddox, *Responsible Grace*, 222. Colin Williams understands it as preparation (infant baptism) and fulfillment (new birth). See Williams, *John Wesley's Theology*, 119–22.

83. Felton, *Gift of Water*, 39.

84. Wesley believed they did not always coincide. In his sermon, "The New Birth," Wesley is clear: "A man may possibly be 'born of water' and not yet 'born of the Spirit.' There may sometimes be the outward sign where there is not the inward grace" (74). When the inward grace is present, there is repentance, faith, hope, love, and victory over sin. Felton writes, "There is no automatic connection between the outward and inner aspects; it is quite possible for them to be severed and they must always be understood as discrete. Herein Wesley asserted his conviction of the freedom of God who may act through the sacraments or who may transcend them." Felton, *Gift of Water*, 33.

85. Wesley is clear that the new birth is not the same as sanctification. Rather, the new birth is merely the beginning of holiness. See Wesley, "Sermon 45, 'The New Birth,'" 195–196.

86. "The being born of God . . . implies not barely the being baptized, or any outward change whatever; but a vast inward change, a change wrought in the soul by the operation of the Holy Ghost." Wesley, "Sermon 19, 'The Great Privilege,'" 432.

Holy Spirit. The water of the Spirit leads us in baptism to the cross where we participate in Christ's death, burial, and resurrection, dying to the old life of sin and rising to the new life in Christ as a new creation (Rom 6). Wesley directs us to the purpose of regeneration:

> Wherefore, to what end, is it necessary that we should be born again? It is easily discerned, that this is necessary, first, in order to holiness . . . what is holiness . . . no less than the image of God stamped upon the heart . . . the whole mind which was in Christ Jesus.[87]

In a Wesleyan theology of baptism, it is essential that the sacrament is understood in catechesis and praxis as water and Spirit because it is the Spirit that vivifies the sacrament for God's restorative mission, a new creation transformed in the *eikon* of God in Christ. From the creation account in Genesis onward, the *missio Spiritus* works through the ontology of sacrament. The Spirit has ignited creation with life from the vast expanding cosmos, to the formless earth, to pillars of cloud and fire, to the glory of the tabernacle and temple, to the Incarnation, to Pentecost, and to the new creation. The invisible grandeur, power, and beauty of the divine are manifest in visible created things. The Spirit working with creation utilizes its forms, like water, which are signs of heavenly things, as channels and means for embodiment. In baptism, the Spirit sanctifies the elements with his real presence. The water washes and regenerates when accompanied with the wind of the Holy Spirit. So, through the dynamic unity of sacrament, the Spirit conceives in the element of water, a new creation, born of water and the Spirit. The vital connection between water and Spirit yields a sacrament with efficacy for the faithful.

Looking Forward: Restoring the Power to the Form

The sacramental-evangelical tension in baptism that Wesley attempted to hold together was not sustained in the Methodist church in North America. Early American Methodism, led often by laity in class meetings, had limited access to elders to minister the sacraments in the fledgling nation. The rapid evangelization of the emerging frontier emphasized the dynamic of conversion over the institutional sacrament. As a result of these and other factors, the significance of baptism diminished. Later, an acculturated, institutional Methodism through the influence of classical

87. Wesley, "Sermon 45, 'The New Birth,'" 194.

liberalism and positivist anthropology embraced a low view of sin and a high view of natural moral development. The need for conversion was minimized, thus draining the sacramental water of its spiritual efficacy.[88] In many cases, the baptismal covenant and rite were reduced to a cultural christening, an infant rite of passage, a dedication, or an initiation into the institutional church apart from any expectancy of spiritual transformation. Methodism possessed the form of sacrament but denied its power.

On the other hand, from the evangelical current would arise the Wesleyan Holiness movement with its emphasis on entire sanctification. With the Arminian influence of human response to free grace, focus shifted to the crises of conversion and sanctification. The "new measures" of revivalism and the camp meetings became the holiness means of grace, replacing the relevance of baptism. An Anabaptist influence on the movement redefined baptism in terms of a divine ordinance that commanded obedience from human agency. The two threads of baptism, the evangelical and the sacramental, became unraveled. A way forward may be the rejoining of the form with the power, the outward with the inward, the water with the Spirit, and the wineskins with the wine. Reclaiming the dynamism of a robust Wesleyan pneumatology rather than relying on mere water or its application could be the catalyst to recovering the transformational DNA of early Methodism. We cannot properly "remember our baptism" if we deny it with our actions. A mere Lutheran remembrance or recalling of the water will not suffice. As Felton reminds us, "baptism could not function as a source of assurance as it did for Luther. In Wesleyan theology to 'remember one's baptism' might well mean to recall what one had lost rather than to be reassured of a present state of grace."[89] An effective baptismal renewal can only occur if remembrance recalls us to repent and be restored in the power of the Spirit. Our baptism then becomes continually renewed when we walk out the consequences of the new birth and are led by the Spirit into holiness and growth in grace.

On the other hand, those who stress the evangelical vigor in baptism need to reclaim the semiotics of their conversion experience that allow it to ground its meaning theologically, historically, and ecclesially. In sacrament, what God has joined together in water and the Spirit is not

---

88. For further information, see Norwood, *Story of American Methodism*; Richey et al., *American Methodism*; Ruth, *Little Heaven Below*; Westerfield Tucker, *American Methodist Worship*.

89. Felton, *Gift of Water*, 40.

to be divided. The signifier, water, is not intended to present merely the signifier but the signified, regeneration. The letter of the water is dead, as the body without the Spirit. But also, our experience of the Spirit is not meant to be an autonomous, docetic, disconnected, undifferentiated qualia of ecstatic sensations unable to touch the earth and unite within the ecclesial hypostasis that is Christ's body. Sacrament as a sign-act would do well to follow the guidance of philosopher Charles Peirce's semiotics and his three-fold theory of the sign: the *signifier*, the *signified*, and *signification*.[90] In baptism, the *signifier*, which mediates, is the water. The *signified* points to the objective reality of regeneration in the Spirit. The *signification* is the subjective interpretation and experience of regeneration. The signification of the experience of regeneration and the confirming inward witness of the Spirit need to be taught and expected. "Signhood" brings us into relation with God through the triadic relation of the water, Spirit, and our experience.

Form and power must come together. For Wesleyans, baptism is "holy water," water that points us to perfection. We would do well to heed Wesley's prophetic warning and admonition from "Thoughts Upon Methodism":

> I am not afraid that the people called Methodists should ever cease to exist either in Europe or America. But I am afraid, lest they should only exist as a dead sect, having the form of religion without the power. And this undoubtedly will be the case, unless they hold fast both the doctrine, spirit, and discipline with which they first set out.[91]

The form and the power may hold together if Methodists retained their doctrine (catechesis in our doctrinal standards), spirit (the Wesleyan emphasis on the presence, the converting, and the sanctifying power of the Spirit), and the discipline (using the means of grace to nurture catechesis and the work of the Spirit in discipleship). The waning of many vital signs in Methodism may prove that we have become or are close to becoming a dead sect, meaning we have not held fast to Wesley's prescription and are in need of a Methodist 2.0 updating.

Such an update has to come from the Holy Spirit. Although Wesley clearly asserted that the Holy Spirit is our agent of entire sanctification and it is an experience subsequent to conversion, he did not seem to use

90. Pierce, *Collected Writings*; Atkin, "Peirce's Theory of Signs."

91. Wesley, "Thoughts Upon Methodism," 258.

Pentecostal or Spirit baptism language to convey that experience.[92] Wesley adhered to the traditional Anglican view, as found even in his *Sunday Service of the Methodists in North America,* that the baptism with water *is* a baptism with the Holy Spirit.[93] Nonetheless, the living waters of the modern Pentecostal-Charismatic movement were ultimately drawn from the wells of Wesley and early Methodism, as attested by the many well-versed accounts.[94] Methodists would do well to receive a charismatic update and upgrade by reclaiming their heritage and rejoining the power of godliness with its sacramental form. Like Pentecostals, Wesleyans need to have faith and expectancy that the same Holy Spirit of the book of Acts will do what he did then now: in this case, be present in the sacrament (Acts 2:38).

One way to reintroduce the person and work of the Holy Spirit to baptism is to begin with more intentional baptismal and confirmation catechesis based off the baptismal liturgy in the *United Methodist Hymnal* (1989) and *Book of Worship* (1992). The liturgy retrieves the ancient apostolic practice of the church of water baptism and the laying on of hands with an option of anointing with oil, joining water and Spirit baptism (chrismation) together (Acts 2:38).[95] A sound and thorough catechesis in

92. There has been much debate as to whether Wesley held to a "Pentecostal" interpretation of entire sanctification, meaning the disciples received entire sanctification at Pentecost. Wesley did explain the roles that Christology and pneumatology play in entire sanctification. Wesley also clearly expressed his conviction that the Holy Spirit, in applying the objective work of the atonement, is the agent of our sanctification, as discussed throughout this essay. See also John Wesley's sermon, "On Grieving the Holy Spirit," 485. Yet, it does not seem that Wesley connected the pneumatic work of the Spirit in entire sanctification with Pentecost, specifically. This position is confirmed by some scholars, such as Herbert McGonigle, Ken Collins, and Donald Dayton, who argue that Wesley did not express holiness in "Pentecostal" or "Baptism in the Spirit" language. On the other hand, Laurence Wood claims Wesley accepted John Fletcher's Pentecostal view of entire sanctification, which later was passed down to the Wesleyan Holiness movement. See McGonigle, "Pneumatological Nomenclature," 61–72; Wood, *Pentecost and Sanctification*; cf. Wood, *Meaning of Pentecost*; Collins, "State of Wesley Studies," 7–38. See also Dayton, "Doctrine of the Baptism," 114–26; Dayton, "Response to Laurence W. Wood," 355–61; and the following conversations between Dayton and Wood: Wood, "Appreciative Reply," 163–72. Dayton, "Rejoinder to Larry Wood," 367–75; Wood, "Can Pentecostals be Wesleyans," 120–30; Dayton, "Final Round with Larry Wood," 265–70.

93. John Wesley, *The Sunday Service of the Methodists in North America,* 138.

94. For example, see Dieter, *Holiness Revival*; Dayton, *Theological Roots*; Synan, *Holiness-Pentecostal Tradition,* and others.

95. See Hippolytus, *On the Apostolic Tradition,* 45–47; cf. Dix, *Theology of Confirmation*; cf. Dix, *Confirmation.*

Methodist baptismal theology and liturgy could ignite a renewal of the Spirit in our sacramental life. Attention is drawn in catechesis and the ministry of the sacrament to the presence and regenerating work of the Spirit as symbolized in the water and the anointing oil. We are reminded though that this or any other program of renewal prescribed must be born and led of the Spirit, or it will bear no fruit. As evident in Methodism's spiritual heirs, the Pentecostal-Charismatic movement, which is sweeping the Global South, any revitalizing of the church and transforming of the world has to come from a new radical emphasis on the work of the third person of the Trinity or it will fail.

Bibliography

Atkin, Albert. "Peirce's Theory of Signs." In *The Stanford Encyclopedia of Philosophy*, edited by Edward N. Zalta. Stanford: Stanford University, 2013. https://plato.stanford.edu/archives/sum2013/entries/peirce-semiotics/.

Baker, Frank. "Practical Divinity—John Wesley's Doctrinal Agenda for Methodism." *Wesleyan Theological Journal* 22.1 (Spring 1987) 7–16.

Bryant, Barry E. "The Doctrine of the Trinity in the Hymns of Charles Wesley." *Wesleyan Theological Journal* 25.2 (Fall 1990) 64–73.

Collins, Kenneth J. "The State of Wesley Studies in North America: A Theological Journey." *Wesleyan Theological Journal* 44.2 (2009) 7–38.

————. *The Theology of John Wesley: Holy Love and the Shape of Grace*. Nashville: Abingdon, 2007.

Dayton, Donald W. "The Doctrine of the Baptism of the Holy Spirit: Its Emergence and Significance." *Wesleyan Theological Journal* 13 (1978) 114–26.

————. "A Final Round with Larry Wood." *Pneuma* 28.2 (Fall 2006) 265–70.

————. "Rejoinder to Larry Wood." *Wesleyan Theological Journal* 27.2 (Fall 2005) 367–75.

————. "Response to Laurence W. Wood." *Pneuma* 27.2 (2004) 355–61.

————. *Theological Roots of Pentecostalism*. Grand Rapids: Baker Academic, 1987.

Dieter, Melvin E. *The Holiness Revival of the Nineteenth Century*. Lanham: Scarecrow, 1996.

Dix, Gregory. *Confirmation, Or Laying On of Hands?* London: S.P.C.K., 1936.

————. *The Theology of Confirmation in Relation to Baptism*. Westminster: Dacre, 1946.

Felton, Gayle Carlton. *This Gift of Water: The Practice and Theology of Baptism Among Methodists*. Nashville: Abingdon, 1993.

Hippolytus. *On the Apostolic Tradition*. Translated by Alistair C. Steward. Crestwood: St. Vladimir's Seminary Press, 2001.

Maddox, Randy L. "John Wesley: Practical Theologian?" In *Wesleyan Theological Journal* 23.1–2 (Spring/Fall 1988) 122–47.

————. *Responsible Grace: John Wesley's Practical Theology*. Nashville: Abingdon, 1994.

McGonigle, Herbert. "Pneumatological Nomenclature in Early Methodism." In *Wesleyan Theological Journal* 8 (Spring 1973) 61–72.

Norwood, Fredrick A. *The Story of American Methodism*. Nashville: Abingdon, 1974.

Osborn, G., ed. *The Poetical Works of John and Charles Wesley.* London: Wesleyan Methodist Conference Office, 1972.

Outler, Albert C. *John Wesley: A Library of Protestant Thought.* New York: Oxford University Press, 1964.

————. "Towards a Re-Appraisal of John Wesley as a Theologian." In *The Wesleyan Theological Heritage,* edited by Thomas C. Oden and Leicester R. Longden, 39–54. Grand Rapids: Zondervan, 1991.

Pierce, Charles Sanders. *Collected Writings.* Edited by Charles Hartshorne et al. 8 vols. Cambridge: Harvard University Press, 1931–58.

Rack, Henry D. *Reasonable Enthusiast: John Wesley and the Rise of Methodism.* Philadelphia: Trinity International, 1989.

Richey, Russell E., et al. *American Methodism: A Compact History.* Nashville: Abingdon, 2012.

Ruth, Lester. *A Little Heaven Below: Worship at Early Methodist Quarterly Meetings.* Nashville: Abingdon, 2000.

Staples, Rob L. *Outward Sign and Inward Grace: The Place of the Sacraments in Wesleyan Spirituality.* Kansas City: Beacon Hill, 1991.

Starkey, Lycurgus. *The Work of the Holy Spirit.* Nashville: Abingdon, 1962.

Synan, Vinson. *The Holiness-Pentecostal Tradition: Charismatic Movements in the Twentieth Century.* Grand Rapids: Eerdmans, 1997.

Tan, Seng-Kong. "The Doctrine of the Trinity in John Wesley's Prose and Poetic Works." *Journal for Christian Theological Research* 7 (2002) 3–14.

The United Methodist Church. *By Water and the Spirit: A United Methodist Understanding of Baptism.* Nashville: General Board of Discipleship, 1996.

Wainwright, Geoffrey. "Why Wesley Was a Trinitarian." *Drew Gateway* 59.2 (Spring 1990) 27.

Wesley, John. "A Farther Appeal to Men of Reason and Religion, Part I." In *Bicentennial Edition of the Works of John Wesley.* Vol. 11, *The Appeals to Men of Reason and Religion and Certain Related Open Letters,* edited by Gerald R. Cragg, 95–202. Nashville: Abingdon, 1987.

————. "John 3:5." In *Explanatory Notes.* Vol. 4, *Upon the New Testament.* Salem: Schmul, 1976.

————. "John Wesley to John Mason, November 21, 1776." In *Works of John Wesley.* Vol. 12, *Letters,* edited by Thomas Jackson, 453. Grand Rapids: Zondervan, 1958–59.

————. "John Wesley to Robert Carr Brackenbury, September 15, 1790." In *Works of John Wesley.* Vol. 13, *Letters,* edited by Thomas Jackson, 9. Grand Rapids: Zondervan, 1958–59.

————. "Large Minutes of Several Conversations." In *Works of John Wesley.* Vol. 8, *Addresses, Essays, Letters,* edited by Thomas Jackson, 299–338. Grand Rapids: Zondervan, 1958–59.

————. "A Letter to the Right Reverend the Lord Bishop of Gloucester [William Warburton] (1747)." In *Bicentennial Edition of the Works of John Wesley.* Vol. 11, *The Appeals to Men of Reason and Religion and Certain Related Open Letters,* edited by Gerald R. Cragg, 459–63. Nashville: Abingdon, 1987.

————. "Letter to a Roman Catholic." In *Works of John Wesley.* Vol. 10, *Letters, Essays, Dialogs, Addresses,* edited by Thomas Jackson, 80–86. Grand Rapids: Zondervan, 1958–1959.

————. "May 24, 1738." In *Bicentennial Edition of the Works of John Wesley*. Vol. 18, *Journals and Diaries I (1735–1738)*, edited by W. Reginald Ward and Richard P. Heitzenrater, 242–50. Nashville: Abingdon, 1990.

————. "Oct. 16, 1756." In *Works of John Wesley*. Vol. 2, *Journals II*, edited by Thomas Jackson, 387. Grand Rapids: Zondervan, 1958–59.

————. "The Principles of a Methodist further Explained." In *Bicentennial Edition of the Works of John Wesley*. Vol. 9, *The Methodist Societies: History, Nature, and Design*, edited by Rupert E. Davies, 160–237. Nashville: Abingdon, 1989.

————. "Serious Thoughts Concerning Godfathers and Godmothers (1752)." In *Works of John Wesley*. Vol. 10, *Letters, Essays, Dialogs, Addresses*, edited by Thomas Jackson, 506–9. Grand Rapids: Zondervan, 1958–59.

————. "Sermon 5, 'Justification by Faith.'" In *Bicentennial Edition of the Works of John Wesley*. Vol. 1, *Sermons I*, edited by Albert Outler, 182–99. Nashville: Abingdon, 1984.

————. "Sermon 10, 'The Witness of the Spirit, I.'" In *Bicentennial Edition of the Works of John Wesley*. Vol. 1, *Sermons I*, edited by Albert C. Outler, 267–84. Nashville: Abingdon, 1984.

————. "Sermon 12, 'The Witness of Our Own Spirit.'" In *Bicentennial Edition of the Works of John Wesley*. Vol. 1, *Sermons I*, edited by Albert Outler, 299–313. Nashville: Abingdon, 1984.

————. "Sermon 16, 'The Means of Grace.'" In *Bicentennial Edition of the Works of John Wesley*. Vol. 1, *Sermons I*, edited by Albert C. Outler, 376–97. Nashville: Abingdon, 1984.

————. "Sermon 18, 'Marks of the New Birth.'" In *Bicentennial Edition of the Works of John Wesley*. Vol. 1, *Sermons I*, edited by Albert Outler, 415–30. Nashville: Abingdon, 1984.

————. "Sermon 19, 'The Great Privilege of Those That Are Born of God.'" In *Bicentennial Edition of the Works of John Wesley*. Vol. 1, *Sermons I*, edited by Albert C. Outler, 431–43. Nashville: Abingdon, 1984.

————. "Sermon 43, 'The Scripture Way of Salvation.'" In *Bicentennial Edition of the Works of John Wesley*. Vol. 2, *Sermons II*, edited by Albert C. Outler, 153–69. Nashville: Abingdon, 1985.

————. "Sermon 45, 'The New Birth.'" In *Bicentennial Edition of the Works of John Wesley*. Vol. 2, *Sermons II*, edited by Albert C. Outler, 186–201. Nashville: Abingdon, 1985.

————. "Sermon 55, 'On the Trinity.'" In *Bicentennial Edition of the Works of John Wesley*. Vol. 2, *Sermons II*, edited by Albert C. Outler, 373–86. Nashville: Abingdon, 1985.

————. "Sermon 60, 'The General Deliverance.'" In *Bicentennial Edition of the Works of John Wesley*. Vol. 2, *Sermons II*, edited by Albert C. Outler, 436–50. Nashville: Abingdon, 1985.

————. "Sermon 63, 'The General Spread of the Gospel." In *Bicentennial Edition of the Works of John Wesley*, volume 2, *Sermons II*, edited by Albert C. Outler, 485–499. Nashville: Abingdon, 1985.

————. "Sermon 64, 'The New Creation.'" In *Bicentennial Edition of the Works of John Wesley*. Vol. 2, *Sermons II*, edited by Albert C. Outler, 500–510. Nashville: Abingdon, 1985.

————. "Sermon 76, 'On Perfection.'" In *Bicentennial Edition of the Works of John Wesley*. Vol. 3, *Sermons III*, edited by Albert Outler, 70–87. Nashville: Abingdon, 1986.

————. "Sermon 85, 'On Working Out Our Own Salvation.'" In *Bicentennial Edition of the Works of John Wesley*. Vol. 3, *Sermons III*, edited by Albert C. Outler, 199–209. Nashville: Abingdon, 1986.

————. "Sermon 138, 'On Grieving the Holy Spirit.'" In *Works of John Wesley*. Vol. 7, *Sermons III*, edited by Thomas Jackson, 485–92. Grand Rapids: Zondervan, 1958–1959.

————. *The Sunday Service of the Methodists in North America*. Reprint ed. Nashville: United Methodist Publishing, 1984.

————. "Thoughts Upon Methodism." In *Works of John Wesley*. Vol. 13, *Letters*, edited by Thomas Jackson, 258–61. Grand Rapids: Zondervan, 1958–59.

————. "A Treatise on Baptism." In *Works of John Wesley*. Vol. 10, *Letters, Essays, Dialogs, Addresses*, edited by Thomas Jackson, 188–201. Grand Rapids: Zondervan, 1958–59.

Westerfield Tucker, Karen B. *American Methodist Worship*. New York: Oxford University Press, 2001.

Williams, Colin W. *John Wesley's Theology Today*. Nashville: Abingdon, 1988.

Wood, Laurence. "An Appreciative Reply." *Pneuma* 27.1 (Spring 2005) 163–72.

————. "Can Pentecostals be Wesleyans?" *Pneuma* 28.1 (Spring 2006) 120–30.

————. *The Meaning of Pentecost in Early Methodism: Rediscovering John Fletcher as John Wesley's Vindicator and Designated Successor*. Lanham: Scarecrow, 2002.

————. *Pentecost and Sanctification in the Writings of John Wesley and Charles Wesley with a Proposal for Today*. Lexington: Emeth, 2018.

PART II

Baptism and the Christian Life

CHAPTER 5

Baptism and the New Testament

Immersed in the Divine Presence

FREDERICK DAVID CARR, NORTHEASTERN SEMINARY

ACCORDING TO OUR EARLIEST sources, followers of Christ have practiced baptism since the church's inception. Historically, however, the church has had diverse understandings of its meaning, its significance, and how it should be performed. Such diversity is hardly surprising given the nature of Scripture's witnesses to the ritual. The Bible does not offer a theological treatise on baptism nor does it give instructions on how Christ-believers should practice the rite. Instead, the New Testament—in which the baptisms of Christ and Christ-followers are discussed—features narratives, metaphors, and brief references on baptism without detailed explanations. We may attempt to convince ourselves and others that our corner of the church has "gotten baptism right," but the impressive range of viewpoints within the global body of Christ should lead us to regular re-examination of our perspectives and practices. For those within Wesleyan traditions, such theological probing begins with Scripture.[1]

The following is an examination of baptism in the New Testament. Various accounts of baptism are considered, ranging from the baptism of

1. For an introduction to baptism in the New Testament and in Wesleyan theology, see Staples, *Outward Sign*, 119–200.

John the Baptist, to Jesus' baptism in the Jordan and Paul's reflections on baptism in his epistles. These accounts offer insight into the meaning(s) of baptism in emerging Christianity, and they prompt us to consider implications for Christian theology and practice today.

John's Baptism in Its Jewish Context

Taken in canonical order, the first New Testament references to baptism appear in the Gospels.[2] The Synoptic Gospels provide the most detail on John the Baptist's practices, including his baptism of Jesus. Although the Gospel writers do not give much background to John's baptism, it was not without precedent. John baptized in a context that featured a variety of immersion rituals.

It is likely that first-century Jews would have understood John's baptism in terms of ritual purification.[3] Such is how Josephus describes it. He labels John a "good man" who "had exhorted the Jews to lead righteous lives, to practice justice toward their fellow Jews and piety toward God, and so doing to join in baptism." John thus baptized not in order for the immersed to gain forgiveness of sins—which was "already cleansed by right behavior"—but to consecrate the body.[4] Although Josephus distinguishes righteous conduct and forgiveness from the practice of baptism, he nevertheless connects the themes of bodily *and* moral purifications in his interpretation of John's baptism.

One can find varied discussions on washing for ritual purification in numerous ancient Jewish writings. According to the book of Leviticus, for example, the people of Israel could become ceremonially unclean from bodily discharges (Lev 15). The resultant uncleanness passed by contact to other people, or to objects such as rugs, beds, or other furniture. For cleansing, bathing both the body and one's clothing in water

---

2. The New Testament uses a number of Greek terms for *baptizing* (verbs) and baptism (nouns), including *bapitzō, baptō, baptisma, baptismos*. It also uses the term *baptistēs* ("baptist" or "baptizer") in reference to John. Often these terms refer not to a ritual but merely to dipping, washing, immersing, or perhaps *dyeing* something. See, e.g., Mark 7:4; Luke 16:24; John 13:26; Rev 19:13. Cf. Judith 12:7; Sir 34:25; Isa 21:4.

3. Thiessen, *Jesus and the Forces of Death*, 21–23; Porter and Cross, "John the Baptist," 25–44.

4. *Ant.* 18.117. Translations of Josephus are from the Loeb Classical Library. Cf. 1 Pet 3:21.

was required (Lev 15:1–33).[5] In a similar fashion, Leviticus prescribes purification with water for high priests and their clothing in preparation for, and as part of, the rites for making atonement (16:4, 24, 26, 28).

Ritual impurity should not be confused with sinfulness; however, Josephus and other Jewish writers relate water immersion to sin and repentance. For instance, Sibylline Oracles instruct "wretched mortals" to "abandon daggers and groanings, murders and outrages, and wash your whole bodies in perennial rivers." He continues, "Stretch out your hands to heaven and ask forgiveness for your previous deeds and make propitiation for bitter impiety with words of praise; God will grant repentance and not destroy. He will stop his wrath again if you all practice honorable piety in your hearts" (4:162–70).[6] While the author does not conflate washing with repentance, he does hold the two together in a process aimed at turning away God's wrath.

Likewise, among the Dead Sea Scrolls the *Community Rule* distinguishes ritual washing from repentance and God's atonement, but it mentions both in a discussion of holistic "purification." Although one's "flesh is cleansed by being sprinkled with cleansing waters and being made holy with the waters of repentance," one will not be "purified by the cleansing waters" nor "made holy by seas or rivers." Instead, "impure will he be all the days he rejects the decrees of God, without allowing himself to be taught by the Community of his counsel." That is so because "it is by the spirit of the true counsel of God" that one experiences atonement, and "it is by the holy spirit of the community, in its truth, that he is cleansed of all his iniquities. And by the spirit of uprightness and of humility his sin is atoned."[7] Here, as seen in other writings, water purifies the body but God cleanses sin.

On a somewhat different note, it is possible, although not completely clear, that some Jews practiced proselyte baptism.[8] It is clear, however, that ancient Jewish writings sometimes stress both ritual purity *and* forgiveness of sins in their discussions of baptism. The Gospel writers

---

5. Cf. Naaman's (spelled Naiman [*Naiman* in Greek] in NETS) immersion (*baptizō*) for cleansing (*katharizō*) leprosy in LXX 2 Kgs 5:13); cf. *Sib. Or.* 3.591–94.

6. Translation from J. J. Collins, in Charlesworth, "Sibylline Oracles," 1.317–472.

7. 1 QS 3:3–9. Translations from Martínez and Tigchelaar, *Dead Sea Scrolls.*

8. For discussion, see Beasley-Murray, *Baptism in the New Testament,* 18–25. Such is likely the case for Greco-Roman mystery religions, as portrayed by Apuleius in *The Golden Ass,* when the main character Lucius is initiated into the cult of Isis (*Metam.* 11.19–29, esp. 11:23).

interpret John's baptism similarly. In particular, they blend themes of repentance, forgiveness, right moral conduct, the work of the "spirit," and, in some sense, initiation in their treatment of baptism.

The Gospels and John the Baptist

All four Gospels describe John and his baptism.[9] The Synoptic Gospels agree that he baptized in the Judean wilderness. Clothed with camel's hair and nourished on locusts and wild honey, he immersed those who went out to him in the Jordan River (Matt 1:1–6; Mark 1:4–6; Luke 3:1–6). Mark and Luke each label John's practice as "a baptism for the forgiveness of sins," and Matthew and Mark record that people underwent baptism while "confessing their sins" (Matt 1:6; Mark 1:5).[10] As with Jewish writers who link immersion or washing with atonement, the authors of the Synoptic Gospels connect John's baptism with confession and forgiveness.

According to the Gospels, John also practiced baptism in conjunction with his prophetic mission.[11] They present John as prophetic in at least two ways. First, he demands that those in his audience turn from their sinful ways (Matt 3:7–10; Luke 3:7–14) and "bear fruit worthy of repentance" (Matt 3:8; Luke 3:8). Second, his proclamation is prophetic in that it points to the arrival of Jesus.[12] In all three Synoptic Gospels, John declares that the one who is coming is more powerful than he is, that he is unworthy even to handle the coming one's sandals, and that this coming figure will baptize "with the Holy spirit and fire" (Matt 3:11–12; Mark 1:7–8; Luke 3:15–18).[13] John recognizes that his baptism of repentance is important in its own right; however, he also acknowledges that his

9. Luke alone narrates John's backstory (1:5–80).

10. Unless noted otherwise, New Testament translations are from the NRSV.

11. Even Chilton (Porter and Cross, "John the Baptist"), who denies that John should be regarded historically as a prophetic figure, acknowledges that the Gospels present him as such (25–39).

12. Such is made clear by the uses of Mal 3:1 and Isa 40:3 in Matt 3:1–3; Mark 1:2–3; Luke 3:3–6.

13. Matt (3:11) and Luke (3:16) add *fire* to Mark's account, which includes only that Jesus will baptize "with the Holy Spirit" (Mark 1:8). The immediate contexts of Mathew and Luke indicate that the addition of fire refers to judgment (Matt 3:12; Luke 3:17–18). See Hartman, "Baptism," 584. The Gospel of John has John assert, "I baptize you with water. Among you stands one who is coming after me; I am not worthy to untie the thong of his sandal" (1:26).

baptism is inferior to and prepares the way for Jesus' messianic mission (Matt 3:3; Mark 1:2–3; Luke 3:4).

The Gospel of John amplifies Jesus' superiority to John the Baptist, as well as the preparatory function of John's baptism. In the fourth Gospel, John testifies to Jesus proclaiming, "This was he of whom I said, 'He who comes after me ranks ahead of me because he was before me'" (1:15; cf. 1:29). John clarifies to the inquiring priests and Levites that he himself is neither the Messiah, nor Elijah, nor "the prophet" (1:19–21); rather, he is the voice crying in the wilderness for the way of the Lord to be made straight (1:23). Upon seeing Jesus, John announces, "Here is the Lamb of God who takes away the sin of the world!" (1:29), and then he explains the purpose of his baptism: "I came baptizing with water for this reason, that he might be revealed to Israel" (1:31). Importantly, despite the differences between John's Gospel and the Synoptics, all accounts indicate that John the Baptist's baptismal practices point to Jesus as the coming Christ.

The Baptism of Jesus

At the start of Jesus' mission to proclaim and enact God's kingdom, he presents himself to John to be baptized—an event that highlights the initiatory role of baptism in the Gospels and Acts. Although the Synoptic Gospel accounts of Jesus' baptism share much in common, they differ in some significant details. Mark, which most scholars argue is the earliest of the canonical Gospels, narrates the story with characteristic brevity: "In those days Jesus came from Nazareth of Galilee and was baptized by John in the Jordan. And just as he was coming up out of the water, he saw the heavens torn apart (*skizō*) and the Spirit descending like a dove on him. And a voice came from heaven, 'You are my Son, the Beloved; with you I am well pleased'" (1:9–11).[14]

Matthew includes these same basic features as Mark: Jesus is immersed; he emerges, and the heavens open (*anoigō*); God's Spirit descends like a dove; and God speaks (3:16–17). Yet Matthew's account differs from Mark's in two striking ways. First, perhaps to clarify why Jesus should be baptized *by John*—an issue Mark leaves unaddressed—Matthew adds an exchange between John and Jesus. After insisting that Jesus should

14. God's declaration to Jesus here echoes LXX Ps 2:7, a coronation psalm, which may indicate that Mark portrays Jesus' reception of the spirit as an anointing for his messianic role. This seems to be how Peter envisages God's giving of the Spirit to Jesus in Acts 10:38.

in fact baptize him, John agrees to baptize Jesus once Jesus explains that such should be done to "fulfill all righteousness" (3:14–15).[15] Second, in Matthew the audience of God's pronouncement differs from that in Mark (and Luke). The heavenly voice announces, "*This* is my Son, the Beloved, with *whom* I am well pleased" (3:17). In lieu of an affirmation from God to Jesus, Matthew has God speak to those in attendance at the event.[16]

Luke, in contrast, retains the same basic features as Mark and Matthew but relocates them to a different context. According to the third Gospel, much as in Mark and Matthew, the heavens are opened (*anoigō*), the "Holy Spirit" descends upon Jesus "in bodily form (*sōmatikō eidei*) like a dove," and God speaks to Jesus with the same affirmation as that in Mark 3:22. Yet, in Luke these events occur not after Jesus emerges from his baptism but at a later time in which he prays (3:21).[17] This relocation shifts attention from the baptism event, with Luke mentioning baptism almost as an afterthought, and emphasizes Jesus' Spirit reception in the context of prayer.[18]

Despite their differences, what the accounts share in common is instructive. Each of the Synoptic Gospels includes John's baptism of Jesus, and each links the immersion with the reception of the Spirit. Each has God speak from heaven with an echo of Psalm 2, (see especially 2:7), and each portrays Jesus' baptism—followed by his testing in the wilderness (Matt 4:1; Mark 1:12; Luke 4:1)—as an initiation into his messianic vocation.

15. For discussion of what it might mean to "fulfill all righteousness" in Matthew, see Luz, *Matthew 1–7*, 141–43; France, *Gospel of Matthew*, 119–21.

16. Uniquely, Matthew ends with Jesus' instructions to his disciples that include a command to baptize (28:18–20, esp. 19).

17. Luke opens the account as follows: "Now when all the people were baptized, and when Jesus also had been baptized and was praying. . . ." Even though John's Gospel includes features that the Synoptic authors associate with Jesus' baptism (1:29–34), it lacks a version of the story. Also, unlike the Synoptic Gospels, John's Gospel indicates that Jesus himself baptized contemporaneously with John the Baptist (3:22–23), though he later clarifies that it was Jesus' disciples, rather than he himself, who baptized others (4:1–2).

18. Prayer is a significant literary and theological theme in Luke-Acts. See Holmes, *Prayer and Vindication*.

Baptism in the Acts of the Apostles

In continuity with the beginning of Luke's Gospel, Acts references baptism in its opening verses. The resurrected Jesus says to his disciples, "This . . . is what you have heard from me; for John baptized with water, but you will be baptized with the Holy Spirit not many days from now" (1:5). In fulfillment of John's prophecy that Jesus would baptize with "the Holy Spirit and fire" (Luke 3:16), Jesus' followers experience tongues of fire resting upon them and receive the filling of the Holy Spirit (Acts 2:3–4; cf. Acts 11:16). Considered alongside John's prophecy, the apostles' experience in Acts indicates that the power of Jesus is present in their "baptism" in the Spirit.

Moreover, in response to the conviction the gathered crowd feels after hearing Peter's proclamation in Acts 2:14–36, the people ask, "What should we do?" Peter responds, "Repent and be baptized every one of you in the name of Jesus Christ so that your sins may be forgiven; and you will receive the gift of the Holy Spirit." With Peter's announcement, Luke again makes a narrative connection with John's baptism. Both stories link baptism with repentance (Luke 3:3, 7–14), forgiveness of sins (Luke 3:3), and receiving the Spirit (Luke 3:16). Likewise, just as Jesus' reception of the Spirit after baptism served as the launching point for his messianic mission, the apostles' prophetic career begins after they receive the Spirit, and the crowd's being "added" to the followers of Jesus coincides with their embrace of Peter's message and their baptism. Luke thus blends the themes of repentance, forgiveness, and Spirit reception with that of initiation into the Jesus movement.[19]

The initiatory function of baptism surfaces in several stories. In Samaria, the crowds—which include Simon who "had previously practiced magic" (8:9)—embrace Philip's message and are "baptized, both men and women" (8:12–13). The Ethiopian eunuch and official of the Candace (i.e., the queen) of the Ethiopians hears the "good news about Jesus" and asks in response, "Look, here is water! What is to prevent me from being baptized?" (8:37). Straightaway, Phillip baptizes the man (8:38–39). So too, Paul undergoes baptism after his Damascus experience, prayer from

---

19. As Luke Timothy Johnson summarizes, "The ritual of repentance associated with John the Baptist . . . is taken over as the ritual of initiation by the messianic community." See Johnson, *Acts of the Apostles*. John Wesley also emphasizes this idea in the first lines of his "Treatise on Baptism" when he calls baptism "the initiatory sacrament which enters us into covenant with God." See Wesley, "Treatise on Baptism," 188.

Ananias for recovery of sight, and the filling of the Spirit (9:17–19). In Caesarea, after Peter's proclamation, gentiles receive the Spirit, and Peter asks, "Can anyone withhold the water for baptizing these people who have received the Holy Spirit just as we have?" (10:47). Peter commands that these gentile believers "be baptized in the name of the Lord Jesus Christ" (*en tō onamati Iēsou Christou*). After their miraculous liberation from confinement in Philippi, Paul and Silas stop a jailer from committing suicide (16:25–29). He asks what he must do to be saved, and they respond, "Believe on the Lord Jesus, and you will be saved, you and your household" (16:31). After the jailer and everyone in the house hear "the word of the Lord . . . he and his entire family were baptized without delay" (16:32–33).[20] Many in Corinth "who heard Paul became believers and were baptized" (18:8), and in Jerusalem Paul defends his conduct with a speech, ending with the exhortation, "And now why do you delay? Get up, be baptized, and have your sins washed away, calling on his name" (22:16). In each instance, baptism accompanies conversion and functions as a rite of initiation for new followers of Christ.[21]

Acts is careful to distinguish John's baptism from baptism that functions as initiation into the community of Christ followers. Multiple times, characters declare that people should be baptized into Jesus' name (2:38; 10:47–48; 19:3–5; cf. 8:16; 22:16). In Ephesus, Paul encounters some disciples who had been baptized "into John's baptism" (19:3). Paul clarifies for them, "John baptized with the baptism of repentance, telling people to believe in the one who was to come after him, that is, in Jesus" (19:4). After this, "they were baptized in the name of the Lord Jesus" (19:5). The implication is straightforward: believers ought to be baptized as part of their initiation into "the Way"—the movement of Jesus Christ, which is distinguishable from, but also the ultimate focus of, John's prophetic immersion practices.

Acts also shows some preoccupation with the order of Spirit reception and baptism. In Samaria, believers were baptized in Jesus' name but

---

20. This passage and others have informed later debates concerning the validity of infant baptism. For works of biblical scholarship that reach opposing conclusions, see Cullmann, *Baptism in the New Testament*; Beasley-Murray, *Baptism in the New Testament*. For discussion of household baptisms in Acts more generally, see Green, "'She and Her Household Were Baptized,'" 72–90.

21. I use the term *conversion* here loosely since it is not clear that Paul or other Jews "converted" to something like a new religion. Increasingly, scholars argue that Paul remained within well within Judaism as a Christ believer. See, e.g., Nanos and Zetterholm, *Paul Within Judaism*.

receive the Spirit some time later, only after Peter and John lay hands on them (8:15–17). In Caesarea, however, gentiles receive the Spirit and are baptized afterward (10:44–48). In the narrative of Acts, the timing of these two phenomena does not follow a prescribed order. Believers might receive baptism along with Spirit reception, before it, or after. Despite featuring mixed sequences, Luke's insistence on including both—and his need to account for those who received one but not the other—reveals the importance he ascribes to believers' experience of each. For him, baptism and the filling of the Spirit are essential and belong together conceptually, even if they occur at different points in time.

Baptism in Paul's Letters

Among New Testament references to baptism, Paul's writings are especially important. Although his letters follow the Gospels in canonical order, they are the earliest of the New Testament writings. Paul's letters thus offer the best evidence for how baptism may have been practiced among the earliest Christ-followers. They also contain evocative metaphors that have shaped perspectives on baptismal practice throughout the church's history. Although Paul makes several references to baptism in his writings, two in particular are germane.[22]

Clothed with Christ at Baptism: Gal 3:27

The first of Paul's writings to be considered is Gal 3:27: "As many of you as were baptized into Christ have clothed yourselves with Christ." When compared with the detailed descriptions of Jesus' immersion in the Gospels and the multiple references to baptism in Acts, the significance of Paul's single statement may not be apparent immediately. Some context is needed to bring its meaning and gravity into view.[23]

In Galatians, Paul addresses what he considers to be a crisis: someone is pressuring gentile, male believers in Galatia to receive circumcision (1:6–9; 3:1; 5:2–6, 7; 6:12–13) and to keep Torah (3:1–5). Prior to Gal 3, Paul describes his own experience of Christ's revelation and his previous interactions with the apostles. He then transitions to a discussion of the

---

22. See 1 Cor 11:13–17; 10:2; 12:13; 15:29; Col 2:12.

23. I first worked out most of the ideas that follow in "Subject of the New Creation." I have further developed them in Carr, *Being and Becoming*.

law and the promises of God. In 3:19–22, he establishes that people live, by default, "under sin" (*hypo hamartian*). He does not mean simply that people sin and cannot quit sinning. Rather, he portrays sin as a cosmic power (3:22) that rules over people.[24] Paul then turns to the law (3:23–25): it formerly functioned as guardian, but only for a set amount of time, namely "until Christ so that we might be justified by faith" (3:23–24).[25] In this scenario, people live under sin's power and under the law's custodianship. After the arrival of Christ, however, believers are liberated from sin and no longer live under the law's guardianship. Although the Galatians were once enslaved to "weak and pitiful elements" (4:8–10), they have become "sons and daughters of God in Christ Jesus" (3:26) and "heirs according to the promise" (3:29).[26]

Rhetorically, Paul establishes a binary with two different spheres of existence.[27] On one side of the binary are those who live in subordination to ruling powers (3:22). Believers in Christ (3:27) have, in contrast, been freed from sin and have no need to live "under a custodian (*hypo paidagōgon*)."[28] They have become adults—sons and daughters of God. Between these before-and-after realities stands the ritual of baptism, an event in which believers are "clothed with Christ" (3:27).

What does it mean to be "clothed" with a person—one who, according to Paul's letters, has been raised from the dead and now reigns with God (1 Cor 15:21–28)? In ancient Jewish and non-Jewish Greco-Roman writings, clothing imagery often symbolizes dramatic transformations of the human self.[29] In Gal 3:27, the Greek verb Paul uses for *clothing* is *enduō*, a term that authors of Septuagint writers use frequently to refer to various changes that a person might undergo, whether they involve alterations of identity, metaphysical changes, or moral transformations.[30]

24. See Martyn, *Theological Issues*, 153; Martyn, *Galatians*, 370–73; Das, *Galatians*, 368; Matera, *Galatians*, 135.

25. Author's translation.

26. Author's translation.

27. Cf. Martyn's discussion regarding discussion of Paul's "antinomies." Martyn, *Theological Issues*, 111–23.

28. Author's translation.

29. See, e.g., LAB, 27:10; cf. 36:2; Jos. Asen. 10:10–16; 15:10; Ovid, Ovid, *Metam.* 7.287–322; Apuleius, *Metam.*, 11.24.

30. For clothing and new regal identity, see Gen 41:42; 1 Macc 10:59–66; Isa 22:20–21; Dan 5:29; 6:3; cf. Jer 26:4. On priestly identity, see Exod 28:41; 29:5–8; 40:13–14; Lev 6:3–4; 8:6–7, 13; 16:2–4, 23–24, 32; 21:10; Num 20:25–29; 5:12; Ezek 42:14; 44:17, 19; 1 Macc 10:18–21; Sir 45:6–13, esp. v. 13. On change in status, see 2 Sam 6:14; Jdt

The term appears twelve times in the Pauline Corpus. Sometimes it is used to encourage an audience to "put on" moral virtues or attributes like faith or hope (1 Thess 5:8; Rom 13:12; Eph 6:11, 14; Col 3:12). Sometimes he uses it to exhort people to "put on the Lord Jesus Christ" (Rom 13:14). Paul employs the verb *enduō* in 1 Cor 15:53–54 to describe a transformation at the resurrection, an event in which "the perishable" will be clothed with "imperishability."[31]

Paul's use of *enduō* in Gal 3:27 signifies a type of transformation.[32] It suggests that a person is joined with Christ when he envelops the person just as a garment covers a body. When this occurs, one is incorporated into a new sphere—the realm of Christ. For Paul, the human self is not an autonomous individual but is determined by the power that rules over it. Thus, when one is clothed with Christ and transferred into the sphere of Christ, she becomes *someone new*. According to Gal 3:28, the Galatians have been changed to the extent that there is "no longer Jew or Greek, there is no longer slave or free, there is no longer male or female." All are "one in Christ Jesus" (3:28). At baptism, gentile Galatians have been transformed into the seed of Abraham as sons and daughters of God.

Significantly, Paul does not erase distinctions like ethnicity or gender in Gal 3:28. In Galatians and other letters, Paul presumes the continuity of ethnic, gender, and status differences present within the body of Christ.[33] Rather, his point in 3:28 seems to be that all are "one in Christ Jesus" regardless of such differences.

In short, Paul portrays baptism as a ritual in which a major transformation occurs. As in Acts, it functions as a rite of passage: it is the entry point into what Paul elsewhere calls "the body of Christ." Furthermore,

---

10:3–4; Ezek 9:2–3; 11; 10:2, 6–7; 16:8–14; 23:5–7, 12; Dan 10:4–5. On clothing and virtues, see Ps 131:9; Job 29:14; Wis 5:18; Sir 6:31; 27:8. On vices, see Zeph 3:3–4. On other qualities or realities, see references to salvation (Ps 131:16; Isa 61:10), strength (Isa 51:9; 52:1; 59:17; Prov 31:26; Sir 17:3), and other attributes (Pss 34:26; 92:1; 103:1; 108:18, 29; 131:18; Prov 31:26; Job 8:22; 29:19; Isa 52:1; Ezek 7:27; Sir 45:8; 1 Esd 5:40; Ps Sol 11:7; 1 Macc 1:28; Bar 5:1). On God's spirit clothing someone, see Judg 6:34; 1 Chr 12:19; 2 Chr 24:20.

31. For fuller discussion of clothing in Paul, see Kim, *Significance of Clothing*.

32. Religious rituals, and especially rites of passage like baptism, often produce experiences of personal transformation. See van Gennep, *Rites of Passage*, esp. 54–115; Turner, *Ritual Process*; Bell, *Ritual Perspectives*, esp. 1–89, 94–101; McNamara, *Neuroscience of Religious Experience*, 212–28.

33. In Galatians he distinguishes between Jewish and gentile believers throughout (see, e.g., 2:11–15).

he claims that Christ envelops the human like a piece of clothing. Baptism is, therefore, the mechanism by which a person becomes united with Christ and transformed as part of the "new creation" (Gal 6:15).

Dying and Rising with Christ: Rom 6:1–11

Next, we turn to Paul's treatment of baptism in Rom 6:1–11. Although Paul's description of baptism in Romans differs from that in Gal 3, the two passages share some important features. Both discuss the ritual of baptism with stark metaphors. Furthermore, Rom 6 shares with Gal 3 an emphasis on union with Christ and human transformation.

Readers of Rom 6 should bear in mind the cosmological context in which the ritual of baptism takes place. Paul opens the pericope in with three queries: "Shall we continue with sin so that grace might increase?" He anticipates the question in response to his claims in 5:18–21. There, he writes that although sin "increased" (*pleonazō*) with the law's entrance onto the scene, "grace" or "the gift" increased all the more (*hyperperisseuō*).[34] After dismissing the question (*mē genoito*), he continues: "How shall we who died to sin still live in it? Or do you not know that all of us who were baptized into Christ were baptized into his death?" (6:2a–3).[35]

With this language of sin and death, Paul alludes to two cosmic forces. As in Gal 3, Romans features sin as a cosmic power (3:9; 6:6, 12–14, 16–18, 20–23; 7:7–9, 11–13, 17–20) that enslaves humanity (6:6, 12–14, 18, 19–23; 7:14; cf. 7:7–9, 11, 12, 25; 8:2–3).[36] Yes, people commit sins, but they do so by "participating" in the power of sin (5:12–13; 6:1–2, 12–14). Similarly, death in Romans refers not merely to biological expiration but to a force with agency that reigns over people (Rom 5:12–21; cf. 1 Cor 15:21, 26, 54–56). Together, these powers *enslave* humanity (see *douleuō* in 6:6). Such is, for Paul, the human condition prior to baptism.

Again, as in Galatians, Paul portrays baptism as a ritual in which a believer transfers from the realm of sin and death to the sphere of Christ. As such, the person is liberated from the oppressive forces of sin (6:3–5).

---

34. On "grace" (*charis*) as "gift," see Barclay, *Paul and the Gift*.

35. Author's translation.

36. For an insightful examination of sin as a power in Romans, see Croassmun, *Emergence of Sin*. For discussion of Paul's "history of sin" in Romans, see Gathercole, "Sin in God's Economy," 158–72.

The transfer produces a transformation so radical that a new person emerges from it. Somehow, Paul's language to describe the event here is even more striking than that which he employs in Galatians. He maps the structure of Jesus' death by crucifixion onto the ritual experience and argues that, through baptism, believers are buried with Christ (6:4). They even experience Christ's death (6:3) and "become united (*sumphutos*) with the likeness of [Christ's] death" (6:5). Paul describes the event as co-crucifixion (6:8; cf. Gal 2:19–20). After baptism "into" Christ and Christ's death, he implicitly suggests that believers undergo a type of resurrection, after which they "walk in the newness of life" (6:4) and can expect to share in the likeness of Christ's resurrection at some point in the future (6:5).[37]

If in Galatians Paul implies that a *new* person emerges from baptism, he makes the claim explicit in Romans. The prebaptized self is in fact so different from the current person that he can label the former as "the old person" (*ho palaios hēmōn anthrōpos*). Baptized believers, in contrast, have died but now are "living with God in Jesus Christ" (6:11). Through baptism, they have been liberated from enslavement to sin (6:6) and now live as new people who are joined to Christ.

Summary

Gal 3:27 and Rom 6:1–11 do not contain all that Paul has to say about baptism, but they offer critical insights. For instance, Paul views the ritual of baptism as a rite of passage in which believers transition from one sphere of existence to another. This transition from enslavement to the power of sin to union with and subjection to Christ involves an experience of transformation so radical that it produces a new person who lives in a new mode of existence. In baptism, believers enter into a "new relational matrix" that determines their selfhood and their moral conduct as members of Christ's body.[38]

---

37. Cf. Col 2:8–15.

38. I borrow the language of a *new relational matrix* from Eastman, *Paul and the Person*, 160.

Baptism in the General Epistles and Revelation

The General Epistles and Revelation also mention baptism, though to a lesser degree than the Gospels, Acts, and Pauline letters. The author of Hebrews, for example, makes a couple of references to baptism (*baptismos*), both of which are brief and ambiguous (6:2; 9:10).[39] Revelation includes one occurrence of the verb *baptō*, but in reference to Jesus' robe having been "dipped" in blood (19:13). We find a more provocative and challenging reference to baptism in 1 Peter.

In particular, 1 Pet 3:18–19 describes Jesus' suffering, death, and proclamation to the "spirits in prison." These spirits to whom Jesus speaks are those "who in former times did not obey, when God waited patiently in the days of Noah, during the building of the ark, in which a few, that is, eight persons, were saved through water" (3:19–20). The theme of deliverance through water then leads Peter to baptism: "And baptism, which this prefigured, now saves you (*hymas . . . nun sōzei*)—not as a removal of dirt from the body, but as an appeal to God for good conscience, through the resurrection of Jesus Christ" (3:21).

The claim that "baptism saves you" may appear at first to suggest that the rite of baptism itself confers salvation. Such a reading, although possible, is probably not the best take. Peter parallels baptism with Noah and company's deliverance, the latter of which occurs not simply by the presence or power of water but, ultimately, by an act of God. Furthermore, the language suggests that salvation occurs not from the removal of water from the body, but rather "through the resurrection of Jesus Christ (*di anastaseōs Iēsou Christou*)."[40] The use of "conscience" (*syneidēsis*) in this context refers less to "a personal subjective untroubled feeling that one is doing right" and more to a type of knowledge concerning what is right and wrong.[41] A "good conscience" here should be understood as "a consciousness of what God wants that will lead one to do it."[42] A "good conscience," understood in just this way, is somehow received in baptism.[43]

---

39. See discussion in Johnson, *Hebrews*, 158–60; cf. 222–27.

40. Cf. John Wesley's distinction between the "outward sign" of baptism with water and the "inward and spiritual grace" that is God's renewal of the inner person in his sermon "The New Birth."

41. Boring, *1 Peter*, 79.

42. Achtemeier, *1 Peter*, 270.

43. Boring, *1 Peter*, 80.

Although washing with water alone does not achieve salvation, it is noteworthy that 1 Peter explicitly connects the two. In fact, the text indicates that salvation is experienced in the rite of baptism. Although the passage is complex, both in its grammar and its meaning, it identifies baptism as soteriologically significant—a feature upon which contemporary readers should reflect.

Implications for Wesleyan Readers

For Wesleyan Christians, baptism is a sacrament, and each generation of believers is responsible to continue the hard work of theological reflection on our beliefs and practices. What features of baptism in New Testament are noteworthy for contemporary Wesleyan audiences to consider? Several points come to mind.

First, the New Testament writings indicate that baptism is a critical practice for Christ followers. Jesus himself underwent immersion, and Acts portrays baptism as a necessary rite, even if it happens out of step with believers' reception of the Spirit. Paul presents baptism as a rite of passage, and Peter describes it as the moment in which God saves people. From our earliest New Testament witnesses to our later ones, those who mention baptism stress its vital importance for followers of Christ.

Second, although our earliest references to baptism in the New Testament come from the Apostle Paul, canonically and chronologically, Jesus' baptism comes first. It is significant that Jesus' baptism appears in Scripture at all. As Matthew's addition to the baptismal episode suggests, it is not obvious that Jesus would need to be baptized. Theologically, then, Jesus' baptism should be understood as foundational for what would later become the Christian movement. Jesus leads the way for all who follow him in their own baptism. Importantly, in all three Synoptic versions of Jesus' baptism (even if Luke's is a step removed from the actual immersion), God's presence is manifest, and Jesus receives the Spirit. Jesus' baptism before God and his reception of the Spirit launch him into his messianic vocation. His baptism thus functions as an initiation of sorts, which is possible because God is powerfully present at the event. Similarly, for much of the church today, the sacrament of baptism functions as an initiation for followers of Christ.

Third, in Acts, one cannot separate the themes of initiation and the reception of the Holy Spirit from baptism, but the narrative recalls John's baptism by stressing repentance as well. Indeed, repentance corresponds with initiation: believers turn *from* their sins and *toward* a new life characterized by devotion to Christ and walking in "the Way" with Christ's followers. For Wesleyans, ongoing reflection on Christian baptism might find ways to relate Wesleyan understandings of repentance, justification, and initiation to the rite of baptism. Moreover, as with Jesus' baptism, one cannot separate the act of baptism from the experience of the divine presence.

Fourth, Paul's writings on baptism are unparalleled among New Testament writers regarding his use of powerful metaphors and his emphases on personal transformation. Much like Jesus' reception of the Spirit in the Gospels, and that of believers in Acts, Paul stresses that when believers are baptized, they experience a real union with the resurrected Christ. They are "clothed with Christ," are baptized "into Christ," and participate in Christ's death and resurrection. This "linking up" with Christ produces a new person. If Wesleyan theology stresses anything, it stresses human transformation in Christ by the Spirit.[44] For Christian traditions that centralize changes like regeneration and sanctification— such as Wesleyan traditions—Paul's striking depictions of human change in the ritual should be sources of ongoing consideration. The supplemental chapters in the current volume offer such reflection.

Fifth, 1 Peter's blunt claim that "baptism saves you" should be taken with the utmost seriousness by Wesleyan readers. I say this not to overemphasize the washing of the body with water, as Peter is quick to do as well. Rather, I say this because particular understandings of salvation lie at the heart of Wesleyan Christianity.[45] If a New Testament witness so explicitly links baptism with salvation, then we need to consider how such is the case and explore the implications for us today.

One can certainly find points of overlap of the biblical themes presented in this chapter with Wesleyan theology and practice. My concern, however, is not an apologetic one. For the ongoing life of the church, it is insufficient to restrict our attention to whether John Wesley read the Bible correctly on baptism, whether Wesleyans have gotten the sacrament right theologically, or whether we can prove that the New Testament supports our perspectives. Rather, our task is to continually re-examine and

---

44. See Wesley, "Sermon 1, 'Salvation by Faith'"; Wesley, "Farther Appeal," 108; Wesley, "Letter to the Right Reverend," 459.

45. See Collins, *Theology of John Wesley*, 4–16.

develop our viewpoints and practices in light of Scripture—just as Wesley did—in order to serve the life of the church.

Bibliography

Achtemeier, Paul J. *1 Peter: A Commentary on First Peter*. Minneapolis: Fortress, 1996.

Barclay, John M. G. *Paul and the Gift*. Grand Rapids: Eerdmans, 2015.

Beasley-Murray, G. R. *Baptism in the New Testament*. Grand Rapids, Eerdmans, 1962.

Bell, Catherine M. *Ritual Perspectives and Dimensions*. Oxford: Oxford University Press, 2009.

Boring, Eugene. *1 Peter*. Nashville: Abingdon, 1999.

Carr, David. *Being and Becoming: Human Transformation in the Letters of Paul*. Waco, TX: Baylor University Press, 2022.

———. "The Subject of the New Creation: Transformation & Selfhood in Paul's Letters." PhD diss., Emory University, 2019.

Charlesworth, James H. "Sibylline Oracles." In *The Old Testament Pseudepigrapha*, translated by J. J. Collins, 1.317–472. Garden City, NY: Doubleday, 1983.

Collins, Kenneth J. *The Theology of John Wesley: Holy Love and the Shape of Grace*. Nashville: Abingdon, 2007.

Croassmun, Matthew. *The Emergence of Sin: The Cosmic Tyrant in Romans*. Oxford: Oxford University Press, 2017.

Cullmann, Oscar. *Baptism in the New Testament*. Translated by J. K. S. Reid. Chicago: Allenson, 1950.

Das, A. Andrew. *Galatians*. St. Louis: Concordia, 2014.

Eastman, Susan Grove. *Paul and the Person: Reframing Paul's Anthropology*. Grand Rapids: Eerdmans, 2017.

France, R. T. *The Gospel of Matthew*. New International Commentary on the New Testament. Grand Rapids: Eerdmans, 2007.

Gathercole, Simon. "Sin in God's Economy: Agencies in Romans 1 and 7." In *Divine and Human Agency in Paul and His Cultural Environment*, edited by John M. G. Barclay and Simon J. Gathercole, 158–72. London: T&T Clark, 2006.

Green, Joel B. "'She and Her Household Were Baptized' (Acts 16:15): Household Baptism in the Acts of the Apostles." In *Dimensions of Baptism: Biblical and Theological Studies*, edited by Stanley E. Porter and Anthony R. Cross, 72–90. London: Sheffield, 2002.

Hartman, Lars. "Baptism." In vol. 1, *The Anchor Bible Dictionary*, edited by David N. Freeman, 585. New York: Doubleday, 1992.

Holmes, Geir O. *Prayer and Vindication in Luke-Acts: The Theme of Prayer within the Context of the Legitimating and Edifying Objective of the Lukan Narrative*. London: T&T Clark, 2001.

Johnson, Luke Timothy. *The Acts of the Apostles*. Collegeville, MN: Liturgical, 1992.

———. *Hebrews: A Commentary*. Louisville, KY: Westminster John Knox, 2006.

Kim, Chŏng-hun. *The Significance of Clothing Imagery in the Pauline Corpus*. London: T&T Clark, 2004.

Luz, Ulrich. *Matthew 1–7: A Commentary*. Hermeneia. Minneapolis: Fortress, 2007.

Matera, Frank J. *Galatians*. Collegeville, MN: Liturgical, 1992.

Martínez, Florentino García, and Eibert J. C. Tigchelaar, eds. *The Dead Sea Scrolls Study Edition.* Leiden: Brill, 1999.

Martyn, J. Louis. *Galatians: A New Translation with Introduction and Commentary.* New York: Doubleday, 1997.

———. *Theological Issues in the Letters of Paul.* London: T&T Clark, 1997.

McNamara, Patrick. *The Neuroscience of Religious Experience.* Cambridge: Cambridge University Press, 2009.

Nanos, Mark D., and Magnus Zetterholm, eds. *Paul Within Judaism: Restoring the First-Century Context of the Apostle.* Minneapolis: Fortress, 2015.

Porter, Stanley E., and Anthony R. Cross, eds. "John the Baptist: His Immersion and His Death." In *Dimensions of Baptism: Biblical and Theological Studies,* 25–44. Translated by Bruce Chilton. London: Sheffield, 2002.

Staples, Rob L. *Outward Sign and Inward Grace: The Place of the Sacraments in Wesleyan Spirituality.* Kansas City: Beacon Hill, 1991.

Thiessen, Matthew. *Jesus and the Forces of Death: The Gospels' Portrayal of Ritual Impurity Within First-Century Judaism.* Grand Rapids: Baker, 2020.

Turner, Victor Witter. *Ritual Process: Structure and Anti-Structure.* Ithaca: Cornell University Press, 1969.

van Gennep, Arnold. *The Rites of Passage.* Chicago: University of Chicago Press, 1960.

Wesley, John. "A Farther Appeal to Men of Reason and Religion, Part I." In *Bicentennial Edition of the Works of John Wesley.* Vol. 11, *The Appeals to Men of Reason and Religion and Certain Related Open Letters,* edited by Gerald R. Cragg, 95–202. Nashville: Abingdon, 1987.

———. "Letter to Dr. Warburton, Bishop of Gloucester, Nov. 1762." In vol. 4, *The Letters of the Rev. John Wesley,* edited by John Telford, 357. London: Epworth, 1931.

———. "A Letter to the Right Reverend the Lord Bishop of Gloucester [William Warburton] (1747)." In *Bicentennial Edition of the Works of John Wesley.* Vol. 11, *The Appeals to Men of Reason and Religion and Certain Related Open Letters,* edited by Gerald R. Cragg, 459–63. Nashville: Abingdon, 1987.

———. "Sermon 1, 'Salvation by Faith.'" In *Bicentennial Edition of the Works of John Wesley.* Vol. 1, *Sermons I,* edited by Albert C. Outler, 109–30. Nashville: Abingdon, 1984.

———. "Sermon 45, 'The New Birth.'" In *Bicentennial Edition of the Works of John Wesley.* Vol. 2, *Sermons II,* edited by Albert C. Outler, 186–201. Nashville: Abingdon, 1985.

———. "A Treatise on Baptism." In *Works of John Wesley.* Vol. 10, *Letters, Essays, Dialogs, Addresses,* edited by Thomas Jackson, 188–201. Grand Rapids: Zondervan, 1958–59.

CHAPTER 6

Baptism and Discipleship

Initiating and Cultivating Holy Love

JONATHAN A. POWERS, ASBURY THEOLOGICAL SEMINARY

THERE IS AN INDIVISIBLE relationship between discipleship and the sacrament of baptism. Jesus Christ himself confirms this correlation in the commission he gives his disciples in Matt 28:18–20:

> Then Jesus came to them and said, "All authority in heaven and on earth has been given to me. Therefore go and make disciples of all nations, baptizing them in the name of the Father and of the Son and of the Holy Spirit, and teaching them to obey everything I have commanded you. And surely I am with you always, to the very end of the age."[1]

Notice Jesus' directive in the above passage. While at first it may seem that he issues three imperatives in his commission—*go, baptize,* and *teach*—he in fact offers only one—*disciple*. The main verb he uses (*disciple*) describes the goal of the work he sends his disciples out to do. The participles he applies (*baptizing* and *teaching*) qualify the means his disciples are to use to reach this end. Basically, Jesus' sole command to his disciples is to go forth and disciple others. The manner by which they are to do the discipling is baptizing and teaching, specifically baptizing into

---

1. All Scripture references in this chapter are in the NKJV unless otherwise noted.

the name of the Trinity and teaching obedience to Christ's commands. Baptism and education (i.e., catechesis) thus play a central role in the disciple-making process.[2]

The way Jesus orients discipleship in the Matt 28 commission is noteworthy, especially inasmuch as he diverges from previous forms of discipleship. In the ancient Jewish context, it was common for rabbis to take on and educate disciples who might in turn become rabbis and pass down traditions to their own students.[3] The highest hope, honor, and privilege of a student in a rabbinic school was to become a rabbi with one's own disciples to instruct. As new rabbis became teachers for new generations, they began new schools where they would foster their own new disciples. In Matt 28, however, Jesus initiates a different paradigm. He begins by reminding his disciples that he has the ultimate authority; therefore, he is the one, true teacher.

He then commissions his disciples to go forth, not making disciples of themselves, but making disciples who are identified in the name of the Triune God (conferred in baptism) and who are obedient to his commandments (learned through catechesis). In doing so, Jesus establishes himself as the standard of discipleship.[4] In other words, all discipleship points back to him. To be a disciple requires submission to his authority and to his teaching. His disciples never take on the role of rabbi themselves; instead, their status as a disciple is perpetual. Nonetheless, Jesus still empowers his disciples for disciple-making. In particular, Jesus introduces a model whereby discipleship requires disciples investing in one another. His disciples are not broken into separate schools but rather remain united as a body. Discipleship is done communally and takes place

---

2. In the earliest days of Christianity, the words "catechesis" and "catechism" indicated instruction one received in preparation for baptism. The "catechumenate" is the term used for the process of initiation. These terms are still often used today in the church to describe teaching and education. Originating from the ancient Greek word κατηχισμός, the word catechism is literally translated "to echo down," which has been implied as "to sound again" or "to instruct." For a study on historic models of catechesis, see Powers, "*Ecclesia Semper Sanctificanda*," which examines the *Didiche* and Hippolytus' *Apostolic Tradition*—in addition to Wesley's Methodist structure—as models that exemplify the cultivation of holiness through ecclesial discipleship. The final two sections of this chapter build off of my work in that article: Powers, "*Ecclesia Semper Sanctificanda*," 85–107.

3. For more on discipleship in an ancient Jewish context, see Grassi, *Jesus as Teacher*.

4. See Ferguson, *Baptism in the Early Church*, 138.

within a relational context. Everyone has equal standing as they devote themselves to mutual growth in Christ-likeness.

This communal nature of discipleship illumines the final words Jesus speaks to his disciples in Matt 28. Specifically, he concludes his commission with a promise that his presence will be with his disciples always, even to very end of the age. His words here are more than an afterthought, however, and directly tie to his previous mandate of discipleship. Surely Jesus seeks to reassure his disciples that his presence will be with them personally in an ongoing, spiritual manner; however, there is also an ecclesial implication to his statement.

Although he does not explicitly name the church in Matt 28:20, Jesus' preceding commission infers he will be present with his disciples through his complete and absolute union to his body, the church. He is the head of the church and his presence persists in the world by virtue of his body, i.e., the collective of his disciples who have been baptized into his name, who follow his teachings, who live obedient to his commands, and who thus bear his image to the world.[5] Since Jesus is the perfect one who submitted to baptism in order to "fulfill all righteousness," his disciples follow him in baptism and conform to his way of righteous living and holy love.[6] United with him in baptism, Jesus' disciples are made

---

5. This idea is best explained through the concept of *totus Christus*, i.e., the "whole Christ"—Jesus as head and the church as his body. The relationship between Christ and his church thus bears a resemblance to the relationship between the head and the members of a physical body. The two cannot be separated from one another. *Totus Christus* is a Christological ecclesiology put forth by Augustine of Hippo based on 1 Cor 12:12–13. Augustine claims that Christ and the church are one spiritual entity; thus, Paul's statement that "the Church is Christ's body" is not an empty metaphor but rather claims the church as Christ's body in a very real way. J. David Moser sums up the basic features of Augustine's *totus Christus* ecclesiology well: "First, *totus Christus* denotes a spiritual union between Christ and the church so that, out of the two, one spiritual entity, head and members, comes to be. The union is spiritual because the Holy Spirit brings it about. Second, *totus Christus* is a metaphysical union between Christ and the church. Third, the metaphysical union in the *totus Christus* is qualitatively distinct from the hypostatic union and from the unity of the three divine persons. The Logos is hypostatically united to his flesh so that his flesh truly is his own, that is, it belongs to his person. But his union with his church, though metaphysical, is decidedly different and non-hypostatic. Fourth, *totus Christus* denotes a kind of metaphysical identity between Christ and the church, such that the "whole thing" (*totum*) is Christ. But this spiritual entity is not composed of two distinct entities that become numerically identical, or one and the same thing. Christ and the church are distinct in one way and united in another: distinct in their being, we might say, since God and creatures are distinct, but united by the Holy Spirit." See Moser, "Totus Christus," 3–30.

6. See Matt 3:13–17.

part of his body. Within this body of the church, through the power of the Holy Spirit, his disciples are transformed into his likeness as they grow in holiness. Thus, as his disciples participate in disciple-making through baptism and catechesis, they are active in extending his representative body on earth.[7] Together, as the body of Christ, disciples mutually and continually grow in the image of Christ, following Christ in life, death, and resurrection.

Baptism as Christian Death and Life

Christian discipleship is nothing less than learning how to live into and live out one's baptism. Put another way, discipleship is learning to live in constant remembrance of one's baptism. Joined with Christ in the waters that he once and for all sanctified, baptism is the sacramental act of initiation and conversion. It is the gateway through which a person enters into life with Christ, life in the church, and the lifelong pursuit of holiness. Discipleship is essential to baptism, therefore, because discipleship is the process through which holiness (based in union with Christ) is cultivated and maintained. Simply put, baptism initiates discipleship, and discipleship is the constant process of being converted into what baptism represents.

Primarily, baptism is both initiation and conversion into the death and resurrected life of Jesus Christ. The person and work of Jesus and the meaning of his death and resurrection are the principal emphases of the rite. The Apostle Paul claims as much in his treatment of baptism in Rom 6:3–4:

> do you not know that as many of us as were baptized into Christ Jesus were baptized into His death? Therefore we were buried with Him through baptism into death, that just as Christ was raised from the dead by the glory of the Father, even so we also should walk in newness of life.

In this passage, Paul contends that the act of baptism exemplifies and embodies a Christological reality that gives perspective to the entirety of the Christian life. Likewise, baptism makes serious claims about the Christian approach to death. On the one hand, baptism is indicative of

---

7. Perhaps, in this regard, in Matt 28:20 Jesus reaffirms the statement he made to Peter in Matt 16:18 that even "the gates of Hades"—i.e., death—will not prevail against the church.

the physical death and new, resurrected life the Christian will one day experience in the corporeal body. The act serves as a reminder to the Christian that death is prevalent and will one day claim them. However, it also offers comfort, acknowledging that death does not have the final word. Since the Christian has been united with Christ in his death, they will also be united with him in his resurrection. Every Christian funeral is thus representative of baptism. The deceased is identified as one who has now entered into the fullness of their baptism. They have reached complete union with Christ who has accepted them into his death so as to be purified, healed, and freed of death itself.[8] Likewise, the Christian has joined Christ in new, resurrected life, following in both death and resurrection where Christ has first led.[9]

On the other hand, baptism signifies a spiritual death and life—death to sin and the reality of new life known in Christ.[10] It is indicative of the saving work of Christ in the present moment. While the act of baptism itself is not salvific, its proper observance places an individual in a context where salvation is realized and actualized, namely relationship to Jesus Christ and Christ's mystical body, the church. As Ole Borgen observes, "the task of baptism is to be the starting point on the road to salvation."[11] Accordingly, baptism is the proleptic event that points to God's work of salvation through grace, a salvation that saves both from future perdition but also saves "to the uttermost" in the here and now, freeing the Christian from the guilt and power of sin.[12] When Christians make use of the grace of God initiated in baptism, they find themselves converting from a life of sin to a life of holy love. Such growth in grace and love persists throughout the entirety of the Christian's life, leading the Christian on to perfection and ultimately to glorification. Baptism thus functions alongside discipleship in the Christian life as an effective sign of salvation, an effective means of grace, and an effective pledge of the glory to come.[13]

8. See Schmemann, *Liturgy of Death*, 90.

9. As Charles Wesley writes: "Soar we now where Christ has led, Alleluia! / Following our exalted head, Alleluia! / Made like him, like him we rise, Alleluia! / Ours the cross, the grave, the skies, Alleluia!" See Wesley, "Hymn for Easter Day," 209–10.

10. See Wesley, "Treatise on Baptism," 188–201.

11. Borgen, "No End Without the Means," 74.

12. See Wesley, "And Are We Yet Alive," 553.

13. See Borgen, *John Wesley on the Sacraments*, 46–47.

In his *Explanatory Notes* on Rom 6:3–4, John Wesley reflects on the requisite relationship between baptism and the Christian life:

> *As many as have been baptized into Jesus Christ have been baptized into his death*—In baptism we, through faith, are engrafted into Christ; and we draw new spiritual life from this new root, through his Spirit, who fashions us like unto him, and particularly with regard to his death and resurrection. . . . *That as Christ was raised from the dead by the glory*—Glorious power. Of the Father, so we also, by the same power, should rise again; and as he lives a new life in heaven, so we should walk in newness of life. This, says the apostle, our very baptism represents to us.[14]

For Wesley, Paul's association of baptism with Christ's death and resurrection in Romans 6 presents baptism as the act by which new spiritual life is drawn. Through faith, the baptized person is "engrafted" into Christ, and through his Spirit "fashioned" into Christ-likeness. This union with Christ in baptism has a specific consequence: walking in newness of life.[15] Wesley thus concludes that baptism is representative not only of a future, resurrected reality but also of the present and active commitment to Christ showcased through Christlike (i.e., holy) living. The disciple gradually grows in holiness until perfected in love. Thus, the sacrament of baptism instigates what discipleship develops and preserves, namely a life of saving faith and holy love.[16]

Baptism and Ecclesial Discipleship

Discipleship cannot be done in isolation, but rather requires a community. This is why baptism must be understood not only as initiation

14. Wesley, "Romans 6:3–4," 376.

15. The liturgical theologian Robert Webber reflects on this idea in a similar manner: "[Obedience in baptism] begins by demanding the full identification of the believer with Christ by baptism. . . . To be baptized into Christ means to identify with his suffering, to enter into his death, and to be raised to new life in him. In this way the Christian participates in the victory of Christ over evil and is called in his body, the church, to continue to wage war against evil, wherever it is found, in the name of Christ—in his power and authority." Webber, *Common Roots*, 194.

16. Baptism is similar to marriage in this regard. The wedding of a bride and groom take place in the moment of a ceremony. The remainder of the bride and groom's life together is to be spent learning how to live into what occurred in the moment they were wed. Baptism, then, serves as that moment of wedding the Bride of Christ, i.e., the church, to its groom, i.e., Christ himself.

and conversion into life with Christ, but also as initiation into Christ's body—the church—where continuous conversion into Christ-likeness takes place. In his "Treatise on Baptism," John Wesley calls baptism "the initiatory sacrament," stating that baptism initiates a person into life with God and into relationship with his church.[17] It is situated within these two relationships that a person is discipled in order to grow in holiness. Through the regenerative work and grace of God, the holiness of heart and life instigated by baptism is continuously realized and actualized in Christian community. Through the process of ecclesial discipleship, one discovers what it means to be a baptized Christian—i.e., one who is identified with Christ, who is part of Christ's mystical and ecclesial body, and who is expected to exhibit Christ-likeness in the world.

One of the hallmark features of the Wesleyan tradition is its commitment to the doctrine of Christian perfection. For Wesley, Christian perfection—i.e., holiness or sanctification—relates to the state of perfect, holy love to the exclusion of all inward and outward sin. The work of Christ's death and resurrection in a person's life makes it possible for the person not only to be saved by grace but also for them to be restored to the image of God and made perfect in holy love of God and neighbor. As God's grace is infused into the soul through the Holy Spirit, one's love for God and others is made pure and complete. The person grows in virtue as their faith is expressed in loving, selfless actions.

In his sermon "The Scripture Way of Salvation," Wesley frames it this way: "[Perfection] is love excluding sin; love filling the heart, taking up the whole capacity of the soul."[18] To put it simply, Christian perfection is nothing less than the reality of love replacing sin in the Christian. It is the natural trait of a purified heart filled with holy love. As Kenneth Collins reflects:

> The creature, once steeped in sin, now reflects the goodness of the Creator in a remarkable way. . . . Christian perfection, then, is another term for holy love. It is holy in that believers so marked by this grace are free from the impurities and the drag of sin. It is loving in that believers now love God as the goal of their being, and they love their neighbors as they should.[19]

---

17. Wesley, "Treatise on Baptism," 191.

18. Wesley, "Sermon 43, 'The Scripture Way of Salvation,'" 160.

19. Collins, *Theology of John Wesley*, 302–3.

A year before his death, John Wesley claimed Christian perfection to be "the grand depositum which God has lodged with the people called Methodists," stating it was for the proliferation of the doctrine that God raised up the Methodist movement.[20] Thus, throughout his writings and teachings, Wesley consistently promotes holiness as a defining characteristic of Methodism and of the people called Methodists.[21] Moreover, he insists holiness as a necessary and fundamental part of every Christian life.[22] Perfection is obtainable for every believer, Wesley claims, because holiness is the fruit of true scriptural Christianity.[23] Christian perfection is not optional, nor should it be relegated to a certain segment of pious Christianity. Rather, for Wesley, holiness of heart and life is expected of all baptized Christians.[24]

Wesley's concept of holiness as a standard for any Christian disciple is exemplified in his sermon "Of the Church" as he reflects on the reason for why the church is called "the holy catholic church" in the Apostles' Creed. Wesley writes, "the church is called 'holy' because it is holy; because every member thereof is holy, though in different degrees, as he that called them is holy."[25] In this sermon, Wesley plainly and definitely affirms that the holy character of the church is directly correlated to the holiness of those baptized into the church. Simply put, the church is called holy because its members are holy. Holiness depicts ecclesial identity.

Wesley makes an important qualification in his sermon, however, stating that holiness subsists in "different degrees." While holiness is a defining characteristic of the church and necessary for the Christian life, Wesley recognizes that those who receive God's gifts of regeneration in baptism and justifying grace in the new birth must also grow in holiness. To put it another way, the holiness instigated in baptism continues to be cultivated throughout the entirety of a Christian's life. Regardless of whether one is baptized as an infant, adolescent, or adult, the sacrament of baptism is the beginning of the life of holiness that the baptized individual is to pursue for the remainder of their life.[26] Even when Christian

20. Wesley, "John Wesley to Robert Carr Brackenbury," 9.

21. See Wesley, "Principles of a Methodist," 227.

22. Watson, *Pursuing Social Holiness*, 39.

23. Wesley, "Minutes of Several Conversations," 845.

24. Wesley, "Principles of a Methodist," 227.

25. Wesley, "Sermon 74, 'Of the Church,'" 55–56.

26. Ole Borgen makes an important qualification at this point: "Wesley believes that infants are 'born again' through the means of baptism. But he rejects the

perfection is achieved, growth in grace still occurs. Just as Jesus grew in wisdom and grace, continual growth is necessary for the Christian as well. However, such growth only occurs in a pure heart that continues to be nurtured in the favor of God.[27]

Since holiness is expected of any baptized Christian, and because Wesley describes perfection and holiness in terms of pure and perfect love, perfection and holiness must be understood in a social and relational way. In other words, there is a necessary social and relational feature to discipleship. This is the primary principle underlying John Wesley's concept of "social" holiness: holy love needs others in order to be cultivated and maintained. There is no division between personal and social piety, which is why in his fourth discourse on the Sermon on the Mount Wesley condemns solitary religion, i.e., religion that exists "without living and conversing with other men."[28] He writes, "Christianity is essentially a social religion; to turn it into a solitary one is to destroy it. When I say, This is essentially a social religion, I mean not only that it cannot subsist so well, but that it cannot subsist at all, without society."[29] Likewise, in his preface to the 1739 edition of Sacred Hymns and Poems, Wesley pens the following words:

> "Holy Solitaries" is a phrase no more consistent with the gospel
> than Holy Adulterers. The gospel of Christ knows of no religion,
> but social; no holiness but social holiness. Faith working by love,

---

suggestion that infants believe, aided by the faith of others, as Luther proposed. When Calvin teaches that God acknowledges infants as His children directly from their birth, that they receive sanctification from their parents, and consequently, are baptized because they already belong to Christ, Wesley differs at several points. For Calvin these privileges belong only to those born within the covenant while, as Wesley sees it, this prevenient grace is given to all. Furthermore, Wesley would agree with Luther that children are born again through baptism, and not only given the sign as seal and assurance of something which has already taken place. He would, nevertheless, agree with Calvin when he says: 'Infants are renewed by the Spirit of God, according to the capacity of their age, till that power which was concealed within them grows by degrees and becomes fully manifest at the proper time.' Wesley would insist that God work this 'renewal,' or at least its beginning, through the means of baptism." See Borgen, "No End Without the Means," 77; cf. Luther, Three Treatises, 187; Calvin, Institutes, IV.15.22:1323; 16.15:1337; 16.32:1359; Calvin, Commentary on a Harmony, 2:390.

27. See Wesley, "Plain Account of Christian Perfection," 366–446; Wesley, "Sermon 40, 'Christian Perfection,'" 97–125; and Wesley, "Sermon 43, 'The Scripture Way of Salvation,'" 153–69.

28. Wesley, "Sermon 24, 'Upon Our Lord's Sermon,'" 531–49.

29. Wesley, "Sermon 24, 'Upon Our Lord's Sermon,'" 534.

is the length and breadth and depth and height of Christian perfection. This commandment have we from Christ, that he who love God, love his brother also: And that we manifest our Love, by doing good to all men; especially to them that are of the household of faith. And in truth, whoever loveth his brethren not in word only, but as Christ loved him, cannot but be zealous of good works. He feels in his soul a burning, restless desire, of spending and being spent for them.[30]

In the above writings, Wesley counters an individualized and privatized notion of the Christian faith by speaking to the necessity for Christian fellowship. He sets forth the idea that one cannot know holy love disconnected from other Christians in the church; instead, Christians need one another for the cultivation and maintenance of holiness.

It is only within Christian community that holiness of heart and life is realized and actualized. This relational and social dynamic is the ecclesial framework of discipleship. The church is to be the community where baptism and discipleship take place. Moreover, disciples are encouraged to watch over one another in love in the mutual pursuit of holiness. This is why the vows taken in baptism are of the utmost importance. Similar to marriage, in baptism a commitment to a relational covenant is made. The vows taken in the covenantal ceremony announce the relationship between the Triune God and the Christian. They also illustrate the promise and responsibility of the church to invest in the baptized Christian's life. As part of the church—the body of Christ and the family of God—Christians learn together how to live and to love. As William Willimon reflects:

> Baptism is Christian initiation. The goal of this process and its culminating rite is not some individualized, purely personal experience. The goal of baptism is initiation into a community of faith, a church. It is entrance into a way of life together, not a rite to do something to or for an individual in private. It asserts from its beginning that to be a follower of Christ means to be grafted into the Body of Christ. There is no Christian without church, no faith outside the community of faith.[31]

---

30. Wesley, *Hymns and Sacred Poems*, viii–ix.
31. Willimon, *Remember Who You Are*, 22–23.

Wesley's Model of Ecclesial Discipleship

One of John Wesley's most enduring legacies is his emphasis on small group formation. In fact, it has been claimed that Wesley's insistence on small groups was an essential component to the growth of the eighteenth-century British revivals.[32] In the early years of his ministry in England, John Wesley came to the stark realization that holiness of heart and life did not characterize the baptized Christians he met day-to-day. Further-more, Wesley discovered that very few of his fellow Christians in the Church of England had a proper understanding of Scripture, theology, and doctrine, much less recognized the significance of their baptism as it pertains to their life as a disciple of Jesus Christ.

Wesley was convinced something needed to be done to spark re-newal in the Church of England. He thus established a system of small groups and societies as a model of discipleship to incite growth in holi-ness. Although his model existed as a movement within the Church of England, it functioned practically as a group of smaller "churches" within the larger church. It should be noted that while John Wesley's model was not a sanctioned system in the Church of England, for him, the model was always connected to the ecclesial life of the church. It was never in-tended to replace the church or stand apart from the regular, ecclesial gathering.

Wesley believed that as long as a person is part of the church, they will draw spiritual life from it; therefore, he established a means of culti-vating attachment to the church through small group discipleship. To be sure, Wesley always aspired for Anglican renewal; however, he understood renewal must take place within people for it to take place in the church. For it to take place within people, as has been noted, Wesley maintained a social and relational dynamic is necessary. This is why Wesley established smaller, more intimate settings—so the early Methodists could learn to "watch over one another in love" in their commitment to one another and in their mutual pursuit of holiness.[33] Wesley's discipleship model can be considered "ecclesial," then, because it took place within the context of Christian community for the purpose of edifying a holy people who con-stitute a holy church. The smaller gatherings provided a more intimate ecclesial setting whereby growth in holiness could occur.

32. Watson, *Class Meeting*, 20. For a very fine and more exhaustive treatment of Wesley's discipleship model, see Watson, *Pursuing Social Holiness*.

33. Wesley, "Nature, Design, and Rules," 69.

Wesley based his system of discipleship in three key structures: the society meeting, the class meeting, and the band meeting. Each of these give significant insight to Wesley's methodical approach to discipleship as well as implications for discipleship in the church today. First, Wesley arranged Societies, which were structured as a gathering of people from a particular region or parish who met periodically for Bible study, prayer, mutual encouragement, and preaching. Usually these gatherings were held during the week so members could attend services in their local parish churches. In Societies, leaders taught key Methodist doctrines since one of the aims of the gathering was to present scriptural truth in a clear and compelling manner.

Within the Methodist Societies, smaller groups called Bands and Classes met. Every member of a Society was also a member of a Class Meeting and/or Band Meeting. Classes provided an entry-level experience of discipleship for the early Methodists and were mixed regarding age, spiritual maturity, gender, marital status, and social standing.[34] The primary focus of the Class Meeting centered on behavioral change through examination of the status of one's soul and the person's life with God. Growth in love was the ultimate goal of the Class Meeting. Band Meetings, however, were for those who desired to grow in love, holiness, and purity of intention, i.e., Christian perfection.

The Bands consisted of four to six members of the same sex and social status. In the Band Meeting, members "sought to improve their attitudes, emotions, feelings, intentions, and affections."[35] Bands committed to the regular confession of sin in order to grow in Christian perfection. Members were accountable to one another regarding life and sin, they prayed for one other, and encouraged one another toward love, good works, and holy living. Kevin Watson claims that the Band Meeting "was the engine of holiness in early Methodism."[36] Since Wesley realized that the grace of God manifest through love for others was essential to perfection, and because he understood that disciples grew through the communal pursuit of holiness, the Band Meeting provided an ideal environment for intimate ecclesial discipleship to take place.

John Wesley also firmly believed in the sanctifying work of God. He thus desired to see dedication to an altered life—namely from sin to holy

---

34. Watson and Kisker, *Band Meeting,*14.

35. Maddix, "John Wesely's Small Groups."

36. Watson and Kisker, *Band Meeting,* 86.

love—in those baptized Christians who wished to be part of the Methodist movement. In this vein, Wesley writes in his "Plain Account of the Methodist Societies": "There is only one condition previously required in those who desire admission into this Society, a desire to flee from the wrath to come, and to be saved from their sins."[37]

All members of the Methodist Societies were expected to show dedication to repentance of sin and commitment to holiness, two aspects of Christian life that baptism demands. If one truly desired to "flee from the wrath to come," Wesley believed it would be exhibited through proper reorientation of life from sinful behavior to Christ-like ways of love. Wesley writes, "wherever this desire is fixed in the soul, it will be shown by its fruits. It is therefore expected of all who continue therein that they should continue to evidence their desire of salvation."[38] Specifically, Wesley believed desire for salvation was made manifest through what he called the "General Rules," i.e., do no harm, do good, and attend upon the ordinances of God.[39] For Wesley, growth in holiness produced the fruit of holy love. This is the kind of ongoing discipleship, i.e., "walking in newness of life," signified in baptism.

Every Methodist was thus expected to keep the three general rules. Once a person was accepted as a member of a Methodist Society, they were placed in a Class in order to submit to the continual examination of life and confirm their commitment to growth in holiness. Every quarter, all members of Methodist Societies who showcased proper Christian living were issued a ticket allowing them entry into the Society meeting. Accountability in the smaller Band and Class meetings became the means of discerning proper from improper persons. Wesley reflects:

> In a while some of these informed me they found such and such an one did not live as he ought. . . . I called together all the *Leaders* of the *Classes* . . . and desired that each would make particular inquiry into the behavior of those whom he saw weekly. They did so. Many disorderly walkers were detected. Some turned from the evil of their ways. Some were put away from us.[40]

Undeniably, as has been explained, John Wesley sought to make disciples in the way of life that baptism demands. Though he believed

37. Wesley, "Plain Account," 257.
38. Wesley, "Plain Account," 257.
39. Wesley, "Plain Account," 257.
40. Wesley, "Plain Account," 260–61.

it was not necessary for a Christian to sin, he recognized that Christians often did sin after coming to the faith. His concern was that unconfessed and unrepentant sin would fester and devolve into more devastating sin. For this reason, if someone was unwilling to submit to the examination of life in a Class or Band Meeting, or if their life did not reflect growth in holiness, the person was removed from the Methodist Society.

Because such earnest commitment to holiness requires constant examination and cultivation, Wesley set leaders in place to foster growth in Class Meetings. The Class leader was a crucial position in the early Methodist movement as they had the role of being the spiritual leader of the people in the Class. The leader kept track of attendance and visited anyone who missed the weekly gathering. Additionally, the Class leader fostered discussion, modeled vulnerability, and provided encouragement and support to those in the group as it was needed. In essence, the Class leader cultivated the relationships necessary for growth in ecclesial discipleship. Kevin Watson reflects on the nature of the Class meetings:

> The phrase that best captures what the Methodists believed was so important about the class meeting was "watching over one another in love." Early Methodists were asked to invite others into their lives and to be willing to enter deeply into the lives of other people so that together they would grow in grace. They were committed to the idea that the Christian life is a journey of growth in grace, or sanctification. And they believed that they needed one another in order to persevere on this journey.[41]

Wesley was convinced the Class and Band Meetings were "the sinews" that held together the Methodist Societies.[42] He believed Bands and Classes were crucial for growth in holy life and love and was afraid their decline in practice would result in the diminishment of Methodism itself. In his "A Plain Account of Christian Perfection," Wesley urges, "Never omit meeting your Class or Band. . . . These are the very sinews of our Society; and whatever weakens, or tends to weaken, our regard for these, or our exactness in attending them, strikes at the very root of our community."[43] For Wesley, then, failing to practice ecclesial discipleship was to eradicate the very foundation of the Methodist movement and stifle its potentiality for church renewal.

---

41. Watson, *Class Meeting*, 26.
42. Wesley, "Plain Account," 433.
43. Wesley, "Plain Account," 433.

Ecclesial Discipleship Today

To reiterate what was stated at the onset of this chapter, there is an indivisible relationship between discipleship and baptism. Specifically, baptism is the sacramental act of initiation and conversion. It instigates what discipleship develops and preserves—a life of saving faith and holy love. However, for holy life and love to persist in disciples, intentional and continual cultivation by the church is needed. If the church is to take seriously the task of discipleship, then it needs to cultivate disciples in the holy life and love that baptism demands. In doing so, the church serves as a constant aid in helping the disciple to remember their baptism and to be constantly thankful for the benefits received therein.[44]

The early Methodist small group structure provides an exemplary model of how the cultivation of holiness can occur through continual and intentional commitment to ecclesial discipleship. It has much to teach the church today. Wesley's model was based in social investment, i.e., disciples making disciples who encouraged one another toward growth in Christ-likeness. The devotion of the early Methodists to one another in these groups established reciprocal relationships in the cultivation of holiness. Through mutual care for one another holy love begat holy love.

A central feature of Wesley's discipleship model that cannot be overlooked is his acknowledgement that continual growth in grace cannot occur without repentance. Since all are born into the sinful nature, holiness requires death to sin, including both wrongful actions and evil desires. The sin present in a person's life blocks their relationship with God, harms them, and harms others; thus, the grace of God at work through the redeeming work of Jesus Christ and the transformative power of the

---

44. The implication made in the following material regarding baptism and discipleship in the church today are connected to the historic vows and liturgical pattern of baptism. Typically included in the liturgical content of baptism are: the promises of God to the baptized individual; the renunciation of sin; the identification with the baptized person in the death and resurrection of Jesus Christ; the commitment to no long yield one's self to Satan, his powers, or principalities; the affirmation of the historic faith of the church through the creeds; the commitment to follow in the ways of Christ; the pledge to (and by) the Christian community to grow together as a community of love and grace; and the welcoming of the new disciple into the church. For two fine examples of how baptismal liturgy embodies these commitments, see: Hippolytus, *On the Apostolic Tradition*, 105–27; and General Board of Discipleship of the United Methodist Church, "Baptismal Covenant I," 86–94.

Holy Spirit is needed in the disciple to reorient them in holy life and love.[45]

To be a baptized disciple of Jesus Christ requires the commitment to turn away from sin (i.e., "to flee from the wrath to come") toward Christ-like holiness. Discipleship today, then, should help disciples acknowledge all things contrary to Christ, namely sin and its motivating factors. Furthermore, discipleship should teach disciples to name and confess their sins as they seek change through God's grace. The natural byproduct of such confession is a greater comprehension of and value for forgiveness and grace. In particular, the grace first received in baptism can be seen permeating all of life and empowering the disciple as they encounter the great love and mercy of God. Likewise, as the disciple experiences pardon with God, they also participate in the tender care of the Christian community. Through the acknowledgment and confession of sin, the church learns to grow together as Christ's body and as a community of love and forgiveness.

Accompanying an emphasis on death to sin through repentance is the affirmation of the baptized disciple's new life with Christ, which comes through healing and deliverance. In this regard, discipleship today should stress deliverance through the intentional purgation of evil in the heart, mind, and life of the disciple as well as the spiritual freedom that comes through God's grace. While the working of God's grace is not a guarantee that every mental, emotional, and physical ailment will be removed from the disciple in this life, it does promise spiritual freedom and peace. Particularly, the atoning work of Christ attended by the Holy Spirit in the disciple's life brings freedom from the guilt of sin and freedom for holy life and love. Exorcism of evil results in purity of desire in the heart as the grace of God brings healing, wholeness, and rest. Discipleship must therefore emphasize not only deliverance from spiritual forces of evil but also freedom for holiness and peace with God in the present life.

Likewise, discipleship today should affirm not only deliverance from spiritual sin but also final freedom from death. Baptism signifies the disciple's union with Christ in death so as to be united with him in the bodily resurrected life. The disciple has no need to fear death, then, because in Christ they have been purified, healed, and freed of death's sting. In their own death they find rest in Christ's death, and ultimately victory over death in his resurrection. When this eschatological feature

45. Watson and Kisker, *Band Meeting*, 44.

of baptism is kept forefront, discipleship not only prepares the disciple for life on earth but also orients them toward eternal life in the kingdom.

In the current life, however, discipleship should impart a distinct Christian ethos that preserves Christian purity of behavior and love. Naturally, an ethos is not something merely known and accepted but rather is a standard to be lived; thus, a focus on Christian behavior is necessary in discipleship, especially concerning how Christian life stands in distinct contrast to secular life. If disciples old and new are to maintain a Christian ethos, constant examination of life is needed. Not only should sin be addressed, but disciples should aid one another in the examination of life habits and practices, gathering together frequently and correcting one another in peace.[46] The goal is not simply to cease from sinful behavior but also to practice virtue through acts of mercy and charity.[47] Thus, discipleship today must work to instill a distinct Christian ethos in disciples through mutual admonition of obedience to Christ-like ways of life and love.

Communal discipline is one way the church can work to develop a distinct Christian ethos. Notedly, a foundational facet of communal discipline is learning the content of the faith with one another. At minimum it is important for disciples both old and new to commit to growth in knowledge of the Triune God through Scripture and theological study. Another significant feature of communal discipline is mutual commitment and adherence to Christian practices, i.e., communal means of grace. In particular, the church commits to growth in holiness by regularly joining together in practices such as prayer, fasting, abstinence, and almsgiving. While there is value in practicing these disciplines individually, it is important to incorporate such practices in an ecclesial way. When done communally, they serve as formative disciplines that bind the community together in the pursuit of Christ-like life and love.

In conclusion, similar to Wesley's model of Societies, Classes, and Bands, discipleship today should strive to foster devotion to Christ and to Christ's body. It should also expect and assert commitment by disciples to total and continual transformation of heart and life in the image of Jesus Christ. If the world is to behold a holy church, then continual and

46. For more on how this practice was done in the early centuries of the church, see Lightfoot and Harmer, "Didache or Teaching," 257–67.

47. For examples of such practices, see Wesley, "Sermon 16, 'Means of Grace,'" 376–97.

intentional dedication to growth in holiness must be given by those who have been baptized into Christ and exist as his representative body on earth.

Bibliography

Borgen, Ole E. *John Wesley on the Sacraments: A Theological Study*. Nashville: Abingdon, 1973.

———. "No End Without the Means: John Wesley and the Sacraments." In *The Asbury Journal* 46.1 (Spring 1991) 63–86.

Calvin, John. *Commentary on a Harmony of the Evangelists*. Translated by W. Pringh. Edinburgh: The Calvin Translation Society, 1845.

———. *Institutes of the Christian Religion*. Library of Christian Classics 20–21. Edited by J. T. McNeill. Philadelphia: Westminster, 1960.

Collins, Kenneth J. *The Theology of John Wesley: Holy Love and the Shape of Grace*. Nashville: Abingdon, 2007.

Ferguson, Everett. *Baptism in the Early Church: History, Theology, and Liturgy in the First Five Centuries*. Grand Rapids: Eerdmans, 2009.

General Board of Discipleship of the United Methodist Church. "Baptismal Covenant I." In *The United Methodist Book of Worship*, 86–94. Nashville: United Methodist Publishing, 1992.

Grassi, J. A. *Jesus as Teacher: A New Testament Guide to Learning "the Way."* Winona, MN: St. Mary's College Press, 1978.

Hippolytus. *On the Apostolic Tradition*. Translated by Alistair C. Steward. Crestwood: St. Vladimir's Seminary Press, 2001.

Lightfoot, J. B., and J. R. Harmer, eds. "The Didache or Teaching of the Twelve Apostles." In *The Apostolic Fathers*, 257–67. Grand Rapids: Baker, 1992.

Luther, Martin. *Three Treatises*. Philadelphia: Muhlenberg, 1943.

Maddix, Mark A. "John Wesley's Small Groups: Models of Christian Community." *Holiness Today* (November/December 2009). https://holinesstoday.org/imported-news/john-wesleys-small-groups-models-christian-community.

Moser, J. David. "*Totus Christus*: A Proposal for Protestant Christology and Ecclesiology." In *Pro Ecclesia: A Journal of Catholic and Evangelical Theology* 29 (2020) 3–30.

Powers, Jonathan A. "*Ecclesia Semper Sanctificanda*: Historic Models of Catechesis and the Cultivation of Social Holiness." In *The Asbury Journal* 74.1 (2019) 85–107.

Schmemann, Alexander. *The Liturgy of Death*. Yonkers: St. Vladimir's Seminary Press, 2016.

Watson, Kevin M. *The Class Meeting: Reclaiming a Forgotten (and Essential) Small Group Experience*. Franklin, TN: Seedbed, 2014.

———. *Pursuing Social Holiness: The Band Meeting in Wesley's Thought and Popular Methodist Practice*. Oxford: Oxford University Press, 2014.

Watson, Kevin, and Scott Kisker. *The Band Meeting: Rediscovering Relational Discipleship in Transformational Community*. Franklin, TN: Seedbed, 2017.

Webber, Robert. *Common Roots: The Original Call to an Ancient-Future Faith*. Grand Rapids: Zondervan, 2009.

Wesley, Charles. "And Are We Yet Alive." In *The United Methodist Hymnal: Book of United Methodist Worship*, 553. Nashville: United Methodist Publishing, 1989.

————. "Hymn for Easter Day." In *Hymns and Sacred Poems*, 209–10. London: William Strahan, 1739.

Wesley, John. *Hymns and Sacred Poems*. London: William Strahan, 1739.

————. "John Wesley to Robert Carr Brackenbury, September 15, 1790." In *Works of John Wesley*. Vol. 13, *Letters*, edited by Thomas Jackson, 9. Grand Rapids: Zondervan, 1958–59.

————. "Minutes of Several Conversations between the Reverend Mr. John and Charles Wesley, and Others." In *Bicentennial Edition of the Works of John Wesley*. Vol. 10, *The Methodist Societies: The Minutes of Conference*, edited by Henry Rack, 845. Nashville: Abingdon, 2011.

————. "The Nature, Design, and Rules of the United Societies in London, Bristol, Kingswood, and Newcastle upon Tyne." In *Bicentennial Edition of the Works of John Wesley*. Vol. 9, *The Methodist Societies: History, Nature, Design*, edited by Rupert E. Davies, 69. Nashville: Abingdon, 1989.

————. "A Plain Account of Christian Perfection." In *Bicentennial Edition of the Works of John Wesley*. Vol. 13, *Doctrinal and Controversial Treatises II*, edited by Paul Wesley Chilcote and Kenneth J. Collins, 132–91. Nashville: Abingdon, 2012.

————. "A Plain Account of the People called Methodist in a Letter to the Rev. Mr. Perronet, Vicar of Shoreham in Kent." In *The Works of John Wesley*. Vol. 9, *The Methodist Societies: History, Nature, Design*, edited by Rupert E. Davies, 257. Nashville: Abingdon, 1989.

————. "The Principles of a Methodist further Explained." In *Bicentennial Edition of the Works of John Wesley*. Vol. 9, *The Methodist Societies: History, Nature, and Design*, edited by Rupert E. Davies, 160–237. Nashville: Abingdon, 1989.

————. "Romans 6:3–4." In *Explanatory Notes*. Vol. 4, *Upon the New Testament*, 376. Salem: Schmul, 1976.

————. "Sermon 16, 'The Means of Grace.'" In *Bicentennial Edition of the Works of John Wesley*. Vol. 1, *Sermons I*, edited by Albert C. Outler, 376–97. Nashville: Abingdon, 1984.

————. "Sermon 24, 'Upon Our Lord's Sermon on the Mount, IV.'" In *Bicentennial Edition of the Works of John Wesley*. Vol. 1, *Sermons I*, edited by Albert C. Outler, 531–49. Nashville: Abingdon, 1984.

————. "Sermon 40, 'Christian Perfection.'" In *Bicentennial Edition of the Works of John Wesley*. Vol. 2, *Sermons II*, edited by Albert C. Outler, 97–124. Nashville: Abingdon, 1985.

————. "Sermon 43, 'The Scripture Way of Salvation.'" In *Bicentennial Edition of the Works of John Wesley*. Vol. 2, *Sermons II*, edited by Albert C. Outler, 153–69. Nashville: Abingdon, 1985.

————. "Sermon 74, 'Of the Church.'" in *Bicentennial Edition of the Works of John Wesley*. Vol. 3, *Sermons III*, edited by Albert C. Outler, 45–57. Nashville: Abingdon, 1986.

————. "A Treatise on Baptism." In *Works of John Wesley*. Vol. 10, *Letters, Essays, Dialogs, Addresses*, edited by Thomas Jackson, 188–201. Grand Rapids: Zondervan, 1958–59.

Willimon, William H. *Remember Who You Are: Baptism, a Model for Christian Life*. Nashville: Upper Room, 1980.

CHAPTER 7

Baptism and Evangelism

Reimagining the Great Commission

DANIEL D. SHIN, DREW THEOLOGICAL SCHOOL

EVANGELISM HAS BECOME A bad word, at least in certain communities where it has fallen on hard times and is looked upon with suspicion, if not outright contempt. In stark contrast, there are Christian communities where evangelism still holds a place of honor among people who remain deeply passionate and convicted of its necessity. Then there are those who fall somewhere in between with a sense of ambivalence, not knowing what to make of it all.[1] Like it or not, the present reality is a deeply divided one on the subject of evangelism. No doubt each respective position has good reasons for its stance, but it is critical to not lose sight of the forest for the trees. To move beyond the current impasse will require a radical transformation, one that will involve robust conversations with biblical, historical, theological, and interdisciplinary studies that enable assessment, correction, and enlargement of the horizon. This urgent task of reimagination through critical, constructive, and creative engagement is no easy feat, but it offers a fighting chance to transform evangelism and reclaim it for the contemporary church.

---

1. For an excellent discussion about this tension concerning evangelism and also a thoughtful proposal based on the notion of communication, see Pickard, "Evangelism," 135–58.

The current chapter undertakes such reimagination. Beginning with a discussion on the Great Commission, it considers problematic receptions of Jesus' final command to his disciples at the end of Matthew and attempts to repair the damage caused by misreadings. The chapter then explores the connection between evangelism and the overall complex of the Christian tradition. Special attention is given to the relation between evangelism and baptism—which is usually the most immediate rite following on the heels of evangelism—by examining John Wesley's "Treatise on Baptism" in light of his understanding of the *via salutis* and through analysis of William Abraham's and Bryan Stone's proposals on evangelism.

The Great Commission and the Great Commandments

It is natural to begin the present exploration of evangelism with a discussion about the Great Commission for two reasons: one, the Great Commission has played such a central role in modern and contemporary Christian mission and evangelism; and two, the imperative "to go and make disciples" includes an explicit charge to baptize and teach obedience to Jesus' teachings.[2] There has been no shortage of sermons, Bible studies, evangelistic programs, and para-church conferences that have invoked the Great Commission to promote Christian ministries worldwide. Unfortunately, the Great Commission has been misused when interpreted out of context and turned into a mere slogan to spread toxic expressions of Christianity around the globe. At the root of this problem lies poor exegetical practices performed in isolation from the overall message of Matthew.[3] Without being deeply rooted in what the body of

2. For further discussion on Matthew's understanding of baptism in the Great Commission, see Keener, "Matthew's Missiology," 3–20; Capes, "Intertextual Echoes," 37–49; and Meier, "John the Baptist in," 383–405.

3. There is no shortage of examples, but a contemporary rendition is a work by Hattaway, *Back to Jerusalem*. Also see a discussion about the Back to Jerusalem movement by Park, "Chosen to Fulfill the Great Commission?" For a recent evangelical appeal to the Great Commission, see Klauber and Manetsch, *Great Commission*. Also see the following for different perspectives on the Great Commission from a wide spectrum of viewpoints: Payne and Beazley, *Reclaiming the Great Commission*; Hertig, "Great Commission Revisited," 343–53; Rundle and Steffen, *Great Commission Companies*; Raschte, *GloboChrist*; Yong and Clarke, *Global Renewal*; Woodford, *Great Commission*; Borthwick, *Great Commission*; Chung, "Postcolonial Reading of the Great Commission," 276–88; Nkansah-Obrempong, "Africa's Contextual Realities," 280–94; Onyinah, "Meaning of Discipleship," 216–27.

the text actually says, the likelihood of doing violence to the passage and to people runs high.

In order to rightly understand the Great Commission, it is important to come to terms with the life-in-setting of the text. According to David Bosch, it is highly probable that the original community Matthew addressed had been uprooted from Judea and transplanted in a foreign environment where they were experiencing a growing presence of Gentiles in their midst. There were two opposing positions on the question about Gentile incorporation to Christianity: whereas legalists argued that faithfulness to the Mosaic law is non-negotiable, enthusiasts were adamant that what is paramount is life in the Spirit and miracles. As if this was not enough, tension was building between the Matthean community and the larger Jewish religious community. Hence, the Matthean community was relatively a young community learning and searching for direction, but it was beset with challenges and uncertain about its identity and future.[4] It was precisely in this liminality that Matthew sets forth a missional theology to help the community embrace mission as its identity and its identity as mission.[5]

How does Matthew do this? He displays both superb pastoral sensitivity and uncompromising prophetical fire in challenging its members to become a missional church, sometimes with uncompromising firmness and very explicit means—as seen in the references to four non-Israelite women in Jesus' genealogy, the magi, the Roman centurion, the Syrophoenician woman, and the eschatological discourses—and sometimes with masterful subtlety; for instance, the commissioning of the disciples in Galilee and Jesus' teaching about the salt of the earth and the light of the world. Matthew masterfully prepares the community to reinterpret their communal life and identity in light of their mission in the reign of God.[6] Their mission is to embody and invite people into the reign of God by obeying God's will through the twofold love of God and neighbor, the latter being the litmus test for the former. This pursuit of love entails costly discipleship because it is about seeking God's righteousness/justice for all—especially the poor, sick, and marginalized—through which disciples fulfill the law and become perfect.[7] If this is what the body of Mat-

---

4. Bosch, *Transforming Mission*, 58–66.

5. Turner, *Ritual Process*, 94–97.

6. Bosch, *Transforming Mission*, 84.

7. Bosch, *Transforming Mission*, 66–80.

thew is about, then mission and evangelism are not about "soul winning" accompanied by blessed assurance, but instead mission and evangelism are about making disciples who demonstrate and teach God's love for the world. The Great Commandments are thus at the core of the Great Commission. Without love, evangelism and mission are empty and hollow.

Global Ambitions and the Great Commission

If the Great Commission is about love, what is not to like? Something has gone wrong, however. Terribly wrong. Without the fundamental understanding of the Great Commission through the lens of the Great Commandments, the centrifugal thrust of worldwide Christian movement can be and has been too often co-opted by regimes of violence and destruction. It is now old news that the modern Western missionary movement has frequently been an accomplice in rolling out Western colonial campaigns.[8] Charges of collusion are indisputable and have been recorded in the annals of history, perhaps most famously by Bartolome de Las Casas in his *The Devastation of the Indies*.[9] Unfortunately, the biblical passage under discussion has been implicated in the expansionist movement of the West. For instance, in her essay "Go, Therefore, and Make Disciples of All Nations?", Musa Dube points out that the evangelistic imperative in Matt 28:16–20 issues a universal, unrestricted passport for Western missionaries to enter foreign lands to pauperize their cultures and societies.[10] Innocent people have been wrenched from their culture and land through racist ideologies of instruction that portrayed the colonized as savage, infantile, inferior, and in need of salvation. This politic of knowledge has annihilated people's belief in their names, languages, environment, and heritage of struggle, making them see their past as one

8. For a helpful discussion about this in the context of Latin America, see Burnett, "Central America and the Caribbean," 154–70.

9. de Las Casas, *Devastation of the Indies*. For further reading on the relation between mission and Western expansionist movements, see the following: Sanneh, "Christian Missions," 331–34; van den Berg, *Constrained by Jesus' Love*; Comaroff and Comaroff, *Of Revelation and Revolution*; Hastings, *Church in Africa*; Fischer-Tine and Mann, *Colonialism as Civilizing Mission*; Robert, *Converting Colonialism*; Elbourne, *Blood Ground*; Forster, *Faith in Empire*; and Sharkey, *American Evangelicals*.

10. Dube, "'Go Therefore and Make Disciples," 224–46.

wasteland of non-achievement to be disposed of in exchange for the new and better world of the West.[11]

When off course, evangelism as a weapon of Western colonization takes aim at any area of the world: Africa, Latin America, Asia, as well as Europe and North America.[12] For instance, Mitzi Smith's essay "US Colonial Missions to African Slaves" in *Teaching All Nations: Interrogating the Matthean Great Commission* details the troubling history of the use of catechesis in the institution of slavery.[13] During the antebellum era, Christian teachings were systematically reworked to make slaves internalize the values that made them better slaves, such as submission, humility, and sacrifice. Instead of proclaiming and incarnating the good news of liberation, evangelism was turned into indoctrination that further fortified an evil system by making slaves accept their lot on earth under their masters. The contents of the catechism—such as the Apostles' Creed, the Lord's Prayer, the Commandments, prayers, and hymns—were bent and twisted to teach that God had ordained slavery because of the sins of the African people, and they must therefore obey their earthly masters as a sign of obedience to their heavenly Master.[14] Smith underscores that such practices of evangelism continued to traumatize both the bodies and the spirits of slaves causing severe mental, emotional, and physical damage. Such catechesis of black slaves led to countless conversions and baptisms, which may have changed their spiritual status but not their socioeconomic and political status as the color white remained an ontological symbol of election before God and black a stigma of sin and inferiority. Though mission to the slaves was initially embarked upon as a viable

11. Dube proposes postcolonial biblical interpretation that enables the pursuit of life-enhancing, noncoercive knowledge in the interest of human freedom. This entails listening respectfully to the perceptions of the divine or the sacred found in a variety of different people groups, nations, and continents beyond the walls of the church to include all cultures. For further reading on postcoloniality and biblical interpretation, see Moore and Segovia, *Postcolonial Biblical Criticism*; and Sugirtharajah, *Postcolonial Reader*. For helpful introductions to postcolonial studies, see the following: Young, *Postcolonialism*; Ashcroft et al., *Postcolonial Studies Reader*; Fanon, *Wretched of the Earth*; Memmi, *Domesticated Man*; Said, *Orientalism*; and Bhaba, *Location of Culture*.

12. See the following for discussions about the history of interaction between Christianity and western colonialism in the Americas and the Caribbean: Boxer, *Church Militant*; Lockhart and Schwartz, *Early Latin America*; Todorov, *Conquest of America*; Rivera, *Violent Evangelism*; Greer, *Jesuit Relations*; and Castro, *Another Face of Empire*.

13. Smith, "US Colonial Mission," 57–85.

14. Smith, "US Colonial Mission," 71.

Christian alternative to options such as abolition, non-interference, or maintenance of the status quo, it actually turned out to be a monstrous tool of dehumanization strengthening the grip of slavery.

In light of these atrocities, it must be asked whatever happened to the Great Commandments of love as the foundation of the Great Commission? The latter without the former not only commits textual violence but also turns the Great Commission into a text of horror.[15] The trouble in splitting the two is that the bifurcation causes a dissolution in interpretation that leads to illegal trespasses and subjugation of people and societies. Warren Carter's reading of Matthew in relation to the Roman imperial powers offers a fresh perspective on the problem of dissociation between the Great Commandments and the Great Commission.[16] Carter interprets the plot in Matthew to be about imperial negotiations by the Matthean community.

The Roman Empire is the political stage on which unfolds the story about God's kin(g)dom, which is marked by worship, mercy, peaceful resistance, not ruling over others, healing, and giving life to all. The mission of God's community is to reverse the personal, social, economic, and political damages of the imperial power as it is informed by Jesus' actions and teachings.[17] For instance, the feeding of the five thousand is about repairing the imperial damage of poverty and hunger by providing food and sustenance in abundance. But the flipside of Jesus' annunciation of the good news of God's reign is denunciation of Rome's oppressive regime. Inevitably, visions of mercy, healing, and material support antithetical to Roman occupiers and imperially aligned religious and political authorities lead to conflict, suffering, and his death on the cross. But Jesus' resurrection shows the limits of imperial power. It is God's empire of life-giving power that ultimately triumphs, and this is the thrust behind the church's worldwide mission.

While highlighting the contestation of Matthew's alternative community against the empire, Carter is careful to point out that ironically their protest illustrates the hybridity of unequal power relations that gives way to yearning for and even imitating the power of oppressors they despise, succumbing to imperial ways all the while mocking and menacing them at the same time. The accommodationist language of Matthew

---

15. Tribble, *Texts of Horror*, 93–118.

16. Carter, *Matthew and the Margins*; Carter, *Matthew and the Empire*.

17. Carter, *Matthew and the Margins*, 119–248.

shows how the gospel employs the very imperial framework it seeks to overcome due to its embeddedness in the empire. Herein lies the clue to the problem of dissociation between the Great Commandments and the Great Commission: the commandments to love are certainly there but so is the imperial language of power and universal expansion. If this is the case, then the possibility of misreading fuels religious subjugation on a global scale, making it all the more urgent and necessary to read the Great Commission in its full context.

Evangelism, Baptism, and the Via Salutis

Reconnecting the Great Commandments and the Great Commission through a textual and hermeneutical approach is certainly one viable way to disentangle evangelism from colonialist and imperialist readings and practices. A more comprehensive effort would involve repairing the connection between evangelism and the larger complex of the world of Christian tradition, including but not limited to baptism, which is the Christian rite tied most closely to evangelism in the continuum of Christian initiation. The argument below is an attempt to reattach evangelism to baptism in a way that ensures its advancement toward the larger complex of the Christian tradition. Of course, there is no fail-proof method to prevent evangelism from relapsing, but something must be done in order for evangelism to have a chance to move forward properly.

John Wesley's thoughts on baptism particularly offer clues to connect evangelism to baptism in a larger framework of Christian life.[18] In his work "A Treatise on Baptism," John Wesley clearly lays out his understanding of baptism as "an initiatory sacrament which enters us into covenant with God."[19] While Wesley addresses various dimensions of baptism, what emerges as significant for the present reflection on the work of evangelism in the overall context of Christian life are the following symbolic functions of baptism: sanctification and the cleansing or washing away of the guilt and disease of original sin, being buried and raised with Christ, entrance into covenant with God, regeneration of heart and spirit, admission into the church, and being united with Christ as joint heirs of God's kingdom. Baptism is understood as a saturated

18. For a discussion about evangelism in the Wesleyan tradition, see Outler, *Evangelism and Theology*.

19. Wesley, "Treatise on Baptism," 188.

event with pluriform functions and benefits, and they are conditional upon one thing, "if we live answerable thereto—if we repent, believe, and obey the gospel."[20]

For Wesley, to live "answerable thereto" means taking into account of the entire *via salutis* that includes conversion from the condition of sin, justification/regeneration, and especially sanctification in love as he underscores that Christ gave himself for the church that he might "sanctify and cleanse" through the work of the Holy Spirit.[21] Similar to Calvin's strategic placement of sanctification before justification in his *Institutes*, Wesley lists sanctification before cleansing lest people would remain satisfied merely with cleansing and not advance forward in perfection![22] Hence, to more fully appreciate Wesley's understanding of baptism, we turn to his construal of the *via salutis*.[23]

God's prevenient grace is universal and invites people to be renewed in love along with the rest of God's creation. This process entails people awakening by God's prompting to a knowledge of themselves as sinners, developing a conviction about their state, and desiring change.[24] Progressing in the movement of grace, justification understood as forgiveness of sin is given by grace and received through faith. At this stage God is experienced as being for us, not against us, and imputes righteousness that is juridical in character and brings about relative change.[25] While justification is distinct from regeneration conceptually and the latter follows the former logically, they occur simultaneously in experience, and it is best that they are held together as in the expression "justification/regeneration" so that those who are justified cannot not move from being born again to growth and maturity in sanctification.[26] In contrast to justifying grace, God's sanctifying grace imparts actual righteousness as

20. Wesley, "Treatise on Baptism," 192.

21. Wesley, "Treatise on Baptism," 191.

22. Calvin, *Institutes*, 537–88.

23. For further reading on the *via salutis* approach to Wesley's soteriology, see Maddox, *Responsible Grace*, 157–91.

24. Wesley, "Sermon 9, 'The Spirit of Bondage,'" 255ff.

25. Wesley, "Sermon 5, 'Justification by Faith,'" 182–99.

26. Wesley, "Sermon 18, 'Marks of the New Birth,'" 417–30; and Wesley, "Sermon 45, 'The New Birth,'" 186–201. According to Outler and Heitzenrater, "Wesley understood regeneration as the act of grace concurrent with justification but not at all identical to it—a 'vast inward change' that opens up the lifelong quest for holiness." See their introduction to Wesley, "Sermon 19, 'The Great Privilege,'" 183.

real change takes place through the therapeutic work of God who not only is for us but also in us.[27] Growth in sanctification is absolutely central in Wesley's *via salutis* as is made unmistakably clear in the following house analogy used by Wesley. If prevenient grace is like the inviting porch of a house, justifying/regenerating grace is like the door through which we enter the house, and sanctifying grace is like the very rooms of the house. What then is the point of justification/regeneration if not ultimately sanctification?[28] Otherwise, justification turns out to be a revolving door rather than an entrance into a deeper love of God and neighbor. This is not to trivialize justification/regeneration since it is the threshold through which the work of sanctification begins. While the two are inseparably connected together in the *via salutis*, they are also distinct from one another. If justification is marked by faith, then sanctification is marked by love. Faith is only a handmaiden of love.[29] Since God's love has been shed abroad in our hearts in the giving of the Holy Spirit (Rom 5:5), Christians are to increase in love by having the mind of Christ and walking as Christ walked, engaging in works of piety and works of mercy.[30]

Moreover, warning against antinomian or Moravian tendencies toward stillness and retreat to inward spirituality, Wesley exhorts Christians toward attentiveness to the laws of God, especially responsibility to the pedagogical use of the law that nurtures both personal and social holiness.[31] For Wesley, there is no separation between personal piety

27. For Wesley's understanding of the therapeutic dimension of grace, see Wesley, "Sermon 44, 'Original Sin,'" 170–85; Wesley, "Sermon 17, 'The Circumcision of the Heart,'" 398–414; Wesley, "Sermon 146, 'The One Thing Needful,'" 351–59; and Wesley, "Treatise on Baptism" 188–201.

28. In the analogy, he explains that prevenient grace is like the porch, justifying-regenerating grace is like the door, and sanctifying grace is like the rooms of the house in order to argue that sanctification is the goal of the dynamics of grace. Wesley, "Sermon 43, 'The Scripture Way of Salvation,'" 153–69.

29. On Wesley's thoughts on love in the *via salutis*, see especially his sermons: "Sermon 17, 'The Circumcision of the Heart,'" 398–414; Wesley, "Sermon 36, 'The Law Established Through Faith: Discourse II,'" 33–43; and Wesley, "Sermon 146, 'The One Thing Needful,'" 351–59.

30. Wesley defines Christian perfection as "having the mind of Christ and walking as Christ walked." Wesley, "Plain Account of Christian Perfection," 367. For further discussion on works of piety and mercy, see Wesley, "Sermon 85, 'On Working Out Our Own Salvation,'" 199–209.

31. For Wesley's understanding of the different uses of the law, see the following: on ceremonial and moral use, Wesley, "Sermon 35, 'The Law Established Through Faith: Discourse I,'" 20–32; Wesley, "Sermon 1, 'Salvation by Faith,'" 109–30; on theological

and the mission of the Methodist movement "to reform the nation and, in particular, the Church; to spread scriptural holiness over the land."[32] Personal piety and social holiness go hand in hand, held together by the love of God that encompasses all spheres of human life in the world. In light of Wesley's *via salutis*, what then does it mean to be baptized in the Wesleyan tradition? What then does it mean for Wesleyans to be about the work of evangelism? Simply put, all of the above.[33]

While evangelism and baptism can point independently to the overall vision of the Christian tradition, together they can better route peoples' attentions to what is ultimately at stake.[34] This move is similar to how Aidan Kavanagh has argued persuasively that baptism, confirmation, and Eucharist are considered sacraments of initiation, which are flanked by pre-catechumenal and catechumenal catechesis on the one hand and post-baptismal catechesis on the other, in the interest of protecting the church as well as individuals undergoing the initiation process.[35] Connecting evangelism to baptism and then to the whole gamut of Christian teaching and practice, especially regarding growth in love based on the Great Commandments, enables its practitioners to break

---

use, see Wesley, "Sermon 9, 'The Spirit of Bondage and Adoption,'" 248–60, and Wesley, "Sermon 36, 'The Law Established Through Faith, Discourse II,'" 33–43; Wesley, "Sermon 5, 'Justification by Faith,'" 181–99; and on pedagogical use, see Wesley, "Upon the Lord's Sermon on the Mount: Discourse IV," 531–49.

32. Wesley, "Large Minutes of Several Conversations," 299, Q.3. For a helpful discussion on baptism as it relates to the Wesleyan movement, see Meadows, *Remembering Our Baptism*.

33. This is in agreement with Barth's understanding of baptism as a symbol of the gospel. See Barth, *Word of God*, 50; McMaken, "Authority, Mission, and Institution," 345–61. On the relation between baptism and evangelism, see also works by Orlando Costas, Carl Braaten, and Walter Brueggemann in Chilcote and Warner, *Study of Evangelism*, 33–45, 159–170, and 219–234.

34. In conversation with Martin Hengel and Martin Kähler among others, Bosch has rightly called our attention to the challenge of mission on the theological development of the early church, and this insight holds true for each generation. See Bosch, *Transforming Mission*, 15–16.

35. Kavanagh, "Christian Initiation," 1–6. The period known as pre-catechumenate includes a time for the seekers to make inquiry, investigate, and solidify his or her purpose as well as the local church to establish trust and communication with the inquirer and evangelize by living well its own life of faith. It is intended to ground the candidates in the basics of spiritual life and Christian teaching. During the catechumenate, the seekers make their intention known publicly, carry out its apostolic mission, and are granted admission into membership. For further discussion on "The Rites of Adult Initiation," see Kavanaugh, *Shape of Baptism*, 126–47.

out of isolated understandings of evangelism and address larger questions about the very scope and nature of the Christian tradition. In that endeavor, baptism functions as a gateway for evangelism to the larger complex of Christianity. Conversely, evangelism can also play a similar role in illuminating what lies beyond baptism to the overall Christian tradition. Interfacing evangelism with major dimensions of the Christian tradition is long overdue and is much needed to address the concerns raised earlier by Bosch, Dube, Smith, and Carter.

The Arc of Evangelism

In his groundbreaking work *The Logic of Evangelism*, William Abraham makes such a move in projecting an overarching arc of evangelism that encompasses conversion, baptism, and moral formation. He begins with a critical assessment of the study and practice of evangelism and notes severe deficiency in substantive theological and critical reflection. Abraham then sets forth a roadmap with a definition of evangelism as intentionally "initiating people into the kingdom of God for the first time."[36] He does not deny proclamation as a vital part of evangelism, but rather offers an important course correction that proclamation should not exclusively define what evangelism is, especially as seen in the New Testament, in the early church, and in Wesleyan and other Christian traditions.

Understanding evangelism as initiation means taking into account polymorphous evangelistic activities such as proclamation, basic instruction in creeds, moral formation, spiritual disciplines, or small groups. The overall thrust of evangelism as initiation into the reign of God is also strategic in underscoring the temporal process of conversion that involves the following: one, admittance to the Christian community; two, instruction in cognitive-propositional claims of Christianity; three, projection of a particular moral vision; four, cultivation of certain experiences, dispositions, and emotions; five, development of gifts and capacities as agents of God; and six, nurture of basic spiritual disciplines essential

---

36. Abraham, *Logic of Evangelism*, 95. Abraham draws attention to the ancient practice of initiation, which became dismembered or disintegrated in the history of the Western church. See also Mitchell, "Dissolution of the Rite," 50–82. And for a thoughtful treatment of initiation in the Reformation period, see essays by Leonel Mitchell and Daniel Stevick in *Made, Not Born*, 83–117. In addition, see John Westerhoff, "Evangelism, Evangelization, and Catechesis," 235–45.

for joyful obedience.[37] This entire process is indispensable in handing over the Christian way of life informed by deep knowledge of its internal grammar, structure, and constraints, the very logic of Christianity, along with "interlocking convictions, commitments, covenants, emotions, affections, and experiences that form the matrix of Christian initiation."[38]

If Abraham's discussion about initiation thus far has seemed more formal, it is worth noting he addresses substantive matters through the initiation continuum of conversion, baptism, and moral formation. Conversion is traditionally understood to be about personal and existential encounter with the gospel of Jesus Christ through the work of the Holy Spirit, which brings about knowledge of one's sins, the compassion of a holy God, and the decision to choose life over death leading to a new birth in relationship with God and others. Unfortunately, conversion understood as such has been taken to be about introspective anthropocentric piety separated from a theological and moral vision of the new age of God.[39] While fully recognizing this, Abraham suggests the language of conversion should be maintained but rehabilitated due to its significance regarding the personal and experiential dimension of "entry into the dynamic rule of God." As a measure to safeguard against anthropocentric piety, Abraham welcomes José Bonino's proposal that accentuates embodiment in specific historical relations. Bonino asserts: "To put it very simply, evangelism must deal with the question: what does it mean, concretely and specifically, in thought and in action, today, to follow Christ?"[40] Abraham agrees social analysis of the situation, examination of the relation between conversion and particular moral, political,

---

37. Abraham, *Logic of Evangelism*, 101–3.

38. Abraham, *Logic of Evangelism*, 83, 96. For additional discussion on catechetical instruction about dispositions, doctrines, Christian association, sacramental participation, and mission in the world, see Kavanagh, "Christian Initiation," 118–37. He offers a comprehensive discussion about evangelization and pre-catechumenate, the catechumenate, purification and enlightenment, sacraments of initiation, post-baptismal catechesis, or *mystagogia*.

39. For an extended discussion on anthropocentric piety versus theocentric piety, see Gustafson, *Ethics from a Theocentric Perspective*.

40. Abraham, *Logic of Evangelism*, 127. For a full discussion, see José M. Bonino, "Conversion, New Creature and Commitment," 324–32; Bonino, *Toward a Christian Political Ethics*. On liberation theology in the Latin American context and evangelism, see Costas, "Evangelism and the Gospel of Salvation"; and Mortimer Arias, "Contextual Evangelization in Latin America," 33–45, 384–404. I have addressed the significance of Christian discipleship in the public world in Daniel D. Shin, *Theology and the Public*.

and philosophical agendas, and ontological construal of human beings as social agents who are inextricably shaped by and demonstrate their freedom in "the web of their relationships" are in order. Such explicit focus on the socioeconomic and political realities of history is not extraneous to but inherently necessitated by the new rule of God into which people are initiated. To do otherwise is to escape into a world of inward and otherworldly piety.

Having established a historical and social understanding of conversion, Abraham then transitions to the topic of baptism and says, "It means that the evangelist must give far more attention to baptism as a means of concrete initiation into the flesh and blood of Christian community than is currently the case."[41] To be sure, Abraham is careful not to equate the reign of God with the church. The former is not merely some abstract ideal but takes on flesh and blood in an eschatological community, i.e., the church. If this is the case, then baptism is not a dead ritual in which we simply rehearse archaic formulas and mechanics, but rather it is a decisive event of initiation into the new eschatological rule of God through "physical incorporation into the church."[42] Baptism as such signifies the deep historical, social, communal, and material character of initiation into the reign of God, which echoes the concerns of Bonino. Baptism is a sacrament that allows entrance into an eschatological community where not only the presence of the Holy Spirit is experienced in mysterious ways, but the character of the reign of God is interpreted and embodied in concrete and specific ways through the church's traditions, visions, rites, ethos, and its social commitments in the world. It is none other than a means of grace that incorporates people into the church for the sake of its public service and witness in the world.

Following incorporation into the church through baptism is moral formation into the new rule of life, the final aspect of the initiation continuum.[43] As the eschatological community, the church is a peculiar entity that both demonstrates and is constituted by its love of God, of one's self, and of its neighbors. In fact, the rule of love is so central that without its enactment in historical embodiment, the eschatological identity of

---

41. Abraham, *Logic of Evangelism*, 128. The topic of infant baptism is not addressed in the present investigation. For a helpful discussion on infant baptism/baptism, confirmation, and catechumenate, see Grant, "Development of Christian Catechumenate," 32–49.

42. Abraham, *Logic of Evangelism*, 130.

43. Abraham, *Logic of Evangelism*, 110.

individuals and communities would not be recognizable. This emphasis on the church's social ethic should be understood as a natural extension of one's encounter with God in conversion represented symbolically in baptism. Conversion, baptism, and moral formation are synchronized in the initiation continuum so that fundamental beliefs and practices of the Christian heritage continue to be handed over. What are conversion and baptism if not the continual process of dying a life of misdirected love and rising again with Christ in the reign of God's love? During the entire process of initiation, the Christian moral imperative of love shapes and guides the catechumen for the journey ahead.

Theopolitical Imagination and Evangelism

In *Evangelism after Christendom*, Bryan Stone, one of the leading voices in the contemporary study of evangelism, offers a truly substantive proposal, including an in-depth discussion about the relation between evangelism and baptism in light of socioeconomic and political concerns raised above.[44] Stone thinks the theological failure and bankruptcy of evangelism has to do with a deeper problem of the church's departure from its Christian specificity rooted in its tradition, narrative, communal existence, and virtuous practice to other competing narratives and social imaginaries in opposition to its own. The church has a peculiar vision of the world accompanied by distinctive Christian practices, but it has become wrenched from that form of life. Stone identifies the Constantinian story and the story of modernity as the rival narratives that have subverted the church's own theopolitical imagination.[45] Though the church's existence was to be about an alternative social arrangement defined by humility and service patterned after Jesus Christ, the Constantinian union of the church and the state led to the sacralization of dominative power structures, military apparatus, and imperial aspirations. The church's failure to configure the world differently through its radical discipleship continued in modernity as it accommodated the Enlightenment project.[46]

Reacting against authoritarian, superstitious religious traditions, Enlightenment thinkers constructed the self as autonomous and empty

---

44. Stone, *Evangelism after Christendom*, 171–276.
45. Stone, *Evangelism after Christendom*, 115–30.
46. Stone, *Evangelism after Christendom*, 131–70.

of social constraints. This resulted in the modern understanding of the self as an individual who contracts voluntarily to social arrangements that somehow coordinate disparate interests for self-fulfillment through bureaucratic management. The church accommodated to this social imagination in a soteriology that is privatistic, individualistic, and decisionistic in character. Moreover, in response to Enlightenment's epistemological turn away from authority and tradition to autonomous rationality in search of meaning and truth, the church translated its truth claims according to universal criteria of rationality. Apologetics became the order of the day.

Stone proposes a different view of evangelism, setting it as a practice understood as the context for the identity of a tradition to be constituted, its narrative enacted, and its ecclesial character further displayed and expanded.[47] Biblical narratives about the shalom and the reign of God for both human and non-human forms of life inform the practice of evangelism by providing a sense of unity, meaning, and direction and establishing its *telos*.[48] Reclaiming these narratives enables the church to be an evangelistic community, which demonstrates the new order of God as social, visible, and material in embodiment befitting an alternative theo-political imagination through its core practices of worship, forgiveness, hospitality, and economic sharing. In the course of ecclesial life together, distinctive virtues are formed and exhibited before a watching world. As a stark opposition to the rival narratives discussed earlier, Stone is after the creation of a new people who live into the alternative story of God's reign embodied concretely in the church's eccentric living. Evangelism is not about salvation in service of anthropocentric piety; it is about inviting people to an alternative way of life that subverts or even assaults the present order to create a new peoplehood who practice common meals, economic leveling, and interethnic and gender inclusion.[49]

47. Having provided a historical assessment of evangelism, Stone sets forth a proposal, both substantively and methodologically, to rectify the situation. The principle interlocutor is Alasdair McIntyre whose definition of practice anchors his turn to the specificity of Christian faith and practice. See Stone, *Evangelism after Christendom*, 29–53. Also see McIntyre, *After Virtue*.

48. On the significance of shalom for evangelism, see Russell, "Liberation and Evangelism," 416–23.

49. The kind of conversion Stone has in mind is that which is a comprehensive socialization over a course of time through apprenticeship during which the whole person is remade, including the heart, mind, allegiances, habits, and identity, after the pattern of Christ. For further discussion on evangelism as socialization, see Lindbeck,

During the process of incorporation into ecclesial existence, Stone claims baptism functions as the central ritual that inducts people into an alternative polis with a distinct social body and identity.[50] If conversion has fundamentally altered one's old way of life, then it is baptism that initiates persons into the new order by the power of the Spirit. Two claims need to be underscored at this point. One, Stone clearly rejects symbolic understanding of baptism as forgiveness of original sin and opts for political induction into the body of Christ. Baptism is essentially a political act of inclusion that relativizes prior boundaries based on race, class, and gender because the reign of God involves a different politics of identity in a new social order.[51] Two, Stone is careful to point out that inclusion in the church does not mean ecclesiocentrism, because the scope of God's redemption is the world. Salvation is both personal and political; therefore, the church must return to the world and maintain a unity of the sacred and profane rather than absolutizing the difference between the two.[52]

The full significance of Stone's understanding of baptism as political inclusion does not come into view without his discussion of about the Eucharist as the central ritual of the church's economics, which includes hospitality, debt forgiveness, Sabbath, simplicity, gratitude, compassion, and justice.[53] This peculiar economic system is best described as eucharistic economics and is embodied in shared communal meals and

---

Nature of Doctrine. And on evangelism as entering into a new story or another social imaginary, see Barth, "Strange New World," 28–50; Brueggemann, "Evangelism and Discipleship," 219–34; and in terms of social imaginary, see Anderson, *Imagined Communities*; Cavanaugh, *Theopolitical Imagination*; and Taylor, *Modern Social Imaginaries.*

50. On baptism as insertion or addition of adherents into the post-paschal eschatological community, see Fuller, "Christian Initiation," 7–31.

51. While Stone's stress on the political dimension of baptism cannot be appreciated enough, it seems to eclipse a more comprehensive understanding of baptism, such as the one that Wesley provided. For a contemporary, ecumenical discussion on the various dimensions or benefits of baptism see, World Council of Churches, *Baptism, Eucharist, and Ministry.*

52. Stone's singular focus on the interior life of the church that embodies its own theopolitical imaginary is indeed a major achievement. If this is the first act of evangelism, then the second act would be the church's public witness. See McBride, *Church for the World.*

53. Stone, *Evangelism after Christendom*, 197–221. For further discussion about the economic dimension of Eucharist, see Hellwig, *Eucharist and the Hunger*; Moltmann, *Church in the Power.*

expresses the solidarity and unity that level all ranks and status. If baptism is a political ritual of inclusion, economics deepens and continues what baptism has started in the new reality of the reign of God. In fact, the church's economics is its politics. Stone proposes that when evangelism is virtuously embodied in the church's theopolitical imagination and existence shaped by its own story of God's reign of peace and empowered by the Spirit, what should emerge is the beauty of holiness integral to the church's service and witness in the world.

Conclusion

Given the troubling history of evangelism in collusion with Western colonialism around the globe and promotion of otherworldly, individualistic, and inward understanding of salvation, the very first act of evangelism ought to be confession and repentance that fully comes to terms with its checkered past. It must be remade by traversing the entire continuum of initiation through conversion, baptism, and moral formation that entails biblical, historical, theological, and critical reflections. Business as usual without transforming evangelism by connecting it organically and intentionally to baptism and the larger universe of the Christian tradition, including growth in the Great Commandments, will result in further ambivalence, resistance, and antagonism as well as naïve expressions to the detriment of Christian witness in the global context. There is no room for reckless evangelism and there is no time for putting off the good work of the Great Commission. Setting aside differences is long overdue. It is high time for the church to come together and grapple with Wesley's question about what it means to live "answerable thereto."

Bibliography

Abraham, William J. *The Logic of Evangelism*. Grand Rapids: Eerdmans, 1989.

Anderson, Benedict. *Imagined Communities*. London: Verso, 1996.

Arias, Mortimer. "Contextual Evangelization in Latin America: Between Accommodation and Confrontation." In *The Study of Evangelism*, 384–404. Grand Rapids: Eerdmans, 2008.

Ashcroft, Bill et al. *The Postcolonial Studies Reader*. London: Routledge, 1995.

Barth, Karl. "The Strange New World within the Bible." In *The Word of God and the Word of Man*, edited by Douglas Horton, 28–50. Cleveland: Pilgrim, 1928.

———. *The Word of God and the Word of Man*. Gloucester: Peter Smith, 1978.

Bhaba, Homi. *The Location of Culture*. London: Routledge, 1994.

Bonino, José M. "Conversion, New Creature and Commitment." *International Review of Missions* 72 (1983) 324–32.

———. *Toward a Christian Political Ethics*. London: SCM, 1983.

Borthwick, Paul. *Great Commission, Great Compassion*. Downers Grove, IL: Intervarsity, 2015.

Bosch, David. *Transforming Mission*. Maryknoll, NY: Orbis, 2011.

Boxer, C. R. *The Church Militant and Iberian Expansion, 1440–1770*. Baltimore: Johns Hopkins University Press, 1978.

Brueggemann, Walter. "Evangelism and Discipleship." In *The Study of Evangelism*, 219–34. Grand Rapids: Eerdmans, 2008.

Burnett, Virginia Garrard. "Central America and the Caribbean." In *Introduction to World Christianity*, 154–70. Oxford, UK: Blackwell, 2012.

Calvin, John. *Institutes of the Christian Religion*. Library of Christian Classics 20–21, edited by J. T. McNeill. Philadelphia: Westminster, 1960.

Capes, Dave. "Intertextual Echoes in the Matthean Baptismal Narrative." *Bulletin for Biblical Research* 9 (1999) 37–49.

Carter, Warren. *Matthew and the Empire*. Harrisburg: Trinity International, 2001.

———. *Matthew and the Margins*. Maryknoll, NY: Orbis, 2000.

Castro, Daniel. *Another Face of Empire*. Durham: Duke University Press, 2007.

Cavanaugh, William. *Theopolitical Imagination*. London: T & T Clark, 2002.

Chilcote, Paul W., and Laceye C. Warner, eds. *The Study of Evangelism: Exploring a Missional Practice of the Church*. Grand Rapids: Eerdmans, 2008.

Chung, Yonghan. "A Postcolonial Reading of the Great Commission (Matt 28:16–20) with a Korean Myth." *Theology Today* 72.3 (October 2015) 276–88.

Comaroff, Jean, and John Comaroff. *Of Revelation and Revolution*. 2 vols. Chicago: University of Chicago Press, 1991.

Costas, Orlando. "Evangelism and the Gospel of Salvation." In *The Study of* Evangelism, 33–45. Grand Rapids: Eerdmans, 2008.

de Las Casas, Bartolome. *The Devastation of the Indies*. London: Penguin, 1992.

Dube, Musa. "'Go Therefore and Make Disciples of All Nations' (Matt 28:19a)." In *Teaching the Bible*, edited by Fernando Segovia and Mary Ann Tolbert, 224–46. Minneapolis: Fortress, 1998.

Elbourne, Elizabeth. *Blood Ground*. Montréal: McGill University Press, 2008.

Fanon, Frantz. *The Wretched of the Earth*. New York: Grove, 2005.

Fischer-Tine, Harald, and Michael Mann. *Colonialism as Civilizing Mission*. London: Anthem, 2004.

Forster, Elizabeth. *Faith in Empire*. Stanford: Stanford University Press, 2014.

Fuller, Reginald. "Christian Initiation in the New Testament." In *Made, Not Born*, 7–31. Notre Dame: University of Notre Dame Press, 1976.

Grant, Robert M. "Development of Christian Catechumenate." In *Made, Not Born*, 32–49. Notre Dame: University of Notre Dame Press, 1976.

Greer, Allan, ed. *The Jesuit Relations*. Boston: Bedford/St. Martins, 2000.

Gustafson, James. *Ethics from a Theocentric Perspective*. 2 vols. Chicago: University of Chicago Press, 1981–84.

Hastings, Adrian. *The Church in Africa, 1450–1950*. Oxford: Clarendon, 1994.

Hattaway, Paul. *Back to Jerusalem: Three Chinese House Church Leaders Share Their Vision to Complete the Great Commission*. Waynesboro, GA: Gabriel Resources, 2003.

Hellwig, Monika. *The Eucharist and the Hunger of the World*. New York: Paulist, 1976.

Hertig, Paul. "The Great Commission Revisited." *Missiology* 29.3 (July 2001) 343–53.

Kavanagh, Aidan. "Christian Initiation." In *Made, Not Born*, 1–6. Notre Dame: University of Notre Dame Press, 1976.

———. *The Shape of Baptism: The Rite of Christian Initiation*. Collegeville, MN: Liturgical, 1991.

Keener, Craig. "Matthew's Missiology: Making Disciples of Nations." *Asian Journal of Pentecostal Studies* 12.1 (2009) 3–20.

Klauber, Martin, and Scott Manetsch, eds. *The Great Commission*. Nashville: Broadman and Holman, 2008.

Lindbeck, George. *The Nature of Doctrine*. Louisville: Westminster John Knox, 1984.

Lockhart, James, and Stuart Schwartz. *Early Latin America*. Cambridge: Cambridge University Press, 1983.

Meier, John. "John the Baptist in Matthew." *Journal of Biblical Literature* 99.3 (1980) 383–405.

Memmi, Albert. *Domesticated Man*. London: Orion, 1968.

Maddox, Randy L. *Responsible Grace: John Wesley's Practical Theology*. Nashville: Abingdon, 1994.

McBride, Jennifer. *The Church for the World*. Oxford: Oxford University Press, 2012.

McIntyre, Alasdair. *After Virtue*. Notre Dame: University of Notre Dame Press, 2007.

McMaken, W. Travis. "Authority, Mission, and Institution: A Systematic Consideration of Matthew 28.18–20 in Karl Barth's Doctrine of Baptism." *Ecclesiology* 5.3 (2009) 345–61.

Meadows, Philip. *Remembering Our Baptism*. Nashville: Discipleship Resources, 2017.

Mitchell, Nathan D. "Dissolution of the Rite of Christian Initiation." In *Made, Not Born*, 50–82. Notre Dame: University of Notre Dame Press, 1976.

Moltmann, Jürgen. *The Church in the Power of the Holy Spirit*. New York: Harper and Row, 1977.

Moore, Stephen, and Fernando Segovia, eds. *Postcolonial Biblical Criticism*. New York: T&T Clark International, 2005.

Nkansah-Obrempong, James. "Africa's Contextual Realities." *International Review of Mission* 106.2 (December 2017) 280–94.

Onyinah, Opoku. "The Meaning of Discipleship." *International Review of Mission* 106.2 (December 2017) 216–27.

Outler, Albert C. *Evangelism and Theology in the Wesleyan Spirit*. Nashville: Discipleship Resources, 1996.

Park, James Sung-Hwan. "Chosen to Fulfill the Great Commission?" *Missiology* 43.2 (April 2015) 163–74.

Payne, Claude, and Hamilton Beazley. *Reclaiming the Great Commission*. San Francisco: Jossey-Bass, 2000.

Pickard, Stephen. "Evangelism and the Character of Christian Theology." In *The Study of Evangelism*, edited by Paul Chilcote and Laceye C. Warner, 135–58. Grand Rapids: Eerdmans, 2008.

Raschte, Carl. *GloboChrist*. Grand Rapids: Baker Academic, 2008.

Rivera, Luis N. *A Violent Evangelism*. Louisville: Westminster John Knox, 1992.

Robert, Dana, ed. *Converting Colonialism*. Grand Rapids: Eerdmans, 2008.

Rundle, Steve, and Tom Steffen. *Great Commission Companies*. Downers Grove, IL: InterVarsity, 2003.

Russell, Letty. "Liberation and Evangelism—A Feminist Perspective." In *The Study of Evangelism*, edited by Paul Chilcote and Lacey Warner, 416–23. Grand Rapids: Eerdmans, 2008.

Said, Edward. *Orientalism: Western Conceptions of the Orient*. New York: Randon House, 1978.

Sanneh, Lamin. "Christian Missions and the Western Guilt." *The Christian Century* 104.11 (April 8, 1987) 331–34.

Sharkey, Heather. *American Evangelicals in Egypt*. Princeton: Princeton University Press, 2015.

Shin, Daniel D. *Theology and the Public*. Lanham: Lexington Books, 2019.

Smith, Mitzi. "US Colonial Mission to African Slaves." In *Teaching All Nations*, edited by Mitzi Smith and Jayachitra Lalitha, 57–85. Minneapolis: Fortress, 2014.

Smith, Mitzi, and Jayachitra Lalitha. *Teaching All Nations: Interrogating the Matthean Great Commission*. Minneapolis: Fortress, 2014.

Stone, Bryan. *Evangelism after Christendom*. Grand Rapids: Brazos, 2006.

Sugirtharajah, R. S. *The Postcolonial Reader*. Malden, MA: Blackwell, 2006.

Taylor, Charles A. *Modern Social Imaginaries*. Durham: Duke University Press, 2004.

Todorov, Tzvetan. *The Conquest of America*. New York: Harper Torchbooks, 1984.

Tribble, Phllis. *Texts of Horror*. Philadelphia: Fortress, 1984.

Turner, Victor Witter. *Ritual Process: Structure and Anti-Structure*. Ithaca: Cornell University Press, 1969.

van den Berg, Johannes. *Constrained by Jesus' Love*. Kampen, NL: J.H. Kok n.v., 1956.

Wesley, John. "Large Minutes of Several Conversations." In *Works of John Wesley*. Vol. 8, *Addresses, Essays, Letters*, edited by Thomas Jackson, 299–338. Grand Rapids: Zondervan, 1958–1959.

———. "A Plain Account of Christian Perfection." In *Bicentennial Edition of the Works of John Wesley*. Vol. 13, *Doctrinal and Controversial Treatises II*, edited by Paul Wesley Chilcote and Kenneth J. Collins, 132–91. Nashville: Abingdon, 2012.

———. "The Principles of a Methodist further Explained." In *Bicentennial Edition of the Works of John Wesley*. Vol. 9, *The Methodist Societies: History, Nature, and Design*, edited by Rupert E. Davies, 160–237. Nashville: Abingdon, 1989.

———. "Sermon 1, 'Salvation by Faith.'" In *Bicentennial Edition of the Works of John Wesley*. Vol. 1, *Sermons I*, edited by Albert C. Outler, 109–30. Nashville: Abingdon, 1984.

———. "Sermon 5, 'Justification by Faith.'" In *Bicentennial Edition of the Works of John Wesley*. Vol. 1, *Sermons I*, edited by Albert Outler, 182–99. Nashville: Abingdon, 1984.

———. "Sermon 9, 'The Spirit of Bondage and Adoption.'" In *Bicentennial Edition of the Works of John Wesley*. Vol. 1, *Sermons I*, edited by Albert C. Outler, 248–66. Nashville: Abingdon, 1984.

———. "Sermon 17, 'The Circumcision of the Heart.'" In *Bicentennial Edition of the Works of John Wesley*. Vol. 1, *Sermons I*, edited by Albert C. Outler, 398–414. Nashville: Abingdon, 1984.

———. "Sermon 18, 'Marks of the New Birth.'" In *Bicentennial Edition of the Works of John Wesley*. Vol. 1, *Sermons I*, edited by Albert Outler, 415–30. Nashville: Abingdon, 1984.

————. "Sermon 19, 'The Great Privilege of Those That Are Born of God.'" In *Bicentennial Edition of the Works of John Wesley.* Vol. 1, *Sermons I,* edited by Albert C. Outler, 431–43. Nashville: Abingdon, 1984.

————. "Sermon 24, 'Upon Our Lord's Sermon on the Mount, IV.'" In *Bicentennial Edition of the Works of John Wesley.* Vol. 1, *Sermons I,* edited by Albert C. Outler, 531–549. Nashville: Abingdon, 1984.

————. Sermon 35, "The Law Established Through Faith: Discourse I." In *Bicentennial Edition of the Works of John Wesley,* volume 2, *Sermons II,* edited by Albert C. Outler, 20–32. Nashville: Abingdon, 1985.

————. "Sermon 36, 'The Law Established Through Faith: Discourse II.'" In *Bicentennial Edition of the Works of John Wesley.* Vol. 2, *Sermons II,* edited by Albert C. Outler, 33–43. Nashville: Abingdon, 1985.

————. "Sermon 43, 'The Scripture Way of Salvation." In *Bicentennial Edition of the Works of John Wesley.* Vol. 2, *Sermons II,* edited by Albert C. Outler, 153–69. Nashville: Abingdon, 1985.

————. "Sermon 44, 'Original Sin." In *Bicentennial Edition of the Works of John Wesley.* Vol. 2, *Sermons II,* edited by Albert C. Outler, 170–85. Nashville: Abingdon, 1985.

————. "Sermon 45, 'The New Birth." In *Bicentennial Edition of the Works of John Wesley.* Vol. 2, *Sermons II,* edited by Albert C. Outler, 186–201. Nashville: Abingdon, 1985.

————. "Sermon 85, 'On Working Out Our Own Salvation." In *Bicentennial Edition of the Works of John Wesley.* Vol. 3, *Sermons III,* edited by Albert C. Outler, 199–209. Nashville: Abingdon, 1986.

————. "Sermon 146, 'The One Thing Needful.'" In *Bicentennial Edition of the Works of John Wesley.* Vol. 4, *Sermons IV,* edited by Albert C. Outler, 351–59. Nashville: Abingdon, 1987.

————. "A Treatise on Baptism." In *Works of John Wesley.* Vol. 10, *Letters, Essays, Dialogs, Addresses,* edited by Thomas Jackson, 188–201. Grand Rapids: Zondervan, 1958–59.

Westerhoff, John. "Evangelism, Evangelization, and Catechesis." In *The Study of Evangelism,* 235–45. Grand Rapids: Eerdmans, 2008.

Woodford, Lucas. *Great Commission, Great Confusion, or Great Confession?* Eugene, OR: Wipf and Stock, 2012.

The World Council of Churches. *Baptism, Eucharist, and Ministry.* Geneva: World Council of Churches, 1982.

Yong, Amos, and Clifton Clarke, eds. *Global Renewal, Religious Pluralism, and the Great Commission.* LaVergne, TN: Emeth, 2011.

Young, Robert J. C. *Postcolonialism: An Historical Introduction.* Oxford: John Wiley & Sons, 2016.

CHAPTER 8

Baptism and Social Justice

A Theological Framework for Flourishing

LAURA GARVERICK, CALVIN THEOLOGICAL SEMINARY

WHILE AT FIRST GLANCE the practices of corporate worship and social justice may seem to be unrelated topics, it is the biblical witness that first testifies to the interrelated nature of the two. Amos 5:21, 23–24 reads:

> I hate all your show and pretense—
> the hypocrisy of your religious . . . assemblies.
> Away with your noisy hymns of praise!
> I will not listen to the music . . .
> Instead, I want to see a mighty flood of justice . . .[1]

The timelessness of this divine critique poses afresh the following question to today's worshipping community: *What relationship do the practices of corporate worship have to God's design and desire for justice? More specifically, what relationship does baptism—as a particular act of corporate worship—have to God's design and desire for justice?* To answer this question, the following chapter will search the baptismal theology of John Wesley to construct a theological framework that both clarifies the relationship between baptism and social justice and names social justice as a necessary outworking of transforming, baptismal grace.

---

1. Amos 5:21, 23–24 (NLT).

Before turning to this task, however, a brief word of methodology will be helpful. Many contemporary discussions of social justice exhibit a subtle tendency: the tendency to begin with *praxis*. This pragmatic leaning is understandable since social justice inherently requires concrete action. However, whether one looks to John Wesley and the social reforms of early Methodism or lauds exemplary endeavors occurring in the church today, starting places such as these nevertheless begin with reflections on *human action*.[2] A theological framework for social justice, on the other hand, must instead begin where all theology begins: with reflection on the person and work of God. Therefore, the bulk of this chapter will be spent surveying the person and work of the triune God as it is understood by John Wesley. Subsequently, this chapter will then offer how Wesley's portrait of God's person and work implicitly issues a call for humanity's practice of social justice.

Proceeding in this manner, the following chapter will advance a twofold argument. Namely, it will argue that: 1) for Wesley, baptism is one's divinely wrought inauguration into a new *internal* reality; and 2) for Wesley, baptism is one's divinely wrought inauguration into a new *external* reality. This argument will unfold in three movements. First, Wesley's understanding of the old internal and external realities left behind at baptism will be narrated using Wesley's *Explanatory Notes* and sermons. This will be a selective and nuanced narration, one which describes Creation and the Fall specifically through the lens of the political image of God. Second, the new *internal* reality inaugurated at baptism will be explored using Wesley's "Treatise of Baptism." Third, the new *external* reality inaugurated at baptism will be examined, using once more Wesley's "Treatise of Baptism." At the end of each section, the implicational task of drawing conclusions for social justice will be undertaken.

Part I: The Divine Community and Mutual Flourishing

It is a stunning portrait that opens Wesley's *Explanatory Notes*: a portrait of nothing less than the world fully ordered according to God's desires for it.[3] Lush, fecund, and teeming, Eden is synonymous with life—life

---

2. For a survey of John Wesley's social reform efforts and early Methodism's reforming impulse, see Thompson, *John Wesley as a Social Reformer*; and Bliss and Binder, "Methodism and Social Reform," 762–65.

3. Wesley, *Genesis Explanatory Notes*, 9–21.

overflowing with more life, life abundant. God has carefully ordered creation so as to provide for the flourishing of all of its members. Eden, therefore, is not merely a portrait of life in general, but a portrait of *mutual flourishing*. Within this scene of mutual flourishing, the needs of every creature have been richly provided for—the poetry of Genesis even goes so far as to detail each sphere of creation that has been given as a gift for creaturely abodes and the sources of food that God, in his careful care, has likewise supplied. Alas, God sits back and delights in the mutual flourishing he has created; and in a very real sense, the mutual flourishing of Eden emulates the inner life of the Trinity. For, the Trinity *"in se"* is likewise a community of distinct members all incomparably alive and flourishing in each other's communion. In this sense, Eden is not only a portrait of God's work, but as is true of all of God's works, it is a reflection of his character and person.

It also reveals something of the triune God's heart for creation that he places within it a Keeper, *one who is tasked with tending and maintaining the order that God has so carefully crafted for the flourishing of all.* Wesley writes that Adam was made "God's vice-regent upon the earth,"[4] meaning that the task of cultivating a world of mutual flourishing was now given to humanity to protect, to steward, and to tend.[5] For, the biblical term "dominion" can never be conceived in terms of selfish instrumentation and domination precisely because it is a sharing of God's own task that humanity is invited into, and God himself never relates to his creation this way.[6] Rather, humanity is invited to be—indeed, commis-

4. Wesley, "Sermon 60, 'The General Deliverance,'" 440. As part of the political image of God, Wesley understood humanity to be conduits of God's care, grace, and blessing to both nonhuman creation and to each other. For this argument, see Collins, *Scripture Way*, 23, 210 n. 24; cf. Collins, *Theology of John Wesley*, 54, 343 n. 30.

5. Though the term "mutual flourishing" is commonly used in a variety of disciplines, I have Norman Wirzba to thank for first connecting the term to a theology of dominion. In his book, *Living the Sabbath*, Wirzba addresses the concept from the perspective of agroecology, emphasizing humanity's relationship with the land in regard to agricultural production: "To be an authentic *adam* is to be intimately tied to the ways of the soil (*adamah*), to be attuned to the soil's limits and possibilities. Farmers do not exercise dominion over their animals and fields by simply imposing or forcing their desires upon them. . . . Indeed, dominion without patient and informed affection quickly leads to ruination, as fields are compromised, and livestock become sick and die. . . . The exercise of dominion is . . . (where) we learn to live patiently and attentively with others so that the mutual flourishing of all becomes possible." See Wirzba, *Living the Sabbath*, 31–34.

6. Collins, *Scripture Way*, 23, 210 n. 24; cf. Collins, *Theology of John Wesley*, 54, 343 n. 30.

sioned to be—extensions of God's own ordering, governing, and tending care within a creation structured for the flourishing of all its members. This profound cooperative reality Wesley terms "the political image of God" in humanity.[7]

Wesley's "political image of God" is often rushed past by theologians hurrying instead to discuss the moral image of God. Admittedly, this is done because Wesley more heavily emphasized the moral image and gave the political image far less ink in comparison. However, as H. Ray Dunning notes, "traditional formulations" of the *imago Dei* explored God's image in twofold terms, distinguishing between the moral and natural image only; thus, Wesley's addition of a third dimension is, in itself, markedly significant.[8] For Wesley's theological interpreters, the task then becomes understanding what this third dimension contributes to Wesley's sketch of human nature. Though the political image can be explicated in many ways, when it is analyzed at its most elemental level, it reveals two truths about humanity. Namely, the political image reveals that: 1) humanity was created to receive God's divine goodness, care, and blessing; and 2) humanity was created to diffuse and communicate God's goodness, care, and blessing to the rest of creation, including each other. When held together, these two truths portray humanity as being both a reservoir and a conduit of the divine, divinely fashioned in this way for the sake of creation's flourishing. Indeed, the task of tending a world established for the flourishing of all its members is one divinely given in Eden and never divinely rescinded. It can, therefore, be rightly called a sacred vocation of humanity which never departs, one woven into the very fabric of what it means to be human beings created in God's image.

In addition to this political image of God, Wesley also describes the moral and natural image as being part of God's viceregents. Imbued with the full moral image of God, God's viceregents were both fully just and fully loving. Writes Wesley, "'God is love': accordingly man at his creation was full of love, which was the sole principle of all his tempers, thoughts, words, and actions. God is full of justice . . . so was man as he came from the hands of his Creator."[9] Therefore, humanity was created to mirror the triune God not only in God's governance and caretaking of all creation's

---

7. Wesley, "Sermon 45, 'The New Birth,'" 188.

8. H. Ray Dunning, *Reflecting the Divine Image*, 56.

9. Wesley, "Sermon 45, 'The New Birth,'" 188, I.1

flourishing (political image of God), but also in God's moral character and holiness (moral image of God). This humanity was able to do freely and faithfully because humanity's will was perfectly aligned with God's own desires for the world (part of the natural image of God).

When one steps back and surveys the threefold image of God from the perspective of the political image, a dynamic interplay becomes logically traceable; that is, what becomes accentuated is how the three dimensions of the *imago Dei* relate or interact within the unity of the human person.[10] From what Wesley affirms of each, it would seem that the presence of the moral and natural images in humanity are what make humanity capable of rightly exercising the political image. For, the moral image makes humanity righteousness and holy, without which God's character, care, and blessing could not be diffused by humanity to creation and each other. Said differently, without the moral image of God in humanity, humanity's capacity to be a conduit of the divine would be utterly bereft of divine content, like a sprinkler disconnected from the source of water. Likewise, the natural image of God—humanity's will, liberty, and understanding—enables humanity to volitionally assume and reasonably enact the role of viceregent. Take away one of the three parts of the natural image and humanity is no longer capable of being a rational and free agent in the service of God. Rather it is together, like a three-stranded cord, that the *moral* image, *natural* image, and *political* image of God make humanity *capable*, *free*, and *called* to participate in God's own work of tending to the mutual flourishing of all creation. When this portrait of Edenic humanity is coupled with Wesley's description of Edenic creation, what emerges is a world divinely ordered for the

10. In making this observation, I here go beyond Wesley's own work, using Wesley's descriptions of the three dimensions to draw a logical conclusion about how those dimensions relate to one another in the unity of the human person. For Wesley, God's image in humanity exists in three dimensions, though it is *one* image of God; like a chord in which three notes are struck. We bear not three images, but one image comprised of three dimensions. This can be seen in Wesley's exclusive use of the term, "image of God" (singular), never "image*s* of God" (plural). (For example, observe this language in his sermon, "Sermon 45, 'The New Birth.'") While it is common to theologically explore the three dimensions severally—and therefore, in some sense, as isolated or discreet entities—the unity of God's image in humanity must never be forgotten. When this three-one nuance is in place, the unitive integrity of the image of God allows one to probe the interrelatedness of the three dimensions: that is, to ask how they work together. This section explores this question from the perspective of the political image specifically.

mutual flourishing of all its members and humanity specially created to be its Keeper.

Though stunning, Wesley's Edenic portrait is a reality now far from our own. For, in the Fall, the face of God in humanity is maimed (political and natural image), and some contours are effaced entirely (moral image).[11] The very next portrait of humanity offered by the biblical canon is one of Edenic antithesis: Cain and Abel. While the Cain and Abel story is often explored through the lens of the lost moral image (and its focus on right relationships) or through the lens of the marred natural image (and its focus on the perverted human will), this story likewise reveals the profound disfigurement of the political image. Namely, humanity's vocation of tending to the mutual flourishing of all creation's members has become mutilated—as mutilated as Abel's murdered body—and has now been supplanted by Cain's violent self-promotion. Violent self-promotion is here the antithesis of working for mutual flourishing. Likewise, humanity's call to be a conduit of God's care to others has become twisted and beclouded, as is evident in Cain's question, "Am I my brother's keeper?" Indeed, in many ways, Cain's question betrays all that is opposite to the Trinity's inner life of loving self-donation to the other. God's response to this profound disfigurement and loss of the divine image in humanity is to create anew in the shell of the old: that is, God's response is to invite fallen humanity into the waters of baptism.

Part II: A New Internal Reality Created in the Shell of the Old

In his "Treatise on Baptism," Wesley describes baptism as being the visible image of an invisible work of God, a work in which God creates anew in the shell of the old. Namely, baptism signifies God's creation of a new *internal* reality in the human soul: *regeneration*. Regeneration is a cataclysmic moment of re-creation. In a single moment, the human soul—both dissevered from the Godhead and dead and decaying in its transgressions—is restored to relational union with the Trinity and infused with the divine life of God. Divine life is breathed into the soul by the Spirit of God, as it was in Eden, once more. And in this very moment

11. Namely, Wesley affirms that the moral image is lost entirely, while the natural and political are disfigured. See Bryant, "Loss of the Moral Image"; and "Marring of the Natural," 531–32; cf. Collins, *Theology of John Wesley*, 61–63; cf. Collins, *Scripture Way*, 29–30.

of divine embrace and divine vivification, the moral image of God is for the very first time returned to the human soul.[12] It is a recovery hitherto untasted by fallen humanity, a reversal of sorts which comes in seedling form; for regeneration's initial renewal of the moral image will be processively "fill(ed) up and deepen(ed)" in sanctification.[13] *However, from the very first moment of regeneration onward, humanity is once again made capable of living according to God's desires for creation.*[14] Indeed, the call to do so has never ceased. Regeneration is therefore a moment which inaugurates a new *internal* reality: the beginning of God restoring what had been lost in Eden, the capacity for humanity to live according to God's desires for creation.

This restoration of the moral image of God makes profound claims for social justice precisely because social justice is, in its broadest sense, humanity's working toward a world ordered according to God's desires for it.[15] When the moral image is renewed in regeneration, the renewed person is once again made capable of personally living according to God's

12. For Wesley's belief that the soul's loss of relational union causes one's loss of spiritual life, see: "He lost the life of God: he was separated from him in union with whom his spiritual life consisted. The body dies when it is separated from the soul, the soul when it is separated from God." Wesley, "Sermon 45, 'The New Birth,'" 189–90. For the soul being restored to relationship in regeneration, see Wesley's description of "This intercourse between God and man, this fellowship with the Father and Son," akin to "a kind of spiritual respiration" by which "the life of God in the soul is sustained." Wesley, "Sermon 45, 'The New Birth,'" 193. For the restoration of divine life to the soul in regeneration, see: "It is that great change which God works in the soul when he brings it into life." Wesley, "Sermon 45, 'The New Birth,'" 192–93. For regeneration being the soul's renewal in the image of God, see: "It is the change wrought in the whole soul by the almighty Spirit of God . . . when it is 'renewed after the image of God.'" Wesley, "Sermon 45, 'The New Birth,'" 194.

13. Pope, *Compendium of Christian Theology*, 3:7; cf. Wesley, "Sermon 45, 'The New Birth,'" 198, IV.3.

14. Wesley gives voice to this reality by using the language of regeneration, breaking the power of sin in the human heart. For examples, see Wesley, "Sermon 8, 'The First-fruits,'" 233–47.

15. This definition, though simple, is broad enough to encompass (and be used by) the wildly diverse forms and expressions that justice assumes in contemporary society; however, it is also specific insofar as it places a crucial limitation on one's definition of justice. Namely, this definition is broad enough to theologically undergird endeavors as varied as working toward racial and gender equality, combating human trafficking, fighting for indigenous persons' land rights, or working toward humane conditions for production line workers in Majority World contexts. However, this definition excludes any conceptions of justice which morally contradict the picture of God's desires for humanity and creation as seen in the biblical portrait of Eden.

desires for the world; and, therefore, Wesley affirms, is tasked to do so.[16] Ever increasingly filled with righteousness, renewed humanity becomes ever more capable of acting righteously toward their neighbor; and is, in equal measure, tasked to do so. Ever increasingly filled with holy love, renewed humanity becomes ever more capable of acting with holiness and love toward their neighbor; and is, in equal measure, tasked to do so. And ever increasingly filled with the justice and the *shalom* of God,[17] renewed humanity becomes ever more capable of diffusing God's justice and wholeness to their neighbor; and is, in equal measure, tasked to do so.

Furthermore, one may logically conclude that the restoration of the moral image likewise enables renewed humanity to more rightly enact the divine vocation related to the political image of God.[18] Since the divinely appointed vocation to serve as God's viceregent and conduit to all of creation has never been rescinded, humanity is still tasked with the twofold vocation of: 1) being the Keeper of God's desired order for creation—a world ordered for the mutual flourishing of all of creation's members; and 2) being a conduit of God's character, care, and blessing to all of creation and each other. Fallen humanity cannot rightly enact this vocation, however, while the soul is relationally disconnected from the life of God, as the Fall made amply clear. But, regeneration's restoration of divine life and the moral image of God to the soul should logically enable the regenerate person to better, albeit imperfectly, fulfill the task of being a viceregent and conduit. For, once again made righteous, holy, loving, and just, now the regenerate person is better equipped to work for the ordering of all creation according to God's desires for it, herself now being ordered according to God's desire for her.

16. Wesley gives voice to this reality in the language of being free from volitional sin and fighting for the mortification of inbred sin which still remains, though no longer reigns, within the renewed person. See Wesley, "Sermon 8, 'The First-fruits'"; cf. Wesley, "Sermon 19, 'The Great Privilege,'" 431–43.

17. Though admittedly a polyvalent term, the world *shalom* is here used to communicate God's vision for the world as it was intended to be and as he desires for it to be, a glimpse of which can be seen in the mutual flourishing of Eden. For a more nuanced definition of *shalom* as it relates to Edenic perfection, see H. Ray Dunning's fourfold exposition in Dunning, *Reflecting the Divine Image*, 47.

18. Here, again, I go beyond *Wesley's* descriptions of the threefold image of God to logically posit how the three dimensions of the one image might interact or relate within the unity of the human person.

Once again filled with the moral image—like a sprinkler reconnected to the source of water—the regenerate person is once again capable of being a conduit of God's desires for, care of, and blessing to all of creation, now that she is herself filled. Though this vocation will not be enacted to the same perfect degree as was seen in Eden,[19] humanity is nonetheless tasked with living in a fallen world according to God's timeless call to the utmost of humanity's abilities as enabled by grace. Regeneration, therefore, means that those bearing the threefold image of God are ever increasingly being made capable of actively, albeit imperfectly, working for a world justly ordered for the flourishing of all its members. Indeed, doing so can rightly be understood as the necessary and active outworking of regenerating, baptismal grace.

Part III: A New External Reality Created in the Shell of the Old

In addition to this new *internal* reality, Wesley's "Treatise on Baptism" also describes baptism as one's inauguration into a new *external* reality. Amid a world no longer ordered according to God's desires for it, God has re-created within the shell of the old a community, a microcosm of humanity, that once again lives according to his desires.[20] Thus, in baptism, humanity is first made capable of living according to God's desires for creation, and then is joined to a community who lives precisely in this way. In his "Treatise on Baptism," Wesley describes this new *external* reality—the called-out community—in three, interrelated ways.[21]

---

19. Wesley affirms that the political image remains in humanity though it is now imperfect as a result of the Fall. See, Bryant, "Marring of the Natural," 532–33. However, Wesley nowhere affirms that the political image is fully restored this side of heaven; therefore, given these two premises, one can only conclude that the political image will be imperfectly enacted by post-Edenic, renewed humanity.

20. "In the ordinary way, there is no other means of entering into the Church . . ." other than baptism. Wesley, "Treatise on Baptism," 192.

21. Notably, the ecclesiological traits described in Wesley's "Treatise on Baptism" are theologically rich, and therefore can be explicated in a variety of different ways. However, the goal of the following discourse is not to offer an exhaustive treatment of these traits' many theological facets. Instead, this chapter takes up the far more focused and therefore limited task of explicating these ecclesiological traits as they pertain to social justice specifically.

The Called-Out Community Lives with Christ as Its Head

The called-out community is first described as being a community that lives under the headship of Christ.[22] Since the concept of headship, within classical theology, assumes and is undergirded by the session of Christ, this statement implicitly throws two opposing realities into sharp relief: 1) that the called-out community exists within a fallen world; and 2) that the called-out community nonetheless lives here and now under the reign and leadership of Christ. The presence of the former will make submission to the latter imperfect in its actualization.[23] However, the responsibility for human effort to partner with divine grace in living out one's submission to Christ ever remains. Therefore, as it regards social justice, to live in a fallen world as those under the headship of Christ means that despite the pressures to kowtow to the norms, powers, and values of the regnant culture, those who are membered in the called-out community live according to the values and ways of King Jesus. In practice, this will manifest in the twin disciplines of *learning* and *unlearning*, or formation and deformation. That is, within the called-out community, effort will partner with grace to *learn* new practices, new sacrifices, and new values (formation), ones both foreign and contrary to the regnant culture marked by the violent self-promotion of Cain. Likewise, within this community, effort will partner with grace to *unlearn* the practices that are contrary to justice and the apathy which neglects to seek justice (deformation).

Such formation and deformation comprise the process of entering into a new way of life, a life ordered according to God's desires for the mutual flourishing of all. Within this community, the extent to which it is possible by grace to live with Christ as their head in a fallen world is precisely the extent to which holy love demands the community do so. As the called-out community pursues a vision of holy love working for justice through the twin disciplines of learning and unlearning, the called-out community enters ever more deeply into all-encompassing submission to the ways and person of Christ; that is, they live with Christ as their head.

---

22. Wesley, "Treatise on Baptism," 191.

23. Submission to the headship of Christ should be understood as imperfect in fallen world because one's submission to Christ will always be marked by what Wesley calls "sin improperly so called." Wesley, "Plain Account," 396.

The Called-Out Community Lives
as Siblings in a Fictive Kinship

Second, Wesley's "Treatise on Baptism" describes the called-out community as being those who live "mystically united" to the person of Christ.[24] Wesley writes that in baptism one enters into "a spiritual, vital union" with Christ, so intimate—if not perichoretic—that one is said to be "made one with him."[25] United to the Eternal Son, the baptized become adopted as children of the Father, "made the children of God by adoption and grace."[26] Notably, Wesley emphasizes that *all baptized persons* are mystically united to Christ in this way: "For 'as many as are baptized into Christ' . . . are mystically united to Christ." While easily overlooked if not carefully read, Wesley's affirmation here introduces a profound reality of great importance for social justice. *Namely, when one becomes united to Christ in baptism, one likewise enters into a fictive kinship with all others to whom Christ is united, for they too have become sons and daughters of the same Father.*[27]

When made sons and daughters, we are simultaneously made fictive kin or siblings to all who share a common Father and participate in a common adoptive sonship[28] through baptism. After his resurrection, Christ himself gave voice to this new *external* reality when he told his followers, "I am ascending to *my* Father and to *your* Father."[29] Thus, the called-out community are those who have been relationally redefined as fictive kin under one Father.

24. Wesley, "Treatise on Baptism," 191.

25. Wesley, "Treatise on Baptism," 191.

26. Wesley, "Treatise on Baptism," 191–92.

27. "The application of the roles and ethos of family to people who are not related is called 'fictive kinship.' . . . A transition between natural kinship and the fictive kinship of the community of disciples is facilitated by the concept of God as Father." deSilva, *Honor, Patronage, Kinship & Purity*, 195–96. For an excellent treatment of how both kinship and fictive kinship were understood within the culture of the New Testament, see chapters 5 and 6 in particular.

28. Note that masculine terminology is used here because it has as its primary referent the gender and relation of the incarnate Son, *not* the gender or relation of the baptized person. When persons are adopted into the family of God, it is by virtue of their union with the Eternal Son, and thereby participation in the Son's sonship. A total avoidance of gendered language eclipses this crucial Christological reality; thus, it is best to combine inclusive language with Christological precision by speaking of both daughters and sons being invited to participate in the sonship of the Son.

29. John 20:17 (ESV), emphasis added.

This profound redefinition of relations makes substantial claims for a Christian commitment to social justice. For, in Christ's Jewish context, kinship dynamics were a primary influence on behavior and ethics; no action was undertaken, no matter how small, without consideration of how it impacted one's kin.[30] In a kinship culture, one's primary identity was one's link to their Father.[31] As extensions of their Father, offspring cared for the well-being of each other as they would for their own selves; a reality born out of the recognition that all share in the same flesh and blood[32] (a concept which today sheds new light on the Eucharist). If one member of the kinship circle suffered, the whole kinship circle suffered, for they shared the same flesh and blood. If one was dishonored, the whole kinship circle bore the dishonor, for they shared the same flesh and blood.[33] If one was in need, the whole kinship circle rallied to meet the need, for they shared the same flesh and blood.[34] And to knowingly perpetrate an injury against one's own kin was the inconceivable sin.[35] *In short, it was a dynamic in which each member cared for and worked for the mutual flourishing of all its members.*

Thus, at baptism, we are once again placed in a dynamic in which we are to care for and to work for the mutual flourishing of all members of the kinship circle. To allow our kin to suffer, to be in need, to be discriminated against or dishonored while we indifferently stand by is no longer a possibility for those mystically united to and through Christ. To perpetrate injustice against our kin—actively or through our insouciance when the other is being oppressed—is no longer a possibility for those mystically united to and through Christ. For, we now share in the same flesh and blood as fellow sons and daughters of the same Father—a new

30. deSilva, *Honor, Patronage, Kinship & Purity*, 165–97.

31. deSilva, *Honor, Patronage, Kinship & Purity*, 163.

32. Within the Greco-Roman context of Christ and the early church, "Special attention is given in this regard to siblings by classical, Hellenistic, and Greco-Roman ethicists. The relationship between siblings is the closest, strongest, and most intimate of relationship in the ancient world. Aristotle considers brotherly love to be a special and augmented form of friendship: 'Brothers love each other as being born of the same parents; for their identity with them makes them identical with each other (which is the reason why people talk of 'the same blood,' 'the same stock,' and so on). They are, therefore, in a sense the same thing, though separate individuals' (*Nic. Eth.* 8.12.3 [1161b30–35])." deSilva, *Honor, Patronage, Kinship & Purity*, 166.

33. deSilva, *Honor, Patronage, Kinship & Purity*, 163, 171.

34. deSilva, *Honor, Patronage, Kinship & Purity*, 170.

35. deSilva, *Honor, Patronage, Kinship & Purity*, 167, 169, 171.

relationality born in and through the waters of baptism—and, therefore, we must care for one another as we do ourselves. Indeed, to be mystically united with, and mutually flourishing with, this very kinship circle will be our eternal reality in heaven, one which we are both charged to, and privileged to, live as members of here and now.

Although the responsibilities of this new relational reality might have been far more familiar to Christ's original hearers than they are to twenty-first-century Western mindsets accustomed to the grammar of individualism, the fictive kinship of the baptized is nonetheless a reality of social and relational responsibility into which God invites us at baptism, and without which we cannot enter into true and full sonship[36] within the family of God.

The Called-Out Community Lives as Heirs

Adoption is also, for Wesley, the link to his third description of the called-out community. Wesley writes that in baptism we are "made children of God . . ." and "*if children . . . then heirs*, heirs of God, and joint-heirs [sic] with Christ . . . of 'a kingdom which cannot be moved.'"[37] Moreover, clarifies Wesley, this heirship is not merely "a title" that guarantees one to a far-off inheritance yet to be received. Rather, it is an heirship which already possesses "an earnest" or deposit of the kingdom here and now; for, this kingdom has come, in part, already.[38] Therefore, the baptized live as heirs, not only in title, but in actual possession.

Whereas headship emphasizes one's submission to Christ's person and ways, heirship is eschatological language. Heirship underscores the eschatological inbreaking of a future reality; that what will one day, in the eschaton, be ubiquitous, is already a reality among us and within us. The called-out community lives as heirs already in possession of a kingdom still to come more fully precisely as it lives according to God's desires for creation. For, by nature, the coming kingdom of God is nothing less than the world conformed to God's desires for it, desires which have been unchanged since Eden. Therefore, the kingdom of God on earth is nothing less than the actualization of God's world restored forever to the mutual

---

36. Here, again, the masculine terminology has as its referent the gender and relation of the incarnate Son, in whose sonship all participate when united to the Son.

37. Wesley, "Treatise on Baptism," 192.

38. Wesley, "Treatise on Baptism," 192.

flourishing for which it was created. This can be affirmed by surveying the book of Revelation's portrait of the kingdom of God come to earth.[39]

Revelation depicts a world in which there is no racism or hatred; all tribes and tongues are gathered as fellow worshippers together. It is a world in which there is no violent self-promotion; all are made level and humbled on bended knee before the throne of the wounded Lamb, who bears the marks of our violence. It is a world in which there is no lack, no unmet need, and as a result, no suffering. As in Eden, Revelation once again depicts a portrait of *mutual flourishing* in which all members are incomparably alive and flourishing in each other's communion. And it is this restored world that is then consummated into the inner life of the triune God, a God who ever exists in himself as a community of divine persons incomparably alive and flourishing in their perichoretic communion.

To be an actual deposit of this coming reality means that the called-out community is not a club which gathers weekly, but a sphere of the created order in which a new world is eschatologically breaking into the old. The called-out community is an eschatological microcosm in which kingdom economics, kingdom equality, kingdom reconciliation, and kingdom justice have already come alive. Within its borders, new anthems are sung, new food is eaten,[40] new rites are administered, new language is spoken,[41] and a new family gathers around one table. Therein, as an "earnest" of eternity, the called-out community acts as a school and training ground within which the baptized become fitted for the new world that will one day be the only world, rather than a microcosm.

As a training ground, the called-out community hosts the ongoing conversion of the regenerate; conversion being not a one-off moment of divine transaction but an ongoing process of ever increasingly *turning away* from the practices and ways of the surrounding culture and *turning to* the practices and ways of Christ (*unlearning* and *learning*). In this sense, the called-out community is both preparation for the coming kingdom and a microcosm of the eternal kingdom already come; and those who live now as its citizens—being conformed to and through it— are its heirs forever.

---

39. Rev 5, 7, 21.

40. I refer here to the body and blood of Christ, the meal of the baptized.

41. I refer here to the language of Scripture as the common vocabulary of the worshipping community's liturgy and prayer.

Conclusion

Richly subtle and nuanced, Wesley's "Treatise on Baptism" reveals baptism to be a divinely wrought inauguration into a new *internal* reality (regeneration) and a new *external* reality (the called-out community). Through this divine work, God is renewing creation according to his original desires for it. First, the Godhead renews the moral image of God in humanity and thereby restores humanity's capacity to once again live according to God's desires for the world (regeneration). This means that as renewed humanity is ever increasingly restored to God's righteousness, holy love, and justice, renewed humanity is made ever more capable of acting with righteousness, holiness, love, and justice toward one neighbor; and is, in equal measure, tasked to do so. Moreover, one may logically conclude that as renewed humanity is ever increasingly filled with the moral image of God, they likewise become better able to faithfully enact the unchanged vocation divinely bestowed in Eden. As God's viceregents upon the earth, renewed humanity can combine effort with grace to care for, tend, and promote God's intended order for creation: a world ordered for the mutual flourishing of all creation's members. And as God's conduits of blessing, grace, and care, renewed humanity can diffuse to the rest of creation God's righteousness, holy love, and justice.[42]

After being given the capacity to once again live according to God's desires for the world, the renewed person is joined to a community who lives precisely in this way: the called-out community. At baptism, one is inaugurated into a community that joins grace with effort to *learn* new practices, new sacrifices, and new values that conform to Christ; and it is also a community that joins grace with effort to *unlearn* practices that are contrary to justice, including the apathy that neglects the seeking of justice. Likewise, one is inaugurated into a community that lives within the joy and responsibilities of a new fictive kinship wrought by mystical union with Christ. Within these new kinship relations, renewed humanity is once again returned to being their "brother's keeper," for kinship is a biblical dynamic in which all members work for the flourishing of the other members. Lastly, as renewed humanity lives under Christ's headship and within Christ's fictive kinship, the community embodies

---

42. As previously noted, this can only be imperfectly enacted as Wesley never affirms that the political image is fully restored in this lifetime. Humanity's task, therefore, is to now faithfully enact their divine vocation to the best of their abilities, as enabled by grace, in a fallen world.

a microcosm of eschatological inbreaking in which the kingdom of God is manifested within fallen creation. Thereby, the called-out community lives as proleptic foretastes and earnests of eternity here and now; that is, they live as heirs already in possession of a kingdom still to come more fully.

For those who have been inwardly renewed and outwardly joined to this community in baptism, failure to exercise holy love in the seeking of social justice is failure to live fully into both the soteriological and ecclesiological realities inaugurated by baptismal waters. For, the full extent to which renewed humanity is capable of exercising holy love through the pursuit of justice is precisely the extent to which renewed humanity is called to do so, both personally and communally. Indeed, when the soteriological and ecclesiological realities inaugurated at baptism are traced to their fullest ends, one can rightly conclude—along with the prophet Amos—that acts of corporate worship are integrally related to the practice of justice. Social justice is, when viewed in this light, nothing short of the active and necessary outworking of transforming, baptismal grace.

Bibliography

Bliss, William Dwight Porter, and Rudolf Michael Binder, eds. "Methodism and Social Reform." *The Encyclopedia of Social Reform,* 762–65. 3rd ed. New York: Funk and Wagnalls, 1910.

Bryant, Barry E. "The Loss of the Moral Image." In *The Oxford Handbook of Methodist Studies,* edited by William J. Abraham and James E. Kirby, 531–32. New York: Oxford University Press, 2013.

———. "The Marring of the Natural and Political Images." In *The Oxford Handbook of Methodist Studies,* edited by William J. Abraham and James E. Kirby, 532–33. New York: Oxford University Press, 2013.

Collins, Kenneth J. *The Scripture Way of Salvation: The Heart of John Wesley's Theology.* Nashville: Abingdon, 1997.

———. *The Theology of John Wesley: Holy Love and the Shape of Grace.* Nashville: Abingdon, 2007.

deSilva, David A. *Honor, Patronage, Kinship & Purity: Unlocking New Testament Culture.* Downers Grove, IL: InterVarsity, 2000.

Dunning, H. Ray. *Reflecting the Divine Image: Christian Ethics in Wesleyan Perspective.* Eugene, OR: Wipf and Stock, 1998.

Pope, William Burt. *Compendium of Christian Theology.* 3 vols. n.p.: Pantianos Classics, 2017.

Thompson, D. D. *John Wesley as a Social Reformer.* New York: Eaton and Mains, 1898.

Wesley, John. *Genesis Explanatory Notes and Commentary.* n.p.: Hargreaves, 2014.

————. "A Plain Account of Christian Perfection." In *Bicentennial Edition of the Works of John Wesley.* Vol. 13, *Doctrinal and Controversial Treatises II*, edited by Paul Wesley Chilcote and Kenneth J. Collins, 132–91. Nashville: Abingdon, 2012.

————. "Sermon 8, 'The First-fruits of the Spirit.'" In *Bicentennial Edition of the Works of John Wesley.* Vol. 1, *Sermons I*, edited by Albert C. Outler, 233–47. Nashville: Abingdon, 1985.

————. "Sermon 19, 'The Great Privilege of Those That Are Born of God.'" In *Bicentennial Edition of the Works of John Wesley.* Vol. 1, *Sermons I*, edited by Albert C. Outler, 431–43. Nashville: Abingdon, 1984.

————. "Sermon 45, 'The New Birth.'" In *Bicentennial Edition of the Works of John Wesley.* Vol. 2, *Sermons II*, edited by Albert C. Outler, 186–201. Nashville: Abingdon, 1985.

————. "Sermon 60, 'The General Deliverance.'" in *Bicentennial Edition of the Works of John Wesley.* Vol. 2, *Sermons II*, edited by Albert C. Outler, 436–50. Nashville: Abingdon, 1985.

————. "A Treatise on Baptism." In *Works of John Wesley.* Vol. 10, *Letters, Essays, Dialogs, Addresses*, edited by Thomas Jackson, 188–201. Grand Rapids: Zondervan, 1958–59.

Wirzba, Norman. *Living the Sabbath: Discovering the Rhythms of Rest and Delight.* Grand Rapids: Brazos, 2006.

CHAPTER 9

Baptism and Social Holiness

Disentangling Social Holiness and Social Justice

Felicia Howell LaBoy,
First United Methodist Church, Elgin, Illinois

Contrary to the popular belief of many Methodists, John Wesley does not equate social holiness with social justice, nor does he equate charity with "Christianized" philanthropic efforts.[1] Rather, for Wesley, growth in holiness requires individuals to be engaged in a community of faith that builds friendships in which persons are mutually accountable to one another and that are thereby designed to help persons in the process of sanctification. As one grows in holiness, social justice is a "fruit." In other words, as God's grace grows one in Christian perfection—ever empowering one for obedience to Christ's commands, and ever manifesting in one a pure and holy love for God and neighbor—social justice is one of the fruits manifested by such love. Baptism is initiation into this

---

1. The primary principle underlying John Wesley's concept of social holiness is that holy love needs others for cultivation. His fourth discourse on the Sermon on the Mount condemns solitary religion, which exists "without living and conversing with other men." He writes: "Christianity is essentially a social religion; to turn it into a solitary one is to destroy it. When I say that this is essentially a social religion, I mean not only that it cannot subsist so well, but that it cannot subsist at all, without society." Wesley, "Sermon 24, 'Upon Our Lord's Sermon,'" 534.

way of Christian growth and living, and therefore is intricately connected to social holiness and its fruit of social justice. In order to better appreciate the relationship between baptism, social holiness, and social justice in Wesleyan thought, however, we must first define each concept within Wesley's thinking.

Social Holiness vs. Social Justice

In his essay "From Societies to Society: The Shift from Holiness to Justice in the Wesleyan Tradition," Andrew C. Thompson contends that in equating "social holiness" and "social justice," Methodists simply confuse and conflate the terms, misinterpreting Wesley's original distinction. With the two terms conflated, it is then assumed that "personal holiness" refers to the spiritual growth of the individual while "social holiness" refers to the work done by holy persons with regard to charity and justice in the world. However, there is a three-fold problem in reducing the terms to these definitions.

First and foremost, equating social justice with social holiness distorts how Wesley understood social holiness to function in the process of sanctification.[2] It places the emphasis on works rather than relationship.

Second, confusing the two terms nullifies the important role of social holiness as a catalyst for social justice, one that is not only concerned with the needs and contemporary plight of the disenfranchised, but also confronts the benevolent, paternalistic attitudes of those who may be engaged in social justice and/or missions work. In this way, confusing and conflating the terms results in a loss of how we understand the role of the church in effecting holiness among its congregants as well as the greater society at large. A better understanding of the relationship between social holiness and social justice challenges the maintenance of patron-client relationships within the church and disrupts the preservation of inequities and injustices in society.[3]

The third problem that arises in equating social justice with social holiness is that the distinction between the work of the church and the work of any other nonprofit or social justice agency is removed. The "ministry" of social justice work thus becomes another "service" that

2. Thompson, "From Societies to Society," 141–72.
3. See 1 Cor 12:12–27.

select groups provide on behalf of the church rather than the ministry that is conducted by the church.

The conflation and confusion of social justice with social holiness also has potential to impact the spiritual growth (what Wesley refers to as "personal holiness") of both benefactors (i.e., the ones providing service) and clients. Wesley maintains that unless friendship is cultivated between benefactors and their clients, then benefactors are not challenged to engage in critical self-reflection with regard to their values of wealth, privilege, and self-love in relation to the gospel. For this reason, Wesley insists that well-to-do members of a church or society meet the poor in their homes so they might get a firsthand look at the causes and effects of poverty.[4] In fact, according to Randy Maddox, as more and more of his members experienced prosperity and embraced the values and views of the culture around them, Wesley pushed against the over-reliance on status, wealth, and privilege claiming it to be an impediment to both spiritual growth and the spread of the gospel.[5]

Although Wesley advocates for the need to develop friendship with the poor so as to meet their needs and to grow in holiness, he perhaps misses what modern sociologists and practitioners have found when benevolence is offered without corresponding mutuality. Clients can also be affected: potentially shifting their reliance from God to patrons or potentially engaging in self-loathing/patron-envy, seeing themselves always in a position of needing assistance. In this way, conflating and confusing social holiness with social justice can work to maintain societal fractures within the body of Christ (1 Cor 12:21–25).

Social Holiness vs. Personal Holiness

Another error many modern Methodists make is to pair personal holiness with social holiness by always linking the two together—i.e., "personal and social holiness" as a sort of shortcut to describe the distinction between works of piety and works of mercy.[6] This error also conflates the idea of social justice with social holiness by focusing on the difference between the adjectives "social" and "personal" to describe the difference between communal/societal and individual effort. The conflation results

4. Newton, "Methodism and the Articulation," 52–53.

5. Maddox, "Visit the Poor," 62–63.

6. Thompson, "From Societies to Society," 155.

in a loss of understanding the role of the church in effecting holiness among its congregants and the greater society at large.[7] Simply put, by pairing personal holiness with social holiness, as in "personal and social holiness," modern Methodists violate the common saying "there is no personal holiness without social holiness."

Personal Holiness

So, what then is the difference between personal holiness and social holiness? A proper way to discern Wesley's meaning of and distinction between personal holiness and social holiness is to first understand that Wesley never said, "There's no personal holiness without social holiness." On the matter of holiness, what Wesley did say can be found in the preface to his 1739 edition of *Hymns and Sacred Poems*: "Directly opposite to this is the gospel of Christ. Solitary religion is not to be found there. 'Holy solitaries' is a phrase no more consistent with the gospel than holy adulterers. The gospel of Christ knows of no religion but social; no holiness but social holiness."[8] So, what does Wesley actually mean by holiness, personal or social, and why does he maintain that there is "no holiness but social holiness"?

First, we have to look at how Wesley defines "holiness" in general. Central to Wesley's theology and practical divinity is that "God is often styled holy, righteous, wise; but not holiness, righteousness, or wisdom in the abstract as he is said to be love; intimating that this is . . . his reigning attribute, the attribute that sheds an amiable glory on all his other perfections."[9] Wesley sees holiness first and foremost as an attribute of God and thus an attribute that humans are meant to share in as creatures created in the image of God. However, because of the power and penalty of sin, humans cannot attain holiness based on their own initiative—it is only attainable by God's prevenient, justifying, and sanctifying grace made available through the person and work of Jesus Christ and by the power of the Holy Spirit.

These are not to be understood as three separate graces given by God but rather as three manners in which God's grace is operative in the life of the believer. God's prevenient grace makes persons aware of their

7. Thompson, "From Societies to Society," 143–44, 155–57.

8. Wesley, *Hymns and Sacred Poems*, viii–ix.

9. Wesley, "1 John 4:8," 637.

sinful nature and the need to be born again (i.e., the New Birth). Justifying grace mediates pardon from sin through the finished and atoning work of Christ such that one's life before God is made righteous (i.e., forgiven and reconciled to God). Sanctifying grace is the working of the Holy Spirit in the life of one who has been forgiven, making them actually righteous and transformed. Simply put, justification effects a relative change in the life of the believer (i.e., the change of one's status before God), while sanctification is the process by which real change occurs (i.e., how one's life is systematically and continuously changed by the power of the Holy Spirit freeing one from all sin). Wesley defines this progressive transformation of believers as growth in "holiness of heart and life."[10]

When Wesley uses the term "personal holiness," he is describing the link between sanctification and justification in the lives of individual believers such that holiness of heart and life is occurring. Wesley further utilizes the term "personal holiness" to emphasize the difference between the holiness of humans and the holiness of God. Second, Wesley uses the term "personal holiness" to signify that justification (i.e., the imputed righteousness from Christ's atoning work) is insufficient for believers to attain the holiness required to see God (Heb 12:14). Wesley makes this point well in his sermon "On the Wedding Garment" when he writes:

> The righteousness of Christ is doubtless necessary for any soul that enters into glory: But so is personal holiness too, for every child of man. But it is highly needful to be observed, that they are necessary in different respects. The former is necessary to entitle us to heaven; the latter to qualify us for it. Without the righteousness of Christ, we could have no claim to glory; without holiness we could have no fitness for it. By the former we become members of Christ, children of God, and heirs of the kingdom of heaven. By the latter "we are made meet to be partakers of the inheritance of the saints in light."[11]

Although Wesley emphasized works of personal piety in the pursuit of personal holiness, he is aware that the pursuit of holiness outside of community is problematic for two reasons. First, it is difficult for one to see one's own faults and make necessary corrections. Second, the quest for holiness could lead to self-deception and/or self-righteousness. For

---

10. Wesley, "Sermon 45, 'The New Birth,'" 194–95.
11. Wesley, "Sermon 120, 'On the Wedding Garment,'" 144.

Wesley, the principle of "social holiness" was a safeguard against the inherent dangers of such an individualistic pursuit of holiness.

Social Holiness

As previously examined, the phrase, "The gospel of Christ knows of no religion but social; no holiness but social holiness," is only utilized in one instance in the corpus of Wesley's work—in the preface to his 1739 edition of *Hymns and Sacred Poems*, cowritten with his brother Charles. Primary aims for Wesley in this work were: 1) to establish his theology of salvation; and 2) to address specific concerns regarding the mysticism of his day, specifically that of the "Mystic Divines" (i.e., "holy solitaries"). Specifically, the phrase is used to contradict the emphasis of the Mystic Divines on separating oneself from community to focus on solitary practices as a means of spiritual growth. Moreover, Wesley sought to challenge their beliefs, which deny the necessity of church doctrine as having any bearing on humans' acceptance before God. For the Mystic Divines, to be right with God one could rely on inner witness and good works as evidence.

For Wesley, growth in holiness requires individuals to be engaged in a community of faith that builds friendships in which persons are mutually accountable to one another. These mutually accountable relationships are designed to help persons in the process of sanctification. While Wesley is sensitive to the need of believers to engage in periodic disengagement from the world for prayer and spiritual renewal, he is certain that the process of spiritual growth is very different from the suggested practice of the Mystic Divines. Thus, he defines and describes the importance of "social holiness" for personal spiritual growth when he writes:

> Whereas, according to the Judgment of our Lord, and the Writings of his Apostles, it is only when we are knit together, that we have Nourishment from Him, and increase with the Increase of GOD. Neither is there any time, when the weakest Member can say to the strongest, or the strongest to the weakest, "I have no need of Thee." Accordingly, our Blessed Lord, when his Disciples were in their weakest State, sent them forth, not alone, but Two by Two. When they were strengthened a little, not by Solitude, but by abiding with him and one another, he commanded them to wait, not separate but being assembled together, for the Promise of the Father. And they were all with one Accord

in one Place, when they received the Gift of the Holy Ghost. Express mention is made in the same Chapter, that when there were added unto them Three Thousand Souls, all that believed were together, and continued stedfastly not only in the Apostles Doctrine but also in fellowship and in breaking of Bread and in praying with one Accord. . . . For contemplation is with them the fulfilling of the law, even a contemplation that "consists in a cessation of all works." Directly opposite to this is the gospel of Christ. Solitary religion is not to be found there. "Holy solitaries" is a phrase no more consistent with the gospel than holy adulterers. The gospel of Christ knows of no religion but social; no holiness but social holiness. "Faith working by love" is the length and breadth and depth and height of Christian perfection. "This commandment have we from Christ, that he who loveth God love his brother also"; and that we manifest our love "by doing good unto all men, especially to them that are of the household of faith." And in truth, whosoever loveth his brethren not in word only, but as Christ loved him, cannot but be "zealous of good works." He feels in his soul a burning, restless desire, of spending and being spent for them.[12]

Wesley understood that growth in holiness happens when Christians are mutually accountable to one another in close relationships within the community of faith.

Social Holiness as a Catalyst for Social Justice

So how does social holiness then relate to social justice? As demonstrated in his preface to *Hymns and Sacred Poems* quoted above, Wesley believed that Christians who have been justified and are in the process of sanctification within Christian community are the ones most equipped to work on the transformation of society. Thus, societal transformation, or what we in the current era refer to as social justice (i.e., the "going about doing good") is the fruit of Christian life and, indeed, of holiness of heart and life in the context of a faith community in which there is friendship, fellowship, and mutual accountability. In this way, social holiness has the potential to serve as a catalyst for a Wesleyan model of social justice that goes beyond Christianized philanthropy and actually challenge the systems that cause people to suffer in the first place.

12. Wesley, *Hymns and Sacred Poems*, vi–ix.

Wesley's system of social justice (i.e., "going about doing good") was indeed comprehensive and well-organized. As is implied above, it was a critical component of his *via salutis* (way of salvation). As such, Wesley defines true religion (i.e., holiness) and true happiness as "in two words, gratitude and benevolence, gratitude to our Creator and supreme Benefactor, and benevolence to our fellow creatures."[13] During his ministry, Wesley was so convinced that practical love of one's neighbor by "going about doing good" was critical to one's growth in holiness, he organized societies around the notion of doing good and mandated their observance of the General Rules. The General Rules, which admonished persons to (1) do no harm/avoid evil, (2) do good, and (3) attend to the ordinances of God, were designed to provide Methodists with a systematized way of growing in the love of both God and of neighbor. So mandatory was the observance of the General Rules that the last paragraph of the General Rules contained severe consequences for those of the early Methodist societies who did not follow them, including expulsions and penitential bands for those removed. As Rebekah Miles notes, the removal of those not following the rules were not for the rules' sake, but rather so that all in the societies would grow in holiness.[14]

In a similar vein, Wesley organized a comprehensive system for doing good to one's neighbor. Not only did he encourage charity in the form of direct aid, but he also urged the edification of others through assistance in increasing their ability to live better lives, especially economically.[15] Likewise, Wesley included a justice component, regularly speaking out in his sermons and writings against the injustices endured by the poor, marginalized, and disenfranchised. In fact, Wesley's social justice model included many initiatives that worked to dismantle the very systems that caused persons to be poor and disenfranchised in the first place.

Wesley's coordinated efforts of charity, economic empowerment, and justice/advocacy are direct results of his understanding of the means of grace and his privileging of works of mercy over works of piety.[16] Jennings argues that even before the terms "preferential option for the poor" or "social justice" were utilized, Wesley is seen concerned with demystifying the dangers of wealth and power to those pursuing a life of holiness.

13. Wesley, "Sermon 120, 'The Unity of Divine Being,'" 66–67.

14. Miles, "Happiness, Holiness," 211–15.

15. For more on Wesley's "evangelical economics," see Jennings, *Good News*.

16. Tuttle, "Review of *Social Justice through the Eyes of Wesley*," 220–21.

In essence, Wesley is creating a new ethic, one befitting the kingdom of God for those within the Methodist societies dedicated to the pursuit of holiness of heart and life. Jennings describes this ethic:

> Wesley is not content merely to condemn injustice. He is also concerned to develop a positive ethic that will alter the given socioeconomic reality. Thus he proposes a view of stewardship that breaks the spell of "private property" and leads to a redistribution of wealth whose criterion is the welfare of the poor. This goes far to lead Wesley to an acceptance of the economic model of the Pentecostal community of Acts 2–4, which "had all things in common" and "made distribution to the poor," as the proper expression of Christian faith that works in love.[17]

Wesley's new economic ethic, driven by his understanding of grace and holiness, not only challenges notions of private property, but also challenges the prevailing notions of benevolence of his day. Randy Maddox notes that Wesley's economic ethic can be summarized in four points all having to do with his theology of grace and the pursuit of holiness: 1) ultimately everything belongs to God; 2) resources are placed in our care to use as God sees fit; 3) God desires that we use these resources to meet our necessities (i.e., providing shelter and food for ourselves and dependents), and then to help others in need; thus, 4) spending resources on luxuries for ourselves while others remain in need is robbing God![18] Wesley's economic ethic is no program of forced "Christian socialism" or redistribution; rather, it is tempered and driven by love of God and love of neighbor. Thus, while Wesley encourages the Methodist societies to earn, save, and give all they can, these were to be tempered by the General Rules.[19]

Whereas Luigi Taparelli, a nineteenth-century Jesuit priest and political theorist, first used the term "social justice" to define a virtue concept based on natural law utilizing concepts from political theory, Wesley based his system on his understanding of the necessity of doing good for one's neighbor and—as a logical progression—for the pursuit of holiness as pursued within the context of the Methodist societies. Taparelli defined social justice as:

---

17. Jennings, *Good News*, 25.
18. Maddox, "Visit the Poor," 62.
19. Maddox, "Visit the Poor," 62.

both a norm and a habit—a social virtue embodied in the political, legal, and cultural institutional conditions obtaining in a
given society—of promoting the common good by encouraging
the free exercise of the rights of persons and particularly of the
intermediary associations they freely form to pursue their own
good, according to the complimentary principles of solidarity
and subsidiarity.[20]

Notably, by basing his definition of social justice on rights, duties and free
exercise, Taparelli leaves open the question of whether or not one will follow his proposal of social justice. For Wesley, for those who are in pursuit
of holiness, there is a mandate, born not of "rights, duties, and free exercise," but rather out of the recognition of the fallen state of all humanity
before a holy and righteous God and the gratitude for the prevenient,
justifying, and sanctifying grace of God that makes salvation possible.

Wesley's ethic of social justice was also not driven by philanthropic
practice but served as a contradiction to it because Wesley's ethic of social
justice served to equalize the privileged and the poor/disenfranchised as
children of God and brethren to one another. In this way, Wesley's system
of social justice challenges methods of social justice and Christianized
philanthropy which maintain the existing dynamics of power, privilege,
and abuse.

At heart of Wesley's system of social justice was his understanding of the way the sacraments were meant to function in the life of the
believer. For the purposes at hand, only the sacrament of baptism will
be examined along with its direct correlation to Wesley's theology and
practice of social holiness and social justice.

Baptism as Sacrament of Initiation and Incorporation

As noted earlier, Wesley does not believe in solitary discipleship, which
includes the rite of baptism. Fundamental to Wesley's theology and practice of baptism was that baptism is the initiation of people into life in
Jesus Christ and into the body of Christ, the church. For Wesley, there is
no baptism without the church because the church is God's primary, chosen vehicle through which one is birthed into the kingdom of God. This
process of initiation is easily seen in the United Methodist "baptismal
covenant" service, which states quite clearly in the introduction of the

20. See Behr, "Luigi Taparelli," 10.

service that baptism is initiation into "Christ's holy church," which is eschatological and spans time and space. Accordingly, for Wesley, baptism is a one-time, once-and-for-all initiation into the body of Christ because in it we enter into the covenant of grace made available by God through Christ's atoning work. Even though we may fail to keep our end of the bargain, God is always faithful. Thus, the covenant we make in baptism between us and God is ultimately based on God and God's grace alone.

Being baptized into Christ's holy church is not only a rite of initiation. Baptism also causes a change of identity because of how sin distorts the image of God within each individual. Gayle Carlton Felton describes vividly the ways this is manifest in us when she writes:

> Through prideful overreach or denial of our God-given responsibilities, we exalt our own will, invent our own values, and rebel against God. Our very being is dominated toward an inherent inclination toward evil which has traditionally be called original sin. It is a universal condition and affects all aspects of life. Because of our condition of sin, we are separated from God, alienated from one another, hostile to the natural world and even at odds with our own best selves.[21]

As we respond to God's justifying grace in our baptism, we are changed from being alienated from God, others, and ourselves. As Wesley further maintains in his "Treatise on Baptism" that in baptism we become sons (and daughters) of God, and heirs and joint heirs with Christ and with other Christians.[22]

However, baptism does not guarantee that we have fully accepted the privileges and responsibilities of being a child of God and joint heir of Christ. This is worked out in our incorporation into Christ's holy church universal and in our incorporation into the local church that receives us. This change of identity is easily seen in the liturgy for The United Methodist Church's "baptismal covenant." Through the "Renunciation of Sin and the Profession of Faith" and in the "Apostle's Creed," we are reminded of our "privileges;" that is, who we are and whose we are across time and space. In our "Reception into The United Methodist Church" and "Reception into the Local Congregation," we are reminded that the change

---

21. Felton, *By Water and the Spirit*, 9.
22. See Wesley, "Treatise on Baptism," 188–201.

of identity also carries with it the responsibility to care for that which we have been incorporated into.[23]

Incorporation vs. Incarnation

Not only are we incorporated into the local and universal church, we are incorporated into the very life of the triune God through our dying and being raised with Christ. This incorporation into the mystical body of Christ does not only pertain to our physical death or the end-times. Based on this, we must ask what does it mean to be incorporated into the body of Christ both mystically (i.e., "dying and being raised with Christ") and materially (i.e., our incorporation into the church, local and universal)? Or, put another way, what does being "incorporated into" the life of the church locally and universally have to do with manifesting the body of Christ (incarnation) to the world? Just as the limbs of our natural body cannot survive without being connected to the overall body, we must be a part of the body of Christ. Our being a part of the body of Christ should not be subsumed such that the diversity is virtually eliminated. Incorporation into the material body of Christ means that we bring our whole selves—regardless of race, ethnicity, gender, sexual orientation, ability, or socioeconomic class—and remain distinct even while unified in purpose.

While this sounds good in theory, it is very difficult to do. In fact, missiologist Andrew Walls asserts that the problem of incorporating difference into the body of Christ has been one of, if not most, significant issues facing the church since its inception. Why? Because often we normalize our way of being born again without considering what is contextual and what is not. For example, as the early church in Acts moved beyond its Jewish roots, it had to discern what was essential to salvation. It also had to be open to the fact that each new people group provided another aspect of God's character and the need for the baptizing congregation to change.[24] Likewise, in many cases, Wesley understood well that the process of sanctification required the elite of his members to see Christ in the other—especially the other that they usually looked down on. But Wesley engaged his members to move beyond "seeing" one another, to actually becoming mutually accountable friends, and this is what made

23. General Board of Discipleship of the United Methodist Church, "Baptismal Covenant I," 86–94.

24. Walls, "Converts or Proselytes?" 2–6.

Wesley unique from other programs of social justice of his day. As noted before, Wesley's program of social justice was the fruit of the quest for holiness. Simply put, Wesley believed that "consistent and faithful social action must be grounded in communal spiritual formation."[25]

For Wesley, the Methodist Societies he established were not merely collectives of individuals seeking to come together, but rather were characterized by personal pursuit of God. They were to be a contemporary manifestation of the early Christian communities in which all believers were mutually dependent on each other and "knit together, [such] that we have Nourishment from Him [Jesus], and increase with the Increase of GOD" (i.e., grow in holiness).[26] In this way, they represented and re-presented the physical body of Christ as made known through the sacraments. Further, this incorporation into the Body of localized believers sought to make Christ known by embracing "lives of self-denial, because self-denial for the sake of the other was a defining characteristic of Christ's life."[27] In this way, Wesley, makes works of mercy (i.e., social justice) an act of spiritual formation in that, along with works of piety, they are responsible for the working out of one's full salvation.

Having looked at how Wesley linked baptism and social holiness, we now turn our attention to how these might inform our modern practices.

The Way Forward: Living into Our Baptismal Vows While Maintaining Our Wesleyan Heritage of Social Holiness

The challenges modern Christians within the Wesleyan heritage face while trying to live into their baptismal vows can be distilled into just a few. First, like many congregations in North America, numerous Methodist (and other Wesleyan) congregations view the church as a place to go rather than as a people, nay a body—i.e., the present re-presentation of the body of Christ sent into the world in the power of the Holy Spirit to continue Christ's mission. Many function like religious stores and volunteer organizations in which members "purchase" services through the giving of their time, talents, and resources. Thus, members within the local church and the community outside it often see baptism as a ceremonial event with no link at all to salvation. Without this link, people

25. Maddox, "Visit the Poor," 64.

26. Wesley, *Hymns and Sacred Poems*, vi.

27. Maddox, "Visit the Poor," 67.

consider the church to be the place to be baptized, married, and buried, but it has no claim on their lives whatsoever.[28] As the congregation and the members go through the liturgy of being received into The United Methodist Church at large as well as the individual congregation, they perceive this as joining any other volunteer club or association. Even though they recite vows to renounce and resist evil, to accept the justifying grace of Christ, and to enter into union with Him and his people so the process of sanctification can continue in their lives, it has no bearing on their daily walk with God.

Thus, as Wesley observed in his day, there are many who had been baptized with water as babies but never experienced baptism by the Spirit (new birth); and there are many churches today—perhaps from a fear of losing members or a discomfort with speaking of sin, salvation, and the need to be born again—that do not emphasize the expectation of sanctification at a person's baptism or during a remembrance of baptismal covenant service. Little to nothing is emphasized to remind them of the link between baptism and the new birth, nor the need for them to come together and be mutually dependent upon one another for spiritual growth (social holiness). In this way, even when churches have small groups, these are simply ways for persons to get together to socialize.

What, then, are we to do? Here are a few suggestions:

1. Preach and teach regularly on baptism and its relationship to the new birth, sanctification, and holiness.

2. Help baptized congregants remember their baptismal covenants with ceremonies of remembrance.

3. Share with the congregation via preaching, small groups, or a Bible study series the latest research regarding the church as "religious store."[29]

4. Create opportunities for congregations to develop relationships that are mutually accountable and diverse across all perceived barriers of race, ethnicity, gender, sexual orientation, socioeconomic status, and theological and political orientation.

---

28. For more on how modern churches in North America function like "religious stores" rather than the body of Christ, see Guder, *Missional Church*, 77–87.

29. See Guder, *Missional Church*, 77–87.

Conclusion

Baptism initiates us into a community of mutually accountable friendships in which growth in holiness of heart and life takes place. This growth in holiness is called personal holiness, but it is brought about within the mutually accountable relationships that exist within the Christian community as those who pursue holiness join together in this pursuit: social holiness. Wesley's emphasis on social holiness as both a catalyst for personal transformation and societal transformation should not be lost in today's churches. It also should also not be confused with other concepts, such as social justice or philanthropy. Social holiness has something to offer the body of Christ and the world that is unique: it is the catalyst for growing in the perfect love of God and neighbor. When John Wesley sought to address the disconnect between baptism and personal holiness, his societies turned the world upside down.

Bibliography

Behr, Thomas C. "Luigi Taparelli and Social Justice: Rediscovering the Origins of a 'Hollowed' Concept." *Social Justice in Context* 1 (2005) 10.

Felton, Gayle Carlton. *By Water and the Spirit: Making Connections for Identity and Ministry.* Nashville: Discipleship Resources, 2003.

General Board of Discipleship of the United Methodist Church. "Baptismal Covenant I." In *The United Methodist Book of Worship*, 86–94. Nashville: United Methodist Publishing, 1992.

Guder, Darrell L., ed. *Missional Church: A Vision for the Sending of the Church in North America.* Nashville: Abingdon, 1990.

Jennings, Theodore. *Good News to the Poor: John Wesley's Evangelical Economics.* Nashville: Abingdon, 1990.

Maddox, Randy L. "Visit the Poor: John Wesley, the Poor and the Sanctification of Believers." In *The Poor and the People Called Methodists*, edited by Richard Heitzenrater, 59–81. Nashville: Kingswood, 2002.

Miles, Rebekah. "Happiness, Holiness, and the Moral Life in John Wesley." In *The Cambridge Companion to John Wesley*, edited by Randy Maddox and Jason Vickers, 207–24. Cambridge: Cambridge University Press, 2010.

Newton, John A. "Methodism and the Articulation of Faith: No Holiness but Social." *Methodist History* 42.1 (October 2003) 52–53.

Thompson, Andrew. "From Societies to Society: The Shift from Holiness to Justice in the Wesleyan Tradition." *Methodist Review* 3 (2011) 141–72.

Tuttle, Robert G. "Review of *Social Justice through the Eyes of Wesley: John Wesley's Theological Challenge to Slavery* by Irv A. Brendlinger." *Wesleyan Theological Journal* 43 (2008) 220–21.

Walls, Andrew. "Converts or Proselytes? The Crisis Over Conversion in the Early Church." *International Bulletin of Missionary Research* 28.1 (January 2004) 2–6.

Wesley, John. *Hymns and Sacred Poems*. London: William Strahan, 1739.

———. "1 John 4:8." In *Explanatory Notes*. Vol. 4, *Upon the New Testament*. Salem: Schmul, 1976.

———. "Sermon 24, 'Upon Our Lord's Sermon on the Mount, IV.'" In *Bicentennial Edition of the Works of John Wesley*. Vol. 1, *Sermons I*, edited by Albert C. Outler, 531–49. Nashville: Abingdon, 1984.

———. "Sermon 45, 'The New Birth.'" In *Bicentennial Edition of the Works of John Wesley*. Vol. 2, *Sermons II*, edited by Albert C. Outler, 186–201. Nashville: Abingdon, 1985.

———. "Sermon 114, 'The Unity of the Divine Being.'" In *Bicentennial Edition of the Works of John Wesley*. Vol. 4, *Sermons IV*, edited by Albert C. Outler, 60–71. Nashville: Abingdon, 1987.

———."Sermon 120, 'On the Wedding Garment.'" In *Bicentennial Edition of the Works of John Wesley*. Vol. 4, *Sermons IV*, edited by Albert C. Outler, 139–48. Nashville: Abingdon, 1987.

———."A Treatise on Baptism." In *Works of John Wesley*. Vol. 10, *Letters, Essays, Dialogs, Addresses*, edited by Thomas Jackson, 188–201. Grand Rapids: Zondervan, 1958–59.

CHAPTER 10

Baptism and the Means of Grace

Initiation into Covenant Community

HENRY H. KNIGHT III, SAINT PAUL SCHOOL OF THEOLOGY

HOW JOHN WESLEY UNDERSTOOD baptism has been a matter of scholarly debate. The reason is that instead of a single, definitive account representing his mature thought, we have instead several discussions of baptism in which Wesley is addressing different misunderstandings. We will say more about Wesley's sacramental and evangelical understandings below, but the varied emphases in these discussions have led some to wonder if Wesley had a coherent theology of baptism. For all the seeming unclarity, Wesley is consistently clear that baptism is a sacrament and a means of grace. "It was," he says, "instituted by Christ, who alone has the power to institute a proper sacrament, a sign, seal, pledge, and means of grace, perpetually obligatory on all Christians."[1] On this he never wavers.

The relation of baptism to means of grace is twofold. As the initiatory sacrament, baptism is the normative link to all other means of grace within the Christian community. But as a sacrament, it is also a means of grace in and of itself. We shall explore each of these points in turn, followed by a discussion of baptism in relation to the Methodist movement in Wesley's day and implications for practice today.

---

1. Wesley, "Treatise on Baptism," 188.

What Are Means of Grace?

First, we need to say a bit more about how Wesley understands means of grace. We can begin with Wesley's own definition: "By 'means of grace' I understand outward signs, words, or actions ordained of God, and appointed for this end—to be the *ordinary* channels whereby he might convey to men preventing, justifying, or sanctifying grace."[2] Thus, sacraments are means of grace, which Wesley's Church of England teaches "is 'an outward sign of inward *grace*, and a *means* whereby we receive the same.'"[3] But means of grace encompass more than the two Protestant sacraments (baptism and eucharist). The means of grace include both works of piety and works of mercy, as well as general means of grace.[4]

General means of grace include such spiritual practices as watching (against temptation and sin, attending to God's will), the exercise of the presence of God (a constant attentiveness to God's presence), self-denial (denying our will when it is contrary to the will of God), and taking up our cross (voluntarily suffering for the sake of God or our neighbor). Wesley believes that, while the other means of grace can be practiced in a routine, "formalistic" manner, these by their very nature cannot be practiced without being beneficial.

Works of mercy are "to the souls and bodies" of persons and are ways "we exercise all holy tempers" and "continually improve them, so that all these are real *means of grace*, although this is not commonly adverted to."[5]

Works of piety include prayer, searching the Scriptures (including both personal devotional reading and public worship), the Lord's Supper, fasting, and Christian conference (conversation together about God, discipleship, and the like). These works of piety are also called by Wesley *instituted* means of grace, meaning that they were specifically ordained by Jesus Christ for Christians to practice. Other means of grace are *prudential*, that is, have proven to also be used by God to enable Christian growth. What is puzzling is that when Wesley lists the instituted means of grace, he never includes baptism, although he is quite clear it too is instituted by Christ and is a means of grace. The most likely explanation for its omission is that baptism is the initiatory sacrament, hence not repeated,

2. Wesley, "Sermon 16, 'The Means of Grace,'" 381.
3. Wesley, "Sermon 16, 'The Means of Grace,'" 381.
4. Wesley, "Sermon 85, 'On Working Out Our Own Salvation,'" 205–6.
5. Wesley, "Sermon 92, 'On Zeal,'" 313.

while the Lord's Supper is the ongoing sacrament that is received again and again.

The means of grace are just that: means through which God works to enable persons to receive and grow in the Christian life. While mainstream Reformation Protestantism had emphasized grace as giving us an alien righteousness and new status before God through justification, Wesley's emphasis falls upon a real change in our hearts and lives through sanctification. Thus, Wesley can say that while the grace of God "is sometimes to be understood that free love, that unmerited mercy, by which I, a sinner, through the merits of Christ am now reconciled to God," Wesley insists that grace is also "that power of God the Holy Ghost which 'worketh in us both to will and to do of his good pleasure.'"[6] This is a strongly trinitarian account of the grace of God. For Wesley, grace is not a "something" from God but the actual presence and power of God. When we participate in the means of grace with any degree of faith, we encounter that divine presence, an encounter that has a transformative effect on our hearts and lives.

It would be hard to overestimate the role of means of grace for Wesleyan theology and practice. They were essential practices for those who sought the promise of salvation. While originally created in the image of the God who is love, Wesley understood our fundamental problem is that we are fallen into sin, which now governs our hearts and lives. Because sin governs our disposition, motivation, and desire, we are unable to save ourselves or even see clearly our condition. We can be saved by grace alone. The way to salvation begins first with prevenient grace that reaches out to all persons, giving them a basic conscience and a limited freedom to respond to God. This gives us the intimation that there is something about our lives that isn't the way it is supposed to be. Through encountering the gospel, convincing grace shows us more clearly the nature of our problem and our need for God if we are to be cured from the disease of sin. Justifying grace forgives us of our sins and reconciles us to God, changing our relationship from that of dutiful obedience (the faith of a servant) to loving obedience (the faith of a child of God). This lays the foundation for sanctification, which for Wesley was the whole point of salvation. Beginning with the new birth (or regeneration) which occurs with justification, sanctification is our growing in the knowledge and love

---

6. Wesley, "Sermon 12, 'The Witness of Our Own Spirit,'" 309.

of God and love of neighbor, until we are perfected in love and restored to the image in which we were created.

Central to the entire way of salvation are means of grace, for it is through these that the Holy Spirit works to bring about this change from sin to love. While God is not limited to means of grace, God has chosen them to be the chief way for us to receive God's transforming power. Without the means of grace, it is hard to see how salvation understood as sanctification would be possible apart from a miraculous act of God.

We can see why they are so vital if we consider that they are intrinsically relational in nature. This not only means that God acts and we respond through means of grace. It also means that, as in any relationship, we come to know God more fully. To know God is not simply to encounter a vague sense of God's presence, an amorphous spirituality, but to know who this God is with whom we have the relationship. This is the God of the Bible, most especially, the God revealed in Jesus Christ. Means of grace are necessary because many of them tell us who God is through accounts of what God has done and promised. Without means of grace like Scripture and sacraments we would be tempted to take our experiences and out of them create a god other than the One Who has been revealed.[7]

It is no wonder, then, that Wesley reacted so strongly against the Moravian Brethren teaching of "stillness" in the Fetter Lane Society in 1740. The Moravians had been instrumental in Wesley's understanding, claiming faith to be a gift of grace that enables us to know and trust God, a teaching that set the stage for his experience at the Aldersgate prayer meeting in 1738. Wesley and other like-minded Anglicans began meeting with Moravians at Fetter Lane. But a Moravian named Philip Henry Molther began teaching that persons should "be still" until they have this faith and the accompanying assurance of salvation, not using means of grace lest they trust in them rather than in Christ.

Nothing could be more subversive of Wesley's understanding of salvation as sanctification, for it cut people off from the means of grace and made salvation primarily a matter of post-mortem destiny rather than a present new life. Wesley and his followers ultimately left Fetter Lane over this issue. But in the process Wesley came to refine his understanding of means of grace. While many Anglicans looked upon sacraments especially as mediating grace and were suspicious of claims for an immediate

---

7. I have argued this in greater detail in Knight, *Presence of God*.

experience of God, the Moravians instead spoke of an immediacy of God's presence apart from any means. Wesley rejected the dichotomy and argued instead for a mediated immediacy. In response to Anglican critics he wrote:

> But all inspiration, though through means, is immediate. Suppose, for instance, you are employed in private prayer, and God pours his love into your heart. God then acts *immediately* on your soul; and the love of him which you then experience is as immediately breathed into you by the Holy Ghost as if you had lived seventeen hundred years ago. Change the term: say, God then *assists* you to love him? Well, and is not this this immediate assistance? Say, His Spirit *concurs* with yours. You gain no ground. It is immediate concurrence or none at all. God, a Spirit, acts upon your spirit.[8]

His word to the Moravians would be the same. Grace, though immediate, is normally through means.

Having now described the means of grace and their essential role for salvation, let us look at how baptism is related to the other means of grace and in what way it is itself a means of grace.

Baptism and the Means of Grace

The linkage between baptism and other means of grace lies in its being the sacrament of initiation. Wesley in "A Treatise on Baptism" (1758) makes this its defining feature, calling baptism "the initiatory sacrament, which enters us into covenant with God."[9] By placing this definition early in the treatise Wesley implies initiation is the aspect of baptism that governs all else.

In the second portion of "A Treatise on Baptism," where he outlines the benefits of baptism, Wesley notes two that directly flow from its initiatory character. First, just as circumcision was the way to enter the old covenant, so baptism is the means of entering the new. Wesley understands this covenant fundamentally as promise: God will give God's people a new heart and remember their sins no more.[10] Second, through "baptism we are admitted into the church and consequently made members

8. Wesley, "Farther Appeal," 171–72.
9. Wesley, "Treatise on Baptism," 188.
10. Wesley, "Treatise on Baptism," 191.

of Christ its head." From this union with Christ "proceeds the influence of his grace on those that are baptized;" from "union with the Church, a share in all its privileges and in all the promises Christ made to it."[11]

The two key words in this set of benefits are "promise" and "grace." We enter into a covenantal community, the body of Christ, in which we are recipients of the promises of God, most especially forgiveness of sins (justification) and a new heart (sanctification). These promises become reality in our lives through grace. While Wesley does not mention means of grace in the "Treatise," as we have seen he is abundantly clear through-out his writings that the normative way "the influence of his grace" is experienced "on those that are baptized" is through means of grace.

Wesley is not insisting in a rigid way that baptism is the precondi-tion for receiving the promise of salvation. Nor does he believe baptism is absolutely necessary for salvation, for "If it were every Quaker must be damned, which I can in no wise believe."[12] Wesley is not mandating a chronological sequence but making a theological connection: the *pur-pose* of baptism is initiation into the covenantal community wherein we find the means of grace. This covenantal community in which baptism initiates us is both itself shaped by means of grace and through means of grace shapes those who are in it. Thus, we can describe this community as that which is shaped by the biblical narrative, relational in nature, and missional in purpose.

First, through the means of grace it is shaped by the story of what God has done in creation and redemption, most centrally in and through Jesus Christ. Scripture preeminently tells this story, which is then taught, preached, and lived out. The Lord's Supper both tells and enacts this story. These, along with prayers and hymns, identify the God we encoun-ter, worship, and serve. Participants in this community are then likewise shaped by the story, seeking the new life it promises and to become the disciples it describes.

Second, means of grace make the community highly relational. Worship itself involves our response to hearing God's word and the in-vitation to God's table. Prayer, at its heart, is conversation with God. But the relational nature of the community is not only manifested in our re-lationship with God, it is also in our relationship with one another. At the Lord's Supper we not only give thanks to God and commune with Christ,

11. Wesley, "Treatise on Baptism," 191.
12. Wesley, "Letters to the Revd. Gilbert Boyce," 425.

we also commune with one another. We also have conversation with one another to enable us to discern what it actually means to love and serve God in our world, and we share testimonies to what God has done and is doing in our lives and in the world. This twofold relationship with God and one another is essential to our growing in the knowledge and love of God as well as in love for our neighbor.

Third, the missional nature of the community is expressed through those means of grace that are works of mercy. These are the primary ways we participate in God's mission in world. Works of mercy move us outside the community as well as deepen community itself. Through evangelism, nurturing the Christian formation of others, meeting the basic needs of others for food, clothing, shelter, medical care and the like, and working to change unjust social conditions, we live out the love of God in the world. As we do this, as in all means of grace, we too are continually transformed by the Holy Spirit, enabling us to increasingly love others as God has loved us.

Baptism as a Means of Grace

It is when we move from the initiatory role of baptism to the consideration of baptism as itself a means of grace that the interpretative difficulties intensify. This is sometimes seen as a tension between a sacramental and an evangelical understanding of baptism, a tension that runs through Wesley's theology but, at least with respect to baptism, he doesn't fully resolve. This is not to say that Wesley himself was incoherent on this subject, only that whatever resolution of the tension he might have had he did not share with his contemporaries and descendants.

In "A Treatise on Baptism," we see Wesley's sacramental side most fully, especially in two of the benefits of baptism he names. The first is that in baptism we "are made children of God" in that by "the water of baptism, we are regenerated or born again." He is careful to note that it is not "the outward washing" but "the inward grace, which added thereto, makes it a sacrament." Through baptism "a principle of grace is infused, which will not be wholly taken away, unless we quench the Holy Spirit of God by long-continued wickedness."[13] Here is an unambiguous claim for baptismal regeneration. The other benefit flows from this one: "In consequence of our being made children of God, we are heirs of the

13. Wesley, "Treatise on Baptism," 191–92.

kingdom of heaven." Thus "as it admits us into the Church here, so into glory hereafter."[14]

One clarification does need to be made about Wesley's language here. As Randy Maddox observes, Wesley's use of the inherited language of "infused grace" is not be literally understood in a way that subverts the essentially relational nature of baptism.[15] What we receive in baptism is the Holy Spirit; not something given by God but the presence of God.

In his more evangelical discussions of baptism, Wesley never repudiates baptismal regeneration. But his emphasis there is not on defending baptism as a sacrament—a means of grace—but in denying that being baptized ensures that one is now a Christian. In "The Marks of the New Birth" (1748), a decade prior to his publication of the "Treatise," Wesley insists, "The question is not what you was made in baptism (do not evade!) but what you are now."[16] A few paragraphs later he makes this exhortation: "Lean no more on the staff of that broken reed, that ye *were* born again in baptism. Who denies that ye were then made 'children of God and heirs of the kingdom of heaven'? But notwithstanding this, ye are now children of the devil; therefore ye must be born again."[17] To be a Christian is to have the marks of the new birth, especially faith, hope, and love. To those who lack those marks Wesley does not deny they were "born of water and the Spirit;" rather, he insists they no longer are children of God.[18]

In his 1760 sermon "The New Birth," written just two years after the "Treatise," Wesley provides the most complete discussion of his "evangelical" understanding of baptism. There he makes two important distinctions. First, he says that "baptism is not the new birth: they are not one and the same thing."[19] With his Church of England Wesley holds that a sacrament consists of two parts: an outward and visible sign and the inward and spiritual grace that is signified. Receiving the outward sign (water) is of no avail if the inward grace (and the new birth it gives) is absent.

---

14. Wesley, "Treatise on Baptism," 192.

15. Maddox, *Responsible Grace*, 225.

16. Wesley, "Sermon 18, 'Marks of the New Birth,'" 428.

17. Wesley, "Sermon 18, 'Marks of the New Birth,'" 430.

18. Wesley, "Sermon 18, 'Marks of the New Birth,'" 428.

19. Wesley, "Sermon 45, 'The New Birth,'" 196.

Wesley imagines a sinner responding to his exhortation to be born again in this way: "I defy your new doctrine; I need not be born again. I was born again when I was baptized. What! Would you have me deny my baptism?"[20] To this Wesley responds, "You have already denied your baptism; and that in the most effectual manner. You have denied it a thousand times and a thousand times; and you do so still day by day. For in our baptism you renounced the devil and all his works. Whenever therefore you give place to him again, whenever you do any of the works of the devil, then you deny your baptism."[21] The issue here is not whether baptism is a means of grace or whether God is faithful to the baptismal covenant. The issue is our faithfulness to that covenant.

The second distinction Wesley makes is "that as the new birth is not the same thing with baptism, so it does not always accompany baptism; they do not constantly go together." The reference here is to adults, not infants, for "our Church supposes that all who are baptized in their infancy are at the same time born again."[22] Thus, for infants baptism is always the means to a new birth; for adults it may or may not be. This in no way disqualifies baptism from being a means of grace, because Wesley is clear that *any* means of grace, when done without a degree of faith, or desire for God, becomes a dead formalism.

Wesley indicated early in his ministry that in the case of adults, baptism did not automatically lead to a new birth. In 1739, for example, Wesley wrote:

> Of the adults I have known baptized lately, only one was at that time born again, in the full sense of that work; that is, found a thorough inward change, by the love of God filling her heart. Most of them were only born again in a lower sense; that is, received the remission of their sins. And some (as it has since too plainly appeared) neither in one sense or the other.[23]

This account reflects Wesley's early failure to distinguish between the new birth and Christian perfection (the love of God filling the heart, what he calls here new birth in the "full sense"). But what it does show is that he sees baptism having varying effects or even none at all upon adults,

20. Wesley, "Sermon 45, 'The New Birth,'" 199.
21. Wesley, "Sermon 45, 'The New Birth,'" 200.
22. Wesley, "Sermon 45, 'The New Birth,'" 197.
23. Wesley, "January 25, 1739," 32.

depending on where they are in the way of salvation and whether or not they had a degree of faith.

In a much later account (1760) Wesley records the baptismal regeneration of an adult: "I baptized a gentlewoman at the Foundery; the peace she immediately found was a fresh proof, that the outward sign, duly received, is always accompanied by inward grace."[24] Here he doesn't doubt that God is at work in baptism, but the element that makes it effectual is that it be "duly received," that is, by faith.

The distinctions Wesley makes in "The New Birth" are not in direct opposition to what we find in the "Treatise." Nonetheless there is a clear difference in emphasis. In "The New Birth" Wesley implies that many if not all persons have fallen away from their baptism. Even more, he stresses the discontinuity between the sign and that which it signifies much more strongly than he does in the "Treatise."

This has led scholars to try to find a theological way to hold together these "sacramental" and "evangelical" emphases in Wesley. Bernard Holland argues for a clear distinction between infant and adult baptism. While Wesley consistently affirms baptismal regeneration in infants, Holland believes this is a new birth in a limited sense, noting that in the "Treatise" Wesley does not mention the benefit of the infusion of a principle of grace when he directly discusses infant baptism. Holland concludes from this that only an adult new birth includes the reception of the Holy Spirit.[25] With regard to adults, baptism, like all means of grace, can convey prevenient or convincing grace as well as justifying or sanctifying; thus, adults may or may not be born anew through baptism. Holland thus holds that while infants have an initial new birth through baptism, all persons, baptized or not, need a full new birth as adults.[26]

Ole Borgen disagrees with Holland, arguing instead that Wesley does not presuppose all of his listeners need a new birth, only those— admittedly a large number—who had by long-continued wickedness lost the grace of their infant baptism.[27] Moreover, nowhere in Wesley do we find a distinction between the new birth in infants and the new birth in adults. There is one new birth, which can be both lost and regained.

24. Wesley, "February 5, 1760," 240.

25. Holland, Baptism in Early Methodism, 56–59.

26. Holland, Baptism in Early Methodism, 73.

27. Borgen, John Wesley on the Sacraments, 157–59, 179–81.

More recently, Ted Campbell has underscored the point that while Wesley

> did speak of regeneration both as a result of infant baptism and as a result of adult conversion, it is not necessary to see these as different things. The opening sentence of the account of Aldersgate seems to imply that what was recovered in the conversion experience was precisely the grace that had been given to Wesley in his baptism and subsequently lost by sin.[28]

In distinguishing between the outward sign and inward grace in such a way that they do not invariably occur together in adult baptism Wesley is reflecting "a consistent hallmark of Reformed sacramental theology and spirituality."[29]

Where, then, does this leave baptism *as* a means of grace? Or, put differently, if baptism is a means of grace, why do so many fall away from their infant baptism and why are the results of adult baptism so inconsistent?

Causes of the Inefficacy of Baptism

Wesley does not consider baptism as ineffective from the standpoint of grace. God is faithful and will be present in baptism. But grace is not irresistible—it enables and invites our response. The problem with baptism has to do with our faithfulness. Wesley states this succinctly in the "Treatise," "baptism doth now save us, if we live answerable thereto; if we repent, believe, and obey the gospel."[30] What is needed on our part, in short, is faith, which is both knowing and trusting in God. Like all means of grace, baptism is relational; while complete as a divine action it remains incomplete without our response in faith.

The problem Wesley saw as prevalent in his own Church of England was the lack of faith, which led to formalism, a kind of going through the motions of Christian practice without actually knowing God. Methodism was designed as a remedy to his situation. Writing in 1743, Wesley describes Methodism's mission this way:

---

28. Campbell, "Conversion and Bap," 167.
29. Campbell, "Conversion and Baptism," 168.
30. Wesley, "Treatise on Baptism," 192.

> We see—and who does not?—the numberless follies and mis-
> eries of our fellow creatures. We see on every side men of no
> religion at all or men of a lifeless formal religion. We are grieved
> at the sight, and should greatly rejoice if, by any means, we
> might convince some there is a better religion to be attained, a
> religion worthy of God that gave it. And this we conceive to be
> no other than love: the love of God and all mankind; the loving
> God with all our heart and soul and strength, as having first
> loved *us*, as the fountain of all the good we have received and of
> all we ever hope to enjoy; and the loving every soul which God
> hath made . . . as our own soul.[31]

It was the absence of this love, of which new birth is the beginning, that so concerned Wesley. This is precisely the life baptism is supposed to give us. However, there were so many who were baptized and yet far from this life of love. Methodism addressed this by proclaiming the promise of new life and then enabling persons to grow in their faith through spiritual disciplines and accountability to those disciplines. Through these disciplines they maintained their focus on relationship with God and their neighbor. In bringing this faith to the church, practices that had once been experienced as formalism now became means of grace through which they encountered the transforming power of God.

This Methodist practice echoes that of the early church, in which persons who were serious inquirers into the Christian faith were enrolled in the catechumenate. These catechumens, or "hearers," attended the preaching of the word but were dismissed prior to the celebration of the Lord's Supper in order to participate in practices of Christian formation. After two to three years, they could make known their desire to profess their faith, become a Christian, and join the covenant community. They then began a more intensive process of formation which culminated in baptism, often during the Easter vigil. It was then the new Christian received the Lord's Supper for the first time. Baptism was clearly the sacrament of initiation for the early church.[32]

Wesley recognized that his societies, classes, and spiritual disciplines, with their focus on a regular participation in the means of grace, were in many ways the functional equivalent of that early Christian catechumenate. In the Wesleys' movement, those awakened to their

31. Wesley, "An Earnest Appeal," 45.

32. For further examination of the catechesis process used in the early church, see Hippolytus, *On the Apostolic Tradition*; Krieder, *Change of Conversion*; Powers, "*Ecclesia Semper Sanctificanda.*"

condition as sinners were enrolled in a class meeting and committed themselves to keep the Methodist discipline. There they entered a formative relationship with God with the goal of knowing that their sins had been forgiven and to receive a new birth. Yet, this was not a replication of the catechumenal process. Membership in a class was lifelong. Moreover, most class members already had been baptized as infants and, as part of their discipline, were expected to receive the Lord's Supper as often as possible.

Implications for a Wesleyan Practice of Baptism

What might this mean for our practice of baptism today? Perhaps the most important thing is to remember that the primary purpose of baptism is *initiation*. Baptism has as its purpose placing us into a community centered on and shaped by the means of grace. But for this initiation to take place, there needs to be a process of Christian formation associated with baptism, ideally as a precondition for adults. That is, we need a set of practices that accomplish something like the catechumenate of primitive Christianity and the classes and discipline of early Methodism. Without something like this, the act of baptism could fall short of its initiatory purpose.

The baptism of children requires a reordering of the process of initiation. Baptized children need something like a post-baptismal catechumenate, through which they participate in a period of Christian formation leading to their own profession of faith. Although Wesley himself did not emphasize a rite of confirmation, many of his descendants have in effect made the confirmation class preparatory to a mature profession of faith. The problem is that confirmation all too often became a matter of learning information rather than an experience of formation that included the heart and the life.

Because it initiates us into the covenant community, baptism is an explicitly Christian act, bringing us into a distinctively Christian way of life. The most important issue this raises for local churches is how the means of grace actually function within the community. It does little good to initiate persons into a community in which the means of grace are practiced infrequently or in a perfunctory way. The process of initiation needs to be organically linked to the means of grace that are themselves faithfully practiced.

Another implication of the initiatory purpose has to do with infant baptism. It suggests that the baptism of infants should be limited to those who are likely to be nurtured in the church. The question to be asked by a pastor when there is a request for infant baptism is: into what will the child be initiated? While the answer is not always clear in particular cases, the norm is that if it is not into a community where God's story is told and God is worshipped and served, then it would be better not to baptize the child.

Sometimes the baptism of infants, regardless of whether the children will be part of a Christian community, is defended by appealing to their receiving prevenient grace. But all infants, whether or not they are baptized, have prevenient grace. Prevenient grace, as a universal grace, is implicitly christological, but baptism is *explicitly* christological—it is a distinctively Christian act through which one enters the covenant community and begins to engage in those practices of worship, community and service that form and shape a Christian life. To baptize someone who will not be part of that community undercuts the purpose of baptism.

Nor is baptism necessary for an infant's eternal destiny. At the time he wrote the "Treatise," Wesley believed it was. The first benefit to baptism he mentions "is the washing away the guilt of original sin by the application of the merits of Christ's death." He specifically includes infants, "for they too die; therefore, they have sinned: but not by actual sin; therefore by original; else what need have they of the death of Christ?"[33] Randy Maddox notes that Wesley may have been uneasy with this claim at the time he published the essay. The "Treatise" was an abridgement of an earlier work by Wesley's father, and Wesley "removed the characterization of this guilt as damning" from his own published version. What is clear is that by 1776 Wesley had decisively rejected this view, arguing instead that the guilt of original sin is universally covered by prevenient grace and the death of Christ for all. As a consequence of this, infants who die go to be with God, baptized or not.[34]

Second, baptism, like all means of grace, is intrinsically *relational*. We can emphasize again the words of Wesley cited earlier, "Baptism doth now save us if we live answerable thereto"—that is, if we respond to God's grace with repentance, faith, and faithful obedience. This speaks to the nature of grace: it is not irresistible but relational; it enables and invites

33. Wesley, "Treatise on Baptism," 190.
34. Maddox, *Responsible Grace*, 224.

our response. Baptism, then, is a gracious act of God that requires a response of faith.

While baptism is intended to be the entrance into a faith relationship with God, the order may vary from person to person. For some, it may lead to an initial relationship with God; for others it may be the occasion of their justification and regeneration, and for others still, it may be the sign and seal of a relationship already begun through a prior conversion. But in all cases, baptism as an action of God requires a response of faith in Jesus Christ to the grace received through the presence of Holy Spirit.

This relational nature of baptism also has implications for baptized infants. They too need faith, but the sequence is different than for adults. Their mature profession of faith will come later, hopefully as a result of their growing up in the midst of the practices and people of a Christian community. If they are in a vital community then it may well be the case that they will always have the sense of knowing God and growing in new life from the time of their baptism.

Baptism is an act of God that initiates us into a covenant. Because God is faithful, we do not re-baptize, as this would call into question God's faithfulness. However, we are not always faithful. Therefore, it is appropriate for us to reaffirm our commitment to the baptismal covenant. The early Methodists did just that. Wesley had an annual Covenant Service—a practice Wesley borrowed from the Puritans—in which the Methodists remembered God's faithfulness, confessed their own unfaithfulness, and renewed their covenant with God. It is clear in Wesley's *Directions for Renewing Our Covenant with God* that the covenant being renewed is the baptismal covenant.[35] Today a number of Christian traditions practice a service more explicitly related to baptism: the renewal of the baptismal covenant. Others practice a version of Wesley's original service, revised by British Methodism to provide for more congregational response. Both of these are ways to reaffirm our faith in Jesus Christ and faithfulness to our baptismal covenant.

Third, baptism as a sacrament is intended as a means to justification and new birth. Baptism is inextricably linked to regeneration. Yet, for Wesley, as we have seen, to have been baptized as an infant or to be baptized as an adult does not guarantee that one now is born anew, and if one is not, one needs to be. This is that tension in Wesley's theology that he never directly addresses but consistently upholds. My suggestion here

---

35. On the covenant service, see Tripp, *Renewal of the Covenant.*

is that Wesleyans need to continue to embrace the tension and adopt the proposal by Ted Campbell mentioned earlier as the best explanation. The key here is to distinguish baptism from the new birth without separating them, to maintain their connection without identifying them as necessarily a single event. Thus, while they may or may not occur together, baptism always signifies the new birth, and the new birth is always the fulfillment of baptism.

With regard to infant baptism, a fruitful way to see how baptism is a means of grace is to emphasize the relational understanding that dominates Wesley's theology. In contrast to the individualistic assumptions we often have, who we are as persons is largely shaped by the story we live out of, the practices we engage in, the relationships we have, as well as the choices we make. This is true for both infants and adults. When infants are baptized, they are brought into a web of relationships and practices shaped by the story of Christ and filled with the presence and power of the Spirit. To be placed in that means of grace environment *is* to be changed, in a real though not deterministic way. Put differently, they would not be the person they are and are becoming if they had not been brought into the Christian community. Could we say this constitutes a new birth? If so, then we can account both for those who grow up always knowing Christ, leading to a mature profession of faith, and those who fall away from that relationship yet return by way of another new birth.

Ideally the church should be, for both infants and adults, a community that nurtures faith and practices love without the need for a Methodist renewal movement. In such a church baptism will be the vital sacrament it is intended to be, initiating persons into a new life of faith, hope and love and in a community formed and shaped by all the other means of grace.

Bibliography

Borgen, Ole E. *John Wesley on the Sacraments: A Theological Study*. Nashville: Abingdon, 1973.

Campbell, Ted A. "Conversion and Baptism in Wesleyan Spirituality." In *Conversion in the Wesleyan Tradition*, edited by Kenneth J. Collins and John H. Tyson, 160–74. Nashville: Abingdon, 2001.

Hippolytus. *On the Apostolic Tradition*. Translated by Alistair C. Steward. Crestwood: St. Vladimir's Seminary Press, 2001.

Holland, Bernard. *Baptism in Early Methodism*. London: Epworth, 1970.

Johnson, Maxwell E., ed. *The Rites of Christian Initiation: Their Evolution and Interpretation*. Collegeville, MN: Liturgical, 1999.

Knight, Henry K., III. *The Presence of God in the Christian Life*. Lanham, MD: Scarecrow, 1992.

Krieder, Alan. *The Change of Conversion and the Origin of Christendom*. Eugene, OR: Wipf & Stock, 1999.

Maddox, Randy L. *Responsible Grace: John Wesley's Practical Theology*. Nashville: Abingdon, 1994.

Powers, Jonathan A. "*Ecclesia Semper Sanctificanda*: Historic Models of Catechesis and the Cultivation of Social Holiness." In *The Asbury Journal* 74.1 (2019) 85–107.

Tripp, David. *The Renewal of the Covenant in the Methodist Tradition*. London: Epworth, 1969.

Wesley, John. "An Earnest Appeal to Men of Reason and Religion (1743)." In *Bicentennial Edition of the Works of John Wesley*. Vol. 11, *The Appeals to Men of Reason and Religion and Certain Related Open Letters*, edited by Gerald R. Cragg, 37–94. Nashville: Abingdon, 1987.

———. "A Farther Appeal to Men of Reason and Religion, Part I." In *Bicentennial Edition of the Works of John Wesley*. Vol. 11, *The Appeals to Men of Reason and Religion and Certain Related Open Letters*, edited by Gerald R. Cragg, 95–202. Nashville: Abingdon, 1987.

———. "February 5, 1760." In *Bicentennial Edition of the Works of John Wesley*. Vol. 21, *Journals and Diaries IV*, edited by W. Reginald Ward and Richard P. Heitzenrater, 240. Nashville: Abingdon, 1992.

———. "Letters to the Revd. Gilbert Boyce, (May 22, 1750)." In *Bicentennial Edition of the Works of John Wesley*. Vol. 26, *Letters II*, edited by Frank Baker, 424–26. Nashville: Abingdon, 1982.

———. "January 25, 1739." In *Bicentennial Edition of the Works of John Wesley*. Vol. 19, *Journals and Diaries II (1738–1743)*, edited by W. Reginald Ward and Richard P. Heitzenrater, 32. Nashville: Abingdon, 1976.

———. "Sermon 12, 'The Witness of Our Own Spirit.'" In *Bicentennial Edition of the Works of John Wesley*. Vol. 1, *Sermons I*, edited by Albert Outler, 299–313. Nashville: Abingdon, 1984.

———. "Sermon 16, 'The Means of Grace.'" In *Bicentennial Edition of the Works of John Wesley*. Vol. 1, *Sermons I*, edited by Albert C. Outler, 376–97. Nashville: Abingdon, 1984.

———. "Sermon 18, 'Marks of the New Birth.'" In *Bicentennial Edition of the Works of John Wesley*. Vol. 1, *Sermons I*, edited by Albert Outler, 415–30. Nashville: Abingdon, 1984.

———. "Sermon 45, 'The New Birth.'" In *Bicentennial Edition of the Works of John Wesley*. Vol. 2, *Sermons II*, edited by Albert C. Outler, 186–201. Nashville: Abingdon, 1985.

———. "Sermon 85, 'On Working Out Our Own Salvation.'" In *Bicentennial Edition of the Works of John Wesley*. Vol. 3, *Sermons III*, edited by Albert C. Outler, 199–209. Nashville: Abingdon, 1986.

———. "Sermon 92, 'On Zeal.'" In *Bicentennial Edition of the Works of John Wesley*. Vol. 3, *Sermons III*, edited by Albert C. Outler, 308–21. Nashville: Abingdon, 1986.

———. "A Treatise on Baptism." In *Works of John Wesley*. Vol. 10, *Letters, Essays, Dialogs, Addresses*, edited by Thomas Jackson, 188–201. Grand Rapids: Zondervan, 1958–59.

CHAPTER 11

Baptism and People
with Developmental Disabilities

The Mysteries of Grace and Transforming Love

DAVID F. WATSON, UNITED THEOLOGICAL SEMINARY

DISCOURSE ON THEOLOGICAL AND biblical topics related to people with disabilities has grown considerably over the last twenty-five years. Nancy Eiesland's 1994 book, *The Disabled God: Toward a Liberatory Theology of Disability*,[1] was a fountainhead in the field of theology as it relates to people with disabilities. The scholarly discussion in this area has flourished since its publication. As we think through baptism in the Wesleyan tradition, we are aided by some of the questions and insights of the ongoing conversation around theology and people with disabilities. About one in five people in the United States lives with some form of disability.[2] About 15 percent of children between the ages of three and seventeen in the United States has some form of developmental disability.[3] According to a 2017 report of the Centers for Disease Control and Prevention, the number of children being diagnosed with developmental disabilities is on

1. Eiesland, *Disabled God*.
2. "Nearly 1 in 5 People Have a Disability."
3. "CDC's Work on Developmental Disabilities."

the rise.[4] Statistics such as these underscore the need both for theological clarity regarding people with disabilities and ecclesiological practices that bring people of all abilities together in the ministries of the church.

The topic of this volume is baptism in the Wesleyan tradition, and this chapter will take up the matter of baptism of people with developmental disabilities. We might begin by asking, first of all, why this is a topic in need of discussion. Does the sacrament of baptism affect people with developmental disabilities differently than it does "typical" people? I will argue that it does not, but the answer is not entirely obvious at first glance. The Wesleyan tradition, at least in its historic and evangelical forms, tends to emphasize personal conversion. We baptize infants, who are unable to understand what is happening to them, but we expect that as they mature, they will make a decision to grow in the grace God poured out upon them at baptism. In other words, we assume the baptized infant will grow into a person who will eventually be able to make a personal decision to follow Jesus. What about people, though, who will never reach a state of intellectual development that will allow them to make a conscious decision to accept Christ? How should we think about the efficacy of baptism in such cases?

My interest in theology and people with disabilities became quite personal after my wife gave birth to our second son, Sean, who has Down syndrome. At the writing of this article, Sean is twelve years old. He speaks in complex sentences, though his speech is difficult to understand. He reads well and knows his multiplication tables. That said, there is no question that he is delayed in many aspects of his development in comparison to "typical" children of his age. Sean is a baptized Christian. He attends church with us each week. He sometimes prays at meals for our family. He loves to watch *VeggieTales*. With regard to his faith development, however, it is difficult to tell what concept he has of God, sin, or salvation. Will Sean ever be able to "make a decision for Christ"? Will he ever own his salvation in a personal way? The answers to these questions are unclear because we do not have a clear sense of the extent to which he will continue to develop intellectually. What, then, is the relationship between his baptism and his relationship to God in light of Wesleyan theology? The question becomes more acute with people whose cognitive impairments are more severe.

The problem I will address in this chapter is: for Wesleyans, what is the significance of baptism for people with developmental disabilities,

---

4. Zablotsky et al., "Estimated Prevalence of Children."

since they function with diminished cognitive capacities compared to "typical" people? I will address this question first by clarifying some terms commonly used in discussion of people with disabilities. I will then move into a discussion of John Wesley's understanding of baptism, both of infants and adults. Next, I will discuss the implications of Wesley's understanding of baptism for people with developmental disabilities, particularly in light of infant baptism.

What Are Developmental Disabilities?

Before going further we should clarify the definition of "developmental disabilities." Scholars who work in the field of disability studies often distinguish between "impairment" and "disability."[5] An impairment is a physical, mental, or emotional condition that is generally considered atypical. Examples of impairments might include a missing limb, a chemical imbalance causing depression, or an extra copy of the twenty-first chromosome (Down syndrome). A disability, however, is the set of social effects caused by the impairment. For example, in the case of a person with a spinal injury requiring him or her to use a wheelchair, the impairment is the injury to the spine. The disability, however, emerges from the fact that our world is not generally "wheelchair friendly." Think about the effect that a few small steps leading up to the front porch of a house can have on this person.

The term "developmental disability" refers to the effects of cognitive impairments. According to John Swinton, this term "refers to a group of human beings who are deemed by the majority within society to have limited communicational skills, restricted or no self-care skills, significant intellectual and/or cognitive difficulties, and who essentially will be dependent upon others for even their most basic needs throughout their lives."[6] This description is inclusive of a wide range of abilities. For example, some people with developmental disabilities might fall into

5. This is sometimes called the "social model" of disability. For a discussion of the most common models used in disability studies, see Moss and Schipper, "Introduction," 3–4.

6. Swinton, "The Body of Christ Has Down's Syndrome," 67. The CDC defines developmental disabilities as "a group of conditions due to an impairment in physical, learning, language, or behavior areas. These conditions begin during the developmental period, may impact day-to-day functioning, and usually last throughout a person's lifetime." See "CDC's Work on Developmental Disabilities."

the category of those with "profound disabilities," which Hans Reinders describes as "a developmental state of mental development that has not gone beyond a toddler's stage of development."[7] On the other hand, some people with Down syndrome will demonstrate the characteristics of this description in much more limited ways. It is not unusual today, for example, for people with Down syndrome to read and write, possess conversational skills sufficient for day-to-day interactions, and live semi-independently. When we refer to people with developmental disabilities, then, we refer to a broad swath of abilities and conditions.

Questions regarding the effects of baptism are most acute when we are confronted with people with profound disability. Some people with developmental disabilities will in time be able to answer for themselves in the acts of baptism, confirmation, and joining the church. Others, however, will never reach this level of intellectual development. Unlike most infants who are baptized, they will at no point in their lives be able to answer for themselves regarding their faith or make a conscious decision to follow Jesus. Yet as we will see, baptism of people with even the most profound disabilities is just as important as the baptism of any other person. Regardless of intellectual ability, every person is the proper recipient of the grace of God mediated through baptism.

Wesley, Baptism, and People with Developmental Disabilities

The category of "disability" did not exist in eighteenth century. In Wesley's day, people with serious cognitive impairments were given labels such as "idiots" or "imbeciles." Fortunately, we have developed language since that time that is more accurate, more sensitive, and simply kinder. The baptism of people with intellectual impairments is not a topic that Wesley took up. Nevertheless, in his "Treatise on Baptism," he provides several key affirmations regarding baptism that are helpful as we think through the significance of baptism for people with developmental disabilities. One of the central concepts of Wesley's "Treatise" is that the primary agent in baptism is God. We do play a part through the liturgy and our obedience to Christ's command to baptize (Matt 28:19). The real action, however, is divine action.

7. Hans Reinders, *Receiving the Gift of Friendship*, 48.

The significance of divine action is especially apparent with regard to the baptism of infants and young children, a practice that corresponds in some ways to the baptism of people with developmental disabilities. The United Methodist teaching document *By Water and the Spirit* clearly makes this connection. It states, "There are no conditions of human life that exclude persons from the sacrament of baptism."[8] Were we to maintain an insistence on baptism only after a profession of faith by the recipient, our perspective might be different. The theological rationale for infant baptism, however, applies to the baptism of people even with the most profound developmental disabilities.

> Through the Church, God claims infants as well as adults to be participants in the gracious covenant of which baptism is the sign. This understanding of the workings of divine grace also applies to persons who for reasons of handicapping conditions or other limitations are unable to answer for themselves the questions of the baptismal ritual. While we may not be able to comprehend how God works in their lives, our faith teaches us that God's grace is sufficient for their needs and, thus, they are appropriate recipients of baptism.[9]

If the power of God is truly "made perfect in weakness" (2 Cor 12:9),[10] we must learn to acknowledge that power at work within those among us whose impairments are most severe.

We may not understand, then, how God's grace is at work in the life of a person with significant developmental disabilities through baptism, but we trust that it is. We certainly do not fully understand how God's grace is at work through baptism in infants and young children, though we may observe the effects of God's grace upon their lives as they get older. Even in adults, however, we never fully understand how God's grace is at work through baptism. Like the Lord's Supper, baptism is a holy mystery, a truth that we know by divine revelation and affirm, yet the depths of which surpass our ability to comprehend. As Wesley put it, "Nor is it an objection of any weight against [infant baptism] that we cannot comprehend how this work can be wrought in infants: for neither can we comprehend how it is wrought in a person of riper years."[11]

---

8. United Methodist Church, *By Water and the Spirit*, 8.

9. United Methodist Church, *By Water and the Spirit*, 9.

10. All Scripture citations in this chapter are from the NRSV.

11. Wesley, "Sermon 45, 'The New Birth,'" 197.

Removal of the Guilt of Original Sin

Despite its mysterious nature, Wesley does affirm several rather specific ways in which God is at work in baptism, whether of infants, children, or adults. First of all, through baptism God removes "the guilt of original sin, by the application of the merits of Christ's death."[12] It is hard to overstate the significance of the doctrine of original sin in Wesley's theological anthropology. His ideas of justification, new birth, and sanctification only make sense with reference to it. Wesley holds that, as the posterity of Adam, all people bear a degree of guilt for that first rebellion against God.[13] Likewise, each of us has inherited a deeply rooted propensity to sin. Wesley writes of "an inward constraining power, flowing from the dictate of corrupt nature."[14] By his death, however, Christ atoned for sin. Charles Wesley puts this beautifully in "Hark! The Herald Angels Sing":

> Come, Desire of nations, come!
> Fix in us Thy humble home:
> Rise, the woman's conqu'ring seed,
> Bruise in us the serpent's head;
> Adam's likeness now efface,
> Stamp Thine image in its place:
> Final Adam from above,
> Reinstate us in Thy love.[15]

Baptism mediates to us the grace by which the image of Christ effaces the image of Adam, thereby reinstating us in the love of God. It is an outward sign of an invisible grace, the mediation to us of the merits of Christ.

Some people with developmental disabilities are so profoundly impaired that they are unable to commit any sin in the sense of "a willing transgression of a known law."[16] Others, like my son Sean, are entirely capable of sinning. They are capable of doing both right and wrong, and, at least in many cases, knowing the difference. Whether or not a person has committed any sin, however, each of us still bears the stain of original sin, which only God can remove. Wesley writes:

12. Wesley, "Treatise on Baptism," 190.
13. See, e.g., Wesley, "Doctrine of Original Sin," 402.
14. Wesley, "Romans 7:21," 545.
15. Wesley, "Hark! The Herald Angels Sing," 240.
16. Wesley, "Plain Account," 19.6.A.

this original stain cleaves to every child of man; and . . . hereby they are children of wrath, and liable to eternal damnation. It is true, the Second Adam has found a remedy for the disease which came upon all by the offence of the first. But the benefit of this is to be received through the means which he hath appointed; through baptism in particular, which is the ordinary means he hath appointed for that purpose; and to which God hath tied us, though he may not have tied himself.[17]

Entrance into Covenant with God

Wesley also teaches that we enter into covenant with God through baptism. In this sense, baptism replaces circumcision as the sign and means of the covenant.[18] The covenant that God established with Israel (Gen 17:7–8) is now available to all humankind through baptism. We may surmise from Wesley's writings that he would affirm this covenant extends to people of all abilities. In fact, he insists that no agency on the part of the baptized person is necessary in order to establish the covenant.

Wesley addresses this question directly in his discussion of infant baptism. Wesley offers for a few reasons that infants are capable of entering into covenants. First, the "custom of nations and common reason of mankind prove that infants may enter into a covenant."[19] In other words, he says, there are examples of infants entering into covenants, though not through their own agency. An infant who is an heir to the throne, for example, would be obliged by, and perhaps benefit from, certain political covenants that others have made on his or her behalf. As we would expect from Wesley, however, an even stronger proof is derived from Scripture, specifically, Deut 29:10–12: "Ye stand this day all of you before the Lord, your captains, with all the men of Israel; your little ones, your wives and the stranger, that thou shouldest enter into covenant with the Lord thy God."[20] Wesley reasons that "God would never have made a covenant with little ones, if they had not been capable of it."[21] For the reader who is not yet convinced, Wesley adds yet another argument that infants and children may enter into covenants, also derived from Scripture. He

17. Wesley, "A Treatise on Baptism," 193.

18. Wesley, "A Treatise on Baptism," 191.

19. Wesley, "A Treatise on Baptism," 193.

20. Wesley, "A Treatise on Baptism," 194.

21. Wesley, "A Treatise on Baptism," 194.

notes that infants were included in the Abrahamic covenant (Gen 17). "They were included in it, they had a right to it and to the seal of it; as an infant heir has a right to his estate, though he cannot yet have actual possession."[22] He continues:

> Now, the same promise that was made to [Abraham], the same covenant that was made with him, was made 'with his children after him.' (Gen. xvii. 7; Gal. iii. 7.) And upon that account it is called 'an everlasting covenant.' In this covenant children were also obliged to what they knew not, to the same faith and obedience with Abraham. And so they are still; as they are still equally entitled to all the benefits and promises of it.[23]

Just as circumcision, and later the law, were signs of God's covenant with Israel, so baptism is now the sign of God's covenant through Christ, and just as infants were able to enter the former, so they are now able to enter the latter.

The arguments that Wesley makes in order to demonstrate that children may properly enter into covenants are not easily applicable to people with developmental disabilities today. We should bear in mind, though, that the problem he is trying to address regarding infants and children entering into covenants is the claim that they do not possess the intellectual capacities and judgments that some might deem necessary to enter into a covenant. Wesley's crucial point is that their inability to make such judgments does not preclude their entrance into covenants. He insists that, as part of a community, others make this decision for them. Our covenant with God through Christ is not a strictly individual relationship. On the contrary, it is unavoidably communal. It is, after all, an admission into the church (discussed below). Like many human covenants, those covenants that God has established, first through Israel and then through Christ, are such that even those who do not possess the necessary agency to enter into them may do so. It follows, then, that like infants and children, people with developmental disabilities may also enter into God's covenant through Christ by virtue of baptism and their place within the community of faith. Regardless of whether or not the baptized person is aware of the covenant into which he or she is entering, the community of faith is aware, and God is aware.

22. Wesley, "Treatise on Baptism," 194.
23. Wesley, "Treatise on Baptism," 194.

Admission into the Church

Third, we are admitted into the church in baptism, and consequently made members of the body of Christ, who is its head. In this act, we are "mystically united to Christ, and made one with him. . . . From which spiritual, vital union with him, proceeds the influence of his grace on those that are baptized; as from our union with the Church, a share in all its privileges, and in all the promises Christ has made to it."[24] This is no less the case for people with developmental disabilities than for anyone else. It is clear from Wesley's description of admission into the church that he is not talking simply about having one's name on the membership rolls of a congregation. Rather, baptism ushers us into the mystical body of Christ (Eph 1:22–23), and we thereby become recipients of the grace that God pours out on the church. The promises God has made to the church are now our promises. Again, the emphasis is upon God's action, not upon ours.

The "vital union" that extends between Christ and the church also inheres between members of the church. We are all mystically drawn together in one body. "In [Christ], the whole structure is joined together and grows into a holy temple in the Lord; in whom you also are built together spiritually into a dwelling place for God" (Eph 2:21–22). There is no reason this should apply any less to people with developmental disabilities than to "typical" people. Like the spiritual union between Christ and his body, the spiritual union between the members of that body is the work of God and independent of human cognition. Put differently, a person who cannot comprehend that he or she has been united with other Christians may be so nonetheless.

It is instructive to apply these theological ideas to a real-life situation. A local residential care center for people with severe intellectual and physical disabilities periodically brings residents to worship at the church I attend. There may be five to seven residents at a time, plus caretakers. All of the residents use motorized wheelchairs. Some seem utterly oblivious to what is happening in worship. Some seem more aware. Sometimes one or more of them will make loud noises during worship that in other contexts might be quite distracting. We have been doing this for so many years at my church, however, the worshipers seem not even to notice. These people with very serious developmental disabilities are simply accepted as part of the worshiping congregation.

24. Wesley, "Treatise on Baptism," 191.

What do they gain from being there? In most cases it is difficult to say with very much specificity. There are two related points, however, that are particularly crucial for understanding the significance of these developmentally disabled people in worship. First, the grace that God pours out on the church is not dependent upon our cognitive capacities. Perhaps a "typical" person will receive more from worship than someone with developmental disabilities, but perhaps not. Whatever we receive is entirely a gift. We do nothing to deserve it. It is simply offered to us out of the love and kindness of God who sought to reconcile himself to us through the cross of Jesus Christ.

Second, the presence of people with severe cognitive disabilities on Sunday morning visibly demonstrates the first point. These worshippers cannot sing, praise, utter prayers, or participate in other ways generally expected of worshippers. Their passivity in worship highlights the centrality of divine action. We are utterly dependent in worship upon the generosity of God. To say that these worshippers are part of the church, then, is not simply a matter of being nice, kind, or inclusive (though these are never bad ideas). Even in their passivity, they contribute to the well-being of the body. They *belong* in worship on Sunday morning, and one part of the body cannot say to another, "I have no need of you" (1 Cor 12:21). Put differently, in worship, the grace of God is at work both *in* and *through* these people with developmental disabilities.

We Are Made Children of God

Fourth, whereas we were once "'by nature children of wrath,'" in baptism we "are made the children of God."[25] In baptism, we are regenerated, "born again" (John 3:5). "[B]eing 'grafted into the body of Christ's Church, we are made the children of God by adoption and grace.'"[26] In baptism, then, there is not simply the relative change of pardon from sin, but a real change in regeneration, or the "new birth." To be clear, baptism and the new birth are not the same thing. Wesley insisted upon this point:

> For what can be more plain, than that the one is an external, the other an internal, work; that the one is a visible, the other an invisible thing, and therefore wholly different from each other?—the one being an act of man, purifying the body; the

25. Wesley, "Treatise on Baptism," 191.
26. Wesley, "Treatise on Baptism," 192.

other a change wrought by God in the soul: So that the former is
just as distinguishable from the latter, as the soul from the body,
or water from the Holy Ghost.[27]

Nevertheless, Wesley holds that the new birth ordinarily follows upon
baptism.

People of all abilities become children of God in baptism. Even when
there is no decision to become a child of God on the part of a person
with cognitive impairments, he or she nevertheless becomes a part of the
divine household. As an analogy, imagine parents who adopt a child with
profound disability. Imagine that, because she does not comprehend her
circumstances, the child is incapable of wishing to enter into the household of the parents, much less of expressing such a wish. Nevertheless,
the parents may adopt the child out of love for her. They will care for her
in ways she does not realize or understand. At some level, she may love
her adopted parents as well. In this circumstance, even though she did
not wish to become (or not to become) a child of these parents and thus
become a part of their household, she was in fact adopted by them. In
the same way, though people with profound disabilities may not have the
capacity to wish to become children of God, God will nonetheless adopt
them as children through the sacrament of baptism.

We Become Joint Heirs

For Christians, the kingdom of God is both a present and future reality.
We have already looked at some of the ways the present kingdom comes
to bear on people with developmental disabilities, and we should also note
its eschatological elements. If we are children of God, we are also "heirs of
the kingdom of heaven."[28] Here Wesley draws upon Rom 8:15–18: "For
you did not receive a spirit of slavery to fall back into fear, but you have
received a spirit of adoption. When we cry, 'Abba! Father!' it is that very
Spirit bearing witness with our spirit that we are children of God, and *if
children, then heirs, heirs of God and joint heirs with Christ*—if, in fact, we
suffer with him so that we may also be glorified with him" (italics mine).
Wesley therefore writes, "Baptism doth now save us, if we live answerable
thereto; if we repent, believe, and obey the gospel: Supposing this, as it

27. Wesley, "Sermon 45, 'The New Birth,'" IV.1.
28. Wesley, "Treatise on Baptism," 192.

admits us into the Church here, so into glory hereafter."[29] Noteworthy in this fifth benefit of baptism is the idea that baptism is a means of salvation *if* we repent, believe, and obey the gospel. By this, Wesley means that although we receive the new birth at baptism, thus becoming children of God and heirs of the kingdom, we can in time reject the gift of salvation if we so choose. He does not mean that a child who is baptized, though does not live long enough to repent, believe, and obey the gospel, cannot be saved. Rather, the baptized child is saved, but while a short life will not provide the opportunity to grow in faith, neither will it afford the opportunity to reject one's salvation.

Interestingly, Wesley does not aver that believer baptism necessarily confers the new birth in the way that infant baptism does. He does hold that the new birth and spiritual adoption "are *ordinarily* annexed to baptism."[30] Nevertheless, he writes, "as the new birth is not the same thing with baptism, so it does not always accompany baptism: They do not constantly go together. A man may possibly be "born of water," and yet not be "born of the Spirit." There may sometimes be the outward sign, where there is not the inward grace." In the case of infants, however, Wesley holds that the new birth always accompanies baptism. He continues, "I do not now speak with regard to infants: It is certain our Church supposes that all who are baptized in their infancy are at the same time born again; and it is allowed that the whole Office for the baptism of Infants proceeds upon this supposition."[31] The capacity to accept or reject God's gift of salvation is pivotal in Wesley's understanding of baptism and the new birth. The default position is that God does renew the nature of the baptized person, opening the way for him or her to grow in grace. Yet Wesley is an Arminian, and the fact that we can reject God's offer of salvation means that even the baptized may persist in an unregenerate state.[32]

Depending on the severity of their impairment and the age at which they are baptized, people with developmental disabilities may not be able to comprehend the fact of their baptism, much less its significance. Yet

29. Wesley, "Treatise on Baptism," 192.

30. Wesley, "Sermon 18, 'Marks of the New Birth,'" 428, italics mine.

31. Wesley, "Sermon 45, 'The New Birth,'" 197.

32. According to G. Stephen Blakemore, "Wesley does not posit as necessary a secondary experience of 'conversion' and repentance, except for those who have lost the grace given in the new birth through their infant baptism." See Blakemore, "By the Spirit," 184.

by analogy with Wesley's understanding of the new birth in infants, we may affirm that people with even profound disability also receive the new birth. Its effects may not be apparent in this life. There may be no capacity to express the marks of the new birth, and their effects may only become apparent in the age to come. In other words, there is a crucial eschatological dimension to baptism especially important for people with significant developmental disabilities. New birth marks us as children of God, and thus heirs of the kingdom of heaven.

Following Baptism

As noted above, the term "developmental disabilities" is quite broad. It may refer to people ranging from those with "profound disabilities" to those who can read, write, and carry on "normal" conversations, though perhaps with more difficulty than "typical" people. Churches should work to create opportunities for the ongoing faith development of people with developmental disabilities as their cognitive capacities allow. As Amos Yong writes, "In the last generation . . . there has emerged the conviction that even the baptism of intellectually disabled infants and children needs to be followed by catechism and confirmation."[33] There are now more curricula than ever before for both children and adults with various forms of cognitive impairments. Most often what is necessary is the will to implement them. In many cases, the extent to which children with cognitive disabilities will develop in their capacities to learn and understand concepts related to the life of faith is unclear. We may in fact be surprised by the extent to which they may grow in the knowledge and love of God.

Another example from the church I attend may help to illustrate how a congregation can invest in the faith development of people with disabilities. A few years ago, our church began a ministry called "Special Friends" for children with all kinds of disabilities, ranging from cerebral palsy to autism. Because the term "disabilities" comprises such a broad range of conditions, individualized, personal attention is key to meeting the needs of children with disabilities and their families in churches. My son Sean, for example, is simply unable to sit still for an hour in worship. Were we to bring him to worship, my wife and I would be unable to participate in any meaningful way, because we would be managing

33. Yong, *Theology and Down Syndrome*, 207.

Sean for most of the service. By the same token, were we simply to place him in the children's program, he could be quite disruptive. Scenarios like this are common among parents with children with disabilities, and many families, unable to find churches that are willing to help, simply quit trying.

The Special Friends program was started by an occupational therapist at our church for families like ours. During worship, Sean is paired with a buddy, and they participate in the children's program together. His buddy, moreover, is normally the same person from week to week (a young man named Zach). They know one another. Zach knows, for example that Sean may try to run out of the classroom and into worship. (Yes, he has done this.) Sean, on the other hand, looks forward to seeing his buddy each week. This makes it easier for us to get him in the car to go to church on Sunday morning. Since its inception, this program has attracted families to our church who have experienced difficulty finding congregations that will do what is necessary to welcome them on Sunday mornings.

Does Sean learn a new Bible verse every Sunday? Has he come home reciting Psalm 23? No. His cognitive impairments mean that he will not learn the faith at the same rate as other kids. Nevertheless, he does learn. The weekly rhythm of church attendance, the songs he sings with other children, the activities he engages in with other kids (with the help of his buddy), the sense of community he experiences—all of these have a formative effect on Sean, just as they would on any child. The church that vowed in his baptism to help him grow in the faith has taken concrete steps to do so, even though it has taken extra effort. In this way, Sean is able to grow in the grace of God that was imparted to him at his baptism, and the church remains faithful in its call to raise up all of its members in the faith in ways appropriate to their abilities.

Just as Sean and other people with disabilities in our congregation are formed by the church, they also help to form the church. Once again, Yong puts the matter eloquently:

> [B]aptism and the Eucharist are not only for the benefit of
> catechumens or their families. Rather, in and through baptism
> of people with intellectual disabilities and their fellowship and
> presence at the Supper the love of God touches also the entire
> congregation. . . . This is because it is the work of the Holy Spirit
> not only to birth new members into the body of Christ but also
> to transform the body of Christ through the addition of new

members. What results with Christian initiation is a fellowship that now includes "us" and "them." This act of naming and
baptising is, after all, never performed individually but is always
communially enacted. In this way, Christian baptism identifies
the church as distinct and set apart from the world.[34]

Sean does not simply receive from the church; he contributes to its
life. He is a regular, ongoing presence in our congregation. He is well
known. People expect him on Sunday mornings. The particularities that
make him who he is, including the fact that he has Down syndrome, help
to shape our community. It was, in part, his presence in the church that
first prompted the Special Friends ministry. As a result, families who were
once kept apart from the church because their children require special
accommodation are now able to attend. They thus enter more deeply into
the knowledge and love of God and enjoy the brotherhood and sister-
hood of Christ that can only be found in the church.

Conclusion

Baptism is a sacrament of the church and should be extended to all people, regardless of ability. We may not always perceive or understand how
God's grace is at work through baptism, but we trust that it is. John Wesley's "Treatise on Baptism" emphasizes again and again that the primary
agent in baptism is God. The pastor, the person baptized, the family, and
congregation all have parts to play, but the primary significance of baptism is in the grace that God pours out through it. Baptism mediates the
merits of Christ to us, cleanses us of the stain of original sin, brings us
into covenant with God, admits us into the body of Christ, and makes us
children of God and heirs of the divine kingdom.

Wesley's emphasis on the centrality of divine action in baptism
means that God is at work in the baptism of people with developmental
disabilities no less than in the baptism of "typical" people. Infant baptism
mediates the benefits of baptism no less than believer baptism. Since infants are not cognizant of what is happening to them in baptism, we can
surmise that even those who live with the most severe developmental
disabilities, and who likewise cannot comprehend what is happening to
them in baptism or make a confession of faith, nevertheless receive the
full benefits of baptism. Whether or not we understand how God is at

34. Yong, *Theology and Down Syndrome*, 212.

work in them is irrelevant. It is not always apparent how God is at work in even able-bodied adults who are baptized. In other words, baptism is a mystery. We may grasp in some ways what God is doing, but the fullness of God's grace in baptism will always surpass our understanding.

Bibliography

Blakemore, Stephen. "By the Spirit through the Water: John Wesley's 'Evangelical' Theology of Infant Baptism." *Wesleyan Theological Journal* 31.2 (1996) 184.

"CDC's Work on Developmental Disabilities." Centers for Disease Control and Prevention, May 16, 2022. https://www.cdc.gov/ncbddd/developmentaldisabilities/about.html.

Eiesland, Nancy. *The Disabled God: Toward a Liberatory Theology of Disability.* Nashville: Abingdon, 1994.

Moss, Candida R., and Jeremy Schipper. "Introduction." In *Disability Studies and Biblical Literature*, edited by Candida R. Moss and Jeremy Schipper, 3–4. New York: Palgrave MacMillan, 2011.

"Nearly 1 in 5 People Have a Disability in the U.S., Census Bureau Reports." United States Census Bureau, July 25, 2012. https://www.census.gov/newsroom/releases/archives/miscellaneous/cb12-134.html.

Reinders, Hans. *Receiving the Gift of Friendship: Profound Disability, Theological Anthropology, and Ethics.* Grand Rapids: Eerdmans, 2008.

Swinton, John. "The Body of Christ Has Down's Syndrome: Theological Reflections on Vulnerability, Disability, and Graceful Communities." *Journal of Pastoral Theology* 13.2 (Fall 2013) 67.

The United Methodist Church. *By Water and the Spirit: A United Methodist Understanding of Baptism.* Nashville: General Board of Discipleship, 1996.

Wesley, Charles. "Hark! The Herald Angels Sing." In *The United Methodist Hymnal: Book of United Methodist Worship*, 240. Nashville: United Methodist Publishing, 1989.

Wesley, John. "The Doctrine of Original Sin: According to Scripture, Reason, and Experience." In *Bicentennial Edition of the Works of John Wesley.* Vol. 12, *Doctrinal and Controversial Treatises II*, edited by Randy L. Maddox, 117–482. Nashville: Abingdon, 2012.

———. "A Plain Account of Christian Perfection." In *Bicentennial Edition of the Works of John Wesley.* Vol. 13, *Doctrinal and Controversial Treatises II*, edited by Paul Wesley Chilcote and Kenneth J. Collins, 132–91. Nashville: Abingdon, 2012.

———. "Romans 7:21." In *Explanatory Notes.* Vol. 4, *Upon the New Testament.* Salem: Schmul, 1976.

———. "Sermon 18, 'Marks of the New Birth.'" In *Bicentennial Edition of the Works of John Wesley.* Vol. 1, *Sermons I*, edited by Albert Outler, 415–30. Nashville: Abingdon, 1984.

———. "Sermon 45, 'The New Birth.'" In *Bicentennial Edition of the Works of John Wesley.* Vol. 2, *Sermons II*, edited by Albert C. Outler, 186–201. Nashville: Abingdon, 1985.

———. "A Treatise on Baptism." In *Works of John Wesley*. Vol. 10, *Letters, Essays, Dialogs, Addresses*, edited by Thomas Jackson, 188–201. Grand Rapids: Zondervan, 1958–59.

Yong, Amos. *Theology and Down Syndrome*. Waco: Baker University Press, 2007.

Zablotsky, Banjamin, et al. "Estimated Prevalence of Children with Diagnosed Developmental Disabilities in the United States, 2014–2016." National Center for Health Statistics Data Brief 291 (November 2017). https://www.cdc.gov/nchs/data/databriefs/db291.pdf.

PART III

Baptism and the Church

CHAPTER 12

Baptism and Ecclesiology

Belonging and Becoming

DION A. FORSTER, STELLENBOSCH UNIVERSITY

WHO ARE YOU? OR, stated slightly differently, to whom do you belong? These are crucial questions in contemporary society, and also in contemporary Christianity. Questions of identity and belonging dominate so much of our lives. Racial identity, national identity, gender identity, religious identity, and a host of other identifiers are coming under scrutiny—some would even say under attack—in today's society. One's appearance, language, nationality, political views, and sexual preference can all be used as means of inclusion or exclusion. This is not only a challenge in society at large, where issues related to migration, political identity, and religious identity feature as central concerns in social and political interaction. Questions of identity have also become central issues of reflection and contention within the Christian faith and the church.

One of the most topical examples of this struggle for identity and belonging in the church is the debate over the ordination of gay and lesbian clergy in The United Methodist Church (UMC).[1] Who is welcome in the church, and what are the theological criteria for belonging? If individuals or groups feel their identity and humanity is not recognized or celebrated within the church, how does this impact upon their relationship with

1. Williams, "Why a Vote on Gay Clergy."

the church or the church's relationship with them? As Christianity has spread throughout the world and different cultural, historical, social, and theological perspectives of the relationship between faith and life have emerged, it is not easy to say what exactly it means to be Christian or to define the identity and nature of the church in a globalized, and increasingly diverse, world.[2]

For Wesleyans, baptism has been an important rite to help us to understand to whom we belong and who we truly are. It is a sacrament of belonging and a sacrament of becoming. This chapter thus considers the sacrament of baptism in relation to Christian identity and ecclesiology (the doctrine of the church) and proposes that reacquaintance with John Wesley's understanding of baptism, in both objective and subjective terms, is foundational in discovering the meaning of belonging and becoming in the church.

The Challenge of a Changing Ecclesiology

What is the church? This is not an easy question to answer definitively. Any answer to the question will first have to be cognizant of various, important historical shifts that have shaped theological understandings of the church. The Nicene Creed confesses Christians believe the church is "one, holy, catholic and apostolic."[3] Yet, as James K. A. Smith points out in his book, *Desiring the Kingdom*, the culture, location, structure, and liturgy of contemporary multinational denominations, such as the UMC, is not easily compared with the churches of the New Testament or the church at the time of writing the Nicene Creed.[4] The Christian church has gone from being a marginal religious sect located on the borders of society and dispersed in homes, to a highly organized, socially powerful, cultural and religious institution with buildings, employees, and media outlets. So, in answering the question, "What is the church?" the history of the church must be considered.

Second, as has already been suggested above, the social and cultural location of the church has changed significantly throughout its history. Moreover, it would be a misnomer to believe the church occupies the same social and cultural location in every society where it exists today.

2. Forster, "New Directions," 267–75.

3. Migliore, *Faith Seeking Understanding*, 248.

4. Smith, *Desiring the Kingdom*, 19–22.

Kirsteen Kim and Sebastian Kim speak of contemporary Christianity as a "transregional" religion that "does not have one single strand of development, one centre, or a linear history but is diffuse, locally divergent and adapted to different contexts."[5] From the small house churches of China or Algeria to the Nigerian and North American mega-churches, there is a great deal of difference in structure, style, polity, and theology. Moreover, in recent decades there have been shifts not only in the diversity of expressions of Christianity and understanding of what it means to be the church, but there has also been a shift in the epicenter of Christian identity.

If one were to visit the average Christian book store, seminary library, or even watch some contemporary Christian television broadcast, one could be fooled into thinking that "Christians are un-black, un-poor, and un-young."[6] It seems that white, Protestant men from Westernized contexts have populated theological libraries with their books, academic articles, sermons, courses, and ideas. However, a significant shift has already taken place in global Christianity, as was witnessed in the February 26, 2019, vote for the "Traditional Plan" at the United Methodist General Conference in St. Louis, Missouri. Some American members of the UMC felt that the denomination had been hijacked by powerful constituencies from outside of the United States whose cultural and theological values are more conservative than the theology and values that had developed in United Methodism in the United States in recent decades.[7]

Philip Jenkins, a sociologist of religion, suggests that events such as these will become more and more common since the "center of gravity in the Christian world has shifted inexorably away from Europe, southward, to Africa and Latin America, and eastward, toward Asia. Today, the largest Christian communities on the planet are to be found in those regions."[8] Undoubtedly, the face, voice, and concerns of the epicenter of Christianity have changed.

Research shows that in the presence of such changes and challenges to theological and ecclesiological identity there are two general responses. First, there is a tendency toward *social and theological protectionism*. Second, some churches respond with a form of *sociotheological*

---

5. Kim and Kim, *Christianity as a World Religion*, sec. 200 of 10074.

6. Jenkins, *Next Christendom*, 1.

7. cf., Birch, "Retired Bible Scholar."

8. Jenkins, *Next Christendom*, 1.

assimilation and transformation.[9] As we shall see, notions of identity lie at the heart of both responses. Those who tend toward *social and theological protectionism* tend to retreat into what are considered to be "traditional" theologies and practices, such as historically held beliefs, religious values, and polity. This is fuelled by a desire to protect what is considered to be an "established" identity—also called an "in-group" identity[10]—against the challenges that emanate from "new" ideas, beliefs, and practices that emerge from forms of cultural or social difference, or persons and groupings that represent the cultural "other."[11]

Those groupings that choose a form of *sociotheological assimilation and transformation*, seek to find ways of retaining aspects of their traditional identity while making some identity shifts in relation to challenges from social, contextual, political, or theological spheres. Examples of this would be "post-congregational" churches in secularizing Western countries that have engaged in Fresh Expressions of church.[12] The life of one of these congregations may be radically different from that of a contemporary suburban church in Atlanta (for example). Some of these churches have no Sunday services, no formal liturgy, preaching, or sacraments. Many do not have buildings or clergy. They may meet in a bar or restaurant for fellowship and discipleship structured around a meal and discussion, with many of the traditional functions of the church absent or relegated to private spaces (such as adult baptisms in homes or the Eucharist as a community love feast).[13] The Fresh Expressions movement, which emerged from the Anglican Church, seems to embody what Paul Avis describes as the "vocation of Anglicanism," seeking "to hold truths together in theology and practice in order that it may hold people together."[14] This is not all that different from what John Wesley aimed to achieve in what eventually became known as Methodism. Randy Maddox writes, "Methodism should be seen, at least in the first instance, as

9. Forster, "New Directions," 267–75.

10. Forster, *(Im)Possibility of Forgiveness?*, 57–78.

11. Forster, "New Directions," 271.

12. Mission and Public Affairs Council (Church of England), *Mission-Shaped Church*; Forster, "New Directions," 272.

13. Sherwood, "As Traditional Believers"; Mission and Public Affairs Council (Church of England), *Mission-Shaped Church*.

14. Avis, *Vocation of Anglicanism*, 182.

a movement *within* the Church of England, rather than as a dissenting movement outside it."[15]

However, churches, whether protectionist or assimilative, present some challenges in relation to traditional theologies and practices of baptism. Methodism has faced this tension between ecclesiological renewal and the sacraments throughout its history. John Wesley, as an Anglican priest, ascribed to relatively traditional views of the practice and theology of baptism.[16] He believed baptism to be a sacrament that was to be administered, as was customary within Anglicanism in England and America at the time, by an ordained priest or bishop within the gathered service of worship on a Sunday.[17] Does this mean that those who stand in the Wesleyan tradition should only ever perform baptism in the same ways as Wesley did in the 1700s?

It can be argued, as some have done, that Wesley was willing to break with traditional practices of baptism as a result of his theological convictions about the importance of the sacrament in a changing church context.[18] John Wesley's commitment to the importance of administering the sacraments (including baptism) as a part of church life and Christian discipleship led him to ordain clergy to serve American Methodist communities. For instance, on September 1–2, 1784, John Wesley ordained Richard Whatcoat and Thomas Vasey to serve as priests and appointed Thomas Coke as a superintendent minister; Coke soon after ordained Francis Asbury as a priest.[19] The ordinations performed by Wesley were prompted by his concern that American Christians were being "starved of the sacraments because of the lack of clergy."[20] Wesley was clearly trying to work out how to continue to serve the sacraments in the midst

---

15. Maddox and Vickers, *Cambridge Companion to John Wesley*, 35.

16. Maddox and Vickers, *Cambridge Companion to John Wesley*, 239.

17. Please see Geordan Hammond's extensive discussion of John Wesley's views, and practice, of baptism in, Hammond, *John Wesley in America*, 67–73.

18. See Thomas C. Oden's discussion of how John Wesley engaged with new members of the Wesleyan societies who came from varied Christian traditions and so did not approach the practice of baptism in the same way: Oden, *John Wesley's Teachings*, 3:185–214.

19. cf., Puglisi, *Process of Admission*, 155; Wigger, *American Saint*, 137; Andrews, *Methodists and Revolutionary America*, 66; Vickers, *Thomas Coke*, 72; Richey, *Methodism in the American Forest*, 22.

20. Grass, *Modern Church History*, 95.

of contextual changes in his own time. He deemed the sacraments, as a "means of grace," essential to what it means to be Christian.[21]

So, to return to where we started, it would seem identity and ecclesiology are in constant conversation with one another in the midst of contextual change. Who we are and what who we aspire to be shapes our faith and our churches. The converse is equally true: how the church constructs its belief and practice shapes its faith and identity. The claim was made earlier that for Wesleyans baptism helps us to understand both to whom we belong as well as who we truly are—it is a sacrament of belonging and a sacrament of becoming. John Wesley's views on baptism clarify in what sense this claim can be substantiated.

John Wesley's View of Baptism as a Means of Grace

The relationship between baptism and ecclesiology is not only complex in broad Christian terms, it is also complex in Methodist and Wesleyan theologies, as has already been shown. This can be related to the complex tension that exists between the objective and subjective understandings of the sacrament in John Wesley's theological views on baptism. Wesley's baptismal theology presents the tension between the subjective and objective understandings of the sacrament by upholding baptism as objective inclusion into the church, which must be held in tension with baptism as the subjective point at which the individual's journey toward salvation begins.[22]

In his 1756 tract, "A Treatise on Baptism," John Wesley offers a fairly common view of baptism for his time.[23] In an objective sense, he states by "baptism we are admitted into the Church, and consequently made members of Christ . . ."[24] As was common among Anglicans of the time, the sacrament of baptism was seen not only as an objective sacrament of belonging to the church (i.e., membership), it was also seen as having salvific (regenerative) efficacy: "By water then, as a means, the water of baptism, we are regenerated, or born again . . ."[25] Yet, also here is a more

---

21. cf., Wesley, "Sermon 16, 'The Means of Grace,'" 381; Wesley, *Plain Account*, 14; Wesley in Williams, *John Wesley's Theology Today*, 238.

22. Maddox and Vickers, *Cambridge Companion to John Wesley*, 239–41.

23. Wesley, "Treatise on Baptism," 188–201.

24. Wesley, "Treatise on Baptism," 190.

25. Wesley, "Treatise on Baptism," 191.

subjective view—namely, that baptism initiates a salvific engagement between God and the baptized person. Wesley did not believe that baptism assured salvation, however. As *The Cambridge Companion to John Wesley* specifies, "By observation, he knew that those who had been baptized in infancy, which was the majority of persons in England, did not always live as if they were children of God and instead appeared more as children of the devil."[26] Wesley believed that baptism initiated the "washing away the guilt of original sin by the application of the merits of Christ's death."[27] However, this did not mean that the person is "regenerated" or "saved" in the act of baptism.

It is not possible to understand Wesley's views on baptism without placing them in the broader context of Wesleyan soteriology, which is a hybrid of Eastern and Western theological influences that engage the doctrines of justification and Christian perfection.[28] A great deal has been written about Wesley's understanding of the *ordo salutis*, (the 'order of salvation') and its rich interplay between God's grace and the choices and actions of human persons. Within Wesley's order of salvation, God's grace operates as "preventing or prevenient grace which elicits a first longing for God; justifying or pardoning grace, by which God brings an individual into a saving relationship; and sanctifying grace, which enables continued growth in faith."[29] For John Wesley, baptism (in a subjective theological sense) was a "means of grace" whereby God begins God's work of regeneration within the baptized person—this is by the operation of God's "prevenient grace."[30] Baptism was thus understood to be the beginning of a lifelong journey, or process, of salvation that starts with inclusion into the body of Christ—a response to God's initiating activity—and is sealed in later life through a personal commitment to the promise of Christ. In short, baptism, from Wesley's theological perspective, is understood as a sacrament of belonging and becoming.

26. Maddox and Vickers, *Cambridge Companion to John Wesley*, 239.

27. Wesley, "Treatise on Baptism," 190.

28. Forster, "On the 250th Anniversary," 1–19.

29. Maddox and Vickers, *Cambridge Companion to John Wesley*, 228.

30. See Karen B. Westerfield Tucker's discussion of the means of grace in Maddox and Vickers, *Cambridge Companion to John Wesley*, 225–44.

On Baptism and (Mis)Recognition

The reception of Wesleyan baptismal theology across the last two centuries in various social, political, and ecclesial contexts has resulted in misunderstandings and misrecognitions of the objective and subjective dynamic of baptism (as discussed in the previous section). In particular, contemporary Methodists and Wesleyans have struggled to hold the objective and subjective views of baptism in a creative theological tension with one another as Wesley did. In large measure, this theological problem has come about because of the way contemporary understandings of the human person have reshaped understandings of personal relationship to social structures, which includes changing views of personal relationship to the community of the church.

In John Wesley's England, human identity, in large measure, was still based on notions of human sanctity and divine dignity.[31] The human person was viewed in relation to religious and political structures of authority that accorded important aspects of identity and being such as rights, freedoms, and value.[32] It is worth remembering this was the beginning of the era that would usher in significant political changes (the American Declaration of Independence of 1776 and the French Revolution of 1789) as a result of emerging ideas on human dignity, equality, and freedom.[33] However, John Wesley's views on human identity and human freedom seem to be somewhat mixed. Some have described him as being "counter enlightenment"[34] and "largely a credulous and overbearing enthusiast whose devotion to biblicism and perfectionism shielded him from practical realities even in his own life."[35] There are others who describe him as a "son of the enlightenment."[36] Regardless of the view one takes, it can be safely concluded that contemporary views of the human person as having individual rights and a largely individual identity, which is free to associate or disassociate from religious and political powers, only came to the fore in the years since John Wesley's death.

---

31. Bauerschmidt, "Being Baptized," 250.

32. Loughlin, *Human Dignity*, 165–69.

33. Loughlin, *Human Dignity*, 167.

34. Thompson, "Anthropology," 41–55.

35. Maddox and Vickers, *Cambridge Companion to John Wesley*, 66; cf., Kent, *Wesley and the Wesleyans*.

36. Maddox and Vickers, *Cambridge Companion to John Wesley*, 66.

This has a significant bearing on engagement of Wesley's under-standing of the human person, as well as Wesley's understanding of the relationship between persons and social structures (such as the church). By extension it also has a bearing on the interpretation of Wesley's sote-riology, ecclesiology, and baptismal theology in relation to very different contemporary social and cultural contexts. The kind of individual identity that is commonplace in contemporary, secularized Western democracies would have been unimaginable for Wesley. Many of the functions that we now associate with the government (the registration of births, mar-riages, and deaths) were functions of the church. As Charles Taylor notes, in that period of history "baptism marked entry into the community" and "[c]onfirmation was a symbolic rite of entry into adulthood."[37] The church played a very different and significant social role in society during Wesley's time—in a sense it can be likened to some of the social functions certain governmental agencies fulfil in contemporary society. As such, it was not only a space of belonging that informed one's faith, it was neces-sary to belong to the church for one's social and political survival! This is no longer the case. As Charles Taylor rightly points out, there is scarcely a country on earth where one's primary identity and one's political be-ing are wholly dependent upon the church. Religious belonging, indeed, religious belief, is now a matter of free choice; and political agency and identity are quite separate from the church—at least in the formal sense. There has quite simply been a shift "from a society in which it was virtu-ally impossible not to believe in God, to one in which faith, even for the staunchest believer, is one human possibility among others."[38]

Whereas in Wesley's time it was the church, and to some extent the state, that defined what it meant to be human, "modern liberal democra-cies establish themselves on the right of individuals to define for them-selves what defines the human."[39] This has led to a crisis of identity since "a human being comes to be defined—paradoxically? incoherently?—by the right to self-definition."[40]

The net result is that in contemporary society we decide who we are and to whom we belong. Without any external claim upon our lives, or any transcending frame of reference for who we are, we have witnessed

37. Taylor, Secular Age, 439, 520, 534.
38. Taylor, Secular Age, 3.
39. Bauerschmidt, "Being Baptized," 251.
40. Bauerschmidt, "Being Baptized," 251.

significant identity struggles and painful misrecognitions. What does it mean to be human? Do all human persons have the same value, and if they do, how do we express this concretely in terms of human rights? Who has the right to decide whether someone is welcome or unwelcome in a country (as we've seen with the significant struggles around migration in Europe and the USA)? How do we deal with persons whose gender identity or sexual preference is expressed in ways that do not represent the historical or social norms of our society?

Francis Fukuyama discusses the consequences of these complex issues in his book *Identity: The Demand for Dignity and the Politics of Resentment*.[41] He suggests that the rise of populist, nationalist movements on the "right" of the political spectrum in the USA, Brazil, France, the Netherlands, Germany, and Sweden, as well as populist and activist movements on the "left," such as #MeToo and #BlackLivesMatter, all reflect a "crisis of meaning" that is a result of misrecognition and a loss of true identity.[42] We are people struggling to answer the questions, "Who am I?" and "To whom do I belong?"

We are haunted by a lack of true identity and a loss of a sense of belonging. This, in turn, has been complicated by the historical repositioning of the identity and role of Christianity and the church in many contemporary societies in which the Wesleyan tradition has taken root. Secularisation, and changes in the way in which the local congregation and the denomination relate to faith life, has had a profound effect on our understanding of baptism.[43] What is the church? Is membership of a local congregation or a specific Christian denomination necessary or important in contemporary Christian faith? If church membership is no longer socially important or theologically linked to Christian faith formation and discipleship, then what is the role and function of baptism as a means of grace that initiates entry into the church? In what sense is entry into the church, and the journey of belonging and formation that accompanies membership in the church, even necessary on the journey toward salvation of the individual and the eschatological intention of creation? These issues have led to baptism being "variously interpreted and often reduced to a ceremony of dedication"[44]—a social ritual or rite

---

41. Fukuyama, *Identity*, 25–37.

42. Fukuyama, *Identity*, 25–37.

43. See for example, Taylor, *Secular Age*; Smith, *How (Not) to Be Secular*.

44. United Methodist Church, *By Water and the Spirit*, 2.

of passage in a nominally Christian culture in which the individual is dedicated to Christ, or socially associated with the Christian religion in some occidental sense, and only very loosely related to the church by means of membership.[45] However, baptism, understood in this sense, has very little to do with faith formation and the formation of Christian identity. Indeed, it has very little to do with how Wesley understood baptism in relation to salvation (soteriology), the church (ecclesiology), and God's intention for creation (eschatology).

Much of contemporary Christian thinking about baptism has thus become focused on the "individual and the spiritual rather than the corporate and the material."[46] We have, mistakenly, understood baptism to be only about the individual (and in the case of infant baptism, the individual's immediate family). Baptism is viewed as a social norm and a rite of passage at worst, and merely as a way for parents or believing individuals to publicly profess their Christian belief and identification with the Christian religion and the church. While this is not entirely wrong, it is also not entirely right as it offers a stunted and jaundiced version of biblical, historical, and Wesleyan baptismal theology. What of God's claim upon our lives? What of the community of the church to which we belong? What of God's will for all of creation?

Baptism a Sacrament of Belonging and Becoming

As has been shown, for the Wesleyan Christian, baptism is intrinsically linked to identity, namely through the sense of belonging and becoming. Who we are and who we are to be as baptized Christians is framed, in Wesleyan theological terms, by soteriology, ecclesiology, and eschatology.

Soteriologically, baptism marks the first response to God's prevenient grace extended toward us. What makes this so beautiful is that it is truly an act of undeserved and unmerited grace. Before we can prove anything about our worth, before we can do anything to make ourselves worthy or unworthy, before we can fully believe or understand, we are

---

45. It is not surprising that after the publication of the resource, *By Water and the Spirit* (1996), a workbook was released to be used by clergy and churches to study aspects of baptism and identity. See Felton, *By Water and the Spirit*.

46. Bauerschmidt, "Being Baptized," 253.

welcomed and chosen by God.[47] It is God who initiates salvation and we who respond to this gracious gift of God.

This is to be held in tension with the ecclesiological emphasis, namely, the life of faith that will develop within the church and the family. Greville Lewis sums up the relationship between "prevenient grace," "justifying grace," and "sanctifying grace" beautifully when he says, "Baptism therefore proclaims that the child is the *inheritor* of God's promises in the Gospel' the later decision, conversion, and reception into full church membership signify that he [sic] now *claims* his inheritance."[48] The provision of an inheritance is God's gracious gift in Christ. The claiming of the inheritance is framed within a dual responsibility. First, it is the responsibility of the Christian community (which includes the parents and family of the baptized person), whose task it is to "so maintain the Church's life of worship and service that *they* [the baptized persons] may grow in grace and in the knowledge and love of God and of his Son Jesus Christ our Lord."[49] The church is the community of belonging in which and through which the baptized learn who they are to become.

Second, it is the responsibility of the baptized person to respond to God's justifying and sanctifying grace in and through the means of grace, thereby truly belonging to Christ and becoming the person they have been created to be. As a member of the church we learn to become who we truly are. Stanley Hauerwas famously said, "the first task of the church is not to make the world just, but to make the world the world."[50] Hauerwas describes the life of the disciples as "growing into your baptism," saying "when Christians live into their baptism they cannot help but be a people of virtue and, for that reason, possessed by joy."[51] What Hauerwas takes from Wesley is the understanding that baptism gives both the promise of salvation and also the responsibility of church discipline, indeed Christian discipleship within the community of the church.

As noted earlier, Wesley differed from some of his contemporaries in the Anglican theological tradition in that he distrusted those who viewed baptism as sufficient for salvation while they continued to live lives that lacked piety, holiness, and justice. It was the church that formed

47. Wesley, "Letter to Dr. Warburton," 357.

48. Lewis, *Approach to Christian Doctrine*, 182, emphasis in the original text.

49. Methodist Church, *Methodist Worship Book*, 94.

50. Hauerwas, *Approaching the End*, xi.

51. Hauerwas, *Character of Virtue*.

the baptized person, first into a believer, and then into a disciple. Wesley understood baptism to be a "covenant relationship with God and the expectation that a life full of love of God would issue forth in works of piety and mercy."[52] For Wesley, belonging to the church had spiritual consequences, but also social and political consequences. For example, he was opposed to slavery for, among other reasons, the belief that by baptism Christians could not view the bodies of other Christians as "property" since they were now members of the same family.[53] Like Wesley, Hauerwas also believes that baptism should have the authority to "reconfigure" all other loyalties and calls upon our person and identity—if we belong to Christ, we are to be Christian.[54] In Wesley's ecclesiology this link is most clearly expressed in his linking of baptism, church membership, and the renewal of our covenant with God. He thus encouraged the original Methodists to continually observe a covenant renewal service, which most often took place at the start of each new calendar year. The service was first introduced by John Wesley in 1755, serving as an opportunity for a recommitment of one's life to Christ and Christ's church, and through that to the responsibilities and tasks of everyday life. It is a remarkable expression of identity and the life that should flow from being in Christ. The Covenant promise begins with the words, "I am no longer my own but yours. Your will, not mine, be done in all things, wherever you may place me, in all that I do and in all that I may endure."[55]

Here is seen radical departure from forms of individualism, self-determination, and self-identification common in contemporary Western societies. The early Methodist emphasis on belonging, in differing forms, was so central to the formation of a new identity. From the Society Meeting to the Class Meeting and the Band Meeting, Wesley established a system for discipleship where each performed an essential task in the formation of true Christian identity—a life that exemplified the character and virtues of Christian faith. D. Michael Henderson suggests that in the worshiping congregation (the Society), Christian faith was taught and witnessed in a "cognitive mode."[56] The Class Meeting sought to engage the "behavioural mode," by instilling practices of accountability, service, and

52. Maddox and Vickers, *Cambridge Companion to John Wesley*, 239.

53. Hauerwas, *Work of Theology*, 204.

54. Stanley Hauerwas, *Hannah's Child*, 268.

55. Methodist Church, *Methodist Worship Book*, 288.

56. Henderson, *John Wesley's Class Meeting*, 83.

discipline in the life of the individual and the community.[57] Finally, the Band sought to engage the "affective" aspects of the life of faith through prayer, worship, confession, and care.[58] What Wesley understood is that belonging to the church is intended to form one into the kind of person that God has created one to be in order to live in such a way as to shape society according to the values of God's kingdom. Here we see, once again, how soteriology, ecclesiology, and eschatology are intricately linked in Wesleyan baptismal theology.

Such a sense of belonging and becoming serves not only to form Christian identity in relation to who God has created persons to be, it also counteracts what Slavoj Žižek identifies as the "nerve centre of liberal ideology," which sustains the destructive myth of the individual "psychological subject" finding fulfilment and flourishing in isolation from other persons and creation.[59] Within the sacrament of baptism, the human person is not a "self-enclosed private domain," rather she or he "is something shared because [she or he] is something surrendered to the Spirit of God."[60] The United Methodist Church's baptismal liturgy states it as follows, "In your baptism, the word of Scripture is fulfilled: 'We love, because God first loved us.'"[61] In this sense, the baptized person is invited into the story of Christ and Christ's work in history and creation. Baptism into the church opens us up to becoming who God has made us to be so we can work alongside Christ to help the world to become what it is created to be. One is invited into the community of church in order to go out in the world to work alongside God in the achievement of the *missio Dei*. As Louis-Marie Chauvet reflects:

> The difference inscribed on the body of every person through Christian initiation is so important that, far from imprisoning one into a clan or cultural group, as some other rites of initiation do, it opens onto the universal: by their baptism, Christians do not become members of a ghetto, but sisters and brothers of all humans in Jesus Christ.[62]

---

57. Henderson, *John Wesley's Class Meeting*, 93.

58. Henderson, *John Wesley's Class Meeting*, 112.

59. Žižek, *On Belief*, 116.

60. Bauerschmidt, "Being Baptized," 254.

61. Methodist Church, *Methodist Worship Book*, 93.

62. Chauvet, *Sacraments*, 111.

So, in this final sense, baptism for the Wesleyan Christian is not only about salvation—belonging to and growing in the body of Christ—it is also about becoming. Baptized persons become what they were created to be. Together with other baptized persons in the church and the world, they live toward the eschatological intention of God's loving act of creation. In John Wesley's soteriology, this is the aim of the Christian life and the purpose of religion; indeed, the very aim for which God "birthed" the Methodists, namely Christian Perfection.[63] It is described as follows:

> The ultimate goal in life . . . was the fullest possible love of God and neighbor—the restoration of the image of Christ in the life of every believer. This restoration is a journey birthed by grace, nurtured by grace, and reaching its ultimate goal through grace: Christian perfection.[64]

When baptism is considered through the theological lens of Methodist soteriology, ecclesiology, and eschatology, it takes on a rich, deep, and textured meaning. It is not only a rite of passage, a cultural practice, or a formulaic requirement for membership of the church. Rather, it is a means of grace by which we discover to whom we belong and learn to become who God has created us to be. In doing so, we learn to live in the world as members of Christ's body, participating with Christ in the renewal and healing of the world toward God's perfect and intended will.

Conclusion

This chapter has argued that we are facing a crisis of identity in contemporary society. We struggle to answer the questions "Who am I?" and "To whom do I belong?" The resources of liberal democracy and Western individualism have proven to be inadequate in providing the necessary resources to help us to become who we are intended to be. A further consequence has been the erosion of our understanding of the identity and purpose of the Christian church. While there is no single, essential form of church that can adequately address the needs of women and men through history or across the many varied contexts of contemporary society, this chapter has proposed that a reacquaintance with John Wesley's understanding baptism, in both objective and subjective terms, could

63. cf., Wesley, *Plain Account*, 14; Wesley in Williams, *John Wesley's Theology Today*, 238; Campbell, "The 'Way of Salvation,'" 5.

64. Wesley, *Plain Account*, 13.

help us discover where we belong and who we are to become. While we may need to consider some variety in contemporary approaches to baptismal liturgy and practice, we should hold to the central Wesleyan baptismal focus on soteriology, ecclesiology, and eschatology.

Bibliography

Andrews, Dee E. *The Methodists and Revolutionary America, 1760–1800: The Shaping of an Evangelical Culture*. Princeton: Princeton University Press, 2010.

Avis, Paul. *The Vocation of Anglicanism*. London: Bloomsbury, 2016.

Bauerschmidt, Frederick Christian. "Being Baptized: Bodies and Abortion." In *The Blackwell Companion to Christian Ethics*, edited by Stanley Hauerwas and Samuel Wells, 250–62. Oxford: Blackwell, 2008.

Birch, Bruce C. "Retired Bible Scholar Withdraws from International Connections." *United Methodist Insight*, March 4, 2019. https://um-insight.net/api/content/b5672766-3c79-11e9-ad77-120e7ad5cf50/.

Campbell, Ted A. "The 'Way of Salvation' and the Methodist Ethos Beyond John Wesley: A Study in Formal Consensus and Popular Reception." *The Asbury Journal* 63.1 (2008) 5–31.

Chauvet, Louis-Marie. *The Sacraments: The Word of God at the Mercy of the Body*. Collegeville, MN: Liturgical, 2001.

Felton, Gayle Carlton. *By Water and the Spirit: Making Connections for Identity and Ministry*. Nashville: Discipleship Resources, 2003.

Forster, Dion A. *The (Im)Possibility of Forgiveness: An Empirical Intercultural Bible Reading of Matthew 18:15–35*. Eugene, OR: Wipf and Stock, 2019.

———. "New Directions in Evangelical Christianities," *Theology* 122.4 (July 1, 2019) 267–75.

———. "On the 250th Anniversary of A Plain Account of Christian Perfection: A Historical Review of Wesleyan Theological Hybridity and Its Implications for Contemporary Discourses on Christian Humanism." *Studia Historiae Ecclesiasticae* 44.1 (April 26, 2018) 1–19.

Fukuyama, Francis. *Identity: The Demand for Dignity and the Politics of Resentment*. London: MacMillan, 2018.

Grass, Tim. *Modern Church History*. London: SCM, 2008.

Hammond, Geordan. *John Wesley in America: Restoring Primitive Christianity*. Oxford: Oxford University Press, 2014.

Hauerwas, Stanley. *Approaching the End: Eschatological Reflections on Church, Politics, and Life*. Grand Rapids: Eerdmans, 2013.

———. *The Character of Virtue: Letters to a Godchild*. Atlanta: Canterbury, 2018.

———. *Hannah's Child: A Theologian's Memoir*. Grand Rapids: Eerdmans, 2012.

———. *The Work of Theology*. Grand Rapids: Eerdmans, 2015.

Henderson, D. Michael. *John Wesley's Class Meeting: A Model for Making Disciples*. Wilmore, KY: Rafiki, 2016.

Jenkins, Philip. *The Next Christendom: The Coming of Global Christianity*. Oxford: Oxford University Press, 2011.

Kent, John. *Wesley and the Wesleyans: Religion in Eighteenth-Century Britain.* Cambridge: Cambridge University Press, 2002.

Kim, Sebastian, and Kirsteen Kim. *Christianity as a World Religion: An Introduction.* London: Bloomsbury Academic, 2006.

Lewis, Greville P., ed. *An Approach to Christian Doctrine.* 3rd ed. Cape Town: Methodist Publishing, 1987.

Loughlin, John. *Human Dignity in the Judaeo-Christian Tradition: Catholic, Orthodox, Anglican and Protestant Perspectives.* London: Bloomsbury, 2019.

Maddox, Randy L., and Jason E. Vickers. *The Cambridge Companion to John Wesley.* Cambridge: Cambridge University Press, 2010.

Methodist Church, ed. *The Methodist Worship Book.* Peterborough: Methodist Publishing, 1999.

Migliore, Daniel L. *Faith Seeking Understanding: An Introduction to Christian Theology.* Grand Rapids: Eerdmans, 2004.

Mission and Public Affairs Council (Church of England). *Mission-Shaped Church: Church Planting and Fresh Expressions of Church in a Changing Context.* London: Church House Publishing, 2009.

Oden, Thomas C. *John Wesley's Teachings.* Vol. 3, *Pastoral Theology.* Grand Rapids: Zondervan Academic, 2013.

Puglisi, J. F. *The Process of Admission to Ordained Ministry: The First Lutheran, Reformed, Anglican and Wesleyan Rites.* Collegeville, MN: Liturgical, 1997.

Richey, Russell E. *Methodism in the American Forest.* Oxford: Oxford University Press, 2015.

Sherwood, Harriet. "As Traditional Believers Turn Away, Is This a New Crisis of Faith?" *The Observer,* August 13, 2016. https://www.theguardian.com/world/2016/aug/13/church-of-england-evangelical-drive.

Smith, James K.A. *Desiring the Kingdom (Cultural Liturgies): Worship, Worldview, and Cultural Formation.* Grand Rapids, MI: Baker Academic, 2009.

———. *How (Not) to Be Secular: Reading Charles Taylor.* Grand Rapids: Eerdmans, 2014.

Thompson, E. P. "Anthropology and the Discipline of Historical Context." *Midland History* 1.3 (January 1, 1972) 41–55.

Taylor, Charles A. *A Secular Age.* Cambridge: Harvard University Press, 2009.

The United Methodist Church. *By Water and the Spirit: A United Methodist Understanding of Baptism.* Nashville: General Board of Discipleship, 1996.

Vickers, John A. *Thomas Coke: Apostle of Methodism.* Eugene, OR: Wipf and Stock, 2013.

Wesley, John. "Letter to Dr. Warburton, Bishop of Gloucester, Nov. 1762." In vol. 4, *The Letters of the Rev. John Wesley,* edited by John Telford, 357. London: Epworth, 1931.

———. *A Plain Account of Christian Perfection, Annotated.* Edited by Randy L. Maddox and Paul W. Chilcote. Kansas City: Beacon Hill, 2015.

———. "Sermon 16, 'The Means of Grace.'" In *Bicentennial Edition of the Works of John Wesley.* Vol. 1, *Sermons I,* edited by Albert C. Outler, 376–97. Nashville: Abingdon, 1984.

———. "A Treatise on Baptism." In *Works of John Wesley.* Vol. 10, *Letters, Essays, Dialogs, Addresses,* edited by Thomas Jackson, 188–201. Grand Rapids: Zondervan, 1958–59.

Wigger, John. *American Saint: Francis Asbury and the Methodists.* Oxford: Oxford University Press, 2009.

Williams, Colin W. *John Wesley's Theology Today.* Nashville: Abingdon, 1988.

Williams, Timothy. "Why a Vote on Gay Clergy and Same-Sex Marriage Could Split the United Methodist Church." *New York Times,* February 26, 2019. https://www. nytimes.com/2019/02/26/us/united-methodist-church-gay-same-sex-marriage. html.

Žižek, Slavoj. *On Belief.* London: Psychology, 2001.

CHAPTER 13

Baptism and Eucharist

Preserving the Sacramental Sequence

R. MATTHEW SIGLER,
SEATTLE PACIFIC UNIVERSITY AND SEMINARY

Toward a Wesleyan Perspective on Font and Table

"THERE ARE TWO THINGS Methodists know about the sacraments," a United Methodist pastor once told me: "We don't re-baptize, and we practice an open table." While it is difficult to verify how pervasive the sentiment is, it undoubtedly represents the thinking of many. Within the last fifty years, the phrase "open table" has been lauded as a hallmark of Methodist eucharistic piety.[1] As it is typically understood and practiced among United Methodists, the phrase "open table" is shorthand for an invitation for all to commune regardless of whether one has been baptized.

This perspective presents a host of problems for sacramental theology and practice. The first is a historical one: for most of the history of the church the Lord's Supper has been understood as a meal for the baptized. In early church practice, baptism was akin to crossing the Jordan River and was immediately followed by the Lord's Supper where the initiate

---

1. For example, see Rieger, "Grace Under Pressure," 42; and United Methodist News Service, "United Methodist View of Communion."

communed for the first time. The "Apostolic Tradition," for example, records that the newly baptized consumed not only bread and wine but also
a cup mixed with milk and honey. Because this traditional link between
the Font and the Table is still maintained by many in the church today,
the practice of an "open table" raises serious questions about ecumenical faithfulness—a second problem. *Baptism, Eucharist, and Ministry*,
adopted by the World Council of Churches, recognizes this sacramental
sequence.[2] When congregations dissolve the link between the Font and
Table, they move out of step with much of the global church. Third, a pastoral problem is presented when one severs the link between baptism and
the Lord's Supper in traditions that do not engage in re-baptism. Parishioners are robbed of the opportunity to remember their baptism every
time they commune at the Table. For denominations, like my own United
Methodist Church, that practice infant baptism, we miss the occasion to
help those who cannot recall their baptism claim for their own the promises made on their behalf at the Font. We also neglect a chance to remind
parishioners of the radical commitment of Christian identity pledged in
the baptismal vows. Much more could be said about the problems that
occur in dissolving the link between baptism and the Lord's Supper, but
the primary focus of this chapter will be to consider a Wesleyan perspective on the topic in hopes of evaluating current practices. As will be seen,
one must question if separating the sacramental sequence of baptism and
Eucharist—and the problems that accompany the practice of an "open
table"—is indeed Wesleyan.

Context

In order to fully appreciate a Wesleyan perspective on the link between
baptism and the Lord's Supper, we must consider first the context in
which the two sacraments were practiced in John and Charles Wesleys'
day. With some notable exceptions like Quakers and Baptists, the majority of the population of Great Britain would have been baptized in
infancy. It is worth mentioning that both the Articles of Religion and
the 1662 catechism of the Church of England sequence their treatment
of sacraments with baptism followed by the Lord's Supper. The historic
connection between Font and Table is clearly indicated in this structure
with one caveat: prior to being admitted to the Lord's Supper, one needed

---

2. World Council of Churches, *Baptism, Eucharist, and Ministry*.

to be confirmed by the bishop. At the time of the Protestant Reformation the rite of confirmation had long been separated from the water bath and served as a means of marking acceptance of the baptismal vows by those who had been baptized in their infancy. Upon confirmation, children were welcomed to the Table. While paedobaptism was the assumed norm, the 1662 *Book of Common Prayer* also included a rubric in the rite of baptism for those of "riper years," which admonished the candidate to be confirmed as soon as possible so she could be admitted to Table. While the connection between baptism and the Lord's Supper was preserved, confirmation was delayed for those baptized as infants in an effort to ensure that recipients were adequately prepared in their understanding of the significance of the Lord's Supper.

Relatedly, self-examination and repentance were emphasized as necessary steps prior to reception of the elements of the Eucharist. For example, the 1662 Catechism includes this question and response:

> Quest. What is required of them who come to the Lord's Supper?
> Answ. To examine themselves, whether they repent them truly of their former sins, steadfastly purposing to lead a new life; have a lively faith in God's mercy through Christ, with a thankful remembrance of his death; and be in charity with all men.

Geoffrey Wainwright argues that the invitation to the Lord's Supper—"Ye that do truly and earnestly repent you of your sins"—is "an invitation to the baptized" for the way it echoes the baptismal vows.[3] So while confirmation and confession were emphasized in the 1662 Catechism and Prayer Book as prerequisites to partaking of the Lord's Supper, both rites point back to baptism. It was in this context that John and Charles Wesley administered the sacrament of Holy Communion as ordained clergy in the Church of England.

During his sojourn in Georgia, John's administering of the sacraments caused controversy at times. Many know of his turbulent relationship with Sophia Hopkey, which ended with his refusal to admit her to the Table. One other incident that bears mentioning is the case of Johann Martin Boltzius, a Lutheran Pietist who fled to Georgia in the 1730s alongside other refugees from Salzburg. John Wesley refused to admit Boltzius to the Table, because he had not been baptized by an episcopally ordained minister. This is one of the main instances where Wesley speaks directly to the link between baptism and the Lord's Supper. And, while

---

3. Wainwright, "Sacraments in a Wesleyan Perspective," 112, 114–17.

he would later openly lament this decision, his regret is primarily over his insistence of episcopal ordination.[4] When one considers that much of John Wesley's aim in Georgia was to experiment in restoring what he called "primitive Christianity," one can understand why baptism by an episcopally ordained minister would have been essential because of Wesley's emphasis at the time on apostolic succession. It remains the case that even the mature Wesley never advocated for dissolving the historic link between the Font and the Table.

In spite of this, much of the discourse around the practice of an "open table" has hinged on arguments that Wesley practiced communing those who had not been baptized. One attempt to substantiate this is the claim that Wesley practiced "field communions" in which thousands likely partook of the Lord's Supper.[5] The central problem with this argument is that it cannot be substantiated. There is no doubt that the early Methodists' eucharistic piety created, at times, tension with the established church because of the numbers of parishioners seeking to commune. In some cases, Methodists were turned away from local Anglican parishes and sought admission to the Table in other locations, such as "sick bed" or hospital Communion.[6] Because those administering the sacrament in such case would have been—for the bulk of Wesley's ministry—ordained in the Church of England, one can easily presume that the norms for admission would have been retained. Even in his later years after ordaining his own Methodist ministers, there is no indication that Wesley abandoned the standards for admission to the Table.

The primary argument offered in defense of an "open table" is that Wesley referred to the Lord's Supper as a "converting ordinance."[7] Here again, context is essential in understanding how Wesley used this term. By early 1740 the society at Fetter Lane was embroiled in the controversy over "stillness" or "quietism." Under the teachings of Moravian minister Alsatian Philipp Heinrich Molther, members of the society were encouraged to wait on the Lord for full assurance of salvation prior to engaging in any of the ordinances. These teachings pitted the Moravians at the society against the Wesleys. On the one side, Molther assumed that faith

4. Wesley, "September 30–Oct 1, 1749," 305.

5. See, for example, Runyon, *New Creation*, 128, 210.

6. See Bowmer, *Sacrament of the Lord's Supper*, 64–66.

7. Many point to John Wesley's journal entry from June 27, 1740: "Experience shows the gross falsehood of that assertion that the Lord's Supper is not a converting ordinance." Wesley, "June 27, 1740," 158.

and assurance were the same. Because justification is a gift that must be received by faith, participation in any ordinance without assurance of salvation is tantamount to working for one's own salvation.

While John and Charles agreed that salvation is by grace and through faith alone, they argued that the means of grace are vital in moving toward full assurance of salvation. It is possible for one to have "degrees of faith" that can be cultivated in the ordinances without such actions becoming a work.[8] With this in mind, John writes in his journal for June 28, 1740:

> I showed at large, 1) that the Lord's supper was ordained by God to be a means of conveying to men either preventing or justifying, or sanctifying grace, according to their several necessities; 2) that the persons for whom it was ordained are all those who know and feel that they want the grace of God, either to restrain them from sin, or to show their sins forgiven, or to renew their souls in the image of God; 3) that inasmuch as we come to his table, not to give him anything but to receive whatsoever he sees best for us, there is no previous preparation indispensable necessary, but a desire to receive whatsoever he pleases to give; and 4) that no fitness is required at the time of communicating but a sense of our state, of our utter sinfulness and helplessness; every one who knows he is fit for hell being just fit to come to Christ in this as well as all other ways of his appointment.[9]

Wesley makes clear that for those in the society seeking assurance of salvation, the longing for God's grace is more than enough to warrant communing at the Table. Note that Wesley assumes that such a desire would be accompanied with an acknowledgement of one's "utter sinfulness and helplessness"—repentance clearly remains an integral component of participating in the sacrament.

What about baptism? John makes little mention of it in his arguments against quietism and this points again to the context in which he was ministering. The Methodist revival centered on a British society that had—the vast majority of them—been baptized as Christians but were living like heathens. Because of this, Methodists preached the necessity of the new birth and assurance of salvation as essential to vibrant faith. In referring to the Lord's Supper as a "converting ordinance," Wesley envisions the sacrament as a vital means of grace for those seeking the new

8. John Wesley, "June 28, 1740," 132–33.
9. John Wesley, "June 28, 1740," 159.

birth. The term, "converting ordinance," was used during the seventeenth century in disagreements between Anglicans and English Dissenters. Some Puritan leaders, such as Richard Baxter, argued that full assurance of faith is required before participating in the sacrament. Others within the Church of England, like John Cheyney, argued in favor of communing those "within the church" who were "unconverted."[10] Writing some sixty years prior to the stillness controversy, Cheyney speaks from the perspective of an "unconverted" Christian in arguing for participating in the Lord's Supper:

> I am willing to obey God's command outwardly, *Do this in re-membrance of me*, and to do the inward part as well as I can, thinking it may be better to do so than wholly forbear, and to cast myself at the feet of God's grace and mercy for conversion if I have it not, and for confirmation and assurance if indeed I am already converted. Salvation, and so God's ordinances, lies at mens [*sic*] doors.[11]

Like Wesley would argue a generation later, the Lord's Supper serves to provide grace for the unconverted and the unassured.

It should be clear that Wesley uses the term "converting ordinance" to indicate his belief that those wrestling for full assurance of salvation should not refrain from participating in the Lord's Supper. In doing so he draws from verbiage utilized in conversations from a previous generation. Both Cheyney and the Wesleys argued that "unconverted" baptized Christians should be advised to partake in the sacrament. As noted above, however, the Wesleyan revival did impact those outside of the Church of England—some of whom did not practice paedobaptism. In such cases, how did the Wesleys practice admission to the Table?

One such episode is recounted in Charles Wesley's journal. In the entry from Sunday, June 16, 1751, Charles relays the story of a person who was among the Methodists but had not yet been baptized. He writes:

> Baptized a young Quaker at Kingswood, and then we all joined in the Lord's Supper. He [God] was mightily present in both sacraments, and afterwards gave me words to shake the souls of those that heard.[12]

10. See Cheyney, *Some Arguments*.

11. Cheyney, *Some Arguments*, 27.

12. See Kimbrough and Newport, *Manuscript Journal*, 609.

Several points are worth offering from Charles' journal entry. First, rather than admitting the Quaker to the Table, Charles preserves the traditional sequence by first offering the sacrament of baptism. This would have been the norm among early Methodists rather than communing the unbaptized at the Table. Second, the sacrament of baptism is immediately followed by the Lord's Supper in which all communed. In effect, this serves as a form of baptismal reaffirmation for the entire community. Lastly, Charles makes clear that sacramental participation was far from a perfunctory act; God's presence was discerned in both sacraments.

This final observation leads to a more fundamental point: both Wesleys had a high view of baptism. One can run the risk of underappreciating this fact since more focus is given to the sacrament of the Lord's Supper as well as the essentiality of the new birth. However, episodes like the one relayed above show that the Wesleyan revival did not minimize the sacrament of baptism. Charles versifies this high piety in one of his hymns on Romans 6:

> Baptized into my Savior's name,
> I of his death partake;
> Buried with Jesus Christ I am,
> And I with him awake.
>
> He burst the barriers of the tomb,
> Rose, and regained the skies;
> And lo! from nature's grave I come,
> And lo! with Christ I rise.
>
> A new, a living life I have;
> And, fashioned to his death,
> His resurrection's power receive,
> And by his Spirit breathe. . . .
>
> I live to God, who from the dead
> Hath me to life restored,
> That I, from sin's oppression freed,
> Might only serve my Lord.[13]

This high baptismal piety is linked to the eucharistic piety of the Wesleys. Charles echoes the above hymn in this selection from his *Hymns on the Lord's Supper* (1745):

13. Wesley, "Romans 6."

By that great sacrifice
Which he for us doth plead,
Into our Saviour's death baptize,
And make us like our head.

Into the fellowship
Of Jesu's sufferings take,
Us who desire with him to sleep,
That we with him may wake:

Plant us into his death
That we his life may prove,
Partakers of his cross beneath,
And of his crown above.[14]

Clearly, both hymns draw upon the baptismal imagery of Romans 6, but the fact that such language is included in this seminal collection of eucharistic hymns illustrates the connection between Font and Table held by the Wesleys.

What about Confirmation?

As mentioned above, the Church of England required that one be confirmed after baptism prior to participating in the Lord's Supper. John Wesley omitted the rite for confirmation in his edition of the *Book of Common Prayer* known as *The Sunday Service of the Methodists in North America*. While he makes no mention as to why he deleted the rite, some historians have speculated that Wesley considered the "new birth" to be more essential and lasting than confirmation.[15] Others have noted the significant logistical challenge presented for Methodists after breaking from the Church of England.[16] Confirmation requires a bishop and even if one understood the office of "superintendent" to be bishop-like, the challenges of travel among the rapidly growing American Methodists would have been daunting. It is interesting to note that others in the Church of England had objected to the rite, calling it superfluous. For example, the Puritans advocated for removal of the rite in the Millenary Petition of 1603. In his "Treatise on Baptism," John Wesley seems to make the same argument:

14. Wesley and Wesley, *Hymns on the Lord's Supper*, 125.

15. See, for example, White, "John Wesley's *Sunday Service*," 405.

16. For example, see White, "John Wesley's *Sunday Service*," 405.

It [Baptism] is the initiatory sacrament, which enters us into covenant with God. . . . From which spiritual, vital union with him,
proceeds the influence of his grace on those that are baptized;
as from our union with the Church, *a share in all its privileges*,
and *in all the promises* Christ has made to it [emphasis added].[17]

Because he deleted the rite of confirmation and made the case that baptism affords one all the rights of the church, it is likely that Wesley would
have communed those who had been baptized but not confirmed.

What about Repentance?

The Communion Rite in the 1662 Prayer Book is inescapably penitential;
a tone that is reflected in the liturgies that predate the Church of England.
Concerns about receiving the sacrament unworthily led to infrequent
communing among the laity for much of the middle ages. In Wesley's
day congregants were required to commune a minimum of three times
a year. While some cathedral and collegiate parishes offered the sacrament weekly, this was not the case in many other parishes.[18] Wesley's
admonition that Methodists practice "constant Communion" was coun-
tercultural in many contexts. In spite of this encouragement for more
frequent reception, Wesley did not jettison the importance of repentance
as a requirement for participating in the Lord's Supper in *The Sunday
Service*. Not only do the rites demonstrate this requirement, but so too
his writings. In "The Duty of Constant Communion," Wesley upholds the
essentiality of repentance and is quick to offer: "we should repent before
we come; not that we should neglect to come at all."[19] Repentance, then,
is an essential requirement for coming to the Table, but fear should not
prevent one from receiving the sacrament. Indeed, Wesley argues in the
same sermon that it is an even greater risk to disobey the Lord's command to "do this. . . ." Just as conviction is a sign of God's gracious work
in our lives, repentance leads to forgiveness and deepening relationship
with the Triune God in the sacrament of the Lord's Supper.

17. Wesley, "Treatise on Baptism," 188.

18. The Communion Rite in the 1662 *Book of Common Prayer* includes the following rubric concerning the frequency of eucharistic reception: "And in Cathedral and
Collegiate Churches, and Colleges, where there are many Priests and Deacons, they
shall all receive the Communion with the Priest every Sunday at the least, except they
have a reasonable cause to the contrary."

19. Wesley, "Sermon 101, 'The Duty of Constant Communion,'" 434.

The early Methodist class and band meetings provided an opportunity for examination and repentance before partaking of the sacrament. Oftentimes, tickets or other tokens were distributed prior to the Lord's Supper to indicate that the communicant was sincere in coming to the Table. It is essential to remember that part of the examination would have included reflection on the love of neighbor. Fencing the Table in this manner was not about exclusivity, but preserving a vibrant witness that was exemplified in personal and communal holiness.[20] The first American Methodist *Discipline*, for instance, barred slaveholding members from participating in the Lord's Supper unless they agreed to free their slaves. These requisite acts of confession and repentance at the Lord's Supper reiterate the baptismal renunciations.

Dissolving the Connection

While the Wesleys assumed that sin was a pervasive reality in their context, by the late nineteenth and early twentieth centuries the emphasis on original sin had become less prevalent among many Methodists. For example, the 1916 *Book of Discipline* for the Methodist Episcopal Church removed all references to original sin and regeneration in the infant baptismal rite. Not only did this shift lead to a minimizing of the importance of repentance prior to participating in the Lord's Supper, it also served to dilute the baptismal connection. Whereas the penitential language in earlier rites for the administration of the Lord's Supper reflects the words of the baptismal rite, liturgies of the early twentieth century mute this link.

On the other hand, evangelicals within Methodist denominations preserved a strong concept of original sin but tended to minimize the efficacy of infant baptism in favor of a near exclusive focus on conversion of the heart. For many, the Lord's Supper became another occasion for experiencing such conversion. In effect the sacramental order became reversed in such communities. Participation in the Lord's Supper could be a means by which one experiences the new birth and then is baptized. Of course, the Wesleys believed in the essentiality of the new birth,

20. The practice of admitting to the Table only those who had been properly examined by an elder or deacon fell into disuse among many late-nineteenth century Methodists. Others within the pan-Methodist family preserved this heritage. The African Methodist Episcopal Church, for example, maintained the stipulation until 1976. See Westerfield Tucker, *American Methodist Worship*, 144–45.

while preserving the historic, sacramental sequence. A century after the Wesleys, many in the pan-Methodist family had departed from this early perspective. In both mainline liberal and evangelical Methodist congregations, the bond between Font and Table was often dissolved, but for very different reasons.

In recent years the sacramental sequence has been interrupted by an additional concern. Many congregations have emphasized hospitality as a defining ecclesial value. This is due to at least two contributing factors. First, inclusivity has become, in many circles, the dominant liturgical motif. In such contexts, exclusion of any form is viewed as anathema to liturgical praxis. Second, in the midst of continued denomination decline, many congregations emphasize hospitality as a means of stemming attrition. Such churches often view corporate worship as a primary place of encounter with the church. Taken together, these trends mean that limiting eucharistic reception to anyone is viewed as incompatible with core liturgical values. In fact, in many congregations an "open table" is understood as the primary litmus test of welcome and inclusion.[21]

A Wesleyan Perspective on the Sequence of Font and Table

It should be clear that the practice of a wide "open table" with no reference to baptism or repentance stands in contrast with the praxis of the Wesleys. Attempts to substantiate the practice of an "open table" by arguing that Wesley advocated for dissolving the historic link between baptism and the Lord's Supper are made on thin ground. What constructive points might be offered regarding a Wesleyan theology of the link between Font and Table?

In the first place, one cannot fully understand a Wesleyan perspective on the sacramental sequence without considering the soteriological focus of the Methodist movement. Assurance of salvation and the new birth were pervasive concerns for the early Methodists—so too was sanctification, but for the purposes of this topic we will limit our focus to

21. For example, see Felton, "Sacraments." The brief statement includes the following: "The 'open table' at Holy Communion has become a beloved hallmark of American Methodism since the nineteenth century.... The table of Holy Communion is the welcome table; it is open to all who come seeking God. . . .

It is a potent expression of United Methodism's unwillingness—even refusal—to get into the dangerous business of judging the spiritual conditions of other people."

the former. The means of grace (including baptism and the Lord's Supper) are given by God to serve in bringing a person into the fullness of God's salvation in Christ. For the Wesleys, assurance and the new birth are not detached from baptism, but are essential, distinct works of God's grace in a person's life. Because the majority would have been baptized as infants in the Wesleys' day, John and Charles encouraged "unconverted" Christians to participate in the Lord's Supper for the way it can lead to the new birth and assurance of salvation. The unconverted Christian, or one whom Charles elsewhere calls the "sleeping Christian" is:

> quiet, rational, inoffensive, good natured professor of the religion of his fathers . . . zealous and orthodox . . . "a Pharisee"; that is, according to the scriptural account, one that "justifies himself," one that labours "to establish his own righteousness" as the ground of his acceptance of God . . . who "having the form of godliness, denies the power thereof"; yea, and probably reviles it, wheresoever it is found, as mere extravagance and delusion. . . . He "fasts twice in the week," uses all the means of grace, is constant at church and sacrament; yes, and "gives tithes of that he has," does all the good he can. "Touching the righteousness of the law," he is "blameless": he wants nothing of godliness but the power; nothing of religion but the spirit; nothing of Christianity but the truth and the life.[22]

Wesley clearly has in mind one who has been baptized—one could not be "constant at sacrament [of the Lord's Supper]" in the Church of England unless one had been baptized. In spite of the fact that a "sleeping Christian" might be "constant at sacrament" to no spiritual benefit, the Lord's Supper remained an integral means of grace in the Wesleyan revival, one given by God alongside other means to awaken the sleeping Christian and then sustain her as she goes on to perfection.[23]

It is telling that Wesley does not include baptism in his official list of the means of grace. This is because the sacrament of baptism could not be repeated as doing so would imply that God's promises were ineffectual. The Table of the Lord's Supper, on the other hand, not only can be repeated, but should be frequented for the opportunity it provided to receive awakening and sanctifying grace. Wesley's understanding of

---

22. Wesley, "Sermon 8, 'Ephesians 5:14,'" 214.

23. This soteriological sequence is narrated quite nicely in John Wesley's sermon on "The Means of Grace." See Wesley "Sermon 16, 'Means of Grace,'" 376–97.

degrees of faith allowed him to admit those who did not yet have assurance of salvation, but nevertheless desired it:

> a man who is not assured that his sins are forgiven may yet have a kind or degree of faith which distinguishes him not only from a devil but also from an heathen, and on which I may admit him to the Lord's Supper.[24]

Susanna Wesley, in fact, experienced assurance while partaking of the Lord's Supper in September of 1739:

> two or three weeks ago, while my son[-in-law] [Westley] Hall was pronouncing these words, in delivering the cup to me, "The blood of our Lord Jesus Christ, which was given for thee," the words struck through my heart, and I knew God for Christ's sake had forgiven *me* all *my* sins.[25]

Susanna was part of the baptized and experienced this deeper work of grace in the sacrament.

Because both Wesley brothers believed that God was sovereign and God's primary work was in bringing full salvation to all, they held out the possibility that God could, and did, work outside of the normal sacramental sequence. "[God] is equally able to work whatsoever pleaseth him by any [means] or none at all," writes Wesley in his sermon on "The Means of Grace."[26] The entire thrust of the sermon, however, is pointing out the "ordinary channels" by which God conveys God's grace. Simply put: God's salvific action is not bound to the means of grace, yet God promises to always meet us in these ordained means. With this in mind, the Wesleys would likely agree that the typical sequence of Font and Table could be interrupted by God's work because of God's sovereignty. Yet because they understood God's central work to be concerned with bringing full salvation to all, such an interruption only makes sense in light of the Wesleyan emphasis on the new birth and assurance. Any such divine break in the sacramental sequence would be the extraordinary work of God not the ordinary means. It is also worth keeping in mind that both John and Charles record incidents of interactions with those who had not yet been baptized. In every recorded case baptism, not the Lord's Supper, was the first sacrament offered to the unbaptized.

24. Wesley, "Letter to Richard Thompson," 575.
25. Wesley, "September 3, 1739," 93.
26. See Wesley, *John Wesley's Sermons*, 160–61.

Problems, in fact, arise when we assume God's extraordinary means of working outside the sacramental sequence are God's ordinary means. This leads to a second point that must be made about a Wesleyan perspective on the link between Font and Table: the Lord's Supper is a meal of the church and one enters the church through baptism. This sacramental sequence is upheld by the Wesleys. As noted above, John Wesley referred to baptism as the sacrament of initiation into the church—a rite "instituted in the room of circumcision."[27] Of course, the outward sign of the covenant must be ratified in the heart, but one must first enter into the covenant through baptism. Here again the Lord's Supper is a means of grace that functions as a type of baptismal reaffirmation for those seeking "circumcision of the heart." We see evidence of this perspective in the liturgical sources produced by the Wesleys. For example, in *Hymns on the Lord's Supper* the sacrament is presented as that which seals the covenant of grace in the heart of the believer.[28]

Third, the link between baptism and the Lord's Supper is accentuated in the rhythms of repentance and receiving grace at the Table. From a Wesleyan perspective, repentance is never an end in itself, but always leads to a restored and deepened relationship with the Triune God. Perhaps the reality is exemplified best at the Lord's Supper because at the Table participants encounter Christ both as judge and priest; conviction and grace go hand in hand. This rhythm anchors us in our baptismal identity as we grow in holiness. The post-Communion prayer in the 1662 Anglican Communion rite, maintained in Wesley's *Sunday Service*, reads:

> And here we offer and present unto thee, O Lord, ourselves, our souls and bodies, to be a reasonable, holy, and lively sacrifice unto thee; humbly beseeching thee, that all we, who are partakers of this holy Communion, may be fulfilled with thy grace and heavenly benediction.

Words of confession and repentance remind the communicant of the vows made at her own baptism, while the sacrament serves as an integral means of grace in God's transforming work.

27. See Wesley, "Treatise on Baptism," 188.
28. For instance, see Wesley and Wesley, *Hymns on the Lord's Supper*, 102–3.

Contemporary Implications

Confusion regarding a Methodist perspective on the link between Font and Table continues to abound. The United Methodist Church's *Book of Worship* states, "We have no tradition of refusing any who present themselves desiring to receive [the Lord's Supper]."[29] While this statement was qualified in an official publication a decade later, contemporary praxis often remains very different from that of the Wesleys. This is due, in large part, to the perception that the Table is the primary place for encountering God's gracious welcome. Just as Christ shared meals with a variety of people, including "insiders" and "outsiders," the Table of the Lord is open to all—so the argument often goes.[30] This, of course, assumes that every episode of table fellowship in the gospels is synonymous with the Lord's Supper. If, in fact, the Lord's Supper was distinct from, say, Christ's sharing a meal with Zacchaeus, then this argument rests on a shaky analogy. Such arguments also tend to overlook the fact that most of those with whom Christ dined were circumcised—the physical sign of entrance into the Jewish community of faith.[31]

A more fundamental consideration lies in the problem created when hospitality is superimposed as the monolithic meaning of the Lord's Supper. Not only does it limit the multivalence of the sacrament, but it tends to circumvent other opportunities for practicing hospitality. One wonders if placing all hopes at being a "hospitable church" on the Lord's Supper actually serves to assuage the urgency of offering radical welcome in other areas.

It should also be noted that many assume that boundaries and hospitality are mutually at odds. Current political discourse heightens this assumption. In an age of border walls, racism, and xenophobia, do boundaries around the Lord's Supper contradict the message of Christ's boundless love for all? Such questions obfuscate the social reality that some boundary-setting is actually productive for hospitality. Without any boundaries, communal identity becomes amorphous and dissonance

29. United Methodist Church, *United Methodist Book of Worship*, 29.

30. See, for example, Felton, *United Methodists*, 71–72. Felton acknowledges that Wesley practiced a more restrictive access to the Table than do United Methodists and grounds her argument in the reasoning enumerated above.

31. This is by no means to advocate for a type of social exclusivity for the faithful—Acts 11, for example, shows that Peter ate with Gentiles—but attempts to argue for breaking the sacramental sequence by drawing a parallel with table fellowship in Scripture do not seem to be adequate.

is created for those seeking entry into the community. When communal boundaries become impermeable, on the other hand, then walls have been erected rather than identity markers delineated. This would certainly be in contrast to a truly Christian ethos that proclaims the gospel is for all and that boundaries serve as thresholds, not impenetrable walls.

Throughout the history of Christian worship, the Lord's Supper has been a definitive marker of the Christian community—a community, for certain, that calls the entire world to enter into the joy of the Lord. In dissolving the traditional sacramental sequence, we conflate a vital marker of the community, the Lord's Supper, with the primary means of entry into the community, baptism. Christ bids all to come to him. How does one come? How does one enter into the body? The Wesleys, along with the bulk of the church, would respond that we come through the waters of baptism.

Relatedly, recovering the sacramental sequence of Font and Table will be even more important in an increasingly post-Christian context. When one places a premium on demonstrating hospitality through the practice of an "open table," one suggests that the Sunday service of Word and Table is the primary place of contact with those who have not yet come to the waters of baptism. In post-Christian areas of the world, we cannot assume that the gathering of the faithful will be the primary "on ramp" to Christianity. Rather, such relationships will likely be cultivated outside the Sunday service. Given this reality, reclaiming the Lord's Supper as a meal for the faithful can serve to strengthen a Christian ethic and identity. This was certainly the perspective of early Methodists. Each time we partake of the Lord's Supper, we renew the vows made in our baptism to resist the works of the devil, die to sin and live to Christ. The vibrant witness of the church is strengthened. When the link between baptism and the Lord's Super is broken, we miss a vital opportunity for regular baptismal reaffirmation.

One brief anecdote might help illustrate the point raised above. I know of a congregation in Boston, Massachusetts, that limits participation in the Lord's Supper to the baptized. Each Sunday the Table is "fenced" as the minister gives the invitation and instructions for distribution. Those who are not yet baptized are "still very welcomed to come forward and receive prayer," but are asked to simply cross their arms to indicate they will not be receiving the elements. Michael (not his real name) was first introduced to this congregation at a neighborhood gardening club of which several parishioners were members. During one club gathering—a potluck held on a roof deck in downtown Boston—Michael began asking questions about Christianity. This initial conversation led to an invitation to dinner with one of the church's neighborhood groups. Michael knew little about Christianity and spent nearly six months coming to weekly dinners with the neighborhood group before attending a Sunday service.

Because he was not yet a Christian, Michael came forward with his arms crossed on his first visit and continued this practice every Sunday for the next year. During this time, he expressed a desire to follow Christ and was baptized on Easter in the midst of the community. Michael took the elements for the first time immediately following his baptism. When asked how he experienced the fencing of the Table, Michael's response was overwhelmingly positive. In the first place, he valued the boundaries enumerated during the Lord's Supper because in fencing the Table the congregation "didn't make presumptions about my faith." At the same time, Michael valued having his own opportunity for participating in the distribution by receiving prayer. As Michael became known better by the ministers, he would offer specific prayer requests as he came forward. Following his own baptism, Michael was overcome with emotion as he received the bread and cup for the first time. As in the case of Michael, the Lord's Supper can be a powerful marker of communal identity—a feast that reinforces the baptismal vows of the Christian community, yet not at the cost of radical hospitality. In preserving the Lord's Supper as a meal for the Body—the baptized community of faith—boundaries placed around the Table need not be impermeable, rather they can lead to full entrance into the community through the Font.

We began this chapter by noting three dilemmas that emerge when the link between Font and Table is dissolved: a historical problem, an ecumenical problem, and a pastoral problem. To these we must also add a fourth: a theological problem. If the Lord's Supper is a meal for the body and if baptism is the entrance into that body, how can one partake of the meal if one is not yet a member of the body? One cannot eat without a physical body and the ecclesiological metaphor leads to a similar conclusion. In limiting the meal of the church to those who have been baptized, are we not simply practicing consistency in our ecclesiology?

Paul's admonition in 1 Corinthians to "discern the body" functions as a double entendre of sorts. One attends Christologically and ecclesiologically to the body in sacramental praxis. While the Lord's Supper calls us to consider the ecclesiological contours of the meal, the feast is also Christ himself who, in his sovereignty, is not bound to the sacramental sequence. Like Wesley, we must resist a recalcitrant sacramentalism that restricts God's salvific work. Nevertheless, in making an "open table" the defining hallmark of a Wesleyan piety we have confused God's extraordinary means with the promised ordinary means of grace in the traditional sacramental sequence. Well intended the practice of an "open table" may be, but in the end it erodes a vibrant baptismal and eucharistic piety. In doing so we move further away from a Wesleyan perspective on sacraments.

Bibliography

Bowmer, John C. *The Sacrament of the Lord's Supper in Early Methodism*. London: Dacre, 1951.

Cheyney, John. *Some Arguments: to prove I. The certain salvation of the christened infants of ungodly . . . II. That unconverted Christians are to receive the Lord's Supper . . . III. That ministers may not repel those of their own parish. IV. That the common sort of sinners are not to be excommunicated, V. With an enquiry into Mr. Baxter's doctrine of particular churches*. London: Printed for J. Robinson, 1680.

Felton, Gayle Carlton. "The Sacraments: Sources of Equality, Liberation, and Justice." Reconciling Ministries Clergy Steering Committee (2005). http://www.rmnetwork.org/newrmn/wp-content/uploads/2015/01/RMC-Sacraments.pdf.

————. *United Methodists and the Sacraments*. Nashville: Abingdon, 2007.

Kimbrough, S. T., Jr., and Kenneth G. C. Newport, eds. *The Manuscript Journal of the Reverend Charles Wesley, M.A.* Vol. 2. Nashville: Kingswood, 2007.

Rieger, Joerg. "Grace Under Pressure: What Really Matters in the Church." *Wesleyan Theological Journal* 47.1 (Spring 2012) 42.

Runyon, Theodore. *The New Creation: John Wesley's Theology Today*. Nashville: Abingdon, 1998.

The United Methodist Church. *The United Methodist Book of Worship*. Nashville: United Methodist Publishing, 1992.

United Methodist News Service. "The United Methodist View of Communion." *United Methodist Insight* (September 28, 2013). http://um-insight.net/in-the-church/the-united-methodist-view-of-communion/.

Wainwright, Geoffrey. "The Sacraments in a Wesleyan Perspective." In *Worship with One Accord: Where Liturgy and Ecumenism Embrace*, 105–25. Oxford: Oxford University Press, 1997.

Wesley, Charles. "Romans 6." In *Hymns and Sacred Poems (1742)*. The Center for Studies in the Wesleyan Tradition at Duke Divinity School. https://divinity.duke.edu/sites/divinity.duke.edu/files/documents/cswt/10_Hymns_and_Sacred_Poems_%281742%29_mod.pdf.

————. "Sermon 8, 'Ephesians 5:14.'" In *The Sermons of Charles Wesley: A Critical Edition with Introduction and Notes*, edited by Kenneth G. C. Newport, 211–24. Oxford: Oxford University Press, 2005.

Wesley, John. *John Wesley's Sermons: An Anthology*. Edited by Albert C. Outler and Richard P. Heitzenrater. Nashville: Abingdon, 1991.

"June 27, 1740." In *Bicentennial Edition of the Works of John Wesley*. Vol. 19, *Journals and Diaries II*, edited by W. Reginald Ward and Richard P. Heitzenrater, 158. Nashville: Abingdon, 1990.

———. "June 28, 1740." In *Bicentennial Edition of the Works of John Wesley*. Vol. 19, *Journals and Diaries II*, edited by W. Reginald Ward and Richard P. Heitzenrater, 132–33. Nashville: Abingdon, 1990.

———. "Letter to Richard Thompson dated July 25, 1755." In *Bicentennial Edition of the Works of John Wesley*. Vol. 26, *Letters II*, edited by Frank Baker, 574–75. Nashville: Abingdon, 1987.

———. "September 3, 1739." In *Bicentennial Edition of the Works of John Wesley*. Vol. 19, *Journals and Diaries II (1738-1743)*, edited by W. Reginald Ward and Richard P. Heitzenrater, 32. Nashville: Abingdon, 1976.

———. "September 30–Oct 1, 1749." In *Bicentennial Edition of the Works of John Wesley*. Vol. 20, *Journal and Diaries III*, edited by W. Reginald Ward and Richard P. Heitzenrater, 305. Nashville: Abingdon, 1991.

———. "Sermon 16, 'The Means of Grace.'" In *Bicentennial Edition of the Works of John Wesley*. Vol. 1, *Sermons I*, edited by Albert C. Outler, 376–97. Nashville: Abingdon, 1984.

———. "Sermon 101, 'The Duty of Constant Communion.'" In *Bicentennial Edition of the Works of John Wesley*. Vol. 4, *Sermons IV*, edited by Albert C. Outler, 427–41. Nashville: Abingdon, 1987.

———. "A Treatise on Baptism." In *Works of John Wesley*. Vol. 10, *Letters, Essays, Dialogs, Addresses*, edited by Thomas Jackson, 188–201. Grand Rapids: Zondervan, 1958–59.

Wesley, John, and Charles Wesley. *Hymns on the Lord's Supper*. Bristol: Printed by Felix Farley, 1745.

Westerfield Tucker, Karen B. *American Methodist Worship*. New York: Oxford University Press, 2001.

White, James. "John Wesley's *Sunday Service* and Methodist Spirituality." In *Wesleyan Theology Today: A Bicentennial Theological Consultation*, edited by Theodore Runyon, 403–5. Nashville: Kingswood, 1985.

The World Council of Churches. *Baptism, Eucharist, and Ministry*. Geneva: World Council of Churches, 1982.

CHAPTER 14

Baptism and Eschatology

Initiation and Journey into the Martyr-Church

Brent D. Peterson, Northwest Nazarene University

Baptism and eschatology perhaps seem like an awkward pairing. In some parts of the Wesleyan tradition, baptism has traditionally emphasized the healing God has done prior to baptism and has been understood as an occasion to give a public testimony of "me going public" for Jesus. Moreover, eschatology among some in the Wesleyan tradition has been reduced to figuring out the details of the "end times" and who will burn in the lake and who will escape to the utopia of heaven. Equally problematic is a view of eschatology in which the kingdom of God coming to earth is simply wishful thinking whereby humans can help the world "get nicer." All of these shortcomings merit a conversation about the crucial links between baptism and eschatology.

After a brief comment about eschatology in the Wesleyan tradition, this chapter will consider first the eschatological imagination of Jesus' baptism in the early church. Second, the conversation will explore the eschatological nature of baptism historically and then consider how a Wesleyan view of salvation is best understood eschatologically. Third, this lens will explore how baptism initiates persons into the martyr-church. Fourth, with this initiation into the martyr-church, funerals will be viewed as a fulfillment of one's baptism on earth. Finally, the chapter will explore how an eschatological baptism in the Wesleyan tradition celebrates healing, not only regarding persons, but also through a cosmic imagination of the full redemption of all creation for the glory of God. It is a primary conviction that baptism in the Wesleyan tradition affirms a robust *already* of God's initial sanctifying work in the life of the person and the world, while also anticipating the *not yet* of healing both for the person and the cosmic redemption of all things.

The topic of eschatology in the Wesleyan tradition is broad and expansive. Randy Maddox notes that several conversations weave together in considering eschatology. Eschatology imagines first, the "last things" in regard to the intermediate state after one's death, resurrection and judgment. Second, eschatology yields debates about Christ's return and all the "millennial" options. Third, eschatology considers "the relations of the Reign of God to present ecclesial and social-political existence."[1] While all three are worthy of consideration, this third area will receive primary focus here. Viewing baptism through this eschatological lens celebrates the tension of the *already* healing of God's redemption while also anticipating in hope the *not yet* cosmic (including persons) redemption.

Jesus' Eschatological Baptism: Inbreaking of the Kingdom

Though found in all four Gospels, Jesus' baptism should be a source of great concern and scandal for the church. Baptism generally, and specifically in the ministry of John the Baptist, was about a cleansing from sin. The answers to why Jesus was baptized are complex and worthy of broader conversation, but it was not because Christ had personal sins that needed cleansing. As the Gospels and specifically Heb 4:15 affirms, Christ was tempted, but did not sin. As the King and head of the Jews (and really of all humanity as the New Adam) "by accepting baptism at the hands of the Baptists, Jesus recognizes that this baptism is the divinely appointed means of passage from the sinful Israel to the Israel promised salvation on the day of judgment."[2] To this end, the Gospels consistently record Jesus' declaration that the kingdom of God was not coming in a far off future, but coming now.[3] "The sign that the kingdom was already present in him was the presence of the Spirit working in and through him

1. Maddox, *Responsible Grace*, 230.
2. McDonnell, *Baptism of Jesus*, 4.
3. Matt 4:17.

in words, healings, and exorcisms."[4] It is the role of the Spirit in the life of Jesus that marks the inbreaking of the kingdom of God. In this way, as part of the Incarnation, the baptism of Jesus forms another powerful celebration that the kingdom of God is here, while also anticipating what is still to come.

There also exists a link to sacrificial death in Jesus' baptism. Both the Gospels of Mark and Luke associate Jesus' baptism with Jesus' laying down his life.[5] This link connects to the broader theme that one's baptism is a uniting in Christ's baptism as a celebration of the kingdom coming and a recognition that salvation comes through initiation into the martyr-church through Christ's death and resurrection. As the Servant of God, it was expected that Jesus would offer forgiveness. "What is entirely new is that Jesus *at the same time* is the Messiah and Suffering Servant, a conception impossible for Judaism. . . . Indeed the Jordan event [Jesus' baptism] reaches out to the future death on the cross when all baptism will find its fulfillment."[6]

If Jesus' baptism was a beginning of his ministry—a present "already" of the kingdom of God here—it also looked forward in anticipation of a life laid down in love and devotion to the Father. As Jesus humbly submitted to the waters of John's baptism, so too would Christ, like a Lamb before the Shearer is silent, lay down his life as an act of love to God and the world. Too often Christians imagine that Christ came simply to do things for us—such as procuring our salvation—while failing to recognize Jesus is not interested in Christians being onlookers and gazers. Rather, Jesus invites persons to be disciples, followers of himself all the way to the cross.

This eschatological lens of Jesus' baptism is not about the killing of Jesus, but demonstrates a consistent willingness of Jesus to kenotically lay down his life in humility and service while also providing a way for all persons, Jews and Gentiles, to find salvation. This salvation only comes through covenantal union with Christ into his martyr-church. As Christ's baptism finds fulfillment as an *already* in his ministry, so too does the *not yet* of his eschatological baptism find completion on the cross, while the hope of the kingdom coming is part of the celebration of the resurrection. Likewise, in this way, all Christian baptisms are eschatological.

4. McDonnell, *Baptism of Jesus*, 3.
5. Mark 10:38–39; Luke 12:50.
6. McDonnell, *Baptism of Jesus*, 18.

Baptism not only points to a saving from sins—the *already*—but it also offers a *not yet* in a willingness of Christians to offer their lives back to God in service to God's kingdom.

To be part of the martyr-church is not about death or being killed. Instead, being part of the martyr-church is to recognize all baptisms are a drowning and death to an idolatrous self. This mindset opens persons up to ministry in the church for the sake of the world, not offering comfortable or calculated compassion, but rather a willingness to lay down one's life in love and service to others, especially the lost, broken, and marginalized.

The Eschatology of Baptism

When baptism is understood as initiation into the martyr-church through Christ's death and resurrection, the eschatological dimension of baptism becomes evident in both Scripture and early Christian testimony. The Gospels recount John the Baptist's proclamation "Change your hearts and lives! Here comes the kingdom of heaven!" (Matt 3:3, CEB). Christian witness in the New Testament is about initiation into the church as part of God's kingdom that is here and will come more fully. James White notes how baptism gives entrance to the kingdom of God by pointing to John 3:5: "unless someone is born of water and Spirit, it's not possible to enter God's kingdom" (CEB).[7] For White, this verse signifies that entrance and participation in the present and coming kingdom occurs through baptism. Thus, when viewed through an eschatological lens, baptism celebrates the *already* of God's cleansing, healing, and restoration, but also anticipates a further healing and cleansing into the *not yet* of the kingdom that will still more fully come. Eschatologically speaking, baptism should be seen as the beginning of the Christian journey and not the end.

White also recounts that throughout the church's history baptism "became the sign of moving into a new age in which one was already a part of the oncoming kingdom. One became part of a new order of creation as a member of a tightly disciplined community. And baptism functioned as the sign of that transition from the old order to the new."[8] This movement from the old to the new, at its best, is not a gnostic attempt to escape

---

7. White, *Sacraments in Protestant Practice*, 54.
8. White, *Sacraments in Protestant Practice*, 54.

creation but rather is part of God's ongoing and persistent redemption of creation. Moreover, an eschatological imagination of baptism considers union with Christ and entrance into the martyr-church as inherently political. One's baptism is initiation into the political citizenship of the kingdom of God, calling Christians to live in the eschatological tension of the *already* present kingdom while also anticipating the kingdom of God *that will come* in fullness. Baptism thus serves as initiation into a new age and new order, one that points to the reality that the Christian life is not an escape from the world but a call to join in Christ's work of redeeming the world. White notes how the *Baptism, Eucharist, and Ministry* ecumenical concord draws upon classic theological prose to celebrate baptism as "a sign of the kingdom of God and of the life of the world to come."[9] Each baptism is thus a new act of healing, of the new creation, and of anticipating the coming of the kingdom in its fullness where all will confess Jesus Christ as Lord.[10]

An eschatological view of baptism also connects the sacraments of baptism and the Lord's Supper. While baptism marks a dynamic beginning of the healing and redemption in the life of each person (the *already*), it also anticipates the ongoing healing and grace of God at work throughout one's life (the *not yet*). The Lord's Supper is the meal of the baptized, an occasion where one's baptismal covenant can be renewed as God offers further healing for the long journey of salvation.

John Wesley's Eschatological Soteriology in Baptism

One of the great challenges the Wesley brothers faced in eighteenth-century England was the problem of *nominalism*. While many in Britain claimed to be Christian, John and Charles greatly grieved how many lives did not demonstrate the love and fruit that should be found among Christians. The Wesleys were concerned that an anemic understanding of baptism was contributing to the problem. Most persons in eighteenth-century England were baptized as infants, and some considered baptism as the only mark needed to confirm their Christianity. Clearly, God's healing through the sacrament of baptism was not the problem; rather, many persons had stopped responding to the grace (i.e., the healing presence of God) given at baptism. While this pastoral concern did not lessen

9. The World Council of Churches, *Baptism, Eucharist, and Ministry*, 3.

10. White, *Sacraments in Protestant Practice*, 54; cf. Phil 2:9–11.

the Wesleys' celebration of baptism, it did cause them to nuance what healing was offered at baptism.

At the beginning of the sermon "Marks of the New Birth" John Wesley states:

> That these privileges, by the free mercy of God, are ordinarily annexed to baptism (which is thence termed by our Lord in a preceding verse, the being "born of water and of the Spirit") we know; but we would know what these privileges are: What is the new birth?[11]

Wesley affirms here the benefits of the new birth are *ordinarily* annexed at baptism. Pastor Wesley recognizes that while there is an *ordo salutis* (order of salvation), every person's journey can be unique. Wesley also identifies how the gift of assurance in the new birth is deeply connected to being a child of God. As a child there is an *already* to this healing, namely power over sin, while the person also anticipates more healing to come, the *not yet*. He writes:

> St. John; particularly with regard to the former branch of it, namely, power over outward sin. After he had been crying out, as one astonished at the depth of the riches of the goodness of God,—Behold, what manner of love the Father hath bestowed upon us, that we should be called the sons of God! Beloved, now are we the sons of God: And it doth not yet appear what we shall be; but we know, that when he shall appear, we shall be like him; for we shall see him as he is.[12]

---

11. Wesley, "Sermon 18, 'Marks of the New Birth,'" 417. John Wesley again affirms the gift of regeneration occurring at baptism in his "Treatise on Baptism." "And this regeneration which our Church in so many places ascribes to baptism is more than barely being admitted into the Church, though commonly connected therewith; being 'grafted into the body of Christ's Church, we are made the children of God by adoption and grace.' This is grounded on the plain words of our Lord: 'Except a man be born again of water and of the Spirit, he cannot enter into the kingdom of God.' (John iii. 5.) By water then, as a means, the water of baptism, we are regenerated or born again; whence it is also called by the apostle, 'the washing of regeneration.' Our Church therefore ascribes no greater virtue to baptism than Christ himself has done. Nor does she ascribe it to the outward washing, but to the inward grace, which, added thereto, makes it a sacrament. Herein a principle of grace is infused, which will not be wholly taken away, unless we quench the Holy Spirit of God by long-continued wickedness." See Wesley, "Treatise on Baptism," 191–92, emphasis added.

12. Wesley, "Sermon 18, 'Marks of the New Birth,'" 420.

Notice the eschatological hope that connects salvation to being renewed into the image of Christ, thus enabling persons to fully see God in God's fullness. Certainly, there is a present healing in baptism, yet there also anticipates the ongoing healing in sanctification.

In celebrating the grace of new birth and regeneration occurring at baptism, John Wesley is being consistent with Article 27, "Of Baptism," in the Anglican Articles of Religion:

> Baptism is not only a sign of profession, and mark of difference, whereby Christian men are discerned from others that be not christened, but it is also a sign of Regeneration or New-Birth, whereby, as by an instrument, they that receive baptism rightly are grafted into the Church; the promises of the forgiveness of sin, and of our adoption to be the sons of God by the Holy Ghost, are visibly signed and sealed; Faith is confirmed, and Grace increased by virtue of prayer unto God.
>
> The baptism of young Children is in any wise to be retained in the Church, as most agreeable with the institution of Christ.[13]

The celebration of the gift of new birth at baptism is inherently eschatological. Persons are grafted into the church and adopted as daughters and sons; faith is confirmed, and grace increased. This is part of the *already*. However, with both the prescription to baptize infants and the *promise of the forgiveness of sins*, baptism also anticipates in hope and joy the full *not yet* of salvation. For, the eschatological nature of regenerating/sanctifying grace is such that the baptized person is ushered into an ongoing process of healing, recovering, and maturing as the person grows in the image of Christ.

Randy Maddox recounts that the new birth is the foundational facet of sanctification for Wesley. Maddox asserts it "addresses the question of our ability for recovering any holiness in our sin-distorted life . . . any such ability is *graciously restored*."[14] Maddox notes that for Wesley to be born again has a wide breadth, "being inwardly changed by the almighty operation of the Spirit of God; changed from sin to holiness: renewed in the image of him that created us."[15] In many ways, this broad definition celebrates the full therapeutic hope of salvation.

13. Wohlers, "Articles of Religion."
14. Maddox, *Responsible Grace*, 176.
15. Wesley, "Doctrine of Original Sin," 308.

Maddox notes that without care the new birth could be equated with entire sanctification.[16] He thus clarifies the distinction between the new birth and entire sanctification in Wesley's teaching: "the first being the rejuvenation of our human faculties that accompanies the restored pardoning Presence of God in our lives, while the second is gradual renewal of our moral nature that is then possible."[17] In other words, the new birth is the beginning to sanctification proper. Both the new birth and sanctification should be identified with regeneration. Within the Wesleyan tradition, it should be affirmed that regeneration (sanctification) occurs eschatologically for the believer. In many ways God at the new birth forgives, adopts, initiates, and prepares the believer for the long journey of sanctification. This is the *already*.

The *not yet* of regeneration celebrates the long journey of sanctification as the ongoing healing into love and maturity in Christ that continues into our death (and perhaps even after) toward glorification. As we respond to God's call for deeper healing, "The New Birth commences further co-operant transformation of our lives, empowered by sanctifying grace."[18] Perhaps Wesley imagines the new birth as initial sanctification that is then expectantly awaiting and anticipating the ongoing fullness of entire sanctification.[19]

Maddox does suggest that Wesley's strong sacramental fervor and pastoral concern about the regnant nominalism of his day together fostered a strong evangelical passion that insisted persons could not simply rely upon the fact that they were baptized, but must respond (and that continually) to God's healing grace. After his encounter with the Moravians and his own revival/conversion experience at Aldersgate,

> Wesley had come to see new birth in terms of a conscious conversion experience. This meant for him that baptismal regeneration could not be presumed past childhood. And so becoming a Christian involved a born-again experience that was not marked by external ceremony or rite but was a life-transforming personal experience.[20]

16. Maddox, *Responsible Grace*, 159.

17. Maddox, *Responsible Grace*, 159.

18. Maddox, *Responsible Grace*, 170.

19. This appears to be what Wesley is suggesting in his "Sermon 45, 'The New Birth,'" 198.

20. White, *Sacraments in Protestant Practice*, 70.

Pastorally, Wesley became agitated by a great deal of nominal Christians who testified to faith by appealing to their baptism but lacked the present fruit and God's love shed abroad in their hearts. This encouraged Wesley not to dismiss the *already* healing at baptism, but also to celebrate the ongoing *not yet* where persons continued to open themselves to God's continual healing. In "The New Birth" sermon, Wesley's growing pastoral concern does prompt him to move away from his earlier teaching—and that of the *Book of Common Prayer*—to suggest that persons may experience the new birth at baptism, but not necessarily so.[21] However, while Wesley suggests that persons can experience the outward sign of baptism but not the inward grace, he clarifies later in "The New Birth" sermon, "I do not now speak with regard to infants: it is certain, our Church supposes that all who are baptized in their infancy are at the same time born again."[22] Infants will certainly receive the new birth at baptism, while for adults it is possible. Yet this celebration of grace for infants is not necessarily eternal.

One can recall from Wesley's journal that on the very day of his Aldersgate experience he notes, "I believe, till I was about ten years old I had not sinned away that 'washing of the Holy Ghost' which was given me at baptism."[23] Rob Staples points to another passage in the earlier sermon, "The Marks of the New Birth," where Wesley talks of the need to restore children: "Those who were made children of god by baptism, but are now children of the devil, may yet again receive power to become sons of God: 'that they may receive again what they have lost.'"[24] So, even infants who receive the gift of new birth at baptism outside of their will and response will need to respond later in their lives to the healing God continues to offer. For children as well as adults, salvation must be imagined eschatologically. There is an *already* for both the infant and adult at baptism, but the *not yet* of future growth, healing, and maturity is mandated for the flourishing of a Christian life.

Wesley's primary concern was to affirm that while persons may get wet at baptism through the outward sign, the inward grace may or may not occur based on the person's response to the salvation offered. This again is central to Wesley's sacramental and soteriological theology. While

---

21. Wesley, "Sermon 45, 'The New Birth,'" 197.
22. Wesley, "Sermon 45, 'The New Birth,'" 197.
23. John Wesley, "May 24, 1738," 242–43.
24. Wesley, "Sermon 18, 'Marks of the New Birth,'" 430.

the healing presence of God is offered at baptism, God also empowers persons to respond to that healing. Yet, if persons fail to respond to that healing, they may thwart the healing God desires to do.[25] Wesleyans can easily deflect any Pelagian charges by noting that all of this is done by the grace of God. Persons do not save themselves but must respond to God's invitation to healing. Moreover, God also empowers humans to respond to the healing offered. It is the movement of God that invites and makes possible the human response. For the Wesleyan tradition today, it seems advisable, pastorally and theologically, to imagine the healing of baptism eschatologically. Indeed, God initiates, adopts, heals, and forgives at baptism, but persons are to continually respond to the ongoing healing God desires to do. This is the journey of sanctification.

Perhaps the analogy of a marriage is helpful. Many marriages begin with a wedding ceremony, some with more or less pomp and circumstance. Many marriages include vows and promises made between the bride and groom in front of family and friends. Certainly, no one would deny the significant commitment and authenticity of the vows offered at the wedding. This is the "already" of a marriage. However, a marriage is much more than a wedding ceremony. A marriage then becomes a daily commitment to live into the wedding covenant and vows. This is the "not yet"—living into the ongoing, ever growing, and flourishing relationship.

Ted Campbell also affirms the two strong strains of sacramental and evangelical passion in John Wesley. Spirituality of the Wesleyan movement in historically Methodist churches is a sacramental evangelicalism. Wesleyan spirituality first shares the conviction of broad catholicity, that the sacraments are divinely appointed, indispensable signs, and means of grace. Second, the evangelical/pietistic tradition emphasizes that no outward act (sacraments included) could suffice in the place of personal conversion to Christ. However, the emphasis on conversion does not deny the objective power of God in salvation. The locus of this objective power, for the pietistic tradition, is located not in the sacraments but in personal, religious experience of transformation. Campbell suggests that the genius is this tension of sacramental and evangelical passions. Baptism is a means of our New Birth and the beginning of our regeneration/sanctification; yet one's experience of conversion is also a means of grace and should be considered eschatological.

25. See Wesley, "Sermon 45, 'The New Birth,'" 199–200.

Wesley saw the New Birth as the ongoing process of repentance and turning to God that is empowered by the grace given at baptism and renewed in participation in the Eucharist. Campbell denies Wesley had two different ideas of regeneration. Campbell argues that regeneration for Wesley was both a result of infant baptism and adult conversion. At Aldersgate, what was recovered or fanned into a flame in the conversion experience was precisely the grace that had been given to Wesley in his baptism and subsequently squelched by sin. While for Wesley baptism is only needed once, Wesley speaks of the need of fresh regeneration. Campbell calls for a convergence of sacramental and pietistic movements. "As churches, we have to take responsibility for the 'ordinary' as well as 'extraordinary' means by which divine grace comes to us."[26] What God has done, is doing, and will do all celebrate the Wesleyan soteriological synergy.

Baptized into the Martyr-Church

It is also important that all Christians recognize their baptism is joining in Christ's baptism, which is also an initiation into the martyr-church, a covenantal joining in Christ's death and resurrection. "Christian baptism makes a double reference: it is both a cleansing and a drowning."[27] For Craig Hovey, this is not an imitation or copying of Jesus; this is being initiated into the body of Christ, a body that bears witness to his life and love and is invited not to fight, or flee, but to follow Jesus in compassionate obedience.[28]

Martyrdom is *not* about wanting or seeking death. At its core, to be a Christian martyr is to bear witness to Jesus Christ. To be baptized into this martyr-church is a willingness to bear witness to the love and grace of the present and coming kingdom, even if that means we are killed for doing so. This is not about being killed but being set free from fear as an embodied gift of the radical eschatological hope. Put negatively, if persons are still afraid to die and thus curtail their compassion and love for sake of their own survival, they are not truly experiencing the deep baptismal hope of the kingdom of God. Put positively, to be baptized into the martyr-church is to bear witness to Christ, to love boldly, with costly

26. Campbell, "Conversion and Baptism," 174.

27. Hovey, *To Share in the Body*, 25.

28. Hovey, *To Share in the Body*, 28, 52.

compassion that allows God to use them to bring the kingdom more fully each day.

Eschatological Hope Necessary for the Martyr-Church

Baptism is a covenant where one is initiated into the body of Christ to pick up their cross with Jesus. Yet, "the church is given no guarantees that following Jesus will achieve anything."[29] Martyrdom is always a result of faithful living and never a strategy. "The church bears its cross when it does not ask what purpose the cross serves."[30] One does not seek death, but one prays for God's strength to be faithful and loving even when it is hard. This is precisely why the eschatological hope is so profound. The eschatological hope of baptism confirms that indeed the kingdom of God will come. With this confidence, one recognizes that her or his existence in this world is not necessary to make the kingdom come. Without this confidence, Christians might be led to violence instead of martyrdom, believing that their lives are necessary to a kingdom that may or may not come unless they maximize their work for the kingdom. However, this eschatological baptism in Jesus says precisely that the kingdom is here and will come, and the primary way to help bear witness to and facilitate its coming is by a willingness to lay down one's life as necessary.

It is also central to note that unlike the cult of martyrs in the early years of the church—in which persons were seeking to be killed in order to receive glory and fame—martyrdom is certainly not the only faithful witness of the church. To seek one's death is, in fact, not martyrdom. The Christian is not to be concerned about whether they are martyred or not; instead, they are simply invited to live a life of faithfulness, come what may. So, with the Apostle Paul, we can pray:

> Rather, I hope with daring courage that Christ's greatness will be seen in my body, now as always, whether I live or die. 21 Because for me, living serves Christ and dying is even better. 22 If I continue to live in this world, I get results from my work. 23 But I don't know what I prefer. I'm torn between the two because I want to leave this life and be with Christ, which is far better. 24 However, it's more important for me to stay in this world for your sake. (Phil 1:20b–24, CEB)

29. Hovey, *To Share in the Body*, 45.
30. Hovey, *To Share in the Body*, 47.

This is the prayer of the eschatological hope of the baptized. To live is Christ and to die is gain.

Funerals as Completion of Eschatological Baptism

In light of the primary thesis of this chapter—that baptism is part of the eschatological beginning of salvation, the "already,"—the Christian funeral in many ways can be seen as a climax and fulfillment of the "not yet." This is not to suggest that at one's death one has no more room for growth in sanctifying grace, nor that persons will not continue to grow and mature moving toward the promise of glorification after death. Because baptism is the beginning of the eschatological pilgrimage of salvation and the Lord's Supper is the meal of the baptized, which renews their baptismal covenant and conveys God's ongoing healing and sustaining grace, funerals can be seen as a key celebration of God's faithfulness in fulfilling saving, baptismal grace.

James White notes that funerals testify to the realities of death and resurrection in the presence of the community. This is the same affirmation and celebration that takes place at baptism as persons are initiated into the church as part of their union with Christ's baptism, and as such, with his death and resurrection. White notes that funerals also "commend the deceased to God . . . each of the baptized has already died and been raised with Christ in baptism (Rom 6:3-4). Now is the time to remember that God has already shown God's acceptance of us, an acceptance first made visible in our baptism."[31] The "Service of Death and Resurrection" in the *United Methodist Hymnal* begins by proclaiming:

> Dying, Christ destroyed our death. Rising, Christ restored our life. Christ will come again in glory. As in baptism *Name* [of deceased] put on Christ, so in Christ may *Name* be clothed in glory. Here and now, dear friends, we are God's children. What we shall be has not yet been revealed; but we know that when he appears, we shall be like him, for we shall see him as he is.[32]

This beautifully celebrates both the ecclesial and eschatological sacramental moments of a Christian's pilgrimage in this life. The eschatological lens is clear with the celebration at baptism that Christ died, is risen, and will come again. So, at one's baptism, a person is initiated into this

31. White, *Introduction to Christian Worship*, 295.
32. United Methodist Church, *United Methodist Hymnal*, 870.

eschatological promise, but also at one's funeral, a person is more fully given into Christ's glory. Moreover, this eschatological link between baptism and funeral is not simply about the individual, for this link holds together ecclesial events.

Just as Christian baptisms must be public for the entire assembly to participate in the celebration as they also remember their own baptismal vows, and just as the Lord's Supper, the meal of the baptized, must be received communally as the church collectively renews their baptismal vows, so too are funerals an ecclesial event; one in which all congregants are reminded of their mortality as they celebrate another sister or brother who—being previously baptized into the death and resurrection of Jesus—is now being given over more fully to God in glory. In this liturgy, all congregants are reminded that our future is beyond what has been revealed to us, which perhaps is now more fully revealed to our departed sister. Therefore, we also in faith anticipate that at our physical death we will be moved to see God as God is.

Baptism as Cosmic Eschatological Redemption

Just as baptisms are not simply about a person, but how God is growing the church, so too baptisms also celebrate the future healing of all creation. One important dimension of the Christian sacraments of baptism and the Lord's Supper is the use of common (profane) parts of creation that are transformed to be holy, infused by God's grace. The use of water, wine, and bread celebrate how God, along with human hands, can transform what is ordinary to become extraordinary. The analogy of the ordinary matter of bread, wine, and water symbolizes (participates in the reality to which it points) how God can take ordinary people and use them in sacramental ways for the further healing and redemption of all creation. This dimension of the sacraments also celebrates how the Wesleyan tradition should reject any sacred and secular dualism, as if God's presence and power are only at work in some spaces and objects while other spaces and objects declared to be secular denote a place or object where God is absent. Such a claim is categorically false. From Genesis to Revelation, the creation comes forth and is blessed by God as good. Certainly, sin is a disease upon creation, which is also longing for its redemption.

> The whole creation waits breathless with anticipation for the revelation of God's sons and daughters. Creation was subjected to frustration, not by its own choice—it was the choice of the one who subjected it—but in the hope that the creation itself will be set free from slavery to decay and brought into the glorious freedom of God's children. We know that the whole creation is groaning together and suffering labor pains up until now. (Rom 8:19–22, CEB).

Therefore, while each baptism is part of the eschatological baptism of persons, it is also part of the eschatological cosmic redemption for which creation groans.

In J. R. R. Tolkien's epic *Lord of the Rings* trilogy, one of the epic narratives is the Battle of Isengard. Encouraged by Meriadoc Brandybuck and Peregrin Took, the Ents (large and powerful talking trees) march against Isengard, which is controlled by Saruman and his armies. The Ents surround Isengard, destroy its gates, tear down its walls, and then break its dam. As the dam breaks, floodwaters pour down the mountainside offering a final drowning to all the defenders of Isengard. Peter Jackson's film adaptation of *The Two Towers* provides a powerful visual of this scene.[33] The waters come down furiously upon the defenders of Isengard, wiping out all of Saruman's army. These floodwaters offer both a drowning and cleansing of the land. Treebeard (the leader of the Ents) exhorts in the film adaptation, "The filth of Saruman is washing away. Trees will come back here—young trees, wild trees."[34] Treebeard was correct. After this battle, the Ents take control of Isengard. After the War of the Ring, it is noteworthy that the Ents turn the land into one of the most beautiful gardens in Middle Earth. In this way, the floodwaters are both a drowning and cleansing, prepped for new creation.

The biblical story of the flood recorded in Genesis 6 also comes to mind. The Lord noted that humanity had become thoroughly evil and all the ideas of their minds were evil. The Lord decided to cleanse the good creation from this evil. Only Noah and his family were spared. It seems fitting to think of the flood as a type of cosmic eschatological baptism, a drowning and cleansing. While this analogy does break down a bit, it can offer an illustration of the way Christians have understood baptism as a cleansing and drowning, not simply for persons, but for creation.[35]

33. Jackson, *Lord of the Rings*.

34. Jackson, *Lord of the Rings*.

35. Hovey, *To Share in the Body*, 25.

H. Paul Santmire notes that the ancient church affirmed cosmic connections to both baptism and the Eucharist. Santmire notes how the architecture of many freestanding baptisteries served to imagine the entire cosmos, often using domed ceilings to point to the heavens. Many had an octagonal shape that often functioned similar to stained glass, in telling the universal history of salvation.[36] More recently, Santmire notes that with the inclusion of flowing water, cosmic imagery, and placing the font near the front and center, some traditions seek to capture again the cosmic nature of baptism. Moreover, baptismal liturgies also illuminate this cosmic redemption. The ELCA includes this prayer in its baptismal liturgy at the "Thanksgiving at the Font":

> Holy God, mighty Lord, gracious Father: We give you thanks, for in the beginning your Spirit moved over the waters and you created heaven and earth.
>
> We give you thanks, O God, for in the beginning your Spirit moved over the waters and by your Word you created the world, calling forth life in which you took delight. Through the waters of the flood you delivered Noah and his family, and through the sea you led your people Israel from slavery into freedom. At the river your Son was baptized by John and anointed with the Holy Spirit. By the baptism of Jesus' death and resurrection you set us free from the power of sin and death and raise us up to live in you.
>
> Pour out your Holy Spirit, the power of your living Word, that those who are washed in the waters of baptism may be given new life. To you be given honor and praise through Jesus Christ our Lord, in the unity of the Holy Spirit, now and forever.[37]

This prayer celebrates the use of waters in God's salvation story. References are made to the flood in Genesis 6, the Israelites passing through the Red Sea in Exodus 14, and Jesus' baptism in the New Testament. Noteworthy is the celebration that Christ "made the water a sign of the kingdom and of cleansing and rebirth." This is seen in Clement of Alexandria, who affirms, "For this reason the Savior was baptized, though he had no need of it, in order to sanctify all the waters for those who would be regenerated."[38] Jesus' baptism proleptically (both for those before and

---

36. Santmire, *Nature Reborn*, 85.

37. Evangelical Lutheran Church in America, *Evangelical Lutheran Worship*, 230.

38. McDonnell, *Baptism of Jesus,* 55, drawing upon Clement of Alexandria, *Selection of Prophetic Writings,* 701.

after him) "joins the creation of the world through water and the Spirit to recreation through water and the Spirit."[39] In this way, Jesus' baptism connects the waters from the first creation to cosmic redemption and healing. According to McDonnell, Irenaeus celebrates the power of Christ's cosmic anointing at his baptism.

> The Father's cosmic anointing of the Word with the Spirit is expressed in the Jordan anointing, which has salvation as its burden. Through two anointings, one eternal, the other at the Jordan, Irenaeus attempts to give a systematic coherence to his doctrine of creation, binding first creation (Genesis) with second creation (redemption) and the Church. The cosmic character of the eternal anointing has echoes in the Jordan anointing.[40]

Yet, just as the eschatological *telos* (goal) of the person is for the glory of God, likewise the eschatological redemption of the cosmos is also for the full glory of God. "The first steps to an eschatological consummation begin at the Jordan where, as Philoxenus would say much later, 'mystically God becomes in all and all in God.'"[41] While this certainly is for the person and the building up of the church, the imagination moves from the church to the cosmos. "The anointing at the Jordan has to do with the fullness and perfection of salvation offered to humankind in the Church, which, as Origen notes, is 'the cosmos of the cosmos.'"[42]

Conclusion

In the Wesleyan tradition, soteriology is best understood eschatologically. This *already, not yet* tension recognizes God's ability to work healing in the world while also empowering persons to continue to live into the healing grace God continues to offer. The *not yet* hope is grounded in what God has done and the full promise of what will come. This is not a Pelagian move where persons heal themselves; God's healing is never coercive but invites and empowers the necessary human response.

Baptism celebrates the *already* of salvation by God's work of regeneration and the new birth, also known as initial sanctification. Yet

---

39. McDonnell, *Baptism of Jesus*, 55.

40. McDonnell, *Baptism of Jesus*, 60, drawing upon Orbe, *La Unción del Verbo*, 521.

41. McDonnell, *Baptism of Jesus*, 66, drawing upon Philoxenus, *Fragments*, 393.

42. McDonnell, *Baptism of Jesus*, 120.

the grace of baptism must continually be responded to throughout one's life along with the continual healing offered through participation in the Lord's Supper. This ongoing response is all part of one's continual growth in love, known by Wesleyans as the process of sanctification. This baptism joins into Christ's life, death, and resurrection as an initiation into the martyr-church. As such, Christians can celebrate a fulfillment of baptism at funerals. Moreover, for the Wesleyan soteriological eschatology this is not simply the healing of persons, this is a cosmic healing for all things whereby God will be all in all. In this way, baptism celebrates God's ongoing healing and redeeming of all things, which still draws and woos persons to keep responding to the healing that God is working in each person, as part of healing God is working in all of creation.

Bibliography

Campbell, Ted A. "Conversion and Baptism in Wesleyan Spirituality." In *Conversion in the Wesleyan Tradition*, edited by Kenneth J. Collins and John H. Tyson, 160–74. Nashville: Abingdon, 2001.

The Evangelical Lutheran Church in America. *Evangelical Lutheran Worship*. Minneapolis: Augsburg Fortress, 2006.

Hovey, Craig. *To Share in the Body: A Theology of Martyrdom for Today's Church*. Grand Rapids: Brazos, 2008.

Jackson, Peter, dir. *The Lord of the Rings: The Two Towers*. DVD. Burbank: New Line Cinema and WingNut Films, 2002.

Maddox, Randy L. *Responsible Grace: John Wesley's Practical Theology*. Nashville: Abingdon, 1994.

McDonnell, Kilian. *The Baptism of Jesus in the Jordan*. Collegeville, MN: Liturgical, 1996.

Orbe, A. *La Unción del Verbo*. Rome: Gregorian University, 1961.

Philoxenus. *Fragments of the Commentary on Matthew and Luke*. Edited by J. W. Watt. Leuven, Belgium: Peeters, 1978.

Santmire, H. Paul. *Nature Reborn: The Ecological and Cosmic Promise of Christian Theology*. Minneapolis: Fortress, 2000.

The United Methodist Church. *The United Methodist Hymnal: Book of United Methodist Worship*. Nashville: United Methodist Publishing, 1989.

Wesley, John. "The Doctrine of Original Sin, Part III (1757)." In *Bicentennial Edition of the Works of John Wesley*. Vol. 12, *Doctrinal and Controversial Treatises I*, edited by Randy L. Maddox, 306–51. Nashville: Abingdon, 2012.

———. "May 24, 1738." In *Bicentennial Edition of the Works of John Wesley*. Vol. 18, *Journals and Diaries I (1735–1738)*, edited by W. Reginald Ward and Richard P. Heitzenrater, 242–50. Nashville: Abingdon, 1990.

———. "Sermon 18, 'Marks of the New Birth.'" In *Bicentennial Edition of the Works of John Wesley*. Vol. 1, *Sermons I*, edited by Albert Outler, 415–30. Nashville: Abingdon, 1984.

————. "Sermon 45, 'The New Birth.'" In *Bicentennial Edition of the Works of John Wesley*. Vol. 2, *Sermons II*, edited by Albert C. Outler, 186–201. Nashville: Abingdon, 1985.

————. "A Treatise on Baptism." In *Works of John Wesley*. Vol. 10, *Letters, Essays, Dialogs, Addresses*, edited by Thomas Jackson, 188–201. Grand Rapids: Zondervan, 1958–1959.

White, James F. *Introduction to Christian Worship*. Nashville: Abingdon, 1990.

————. *The Sacraments in Protestant Practice and Faith*. Nashville: Abingdon, 1999.

Wohlers, Charles. "The Articles of Religion as they Appear in the 1789, 1892, and 1928 Books of Common Prayer." http://justus.anglican.org/resources/bcp/1928/Articles.htm.

The World Council of Churches. *Baptism, Eucharist, and Ministry*. Geneva: World Council of Churches, 1982.

CHAPTER 15

Baptism and Ecumenism

Toward a Sacramental Bond of Unity

KAREN B. WESTERFIELD TUCKER,

BOSTON UNIVERSITY SCHOOL OF THEOLOGY

IN ITS CONCLUDING 2011 report, the International Commission for Dialogue between the Roman Catholic Church and the World Methodist Council appropriated a sentence from its previous final report (2006) to reaffirm that "[o]ur common baptism in' the name of the Father, the Son and the Holy Spirit is our sacramental bond of unity, the visible foundation of the deep communion which already exists between us and which impels us to ever deeper unity with each other and participation in the life and mission of Christ himself."[1] Here the International Commission not only reasserted its understanding of baptism as "the sacramental bond of unity," a phrase drawn from the Second Vatican Council's decree on ecumenism *Unitatis Redintegratio*.[2] They also responded to the call

---

1. International Commission for Dialogue between the Roman Catholic Church and the World Methodist Council, *Encountering Christ the Saviour*, 23, Section 29. Cf. International Commission for Dialogue between the Roman Catholic Church and the World Methodist Council, *Grace Given You in Christ*, 34, Section 78. Digital links to the World Methodist Council dialogue documents mentioned in this essay are at http://worldmethodistcouncil.org/resources/ecumenical-dialogues/.

2. *Unitatis Redintegratio*, Section 22b: "Baptism therefore establishes a sacramental

from the World Council of Churches (WCC) issued in the convergence text *Baptism, Eucharist and Ministry* (1982) to move further toward the mutual recognition of baptism "as an important sign and means of expressing the baptismal unity given in Christ."[3] A more detailed summons appeared subsequently in the WCC study text *One Baptism: Towards Mutual Recognition* (2011). The International Commission's 2011 report went on to specify places of agreement, convergence, and difference regarding baptism, all the while holding to the "one overarching conviction" that "all that happens through baptism is the work of God's grace in Jesus Christ."[4]

According to Thomas F. Best, former director of Faith and Order at the WCC, the "B" section was the "most broadly accepted aspect" of *Baptism, Eucharist, and Ministry* (*BEM*) with many responses to the document reflecting "a growing consensus that baptism was fundamental to the churches' acceptance of one another as members together of the one body of Christ."[5] Perhaps this "growing consensus" created the impetus for subsequent bilateral and multilateral dialogues to focus partially or entirely upon the topic of baptism over the course of the last almost forty years. The signing of the Joint Declaration on the Doctrine of Justification in 1999 by the Pontifical Council for Promoting Christian Unity and the Lutheran World Federation[6]—and the World Methodist Council's affiliation with the document in 2006[7]—along with the 2005

---

bond of unity which links all who have been reborn by it. But of itself baptism is only a beginning, an inauguration wholly directed toward the fullness of life in Christ. Baptism, therefore, envisages a complete profession of faith, complete incorporation in the system of salvation such as Christ willed it to be, and finally complete ingrafting in eucharistic communion."

3. World Council of Churches, *Baptism, Eucharist and Ministry*, 5, Section 15. Also referred to as *BEM*.

4. International Commission for Dialogue between the Roman Catholic Church and the World Methodist Council, *Encountering Christ the Saviour*, 24, Section 31.

5. Best, "Faith and Order Saga," 305–6.

6. The Lutheran World Federation and The Roman Catholic Church, *Joint Declaration*.

7. For the World Methodist Council's Statement of Association, see World Methodist Council, "WMC's Statement." In 2016, the Anglican Consultative Council "affirmed and welcomed" the substance of the Declaration, and a year later the Anglican Communion formally signed an agreement. The World Communion of Reformed Churches signed an association agreement also in 2017. Representatives from all five world communions convened at the University of Notre Dame (South Bend, Indiana, USA) on March 26–28, 2019, to discuss the implications of their agreement

study on the "Ecclesiological and Ecumenical Implications of a Common Baptism" by the Joint Working Group between the WCC and the Roman Catholic Church[8] each stimulated ongoing as well as new national and international conversations. Several consultations and dialogues, in considering the sacramental bond of unity and mutual recognition, aired the necessity for an "acknowledgement of apostolicity in the other. Apostolicity indicates coherence and continuity with the faith, life, witness and ministry of the apostolic community, chosen and sent by Christ."[9]

Of course, determination of apostolicity in baptismal theology and practice is not a simple matter given potential and real differences in the reading of the biblical and patristic sources. In some cases, these differences also exist within a single world communion. The 2018 report of the International Dialogue between the Baptist World Alliance and the World Methodist Council confessed that while Baptists and Methodists discerned commonalities and differences in their discussions relative to baptism and Christian initiation, they also needed to acknowledge "a wide divergence on some issues within each church."[10] Such honesty is essential, and it does create challenges to an ecumenical affirmation of a common baptism when significant differences of theology and practice already exist in one dialogue partner, whether it be within a single denomination or across a confederation of a "family" of ecclesial communities. Such is certainly the case within the membership of the World Methodist Council where among the most significant differences/divergences are regarding baptism's (sacramental) efficacy and its proper recipient. As Methodists and Wesleyans receive and appropriate the ecumenical insights already obtained from their own and others' dialogues, and as they engage further in bilateral dialogue—and in some cases move toward the establishment of full communion with those other communities—they

---

in the context of the growing closeness and collaboration between them. One of the outcomes was an agreement to strengthen their witness to their common bonds of baptism. This author was one of the World Methodist Council representatives engaged in the conversation.

8. Joint Working Group between the Roman Catholic Church and the World Council of Churches, *Eighth Report*, 45–72 (Appendix C).

9. World Council of Churches, *One Baptism*, 4–5, Section 14; cf. "Ecclesiological and Ecumenical Implications of a Common Baptism," in Joint Working Group between the Roman Catholic Church and the World Council of Churches, *Eighth Report*, 65–66, Section 91.

10. International Dialogue between the Baptist World Alliance and the World Methodist Council, *Faith Working Through Love*, Section 66.

may recognize a strategy already at hand for bringing together diverse views on baptism within their own ecclesial family.

Different Interpretations of a Common Heritage

The source of these differences among Methodists and Wesleyans is traceable, in some instances, to the literary output of John Wesley himself. Wesley addressed the topic of baptism not in a thoroughgoing or systematic fashion, but out of the need to validate Anglican/Methodist praxis in a context of increasing ecclesial, theological, philosophical, and social complexity. To keep the people called Methodists from wandering toward the antisacramentalism of the Society of Friends, Wesley stressed the dominical and apostolic origins of water baptism, a position that is the focus of the manuscript essay, "Water Baptism is the Baptism of Christ."[11] In a climate of Baptist critique, he argued for the antiquity and suitability of infant baptism as well as for a definition of *baptizo* inclusive of any mode of washing: submersion, immersion (dipping), affusion (pouring), and aspersion (sprinkling). Wesley may have had the Baptists in mind with the publication of "Thoughts upon Infant Baptism, Extracted from a Late Writer" (1751, itself an "ecumenical" treatise[12]) and "A Treatise on Baptism" (1756), the latter derived from the appendix of his father Samuel's *The Pious Communicant Rightly Prepar'd; or, a Discourse Concerning the Blessed Sacrament . . . To which is added, A Short Discourse of Baptism* (1700).[13] The son's reworking of the father's text—by reorganization, omission, and revision, but absent a strident, polemical tone—seems to have as its primary interest brevity and precision rather than correction. A concern for simplicity thus may explain John's occasional deletion of references to baptismal regeneration from *A Short Discourse*; certainly, the language of regeneration is still present:

11. Bernard G. Holland supplies the text for "Water Baptism," 158–62. Cf. Wesley, "Letter to a Person," 184.

12. This essay draws together material from Anglican William Walls' *History of Infant Baptism* (1705), the sermon "Christian Baptism" by Congregationalist Isaac Watts, Puritan Richard Baxter's *Plain Scripture Proof of Infants' Church Membership and Baptism* (1651), and other writers, likely including Wesley. The "Late Writer" referenced with the title perhaps had already knit together the principal sources, but that author and document remain unknown. Thus, the extent to which this is an "extract" is unclear.

13. Cf. Wesley, "October 19, 1756," 637.

By *Water*, then, as a Means, the Water of Baptism, we are regenerated or born again: Whence it is also called by the apostle,
The Washing of Regeneration. Our Church therefore ascribes no
greater Virtue to Baptism, than *Christ* Himself has done. Nor
does she ascribe it to the *Outward* Washing, but to the *Inward*
Grace, which added thereto, makes it a Sacrament. Herein a
Principle of Grace is infused, which will not be wholly taken
away, unless we quench the Holy Spirit of God, by long-continued Wickedness . . . Baptism doth now save us, if we live
answerable thereto, if we repent, believe and obey the Gospel.
Supposing this, as it admits us into the Church here, so into
Glory hereafter.[14]

Probably operative here as well was a desire to show sensitivity to the
Puritan wing of the Church of England and to keep a distance from understanding (as he considered Roman Catholics to do[15]) the efficacy of the
sacrament *ex opere operato*. Wesley employed similar editorial methods
relative to regeneration in the baptismal liturgies included in his revision
of the 1662 *Book of Common Prayer* under the title *The Sunday Service of
the Methodists* (1784). In both the infant and adult rites, Wesley deleted
post-baptismal references to regeneration, yet he retained references to
the remission of sins and regeneration prior to the imposition of water.
Such a strategy left open the possibility, but not the inevitability, of regeneration during the baptismal washing. By taking this position, Wesley
adhered to the Augustinian distinction between the external sign (*sig-
num*) and that which it signified (*res*), but which also regarded them as
inseparable since together they made a sacrament.[16] Wesley's willingness
to admit that regeneration was "ordinarily annexed to baptism"[17]—infants
were "born anew" from original sin; adult regeneration might occur
during, before or after the rite—explains his retention of the language
of regeneration in his revision of the twenty-seventh Anglican Article

---

14. Wesley, "Treatise on Baptism," 191–92. The 1758 printing of *A Preservative
against Unsettled Notions in Religion*, a collection of essays, also included Wesley's
baptism-related treatise "Serious Thoughts concerning Godfathers and Godmothers,"
171–75.

15. Cf. Q. 54 in Wesley, "Roman Catechism," 113.

16. It is useful to read Wesley's sermon, "Sermon 45, 'The New Birth,'" (IV.1–2)
with the Augustinian distinction in mind. For a more detailed discussion, see my
American Methodist Worship, 87–93.

17. John Wesley, "Sermon 18, 'Marks of the New Birth,'" 417.

of Religion, "Of Baptism," which became the Methodists' seventeenth Article.[18]

While adhering to baptismal regeneration, Wesley nevertheless enjoined, "Lean no more on the staff of that broken reed, that ye *were* born again in baptism. Who denies that ye were then made children of God, and heirs of the kingdom of heaven? But, notwithstanding this, ye are now children of the devil. Therefore ye must be born again."[19] In Wesley's view, persons who had lost the "principle of grace" as the result of "long-continued wickedness" (i.e., actual sin) required another new birth by means of a conscious experience and profession of the grace that saves. For most persons, then, two new births were required: one sacramental and objective (of divine agency) and one experiential and subjective (of human agency). Unfortunately, Wesley did not connect and reconcile these two new births or delineate explicitly that the second was a recovery of what was given in and through baptism. Wesley's strong emphasis on the second birth, coupled with the intention of the Methodist societies to cultivate that "new" new birth (and not the first, which was located with the parish church), seemed to place greater theological and ritual weight on personal profession of faith than on baptismal regeneration in infants.

Methodists/Wesleyans further distanced themselves from baptismal regeneration even before Wesley's death. In the two revisions of *The Sunday Service of the Methodists* made in 1786, one for the United States and the other for Britain (by Wesley or some other hand), references to regeneration, particularly in the infant baptismal rite, are more substantially removed. The introductions to infant and adult rites in both versions retain the quotation from John 3:5 ("none can enter into the kingdom of God, except he be regenerate and born anew of water and of the Holy Ghost"), though by 1792 (the year following Wesley's death), the version for use in the United States supplied a rubric permitting an alternate introductory exhortation. The 1792 baptismal texts in the United States, relocated from a worship book to a book of "doctrine and discipline," appeared with "An Extract on the Nature and Subjects of Christian Baptism," an abridgement made by Methodist book steward John

18. Wesley does not transfer to the Methodist Article the words "whereby, as by an instrument, they that receive baptism rightly are grafted into the Church; the promises of the forgiveness of sin, and of our adoption to be the sons of God, by the Holy Ghost are visibly signed and sealed; faith is confirmed, and grace increased by virtue of prayer unto God."

19. Wesley, "Sermon 18, 'The Marks of the New Birth,'" 430.

Dickins of a work by Congregational minister Moses Hemmenway.[20] The "Extract" made no mention of regeneration and instead focused principally upon the scriptural legitimacy of modes other than immersion and the appropriateness of infant baptism—the latter justified not on the basis of original sin but on the continuity of the Abrahamic covenant in the Christian dispensation. By 1831, John Emory's printing of the first American edition of Wesley's works could boldly assert at the conclusion of section II.4–5 of Wesley's "Treatise on Baptism" (cited in block quotes above) that the "high-churchman" Wesley "used some expressions, in relation to the doctrine of baptismal regeneration, which we at this day should not prefer."[21] In these examples of Dickins and Emory, two shifts are clear: a growing willingness to disconnect original sin and baptism in favor of a defining covenantal theology of baptism; and a readiness to depart from, reinterpret, or give limited focus to the writings of Wesley. Shifts along similar lines also occurred among Methodists/Wesleyans in Britain.

Throughout the nineteenth century and into the twentieth, various factors influenced the theological reflection and liturgical revisions of Methodists and Wesleyans on both sides of the Atlantic. Among these were a stress on the freedom of the individual, an increasingly positive view of human nature and ability, and attention to the place of children and childhood in the social order. Reaction to the theology and practice of other denominations, in particular, Anglicans and Calvinists in Britain, and Baptists and Disciples of Christ ("Campbellites") in the United States, shaped many Methodist/Wesleyan statements and liturgical texts.[22] As a result, the language of regeneration further declined or disappeared from baptismal rites, while references in liturgical texts and theological writings to baptism as adoption, initiation, entrance,

---

20. Dickins' extract of Hemmenway's work (originally written in 1788) was printed in Methodist Episcopal books of *Doctrine and Discipline* from 1790–97.

21. Emory, *Works of the Reverend John Wesley, A. M.*, 15. The printing of the treatise in *A Collection of Interesting Tracts* retains the disclaimer; see page 249. The title page also carries the note "Published by order of the General Conference."

22. During the nineteenth century in the United States, popular staged debates between a Methodist and a disputant of another denomination often took up topics related to baptism—particularly subject and mode. Methodists Orceneth Fisher (author of *The Christian Sacraments* [2nd ed., 1851]) and Jacob Ditzler (whose disputation with Landmarker Baptist J. R. Graves became known as the "Great Carrollton Debate") are among the most documented. See Holifield, "Theology as Entertainment," 499–520.

and covenant proliferated.[23] Infant baptism was still encouraged, though the reality was that despite the utilization of church schools and youth organizations those baptized at infancy often did not make their own commitments later via profession of faith and/or full membership rites. There is also abundant evidence that among many Methodists and Wesleyan denominations infant baptism languished in preference to baptism upon a candidate's profession of faith, and rites of infant dedication were improvised though in many cases not authorized. In practice, human decision, in effect, received priority over divine grace, even though most Methodists/Wesleyans remained vehement in their defense of the legitimacy of infant baptism as a *sacrament*; some of the churches aligned with the holiness movement were exceptions.[24] Methodist/Wesleyan/ holiness churches, in the distinction made between water baptism and Spirit baptism, added another layer to inter-Methodist discussions relative to the sacrament. Missionaries from the United States and Britain transplanted these various theologies, liturgies, and practices of baptism into new contexts, which not only provided the foundations for the mission churches, but also perpetuated tensions on the subject of baptism across congregations within the Methodist/Wesleyan family.

The Descendants of Wesley, the Ecumenical and Liturgical Movements, and Baptism

The involvement of Methodist/Wesleyan students and leaders in various national, regional, and global movements at the turn into and throughout the twentieth century[25] set the stage for Methodist/Wesleyan engagements with the Ecumenical and Liturgical Movements. Each of these two movements has its own distinct history, but they also share a history

---

23. For studies of these liturgical and theological changes during the nineteenth and early twentieth centuries, see, for Britain, Chapman, *Born in Song*, 94–105. For the United States, in addition to my *American Methodist Worship*, 93–117, see Hohenstein, "Revisions of the Rites of Baptism"; and Felton, *This Gift of Water*.

24. See, for example, Cullum, "Gospel Simplicity," 279–82; and Ellis, *Holy Fire Fell*, esp. 164–86. According to Ellis, baptism remains a subject of contention within the Church of the Nazarene.

25. These movements include the national and regional Student Christian Movements, the global World's Student Christian Federation, the International Missionary Council, the Life and Work Movement, and the Faith and Order Movement.

intertwined around the subject of Christian worship.[26] The initially Roman Catholic Liturgical Movement, committed to the restoration of worship as the heart of Christian communities, took as the first of two tasks *ressourcement*, informing the present by a recovery or retrieval of the best of the past, which was defined principally as the patristic period. The second task, *aggiornamento* or updating, looked to revise the liturgy so that it might address the present age and be appropriately inculturated. These two tasks readily spoke to the needs of Protestants—including Methodists and Wesleyans. Already by 1932, a new rubric appeared in the Methodist Episcopal Church's Order for the Administration of Baptism stating that baptisms should take place in the context of congregation and church buildings, correcting the practice of private baptism in domestic settings that had become (and for a time would remain) popular. The adult baptism rite in the 1936 British Methodist *Book of Offices* seems to indicate the normativity of baptism with the candidate's profession, in imitation of biblical and patristic examples, but a departure from previous Methodist/Wesleyan ritual assumptions. Interest in fuller engagement with liturgical renewal prompted the creation in 1935 of the Methodist Sacramental Fellowship in Britain, which sought to recover ancient Christian and early Methodist praxis while also committing to prayer for Christian unity (including the success of the 1932 union that created the Methodist Church). Members of the Methodist Church in the United States followed suit in founding the Brotherhood (later Order) of St. Luke in 1946. Both groups used their publications to disseminate information about liturgical renewal within their denominations and regarding what was happening globally and ecumenically.

The Second Vatican Council's first document, the Constitution on the Sacred Liturgy (*Sacrosanctum Concilium*, 1963), which explicitly connected the promotion of "union among all who believe in Christ" with the "reform and promotion of the liturgy,"[27] realized many of the goals of the Liturgical Movement. The linkage between ecumenism and liturgical reform was not lost on American Methodist and official Council observer Albert C. Outler, who wrote: "What if the Romans teach the world that the essence of worship is the faithful [human] response to God's immediate and real presence in a community of men and women who love each other as they have been loved by God in Christ? Our only

---

26. On the intertwining of these two movements, see Wainwright, "Ecumenical Convergences," 721–54.

27. *Sacrosanctum Concilium*, Section 1.

legitimate reaction would have to be a bold venture in basic liturgical reform ourselves."[28] Methodists and Wesleyans were among the many Protestants who engaged in their own "bold ventures" after Vatican II by deepening their commitments to liturgical renewal based on the liturgical commentaries and texts of the early church and on the rites produced by Roman Catholics and others after the Council.

Interest in the topic of baptism generated prior to the Council took new form as churches gave themselves permission to reexamine their theologies and praxis. Baptism as water bath was coming to be regarded in many churches as only one part of a larger process of "Christian initiation" that reconnected the Lord's Supper to the initiatory process and saw ongoing eucharistic reception as a type of baptismal renewal. To aid this reflection, British Methodist Geoffrey Wainwright brought out in 1969 the study *Christian Initiation* intended "to establish a theology and a practice of initiation acceptable to the denominations at present divided on this as on other issues" and to rethink practices of initiation "so that they may better reflect the present relations between the Church and the world."[29] At the book's conclusion, Wainwright made several bold proposals in light of what he saw as a current ecumenical trajectory, among them: that baptism upon profession of the candidate's faith be the normative practice, but not to the exclusion of infant baptism; and that infant children of active parents be liturgically enrolled in a catechumenate.[30] Three years after the publication of Wainwright's book, the Vatican promulgated the *Rite of Christian Initiation of Adults* (Latin typical edition 1972, English 1974), which assumed the normativity of baptism upon the candidate's profession and included, following examples from the fourth century, a catechumenate for adults as part of the pre-baptismal formative process.[31]

Beginning in the 1970s, the move toward liturgical revisions by many Methodist, Wesleyan, and united denominations—e.g., the Methodist Church in Great Britain, the United Methodist Church, the United

---

28. Outler, *Methodist Observer at Vatican II*, 66.

29. Wainwright, *Christian Initiation*, 5.

30. Wainwright, *Christian Initiation*, 80–84. Cf. Wainwright, "Need for a Methodist Service," 51–60. "A Service for Welcoming a Child as a Hearer" appeared as an "unofficial" option for United Methodist practice in 1996, but it was never widely used. See Benedict, *Come to the Waters*, 130–33.

31. An adult catechumenal process was the core of *Come to the Waters* and its related publications, but similar to the catechumenal process for infants/children, it never received much attention.

Church of Canada, the Uniting Church in Australia—added to the different approaches to baptismal theology and practice already experienced across the Methodist family. In the United States, this variety spanned from the African Methodist Episcopal Church's use of Wesley's 1786 texts, which included a prayer for the adult candidate's receiving in baptism the remission of sins by spiritual regeneration,[32] to the Wesleyan Church's exhortation that the adult coming to baptism would "continually enjoy the washing of regeneration, and the renewing of the Holy Spirit,"[33] to the United Methodist's authorized text for adults that spoke of remission/forgiveness of sin and filling with the Holy Spirit but not specifically of regeneration.[34] Some churches, among them the Free Methodists, permitted infant dedication in practice if not by a specifically approved rite.[35]

It is also during the 1970s that the formal bilateral dialogue between the World Methodist Council and the Roman Catholic Church came into its own following an initial meeting in 1967 in Arricia. Neither the "Denver Report" (1971) nor the "Dublin Report" (1976) mentioned baptism (both did discuss matters related to Eucharist). Only in *The Apostolic Tradition* (1991) would the dialogue take up the topic of baptism following upon other bilateral as well as multilateral conversations (and responses) on the topic, among them those prompted by the work of the WCC.

The World Council of Churches, constituted in 1948, and its Commission on Faith and Order, began discussions on baptism and included a report in *One Lord, One Baptism* (1961), which laid the groundwork for the draft text *One Baptism, One Eucharist, and Mutually Recognized Ministry*, which, after feedback from the churches and subsequent redaction, became *Baptism, Eucharist and Ministry*.[36] Methodist/Wesleyan responses to *BEM* made clear the divergences present within the Methodist

32. African Methodist Episcopal Church, *Book of Discipline*, 72, part V-A, section 5 C.

33. Wesleyan Church, *Discipline of the Wesleyan Church*, 520, paragraph 1611. This language is similar to the rite of the Free Methodist Church of North America, "Of Those in Mature Years" 231, paragraph 904.

34. United Methodist Church, *Book of Worship*, 9.

35. The Evangelical United Brethren Church, at its creation in 1946, included a rite of infant dedication inherited through the Church of the United Brethren, which added the rite a year before the merger. The Evangelical United Brethren's merger with the Methodist Church in 1968 to form the United Methodist Church saw—at least officially—the gradual demise of infant dedication as a ritual option.

36. Methodists were involved in the process leading to *BEM*, with considerable contributions from Geoffrey Wainwright.

family regarding baptism; indeed, the response of the Methodist Church of New Zealand noted that the "B" section of the document summoned them "to continue to grapple with the consequences of differing views on baptism within our church."[37] The New Zealand church joined other Methodists/Wesleyans in lamenting the absence of fuller discussion on the unrepeatability of baptism and the limited emphasis on divine grace, although the United Methodist Church appreciated that "common reference to God's saving grace in Jesus Christ lifts the discussion above external rites and ceremonies."[38]

Several churches expressed concern about what the "B" section said regarding sacramental efficacy and thus the role of a baptismal rite itself. The responders for the Methodist Church of Great Britain were straightforward in their comments:

> There was some difficulty about how the word "baptism" was being used in the text. At one point it appeared to be a purely descriptive term for a particular ritual action apart from any specific theological meaning (e.g., 17). At another point the term is used as having essential theological sense, "incorporation into Christ", "washing away of sin", "new birth", etc., (e.g., 1, 2). There is a certain ambiguity here. For example, is it being said that the rite "effects" these things, or simply that it "signifies" them as being important elements in the Christian life into which the baptized person is initiated? Methodists do not wish to deny efficacy in the sacraments. However, they plead that the nature of this efficacy be clarified, believing that there are some interpretations of the notion which they must reject. Methodists would want to emphasise that the efficacy of the sacraments depends upon God and not upon any supposed automatism in the rite. We have much to gain from the sacramental understanding of sister churches, but it will be easier for us if we proceed slowly without the fear that certain interpretations are taken for granted.[39]

Other churches were more nervous about *BEM*'s seeming presumptions regarding baptismal efficacy. The report of the Evangelical-Methodist Church, Central Conference in the Federal Republic of Germany and

---

37. Thurian, *Churches Respond to BEM*, 1:79.
38. Thurian, *Churches Respond to BEM*, 2:181.
39. Thurian, *Churches Respond to BEM*, 2:220 (4.1.1).

West Berlin cautioned the "danger in over-emphasizing rites and signs."[40] The Methodist Church of Southern Africa pressed the matter further:

> We emphasize the necessity of personal faith for the personal appropriation of the saving work of God in Jesus Christ, and are very suspicious of any suggestion that an outward rite *either* effects salvation irrespective of faith, *or* is necessary for salvation when faith is present.[41]

The Evangelical-Methodist Church, Central Conference in the German Democratic Republic took a similar line in stating, "We reject statements which bring about an identification between baptism and the Christian life. . . . The sacrament of baptism has no legitimate effect from itself. The spirit of God gives life to the sacrament. What is decisive is one's personal encounter with Christ."[42]

Bringing Diverse Views Together

An important statement in *BEM*'s "B" section was the assertion that "baptism is related not only to momentary experience, but to life-long growth into Christ" (Section 9), which became, in many respects, the starting point for the WCC's 2011 study document *One Baptism*. Summed up in this assertion is the desire to find across the churches convergences around baptismal ritual practices, baptismal efficacy, and the relationship between baptism and faith. There is also the intention to find greater convergence between those who affirm baptism only upon a person's profession of faith (credobaptist[43]) and those who also allow for infant baptism (paedobaptist). The process that produced *One Baptism* unfolded over more than a decade and included several ecumenical drafting teams, which over time discerned a threefold scheme in which the majority of baptismal practices could be located.

> Most churches regard the baptismal event as an unrepeatable liturgical rite in which God acts and the Christian faith is professed. However, the unique event of baptism reflects and

40. Thurian, *Churches Respond to BEM*, 4:176.

41. Thurian, *Churches Respond to BEM*, 2:237.

42. Thurian, *Churches Respond to BEM*, 4:169.

43. The current tendency is not to use "believer baptist" as the contrasting term for "infant," since, properly understood, belief is expressed by parents/sponsors/congregation in an infant baptism.

recapitulates the catechumenate, and the processes of nurture and growth guided by the Holy Spirit, that lead to and follow it. In the early church complex patterns of Christian nurture emerged, including instruction in faith before and after baptism, as well as an extended series of liturgical celebrations marking the journey in a growing faith. Later Christian history saw the development of even more diverse patterns of Christian nurture.

> Within this diversity the churches have discerned three elements which encompass the believer's full incorporation into Christ: (1) formation in faith, (2) baptism and Christian initiation . . . and (3) participation in the life of the Christian community, fostering life-long growth into Christ.[44]

Because of the transparency of this work while in process, other ecumenical dialogues were able to draw upon it for their own conversations, particularly the discernment of the three common elements and differences in their patterns. In 2011, the publication year of *One Baptism*, the "Joint Future Church" (*Gemensam framtid*) came into being out of the union of the Baptist Union of Sweden, the United Methodist Church, and the Mission Covenant Church of Sweden; in 2013, they officially became the Uniting Church of Sweden (*Equmeniakyrkan*). The new church, in trying to reconcile obvious issues related to baptism, directly or indirectly drew on the language considered for *One Baptism* that gave room for the different sequences and approaches to baptism: "[Baptism] is a gift of God met by the individual's response in faith. Baptism is the celebration of new life in Christ and implies a unity with him and his Church. Faith, baptism, and membership of a congregation form a union. To live in one's baptism is a process which has to do with growth in faith and imitation of Christ." This statement, from their "Theological Foundation," also recognized that, within this new church formed by bringing together credobaptists and paedobaptists, different baptismal practices intentionally would coexist.[45]

The international dialogue between the World Methodist Council and the Roman Catholic Church were similarly familiar with the preparatory work for *One Baptism*,[46] and drew upon it as one among many

---

44. World Council of Churches, *One Baptism*, 9, Sections 41–42.

45. "Theological Foundation for Uniting Church in Sweden," 5.

46. This author was among the persons from the Methodist/Wesleyan tradition included in the drafting process of *One Baptism*.

sources for their own 2011 report. The document *Encountering Christ the Saviour*, in the chapter on baptism, highlights the threefold elements in an exploration of formation, rite, and growth in faith:

> The prayer: "I believe! Help my unbelief!" (Mark 9:24) witnesses to the ongoing human sense of being called to deepen faith. Personal faith is not a "thing" received all at once. Faith is something which matures and grows in Christian living. The rediscovery of the importance of the catechumenate as the proper approach to baptism, embodied for contemporary Catholics in the *Rite of Christian Initiation of Adults* (RCIA), emphasizes this sense of the journey of faith. That Methodists similarly emphasize the importance of preparation for baptism indicates that our communities are coming together in an understanding of the *process* of faith.
>
> Such an understanding of faith has consequences for how the relationship of faith and baptism is understood. For both Catholics and Methodists, baptism can be celebrated for a person only once; but, if we see faith as a process and a journey, it is easier to accept that this one baptism, as the sacrament of faith, may be celebrated for different individuals at different points in this journey of faith. This would be true within our respective communities as well as between them. The gospel shows Jesus on his way from his baptism in the Jordan to his "baptism" in his death on Calvary (cf. Mark 10:38). This makes it clear that baptism is the call to follow Jesus, a vocation to share his life and his suffering, just as it is a sharing in God's saving acts in Christ's cross and resurrection. Our faith is the openness to live from what God has done through Jesus for us.[47]

The rest of the chapter explores these themes in depth (e.g., baptism and new life; baptism and church), which lead to a summary conclusion in the final chapter:

> The perspective of baptism as a vocation—specifically the call to grow in holiness and mission through participation in the paschal mystery—provides the framework for understanding a number of points of convergence between Methodists and Catholics in this area:
>
> Catholics and Methodists together firmly believe that baptism incorporates those who are baptized into the paschal mystery of the death and resurrection of Jesus Christ.

47. International Commission for Dialogue between the Roman Catholic Church and the World Methodist Council, *Encountering Christ the Saviour*, 29–30, section 44.

In spite of differences of emphasis, they agree that baptism and faith belong inseparably together. Faith asks for baptism and baptism asks for faith. . . . The relationship between faith and baptism is not simple or linear.

Methodists and Catholics also agree that baptism and regeneration are deeply connected. Together they are aware that the sacramental reality of new birth is a gift which has to be claimed anew in different phases of the believer's growth in the baptismal life. Whilst Catholics may be more inclined to emphasize the objective reality of God's act in baptism, they share with Methodists a concern for the subjective fruitfulness of baptism in the lives of Christians. Methodists, for their part, would also hold that the effect of baptism is not only a subjective matter.

Catholics and Methodists are of one mind that baptism makes those who are baptized members of Christ's body, the Church. Baptism brings us into a fundamental communion with one another in Christ.[48]

It is often the case that conversation with another reveals much that one holds deeply, and so it is in ecumenical conversation. The fruits of multilateral and bilateral ecumenical dialogue—dialogues involving one's ecclesial tradition(s) and those that do not—may speak in helpful ways to one's own community, particularly in places where there are internal disagreements.[49] In terms of theologies and practices of baptism, members of the World Methodist family may learn from ecumenical statements to take a new approach in addressing differences related to the baptismal recipient, the role of the baptismal ritual, and baptism's efficacy. Baptism is a critical area to engage since, as the World Methodist/Roman Catholic dialogue asserts (above), "Baptism brings us into a fundamental communion with one another in Christ."

A preliminary and overarching approach is to consider the first "imperative" delineated in the statement made conjointly by the Roman Catholic Church and the Lutheran World Federation in preparation for their common commemoration of the Reformation in 2017. The so-called "Lund Imperative" that is being adopted widely for multilateral and bilateral ecumenical conversation states, "Catholics and Lutherans

48. International Commission for Dialogue between the Roman Catholic Church and the World Methodist Council, *Encountering Christ the Saviour*, 44–45, section 72.

49. For a helpful synthesis of statements emerging from dialogues with the Roman Catholic Church from 1967–2009, see Kasper, *Harvesting the Fruits*. Kasper includes dialogues with the World Methodist Council in his "harvest."

should always begin from the perspective of unity and not from the point of view of division in order to strengthen what is held in common even though the differences are more easily seen and experienced."[50] On the matter of baptism within the World Methodist family, starting from a perspective of unity and not difference may permit the embrace of an insight from the WCC's *One Baptism*: the three recognized components of faith formation, rite, and participation in Christian community to nurture life-long growth into Christ. In this scheme, there are multiple starting points that may begin at any age. Such a holistic approach may reduce fears of "ritualism," for it mitigates views of the completion of initiation or salvation in a single moment and assumes that the faith journey spans a lifetime. It relatedly may address the conviction of some in the World Methodist family that baptism figures more as an ordinance than as a sacrament, for the outpouring of the triune God's grace is seen at every point on the journey of faith. The approach also may forestall actions of rebaptism, since the singular baptism—at any time on a life path—is placed into a broader framework where the "reality of baptism needs to be lived out as a daily experience; again and again, the baptized will need to repent and turn to Christ."[51] Growth into Christ, as a life-long process, thus ends only with the "final profession which is the testimony of a Christian death."[52]

This understanding of faith—and baptism—as a process has the capacity to address the coexistence of rites of infant baptism and infant dedication in the Methodist/Wesleyan family. One means to reframe this coexistence of practices is to revisit the prospect of enrolling all infants and children as "hearers," thereby effectively equalizing the different starting points for baptism and indicating that faith formation and the baptismal process begins even from infancy. Families and the congregation determine the time for baptism. Children whose families desire a delayed baptism participate in what is effectively pre-baptismal formation, while those baptized early in life enter into post-baptismal formation. In actuality, these would be the same as the children, baptized and not, prepare to make public profession of their faith.

In view of a ritual and theological coalescing around related patterns of baptism/initiation, Methodists and Wesleyans can affirm with

50. Lutheran-Roman Catholic Commission on Unity, *From Conflict to Communion*, 87, boxed insert between sections 239 and 240.

51. World Council of Churches, *One Baptism*, 10, section 49.

52. World Council of Churches, *One Baptism*, 9, section 3.

their ecumenical partners that our common baptism is a sacramental bond of unity. "We are travelling on the same road, seeking faithfully to follow the same Lord, desiring to be led by the same Spirit, and yearning to find our identity as children of the same Father. The triune God who calls us to holiness also calls us to unity."[53]

Bibliography

The African Methodist Episcopal Church. *The Book of Discipline of the African Methodist Episcopal Church*. Nashville: A. M. E. Sunday School Union, 1972.

Benedict, Daniel T., Jr. *Come to the Waters: Baptism and Our Ministry of Welcoming Seekers and Making Disciples*. Nashville: Discipleship Resources, 1996.

Best, Thomas F. "A Faith and Order Saga. Towards *One Baptism: Towards Mutual Recognition*." In *Worship and Culture: Foreign Country or Homeland?*, edited by Gláucia Vasconcelos Wilkey, 302–19. Grand Rapids: Eerdmans, 2014.

Chapman, David M. *Born in Song: Methodist Worship in Britain*. Warrington: Church in the Marketplace, 2006.

A Collection of Interesting Tracts, Explaining Several Important Points of Scripture Doctrine. New York: Lane & Scott, 1850.

Cullum, Douglas R. "Gospel Simplicity: Rhythms of Faith and Life among Free Methodists in Victorian America." PhD diss., Drew University, 2002.

Ellis, Dirk R. *Holy Fire Fell: A History of Worship, Revivals, and Feasts in the Church of the Nazarene*. Eugene, OR: Wipf and Stock, 2016.

Emory, John, ed. *The Works of the Reverend John Wesley, A. M.* Vol. 6. New York: J. Emory and B. Waugh, for the Methodist Episcopal Church, 1831.

Felton, Gayle Carlton. *This Gift of Water: The Practice and Theology of Baptism among Methodists*. Nashville: Abingdon, 1993.

The Free Methodist Church of North America. "Of Those in Mature Years." In *The Book of Discipline 1974*. Winona Lake, IN: Free Methodist Publishing, 1974.

Hohenstein, Charles R. "The Revisions of the Rites of Baptism in the Methodist Episcopal Church, 1784–1939." PhD diss., University of Notre Dame, 1990.

Holifield, E. Brooks. "Theology as Entertainment: Oral Debate in American Religion." *Church History* 67.3 (September 1998) 499–520.

Holland, Bernard. "Water Baptism Is the Baptism of Christ." In *Baptism in Early Methodism*, 158–62. London: Epworth, 1970.

International Commission for Dialogue between the Roman Catholic Church and the World Methodist Council. *The Call to Holiness*. Lake Junaluska, NC: World Methodist Council, 2016.

———. *Encountering Christ the Saviour: Church and Sacraments*. Lake Junaluska, NC: World Methodist Council, 2011.

———. *The Grace Given You in Christ: Catholics and Methodists Reflect Further on the Church*. Lake Junaluska, NC: World Methodist Council, 2006.

---

53. International Commission for Dialogue between the Roman Catholic Church and the World Methodist Council, *Call to Holiness*, section 168.

International Dialogue between the Baptist World Alliance and the World Methodist Council. *Faith Working Through Love.* 2018.

Joint Working Group between the Roman Catholic Church and the World Council of Churches. *Eighth Report: 1999–2005.* Geneva: WCC, 2005.

Kasper, Cardinal Walter. *Harvesting the Fruits: Basic Aspects of Christian Faith in Ecumenical Dialogue.* New York: Continuum, 2009.

Lutheran-Roman Catholic Commission on Unity. *From Conflict to Communion: Lutheran-Catholic Common Commemoration of the Reformation in 2017: Report.* Leipzig: Evangelische Verlagsanstalt and Paderborn: Bonifatius, 2013.

The Lutheran World Federation and The Roman Catholic Church. *Joint Declaration on the Doctrine of Justification.* English language edition. Grand Rapids: Eerdmans, 2000. https://www.lutheranworld.org/sites/default/files/Joint%20Declaration%20on%20the%20Doctrine%20of%20Justification.pdf.

Outler, Albert C. *Methodist Observer at Vatican II.* Westminster, MD: Newman, 1967.

Thurian, Max, ed. *Churches Respond to BEM.* Vol. 1. Geneva: World Council of Churches, 1986.

———. *Churches Respond to BEM.* Vol. 2. Geneva: World Council of Churches, 1986.

———. *Churches Respond to BEM.* Vol. 4. Geneva: World Council of Churches, 1986.

Unitatis Redintegratio. November 21, 1964. http://www.vatican.va/archive/hist_councils/ii_vatican_council/documents/vat-ii_decree_19641121_unitatis-redintegratio_en.html.

The United Methodist Church. *Book of Worship for Church and Home.* Nashville: United Methodist Publishing, 1964–65.

Uniting Church in Sweden. "A Theological Foundation for Uniting Church in Sweden." https://equmeniakyrkan.se/wp-content/uploads/2015/12/theological_foundationUCS.pdf.

Wainwright, Geoffrey. *Christian Initiation.* London: Lutterworth, 1969.

———. "Ecumenical Convergences." In *The Oxford History of Christian Worship,* edited by Geoffrey Wainwright and Karen B. Westerfield Tucker, 721–54. New York: Oxford University Press, 2006.

———. "Need for a Methodist Service for the Admission of Infants to the Catechumenate." *London Quarterly and Holborn Review* 193 (January 1968) 51–60.

Westerfield Tucker, Karen B. *American Methodist Worship.* New York: Oxford University Press, 2001.

Wesley, Charles. "October 19, 1756." In *The Manuscript Journal of the Reverend Charles Wesley, M.A.* Vol. 2, edited by S. T. Kimbrough Jr. and Kenneth G. C. Newport. Nashville: Kingswood, 2007.

Wesley, John. "A Letter to a Person Lately Joined with the People call'd Quakers. In Answer to a Letter wrote by Him." In *Works of John Wesley.* Vol. 10, *Letters, Essays, Dialogs, Addresses,* edited by Thomas Jackson, 177–88. 3rd ed. Grand Rapids: Zondervan, 1958–59.

———. "A Roman Catechism, Faithfully Drawn Out of the Allowed Writings of the Church of Rome. With a Reply Thereto." In *Works of John Wesley.* Vol. 10, *Letters, Essays, Dialogs, Addresses,* edited by Thomas Jackson, 88–128. Grand Rapids: Zondervan, 1958–59.

————. "Serious Thoughts Concerning Godfathers and Godmothers (1752)." In *Works of John Wesley*. Vol. 10, *Letters, Essays, Dialogs, Addresses*, edited by Thomas Jackson, 506–9. Grand Rapids: Zondervan, 1958–59.

————. "Sermon 18, 'Marks of the New Birth.'" In *Bicentennial Edition of the Works of John Wesley*. Vol. 1, *Sermons I*, edited by Albert Outler, 415–30. Nashville: Abingdon, 1984.

————. "Sermon 45, 'The New Birth.'" In *Bicentennial Edition of the Works of John Wesley*. Vol. 2, *Sermons II*, edited by Albert C. Outler, 186–201. Nashville: Abingdon, 1985.

————. "A Treatise on Baptism." In *Works of John Wesley*. Vol. 10, *Letters, Essays, Dialogs, Addresses*, edited by Thomas Jackson, 188–201. Grand Rapids: Zondervan, 1958–59.

The Wesleyan Church. *The Discipline of the Wesleyan Church 1972*. Marion, IN: Wesleyan Publishing, 1972.

The World Council of Churches. *Baptism, Eucharist, and Ministry*. Geneva: World Council of Churches, 1982.

————. *One Baptism: Towards Mutual Recognition. A Study Text*. Geneva: World Council of Churches, 2011.

World Methodist Council. "WMC's Statement of Association with the Joint Declaration of the Doctrine of Justification." July 23, 2006. https://worldmethodistcouncil.org/wmcs-statement-of-assocation-with-the-joint-declaration-of-the-doctrine-of-justification/.

APPENDIX A

A Treatise on Baptism

John Wesley, November 11, 1756

CONCERNING baptism I shall inquire, what it is; what benefits we receive by it; whether our Savior designed it to remain always in his Church; and who are the proper subjects of it.

I. What Is Baptism?

1. What it is. It is the initiatory sacrament, which enters us into covenant with God. It was instituted by Christ, who alone has power to institute a proper sacrament, a sign, seal, pledge, and means of grace, perpetually obligatory on all Christians. We know not, indeed, the exact time of its institution; but we know it was long before our Lord's ascension. And it was instituted in the room of circumcision. For, as that was a sign and seal of God's covenant, so is this.

2. The matter of this sacrament is water; which, as it has a natural power of cleansing, is the more fit for this symbolical use. Baptism is performed by washing, dipping, or sprinkling the person, in the name of the Father, Son, and Holy Ghost, who is hereby devoted to the ever-blessed Trinity. I say, by washing, dipping, or sprinkling; because it is not determined in Scripture in which of these ways it shall be done, neither by any express precept, nor by any such example as clearly proves it; nor by the force or meaning of the word baptize.

3. That there is no express precept, all calm men allow. Neither is there any conclusive example. John's baptism in some things agreed with Christ's, in others differed from it. But it cannot be certainly proved

from Scripture, that even John's was performed by dipping. It is true he baptized in Enon, near Salim, where there was "much water." But this might refer to breadth rather than depth; since a narrow place would not have been sufficient for so great a multitude. Nor can it be proved, that the baptism of our Savior, or that administered by his disciples, was by immersion. No, nor that of the eunuch baptized by Philip; though "they both went down to the water:" For that going down may relate to the chariot, and implies no determinate depth of water. It might be up to their knees; it might not be above their ankles.

4. And as nothing can be determined from Scripture precept or example, so neither from the force or meaning of the word. For the words baptize and baptism do not necessarily imply dipping, but are used in other senses in several places. Thus we read, that the Jews "were all baptized in the cloud and in the sea" (1 Cor 10:2); but they were not plunged in either. They could therefore be only sprinkled by drops of the sea-water, and refreshing dews from the cloud; probably intimated in that, "Thou sentest a gracious rain upon thine inheritance, and refreshedst it when it was weary" (Ps 67:9). Again: Christ said to his two disciples, "Ye shall be baptized with the baptism that I am baptized with" (Mark 10:38); but neither he nor they were dipped, but only sprinkled or washed with their own blood. Again we read (Mark 7:4) of the baptisms (so it is in the original) of pots and cups, and tables or beds. Now, pots and cups are not necessarily dipped when they are washed. Nay, the Pharisees washed the outsides of them only. And as for tables or beds, none will suppose they could be dipped. Here, then, the word baptism, in its natural sense, is not taken for dipping, but for washing or cleansing. And, that this is the true meaning of the word baptize, is testified by the greatest scholars and most proper judges in this matter. It is true, we read of being "buried with Christ in baptism." But nothing can be inferred from such a figurative expression. Nay, if it held exactly, it would make as much for sprinkling as for plunging; since, in burying, the body is not plunged through the substance of the earth, but rather earth is poured or sprinkled upon it.

5. And as there is no clear proof of dipping in Scripture, so there is very probable proof of the contrary. It is highly probable, the Apostles themselves baptized great numbers, not by dipping, but by washing, sprinkling, or pouring water. This clearly represented the cleansing from sin, which is figured by baptism. And the quantity of water used was not material; no more than the quantity of bread and wine in the Lord's supper. The jailer "and all his house were baptized" in the prison; Cornelius

with his friends, (and so several households), at home. Now, is it likely, that all these had ponds or rivers, in or near their houses, sufficient to plunge them all? Every unprejudiced person must allow, the contrary is far more probable. Again: Three thousand at one time, and five thousand at another, were converted and baptized by St. Peter at Jerusalem; where they had none but the gentle waters of Siloam, according to the observation of Mr. Fuller: "There were no water-mills in Jerusalem, because there was no stream large enough to drive them." The place, therefore, as well as the number, makes it highly probable that all these were baptized by sprinkling or pouring, and not by immersion. To sum up all, the manner of baptizing (whether by dipping or sprinkling) is not determined in Scripture. There is no command for one rather than the other. There is no example from which we can conclude for dipping rather than sprinkling. There are probable examples of both; and both are equally contained in the natural meaning of the word.

II. The Benefits Received in Baptism

1. What are the benefits we receive by baptism, is the next; point to be considered. And the first of these is, the washing away the guilt of original sin, by the application of the merits of Christ's death. That we are all born under the guilt of Adam's sin, and that all sin deserves eternal misery, was the unanimous sense of the ancient Church, as it is expressed in the Ninth Article of our own. And the Scripture plainly asserts, that we were "shapen in iniquity, and in sin did our mother conceive us;" that "we were all by nature children of wrath, and dead in trespasses and sins;" that "in Adam all die;" that "by one man's disobedience all were made sinners;" that "by one man sin entered into the world, and death by sin; which came upon all men, because all had sinned." This plainly includes infants; for they too die; therefore they have sinned: But not by actual sin; therefore, by original; else what need have they of the death of Christ? Yea, "death reigned from Adam to Moses, even over those who had not sinned" actually "according to the similitude of Adam's transgression." This, which can relate to infants only, is a clear proof that the whole race of mankind are obnoxious both to the guilt and punishment of Adam's transgression. But; "as by the offense of one, judgment came upon all men to condemnation; so by the righteousness of one, the free gift came upon all men, to justification of life." And the virtue of this free gift, the merits of Christ's life and death, are applied to us in baptism. "He gave himself

for the Church, that he might sanctify and cleanse it with the washing of water by the word" (Eph 5:25, 26); namely, in baptism, the ordinary instrument of our justification. Agreeably to this, our Church prays in the baptismal office, that the person to be baptized may be "washed and sanctified by the Holy Ghost, and, being delivered from God's wrath, receive remission of sins, and enjoy the everlasting benediction of his heavenly washing;" and declares in the Rubric at the end of the office, "It is certain, by God's word, that children who are baptized, dying before they commit actual sin are saved." And this is agreeable to the unanimous judgment of all the ancient Fathers.

2. By baptism we enter into covenant with God; into that everlasting covenant, which he hath commanded forever (Ps 111:9); that new covenant, which he promised to make with the spiritual Israel; even to "give them a new heart and a new spirit, to sprinkle clean water upon them," (of which the baptismal is only a figure), "and to remember their sins and iniquities no more;" in a word, to be their God, as he promised to Abraham, in the evangelical covenant which he made with him and all his spiritual offspring (Gen 17:7, 8). And as circumcision was then the way of entering into this covenant, so baptism is now; which is therefore styled by the Apostle, (so many good interpreters render his words), "the stipulation, contract, or covenant of a good conscience with God."

3. By baptism we are admitted into the Church, and consequently made members of Christ, its Head. The Jews were admitted into the Church by circumcision, so are the Christians by baptism. For "as many as are baptized into Christ," in his name, "have" thereby "put on Christ" (Gal 3:27); that is, are mystically united to Christ, and made one with him. For "by one Spirit we are all baptized into one body," (1 Cor 12:13), namely, the Church, "the body of Christ" (Eph 4:12). From which spiritual, vital union with him, proceeds the influence of his grace on those that are baptized; as from our union with the Church, a share in all its privileges, and in all the promises Christ has made to it.

4. By baptism, we who were "by nature children of wrath" are made the children of God. And this regeneration which our Church in so many places ascribes to baptism is more than barely being admitted into the Church, though commonly connected therewith; being "grafted into the body of Christ's Church, we are made the children of God by adoption and grace." This is grounded on the plain words of our Lord: "Except a man be born again of water and of the Spirit, he cannot enter into the kingdom of God" (John 3:5). By water then, as a means, the water of

baptism, we are regenerated or born again; whence it is also called by the Apostle, "the washing of regeneration." Our Church therefore ascribes no greater virtue to baptism than Christ himself has done. Nor does she ascribe it to the outward washing, but to the inward grace, which, added thereto, makes it a sacrament. Herein a principle of grace is infused, which will not be wholly taken away, unless we quench the Holy Spirit of God by long-continued wickedness.

5. In consequence of our being made children of God, we are heirs of the kingdom of heaven. "If children," (as the Apostle observes), "then heirs, heirs of God, and joint-heirs with Christ." Herein we receive a title to, and an earnest of, "a kingdom which cannot be moved." Baptism doth now save us, if we live answerable thereto; if we repent, believe, and obey the gospel: Supposing this, as it admits us into the Church here, so into glory hereafter.

III. Baptism and the Church

1. But did our Savior design this should remain always in his Church? This is the Third thing we are to consider. And this may be dispatched in a few words, since there can be no reasonable doubt, but it was intended to last as long as the Church into which it is the appointed means of entering. In the ordinary way, there is no other means of entering into the Church or into heaven.

2. In all ages, the outward baptism is a means of the inward; as outward circumcision was of the circumcision of the heart. Nor would it have availed a Jew to say, "I have the inward circumcision and therefore do not need the outward too:" That soul was to be cut off from his people. He had despised, he had broken, God's everlasting covenant, by despising the seal of it (Genesis 17:14). Now, the seal of circumcision was to last among the Jews as long as the law lasted, to which it obliged them. By plain parity of reason, baptism, which came in its room, must last among Christians as long as the gospel covenant into which it admits, and whereunto it obliges, all nations.

3. This appears also from the original commission which our Lord gave to his Apostles: "Go, disciple all nations, baptizing them in the name of the Father, of the Son, and of the Holy Ghost; teaching them. And lo! I am with you always, even unto the end of the world." Now, as long as this commission lasted, as long as Christ promised to be with them in the execution of it, so long doubtless were they to execute it, and to

baptize as well as to teach. But Christ hath promised to be with them, that is, by his Spirit, in their successors, to the end of the world. So long, therefore, without dispute, it was his design that baptism should remain in his Church.

IV. The Proper Subjects of Baptism

1. But the grand question is, Who are the proper subjects of baptism? grown persons only, or infants also? In order to answer this fully, I shall, First, lay down the grounds of infant baptism, taken from Scripture, reason, and primitive, universal practice; and, Secondly, answer the objections against it.

2. As to the grounds of it: If infants are guilty of original sin, then they are proper subjects of baptism; seeing, in the ordinary way, they cannot be saved, unless this be washed away by baptism. It has been already proved, that this original stain cleaves to every child of man; and that hereby they are children of wrath, and liable to eternal damnation. It is true, the Second Adam has found a remedy for the disease which came upon all by the offense of the first. But the benefit of this is to be received through the means which he hath appointed; through baptism in particular, which is the ordinary means he hath appointed for that purpose; and to which God hath tied us, though he may not have tied himself. Indeed, where it cannot be had, the case is different, but extraordinary cases do not make void a standing rule. This therefore is our First ground. Infants need to be washed from original sin; therefore they are proper subjects of baptism.

3. Secondly, if infants are capable of making a covenant, and were and still are under the evangelical covenant, then they have a right to baptism, which is the entering seal thereof. But infants are capable of making a covenant, and were and still are under the evangelical covenant. The custom of nations and common reason of mankind prove that infants may enter into a covenant, and may be obliged by compacts made by others in their name, and receive advantage by them. But we have stronger proof than this, even God's own word: "Ye stand this day all of you before the Lord, — your captains, with all the men of Israel; your little ones, your wives and the stranger, — that thou shouldest enter into covenant with the Lord thy God" (Deut 29:10–12). Now, God would never have made a covenant with little ones, if they had not been capable of it. It is not said children only, but little children, the Hebrew word properly signifying

infants. And these may be still, as they were of old, obliged to perform, in after time, what they are not capable of performing at the time of their entering into that obligation.

4. The infants of believers, the true children of faithful Abraham, always were under the gospel covenant. They were included in it, they had a right to it and to the seal of it; as an infant heir has a right to his estate, though he cannot yet have actual possession. The covenant with Abraham was a gospel covenant; the condition the same, namely, faith, which the Apostle observes was "imputed unto him for righteousness." The inseparable fruit of this faith was obedience; for by faith he left his country, and offered his son. The benefits were the same; for God promised "I will be thy God, and the God of thy seed after thee:" And he can promise no more to any creature; for this includes all blessings, temporal and eternal. The Mediator is the same; for it was in his Seed, that is, in Christ, (Gen 22:18; Gal 3:16), that all nations were to be blessed; on which very account the Apostle says, "The gospel was preached unto Abraham" (Gal 3:8). Now, the same promise that was made to him, the same covenant that was made with him, was made "with his children after him" (Gen 17:7; Gal 3:7). And upon that account it is called "an everlasting covenant." In this covenant children were also obliged to what they knew not, to the same faith and obedience with Abraham. And so they are still; as they are still equally entitled to all the benefits and promises of it.

5. Circumcision was then the seal of the covenant; which is itself therefore figuratively termed the covenant (Acts 7:8). Hereby the children of those who professed the true religion were then admitted into it, and obliged to the conditions of it; and when the law was added, to the observance of that also. And when the old seal of circumcision was taken off, this of baptism was added in its room; our Lord appointing one positive institution to succeed another. A new seal was set to Abraham's covenant; the seals differed, but the deed was the same; only that part was struck off which was political or ceremonial. That baptism came in the room of circumcision, appears as well from the clear reason of the thing, as from the Apostle's argument, where, after circumcision, he mentions baptism, as that wherein God had "forgiven us our trespasses;" to which he adds, the "blotting out the hand-writing of ordinances," plainly relating to circumcision and other Jewish rites; which as fairly implies, that baptism came in the room of circumcision, as our Savior's styling the other sacrament the passover, (Col 2:11–13; Luke 22:15), shows that it was instituted in the place of it. Nor is it any proof that baptism did not

succeed circumcision, because it differs in some circumstances, any more than it proves the Lord's supper did not succeed the passover, because in several circumstances it differs from it. This then is a Second ground. Infants are capable of entering into covenant with God. As they always were, so they still are, under the evangelical covenant. Therefore they have a right to baptism, which is now the entering seal thereof.

6. Thirdly. If infants ought to come to Christ, if they are capable of admission into the Church of God, and consequently of solemn sacramental dedication to him, then they are proper subjects of baptism. But infants are capable of coming to Christ, of admission into the Church, and solemn dedication to God. That infants ought to come to Christ, appears from his own words: "They brought little children to Christ, and the disciples rebuked them. And Jesus said, Suffer little children to come unto me, and forbid them not; for of such is the kingdom of heaven" (Matt 19:13, 14). St. Luke expresses it still more strongly: "They brought unto him even infants, that he might touch them" (Luke 18:15). These children were so little that they were brought to him; yet he says, "Suffer them to come unto me:" So little, that he "took them up in his arms;" yet he rebukes those who would have hindered their coming to him. And his command respected the future as well as the present. Therefore his disciples or Ministers are still to suffer infants to come, that is, to be brought, unto Christ. But they cannot now come to him, unless by being brought into the Church; which cannot be but by baptism. Yea, and "of such," says our Lord, "is the kingdom of heaven;" not of such only as were like these infants. For if they themselves were not fit to be subjects of that kingdom, how could others be so, because they were like them? Infants, therefore, are capable of being admitted into the Church, and have a right thereto. Even under the Old Testament they were admitted into it by circumcision. And can we suppose they are in a worse condition under the gospel, than they were under the law? and that our Lord would take away any privileges which they then enjoyed? Would he not rather make additions to them? This, then, is a Third ground. Infants ought to come to Christ, and no man ought to forbid them. They are capable of admission into the Church of God. Therefore, they are proper subjects of baptism.

7. Fourthly. If the Apostles baptized infants, then are they proper subjects of baptism. But the Apostles baptized infants, as is plain from the following consideration: The Jews constantly baptized as well as circumcised all infant proselytes. Our Lord, therefore, commanding his Apostles to proselyte or disciple all nations by baptizing them, and not forbidding

them to receive infants as well as others, they must needs baptize children also. That the Jews admitted proselytes by baptism as well as by circumcision, even whole families together, parents and children, we have the unanimous testimony of their most ancient, learned, and authentic writers. The males they received by baptism and circumcision; the women by baptism only. Consequently, the Apostles, unless our Lord had expressly forbidden it, would of course do the same thing. Indeed, the consequence would hold from circumcision only. For if it was the custom of the Jews, when they gathered proselytes out of all nations, to admit children into the Church by circumcision, though they could not actually believe the law, or obey it; then the Apostles, making proselytes to Christianity by baptism, could never think of excluding children, whom the Jews always admitted, (the reason for their admission being the same), unless our Lord had expressly forbidden it. It follows, the Apostles baptized infants. Therefore, they are proper subjects of baptism.

8. If it be objected, "There is no express mention in Scripture of any infants whom the Apostles baptized," I would ask, Suppose no mention had been made in the Acts of those two women baptized by the Apostles, yet might we not fairly conclude, that when so many thousands, so many entire households, were baptized, women were not excluded? especially since it was the known custom of the Jews to baptize them? The same holds of children; nay, more strongly, on the account of circumcision. Three thousand were baptized by the Apostles in one day, and five thousand in another. And can it be reasonably supposed that there were no children among such vast numbers? Again: The Apostles baptized many families; nay, we hardly read of one master of a family, who was converted and baptized, but his whole family (as was before the custom among the Jews) were baptized with him: Thus the "jailer's household, he and all his; the household of Gaius, of Stephanas, of Crispus." And can we suppose, that in all these households, which, we read, were, without exception, baptized, there should not be so much as one child or infant? But to go one step further: St. Peter says to the multitude, "Repent and be baptized, every one of you, for the remission of sins. For the promise is to you, and to your children" (Acts 2:38, 39). Indeed, the answer is made directly to those who asked, "What shall we do?" But it reaches farther than to those who asked the question. And though children could not actually repent, yet they might be baptized. And that they are included, appears, (1) Because the Apostle addresses to "every one" of them, and in "every

one" children must be contained; (2) They are expressly mentioned: "The promise is to you, and to your children."

9. Lastly. If to baptize infants has been the general practice of the Christian Church in all places and in all ages, then this must have been the practice of the Apostles, and, consequently, the mind of Christ. But to baptize infants has been the general practice of the Christian Church, in all places and in all ages. Of this we have unexceptionable witnesses: St. Austin for the Latin Church, who flourished before the year 400; and Origen for the Greek, born in the second century; both declaring, not only that the whole Church of Christ did then baptize infants, but likewise that they received this practice from the Apostles themselves (Augustine, *On Genesis*, 1. 10, c. 23; Original in Rom 6). St. Cyprian likewise is express for it, and a whole Council with him (Epist. ad Fidum). If need were, we might cite likewise Athanasius, Chrysostom, and a cloud of witnesses. Nor is there one instance to be found in all antiquity, of any orthodox Christian who denied baptism to children when brought to be baptized; nor any one of the Fathers, or ancient; writers, for the first eight hundred years at least, who held it unlawful. And that it has been the practice of all regular Churches ever since, is clear and manifest. Not only our own ancestors when first converted to Christianity, not only all the European Churches, but the African too and the Asiatic, even those of St. Thomas in the Indies, do, and ever did, baptize their children. The fact being thus cleared, that infant baptism has been the general practice of the Christian Church in all places and in all ages, that it has continued without interruption in the Church of God for above seventeen hundred years, we may safely conclude, it was handed down from the Apostles, who best knew the mind of Christ.

10. To sum up the evidence: If outward baptism be generally, in an ordinary way, necessary to salvation, and infants may be saved as well as adults, nor ought we to neglect any means of saving them; if our Lord commands such to come, to be brought unto him, and declares, "Of such is the kingdom of heaven;" if infants are capable of making a covenant, or having a covenant made for them by others, being included in Abraham's covenant, (which was a covenant of faith, an evangelical covenant), and never excluded by Christ; if they have; a right to be members of the Church, and were accordingly members of the Jewish; if, suppose our Lord had designed to exclude them from baptism, he must have expressly forbidden his Apostles to baptize them, (which none dares to affirm he did), since otherwise they would do it of course, according to

the universal practice of their nation; if it is highly probable they did so, even from the letter of Scripture, because they frequently baptized whole households, and it would be strange if there were no children among them; if the whole Church of Christ, for seventeen hundred years together, baptized infants, and were never opposed till the last century but one, by some not very holy men in Germany; lastly, if there are such inestimable benefits conferred in baptism, the washing away the guilt of original sin, the engrafting us into Christ, by making us members of his Church, and thereby giving us a right to all the blessings of the gospel; it follows, that infants may, yea, ought to be baptized, and that none ought to hinder them. I am, in the Last place, to answer those objections which are commonly brought against infant baptism.

Response to Objections Against Infant Baptism

1. The chief of these is: "Our Lord said to his Apostles, 'Go and teach all nations, baptizing them in the name of the Father, the Son, and the Holy Ghost' (Matt 28:19). Here Christ himself put teaching before baptizing. Therefore, infants, being incapable of being taught, are incapable of being baptized." I answer, (1) The order of words in Scripture is no certain rule for the order of things. We read in St. Mark 1:4: "John baptized in the wilderness, and preached the baptism of repentance;" and, verse 5, "They were baptized of him in Jordan, confessing their sins." Now, either the order of words in Scripture does not always imply the same order of things; or it follows, that John baptized before his hearers either confessed or repented. But, (2) The words are manifestly mistranslated. For if we read, "Go and teach all nations, baptizing them, — teaching them to observe all things," it makes plain tautology, vain and senseless repetition. It ought to be translated, (which is the literal meaning of the words), "Go and make disciples of all nations, by baptizing them." That infants are capable of being made proselytes or disciples has been already proved; therefore this text, rightly translated, is no valid objection against infant baptism.

2. Their next objection is: "The Scripture says, 'Repent and be baptized; believe and be baptized.' Therefore, repentance and faith ought to go before baptism. But infants are incapable of these; therefore they are incapable of baptism." I answer: Repentance and faith were to go before circumcision, as well as before baptism. Therefore, if this argument held, it would prove just as well, that infants were incapable of circumcision.

But we know God himself determined the contrary, commanding them to be circumcised at eight days old. Now, if infants were capable of being circumcised, notwithstanding that repentance and faith were to go before circumcision in grown persons, they are just as capable of being baptized; notwithstanding that repentance and faith are, in grown persons, to go before baptism. This objection, therefore, is of no force; for it is as strong against circumcision of infants as infant baptism.

3. It is objected, Thirdly, "There is no command for it in Scripture. Now, God was angry with his own people, because they did that which, he said, 'I commanded them not' (Jer 7:31). One plain text would end all the dispute." I answer, (1) We have reason to fear it would not. It is as positively commanded in a very plain text of Scripture, that we should "teach and admonish one another with psalms, and hymns, and spiritual songs, singing to the Lord with grace in our hearts," (Eph 5:19), as it is to honor our father and mother: But does this put an end to all dispute? Do not these very persons absolutely refuse to do it, notwithstanding a plain text, an express command? I answer, (2) They themselves practice what there is neither express command nor clear example for in Scripture. They have no express command for baptizing women. They say, indeed, "Women are implied in 'all nations.'" They are; and so are infants too: But the command is not express for either. And for admitting women to the Lord's supper, they have neither express command nor clear example. Yet they do it continually, without either one or the other. And they are justified therein by the plain reason of the thing. This also justifies as in baptizing infants, though without express command of clear example. If it be said, "But there is a command, 'Let a man,' . . . 'examine himself, and so let him eat of that bread' (1 Cor 11:28); the word 'man,' in the original, signifying indifferently either men or women:" I grant it does in other places; but here the word "himself," immediately following, confines it to men only. "But women are implied in it, though not expressed." Certainly; and so are infants in "all nations." "But we have Scripture example for it: For it is said in the Acts, 'The Apostles continued in prayer and supplication with the women.'" True, in prayer and supplication; but it is not said, "in communicating:" Nor have we one clear example of it in the Bible. Since, then, they admit women to the communion, without any express command or example, but only by consequence from Scripture, they can never show reason why infants should not be admitted to baptism, when there are so many scriptures which by fair consequence show they have a right to it, and are capable of it. As for the texts wherein God reproves his

people for doing "what he commanded them not;" that phrase evidently means, what he had forbidden; particularly in that passage of Jeremiah. The whole verse is, "They have built the high places of Tophet, to burn their sons and their daughters in the fire, which I commanded them not." Now, God had expressly forbidden them to do this; and that on pain of death. But surely there is a difference between the Jews offering their sons and daughters to devils, and Christians offering theirs to God. On the whole, therefore, it is not only lawful and innocent, but meet, right, and our bounden duty, in conformity to the uninterrupted practice of the whole Church of Christ from the earliest ages, to consecrate our children to God by baptism, as the Jewish Church were commanded to do by circumcision.

APPENDIX B

John Wesley, "Sermon 45: The New Birth"

"Ye must be born again." JOHN 3:7.

1. IF ANY DOCTRINES within the whole compass of Christianity may be properly termed fundamental, they are doubtless these two—the doctrine of justification, and that of the new birth: The former relating to that great work which God does for us, in forgiving our sins; the latter, to the great work which God does in us, in renewing our fallen nature. In order of time, neither of these is before the other: in the moment we are justified by the grace of God, through the redemption that is in Jesus, we are also "born of the Spirit;" but in order of thinking, as it is termed, justification precedes the new birth. We first conceive his wrath to be turned away, and then his Spirit to work in our hearts.

2. How great importance then must it be of, to every child of man, thoroughly to understand these fundamental doctrines! From a full conviction of this, many excellent men have wrote very largely concerning justification, explaining every point relating thereto, and opening the Scriptures which treat upon it. Many likewise have wrote on the new birth: And some of them largely enough; but yet not so clearly as might have been desired, nor so deeply and accurately; having either given a dark, abstruse account of it, or a slight and superficial one. Therefore a full, and at the same time a clear, account of the new birth, seems to be wanting still; such as may enable us to give a satisfactory answer to these three questions: First, Why must we be born again? What is the foundation of this doctrine of the new birth? Secondly, How must we be born again? What is the nature of the new birth? And, Thirdly, Wherefore must we be born again? To what end is it necessary? These questions, by

the assistance of God, I shall briefly and plainly answer; and then subjoin a few inferences which will naturally follow.

I. Why Must We Be Born Again?

1. And, First, Why must we be born again? What is the foundation of this doctrine? The foundation of it lies near as deep as the creation of the world; in the scriptural account whereof we read, "And God," the three-one God, "said, Let us make man in our image, after our likeness. So God created man in his own image, in the image of God created he him." (Gen 1:26, 27). Not barely in his natural image, a picture of his own immortality; a spiritual being, endued with understanding, freedom of will, and various affections—nor merely in his political image, the governor of this lower world, having "dominion over the fishes of the sea, and over all the earth"—but chiefly in his moral image; which, according to the Apostle, is "righteousness and true holiness" (Eph 4:24) in this image of God was man made. "God is love:" Accordingly, man at his creation was full of love; which was the sole principle of all his tempers, thoughts, words, and actions. God is full of justice, mercy, and truth; so was man as he came from the hands of his Creator. God is spotless purity; and so man was in the beginning pure from every sinful blot; otherwise God could not have pronounced him, as well as all the other work of his hands, "very good" (Gen 1:31) This he could not have been, had he not been pure from sin, and filled with righteousness and true holiness. For there is no medium: If we suppose and intelligent creature not to love God, not to be righteous and holy, we necessarily suppose him not to be good at all; much less to be "very good."

2. But, although man was made in the image of God, yet he was not made immutable. This would have been inconsistent with the state of trial in which God was pleased to place him. He was therefore created able to stand, and yet liable to fall. And this God himself apprized him of, and gave him a solemn warning against it. Nevertheless, man did not abide in honor: He fell from his high estate. He "ate of the tree whereof the Lord had commanded him, Thou shalt not eat thereof." By this willful act of disobedience to his Creator, this flat rebellion against his Sovereign, he openly declared that he would no longer have God to rule over him; That he would be governed by his own will, and not the will of Him that created him; and that he would not seek his happiness in God, but in the world, in the works of his hands. Now, God had told him before, "In the

day that thou eatest" of that fruit, "thou shalt surely die." And the word of the Lord cannot be broken. Accordingly, in that day he did die: He died to God—the most dreadful of all deaths. He lost the life of God: He was separated from Him, in union with whom his spiritual life consisted. The body dies when it is separated from the soul; the soul, when it is separated from God. But this separation from God, Adam sustained in the day, the hour, he ate of the forbidden fruit. And of this he gave immediate proof; presently showing by his behavior, that the love of God was extinguished in his soul, which was now "alienated from the life of God." Instead of this, he was now under the power of servile fear, so that he fled from the presence of the Lord. Yea, so little did he retain even of the knowledge of Him who filleth heaven and earth, that he endeavored to "hide himself from the Lord God among the trees of the garden" (Gen 3:8). So had he lost both the knowledge and the love of God, without which the image of God could not subsist. Of this, therefore, he was deprived at the same time, and became unholy as well as unhappy. In the room of this, he had sunk into pride and self-will, the very image of the devil; and into sensual appetites and desires, the image of the beasts that perish.

3. If it be said, "Nay, but that threatening, 'In the day that thou eatest thereof, thou shalt surely die,' refers to temporal death, and that alone, to the death of the body only;" the answer is plain: To affirm this is flatly and palpably to make God a liar; to aver that the God of truth positively affirmed a thing contrary to truth. For it is evident, Adam did not die in this sense, "in the day that he ate thereof." He lived, in the sense opposite to this death, above nine hundred years after. So that this cannot possibly be understood of the death of the body, without impeaching the veracity of God. It must therefore be understood of spiritual death, the loss of the life and image of God.

4. And in Adam all died, all human kind, all the children of men who were then in Adam's loins. The natural consequence of this is, that every one descended from him comes into the world spiritually dead, dead to God, wholly dead in sin; entirely void of the life of God; void of the image of God, of all that righteousness and holiness wherein Adam was created. Instead of this, every man born into the world now bears the image of the devil in pride and self-will; the image of the beast, in sensual appetites and desires. This, then, is the foundation of the new birth—the entire corruption of our nature. Hence it is, that, being born in sin, we must be "born again." Hence every one that is born of a woman must be born of the Spirit of God.

II. How Must We Be Born Again?

1. But how must a man be born again What is the nature of the new birth This is the Second question. And a question it is of the highest moment that can be conceived. We ought not, therefore, in so weighty a concern, to be content with a slight inquiry; but to examine it with all possible care, and to ponder it in our hearts, till we fully understand this important point, and clearly see how we are to be born again.

2. Not that we are to expect any minute, philosophical account of the manner how this is done. Our Lord sufficiently guards us against any such expectation, by the words immediately following the text; wherein he reminds Nicodemus of as indisputable a fact as any in the whole compass of nature, which, notwithstanding, the wisest man under the sun is not able fully to explain. "The wind bloweth where it listeth"—not by thy power or wisdom; "and thou hearest the sound thereof"—thou art absolutely assured, beyond all doubt, that it doth blow; "but thou canst not tell whence it cometh, nor whither it goeth"—the precise manner how it begins and ends, rises and falls, no man can tell. "So is every one that is born of the Spirit"—Thou mayest be as absolutely assured of the fact, as of the blowing of the wind; but the precise manner how it is done, how the Holy Spirit works this in the soul, neither thou nor the wisest of the children of men is able to explain.

3. However, it suffices for every rational and Christian purpose, that, without descending into curious, critical inquiries, we can give a plain scriptural account of the nature of the new birth. This will satisfy every reasonable man, who desires only the salvation of his soul. The expression, "being born again," was not first used by our Lord in his conversation with Nicodemus: It was well known before that time, and was in common use among the Jews when our Savior appeared among them. When an adult Heathen was convinced that the Jewish religion was of God, and desired to join therein, it was the custom to baptize him first, before he was admitted to circumcision. And when he was baptized, he was said to be born again; by which they meant, that he who was before a child of the devil was now adopted into the family of God, and accounted one of his children. This expression, therefore, which Nicodemus, being "a Teacher in Israel" ought to have understood well, our Lord uses in conversing with him; only in a stronger sense than he was accustomed to. And this might be the reason of his asking, "How can these things be" They cannot be literally—A man cannot "enter a second time into

his mother's womb, and be born"—But they may spiritually. A man may be born from above, born of God, born of the Spirit, in a manner which bears a very near analogy to the natural birth.

4. Before a child is born into the world he has eyes, but sees not; he has ears, but does not hear. He has a very imperfect use of any other sense. He has no knowledge of any of the things of the world, or any natural understanding. To that manner of existence which he then has, we do not even give the name of life. It is then only when a man is born, that we say he begins to live. For as soon as he is born, be begins to see the light, and the various objects with which he is encompassed. His ears are then opened, and he hears the sounds which successively strike upon them. At the same time, all the other organs of sense begin to be exercised upon their proper objects. He likewise breathes, and lives in a manner wholly different from what he did before. How exactly doth the parallel hold in all these instances! While a man is in a mere natural state, before he is born of God, he has, in a spiritual sense, eyes and sees not; a thick impenetrable veil lies upon them; he has ears, but hears not; he is utterly deaf to what he is most of all concerned to hear. His other spiritual senses are all locked up: He is in the same condition as if he had them not. Hence he has no knowledge of God; no intercourse with him; he is not at all acquainted with him. He has no true knowledge of the things of God, either of spiritual or eternal things; therefore, though he is a living man, he is a dead Christian. But as soon as he is born of God, there is a total change in all these particulars. The "eyes of his understanding are opened," (such is the language of the great Apostle); and, He who of old "commanded light to shine out of darkness shining on his heart, he sees the light of the glory of God," his glorious love, "in the face of Jesus Christ." His ears being opened, he is now capable of hearing the inward voice of God, saying, "Be of good cheer; thy sins are forgiven thee;" "go and sin no more." This is the purport of what God speaks to his heart; although perhaps not in these very words. He is now ready to hear whatsoever "He that teacheth man knowledge" is pleased, from time to time, to reveal to him. He "feels in his heart," to use the language of our Church, "the mighty working of the Spirit of God;" not in a gross, carnal sense as the men of the world stupidly and willfully misunderstand the expression; though they have been told again and again, we mean thereby neither more nor less than this: He feels, is inwardly sensible of, the graces which the Spirit of god works in his heart. He feels, he is conscious of, a "peace which passeth all understanding." He many times feels such a joy in God as is "unspeakable,

and full of glory." He feels "the love of God shed abroad in his heart by the Holy Ghost which is given unto him;" and all his spiritual senses are then exercised to discern spiritual good and evil. By the use of these, he is daily increasing in the knowledge of God, of Jesus Christ whom he hath sent and to all the things pertaining to his inward kingdom. And now he may be properly said to live: God having quickened him by his Spirit, he is alive to God through Jesus Christ. He lives a life which the world knoweth not of, a "life which is hid with Christ in God." God is continually breathing, as it were, upon the soul; and his soul is breathing unto God. Grace is descending into his heart; and prayer and praise ascending to heaven: And by this intercourse between God and man, this fellowship with the Father and the Son, as by a kind of spiritual respiration, the life of God in the soul is sustained; and the child of God grows up, till he comes to the "full measure of the stature of Christ."

5. From hence it manifestly appears, what is the nature of the new birth. It is that great change which God works in the soul when he brings it into life; when he raises it from the death of sin to the life of righteousness. It is the change wrought in the whole soul by the almighty Spirit of God when it is "created anew in Christ Jesus;" when it is "renewed after the image of God, in righteousness and true holiness;" when the love of the world is changed into the love of God; pride into humility; passion into meekness; hatred, envy, malice, into a sincere, tender, disinterested love for all mankind. In a word, it is that change whereby the earthly, sensual, devilish mind is turned into the "mind which was in Christ Jesus." This is the nature of the new birth: "So is every one that is born of the Spirit."

III. Why Is It Necessary to Be Born Again?

1. It is not difficult for any who has considered these things, to see the necessity of the new birth, and to answer the Third question, Wherefore, to what end, is it necessary that we should be born again It is very easily discerned, that this is necessary, First, in order to holiness. For what is holiness according to the oracles of God; not a bare external religion, a round of outward duties, how many soever they be, and how exactly soever performed. No: Gospel holiness is no less than the image of God stamped upon the heart; it is no other than the whole mind which was in Christ Jesus; it consists of all heavenly affections and tempers mingled together in one. It implies such a continual, thankful love to Him who

hath not withheld from us his Son, his only son, as makes it natural, and in a manner necessary to us, to love every child of man; as fills us "with bowels of mercies, kindness, gentleness, long-suffering." It is such a love of God as teaches us to be blameless in all manner of conversation; as enables us to present our souls and bodies, all we are and all we have, all our thoughts, words, and actions, a continual sacrifice to God, acceptable through Christ Jesus. Now, this holiness can have no existence till we are renewed in the image of our mind. It cannot commence in the soul till that change be wrought; till, by the power of the Highest overshadowing us, we are "brought from darkness to light, from the power of Satan unto God;" that is, till we are born again; which, therefore, is absolutely necessary in order to holiness.

2. But "without holiness no man shall see the Lord," shall see the face of God in glory. Of consequence, the new birth is absolutely necessary in order to eternal salvation. Men may indeed flatter themselves (so desperately wicked and so deceitful is the heart of man!) that they may live in their sins till they come to the last gasp, and yet afterwards live with God; and thousands do really believe, that they have found a broad way which leadeth not to destruction. "What danger," say they, "can a woman be in that is so harmless and so virtuous? What fear is there that so honest a man, one of so strict morality, should miss of heaven; especially if, over and above all this, they constantly attend on church and sacrament?" One of these will ask with all assurance, "What! Shall not I do as well as my neighbours?" Yes, as well as your unholy neighbours; as well as your neighbours that die in their sins! For you will all drop into the pit together, into the nethermost hell! You will all lie together in the lake of fire; "the lake of fire burning with brimstone." Then, at length, you will see (but God grant you may see it before!) the necessity of holiness in order to glory; and, consequently, of the new birth, since none can be holy, except he be born again.

3. For the same reason, except he be born again, none can be happy even in this world. For it is not possible, in the nature of things, that a man should be happy who is not holy. Even the poor, ungodly poet could tell us, Nemo malus felix: "no wicked man is happy." The reason is plain: All unholy tempers are uneasy tempers: Not only malice, hatred, envy jealousy, revenge, create a present hell in the breast; but even the softer passions, if not kept within due bounds, give a thousand times more pain than pleasure. Even "hope," when "deferred," (and how often must this be the case!) "maketh the heart sick;" and every desire which

is not according to the will of God is liable to "pierce" us "through with many sorrows." And all those general sources of sin—pride, self-will, and idolatry—are, in the same proportion as they prevail, general sources of misery. Therefore, as long as these reign in any soul, happiness has no place there. But they must reign till the bent of our nature is changed, that is, till we are born again; consequently, the new birth is absolutely necessary in order to happiness in this world, as well as in the world to come.

IV. Inferences of the New Birth

I proposed in the Last place to subjoin a few inferences, which naturally follow from the preceding observations.

1. And, First, it follows, that baptism is not the new birth: They are not one and the same thing. Many indeed seem to imagine that they are just the same; at least, they speak as if they thought so; but I do not know that this opinion is publicly avowed by any denomination of Christians whatever. Certainly it is not by any within these kingdoms, whether of the established Church, or dissenting from it. The judgment of the latter is clearly declared in the large Catechism: [Q. 163, 165.—Ed.]—Q. "What are the parts of a sacrament A. The parts of a sacrament are two: The one an outward and sensible sign; the other, and inward and spiritual grace, thereby signified.—Q. What is baptism A. Baptism is a sacrament, wherein Christ hath ordained the washing with water, to be a sign and seal of regeneration by his Spirit." Here it is manifest, baptism, the sign, is spoken of as distinct from regeneration, the thing signified.

In the Church Catechism likewise, the judgment of our Church is declared with the utmost clearness: "What meanest thou by this word, sacrament A. I mean an outward and visible sign of an inward and spiritual grace. Q. What is the outward part or form in baptism A. Water, wherein the person is baptized, in the name of the Father, Son, and Holy Ghost. Q. What is the inward part, or thing signified A. A death unto sin, and a new birth unto righteousness." Nothing, therefore, is plainer than that, according to the Church of England, baptism is not the new birth.

But indeed the reason of the thing is so clear and evident, as not to need any other authority. For what can be more plain, than the one is a visible, the and invisible thing, and therefore wholly different from each other—the one being an act of man, purifying the body; the other a change wrought by God in the soul: So that the former is just as distinguishable from the latter, as the soul from the body, or water from the Holy Ghost.

2. From the preceding reflections we may, Secondly, observe, that as the new birth is not the same thing with baptism, so it does not always accompany baptism: They do not constantly go together. A man my possibly be "born of water," and yet not be "born of the Spirit." There may sometimes be the outward sign, where there is not the inward grace. I do not now speak with regard to infants: It is certain our Church supposes that all who are baptized in their infancy are at the same time born again; and it is allowed that the whole Office for the Baptism of Infants proceeds upon this supposition. Nor is it an objection of any weight against this, that we cannot comprehend how this work can be wrought I infants. For neither can we comprehend how it is wrought in a person of riper years. But whatever be the case with infants, it is sure all of riper years who are baptized are not at the same time born again. "The tree is known by its fruits:" And hereby it appears too plain to be denied, that divers of those who were children of the devil before they were baptized continue the same after baptism: "for the works of their father they do." They continue servants of sin, without any pretense either to inward or outward holiness.

3. A Third inference which we may draw from what has been observed, is, that the new birth is not the same with sanctification. This is indeed taken for granted by many; particularly by an eminent writer, in his late treatise on "The Nature and Grounds of Christian Regeneration." To wave several other weighty objections which might be made to that tract, this is a palpable one: It all along speaks of regeneration as a progressive work, carried on in the soul by slow degrees, from the time of our first turning to God. This is undeniably true of sanctification; but of regeneration, the new birth, it is not true. This is a part of sanctification, not the whole; it is the gate to it, the entrance into it. When we are born again, then our sanctification, our inward and outward holiness, begins; and thenceforward we are gradually to "grow up in Him who is our Head." This expression of the Apostle admirably illustrates the difference between one and the other, and farther points out the exact analogy there is between natural and spiritual things. A child is born of a woman in a moment, or at least in a very short time: Afterward he gradually and slowly grows, till he attains to the stature of a man. In like manner, a child is born of God in a short time, if not in a moment. But it is by slow degrees that he afterward grows up to the measure of the full stature of

Christ. The same relation, therefore, which there is between our natural birth and our growth, there is also between our new birth and our sanctification.

4. One point more we may learn from the preceding observations. But it is a point of so great importance, as my excuse the considering it the more carefully, and prosecuting it at some length. What must one who loves the souls of men, and is grieved that any of them should perish, say to one whom he sees living in sabbath-breaking, drunkenness, or any other willful sin What can he say, if the foregoing observations are true, but, "You must be born again." "No," says a zealous man, "that cannot be. How can you talk so uncharitably to the man Has he not been baptized already He cannot be born again now." Can he not be born again Do you affirm this Then he cannot be saved. Though he be as old as Nicodemus was, yet "except he be born again, he cannot see the kingdom of God." Therefore in saying, "He cannot be born again," you in effect deliver him over to damnation. And where lies the uncharitableness now—on my side, or on yours I say, he may be born again, and so become an heir of salvation. You say, "He cannot be born again." And if so, he must inevitably perish! So you utterly block up his way to salvation, and send him to hell, out of mere charity!

But perhaps the sinner himself, to whom in real charity we say, "You must be born again," has been taught to say, "I defy your new doctrine; I need not be born again: I was born again when I was baptized. What! Would you have me deny my baptism." I answer, First, There is nothing under heaven which can excuse a lie; otherwise I should say to an open sinner, If you have been baptized, do not own it. For how highly does this aggravate your guilt! How will it increase your damnation! Was you devoted to God at eight days old, and have you been all these years devoting yourself to the devil Was you, even before you had the use of reason, consecrated to God the Father, the son, and the Holy Ghost And have you, ever since you had the use of it, been flying in the face of God, and consecrating yourself to Satan Does the abomination of desolation—the love of the word, pride, anger, lust, foolish desire, and a whole train of vile affections—stand where it ought not Have you set up all the accursed things in that soul which was once a temple of the Holy Ghost; set apart for an "habitation of God, through the Spirit;" yea, solemnly given up to him And do you glory in this, that you once belonged to God. O be ashamed! Blush! Hide yourself in the earth! Never boast more of what ought to fill you with confusion, to make you ashamed before God and man! I answer, Secondly, You have already denied your baptism; and that in the most effectual manner. You have denied it a thousand and a thousand times; and you do so still, day by day. For in your baptism you renounced the devil and all his works. Whenever, therefore, you give place to him again, whenever you do any of the works of the devil, then you deny your baptism. Therefore you deny it by every willful sin; by every act of uncleanness, drunkenness, or revenge; by every obscene or profane word; by every oath that comes out of your mouth. Every time you profane the day of the Lord, you thereby deny your baptism; yea, every time you do any thing to another which you would not he should do to you. I answer, Thirdly, Be you baptized or unbaptized, "you must be born again;" otherwise it is not possible you should be inwardly holy; and without inward as well as outward holiness, you cannot be happy, even in this world, much less in the world to come. Do you say, "Nay, but I do no harm to any man; I am honest and just in all my dealings; I do not curse, or take the Lord's name in vain; I do not profane the Lord's day; I am no drunkard; I do not slander my neighbor, nor live in any willful sin?" If this be so, it were much to be wished that all men went as far as you do. But you must go farther yet, or you cannot be saved: Still, "you must be born again." Do you add, "I do go farther yet; for I not only do no harm, but do all the good I can?" I doubt that fact; I fear you have had a thousand opportunities of doing good which you have suffered to pass by unimproved, and for which therefore you are accountable to God. But if you had improved them all, if you really had done all the good you possibly could to all men, yet this does not at all alter the case; still, "you must be born again." Without this nothing will do any good to your poor, sinful, polluted soul. "Nay, but I constantly attend all the ordinances of God: I keep to my church and sacrament." It is well you do: But all this will not keep you from hell, except you be born again. Go to church twice a day; go to the Lord's table every week; say ever so many prayers in private; hear ever so many good sermons; read ever so many good books; still, "you must be born again." None of these things will stand in the place of the new birth; no, nor any thing under heaven. Let this therefore, if you have not already experienced this inward work of God, be your continual prayer: "Lord, add this to all thy blessings—let me be born again! Deny whatever thou pleasest, but deny not this; let me be 'born from above!' Take away whatsoever seemeth thee good—reputation, fortune, friends, health—only give me this, to be born of the Spirit, to be received among the children of God! Let me be born, 'not of corruptible seed, but incorruptible, by the word of God, which liveth and abideth for ever;' and then let be daily 'grow in grace, and in the knowledge of our Lord and Savior Jesus Christ!'"